Rick Steves' ®

AMSTERDAM
BRUGES & BRUSSELS
2006

W9-AAN-699

Rick Steves & Gene Openshaw

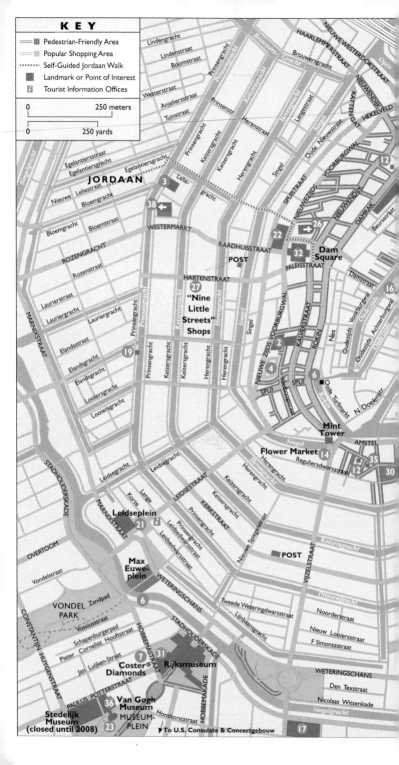

KEY

- Pedestrian-Friendly Area
- Popular Shopping Area
- Self-Guided Jordaan Walk
- Landmark or Point of Interest
- *i* Tourist Information Offices

0 ——— 250 meters

0 ——— 250 yards

NIEUWE WESTERDOKSTRAAT

Lindengracht

Lindenstraat

Boomstraat

HAARLEMMERSTRAAT

Brouwersgracht

Westerstraat

Anjeliersstraat

Tuinstraat

Prinsenstr.

Herenstraat

Langestraat

KATTENGAT

HEKELVELD

NIEUWENDIJK

Egelantiersstraat

Egelantiersgracht

JORDAAN

Nieuwe

Leliestraat

Bloemgracht

Bloemgracht

ROZENGRACHT

Rozenstraat

Laurierstraat

Lauriergracht

Elandsstraat

Elandsgracht

Looiersgracht

Looiersgracht

Egelantiersgracht

Leliegracht

Prinsengracht

Keizersgracht

Herengracht

Singel

SPUISTRAAT

VOORBURGWAL

NIEUWENDIJK

DAMRAK

Beursstraat

3

38

WESTERMARKT

RAADHUISSTRAAT

POST

HARTENSTRAAT

27 "Nine
Little
Streets"
Shops

19

22

26

32

**Dam
Square**

PALEISSTRAAT

NIEUWE ZIJDS VOORBURGWAL

KALVERSTRAAT

ROKIN

Nes

Oudezijds Voorburgwal

Oudezijds Achterburgwal

Oudezijds

Damstraat

16

2

4

6

Oude Turfmarkt

N. Doelenstr.

MARNIXSTRAAT

Leidsegracht

Leidsegracht

LEIDSESTRAAT

KERKSTRAAT

Herengracht

Keizersgracht

Prinsengracht

Nieuwe Spiegelstraat

**Mint
Tower**

AMSTEL

14

Flower Market

Reguliersdwarsstraat

12

35

30

STADHOUDERSKADE

Leidseplein

21 *i*

Korte

Lange

Leidsedwarsstraat

Leidsedwarsstraat

OVERTOOM

**Max
Euwe-
plein**

WETERINGSCHANS

VIJZELSTRAAT

POST

Prinsengracht

Keizersgracht

Vondelstraat

Zandpad

**VONDEL
PARK**

6

STADHOUDERSKADE

Tweede Weteringdwarsstraat

Lijnbaansgracht

Noorderstraat

Nieuw Looiersstraat

F Simonszstraat

Vossiusstraat

Schapenburgerpad

Pieter Cornelisz Hooftstraat

Jan Luijken-Straat

CONSTANTIJN HUYGENSTRAAT

7 **31**

**Coster
Diamonds**

Rijksmuseum

HOBBEMASTRAAT

HOBBEMAKADE

PAULUS POTTERSTRAAT

36

**Van Gogh
Museum**

MUSEUM-
PLEIN

**Stedelijk
Museum**
(closed until 2008)

23

Honthorststraat

►To U.S. Consulate & Concertgebouw

WETERINGSCHANS

Den Texstraat

Nicolaas Witsenkade

Singelgracht

17

Keizersgracht

Prinsengracht

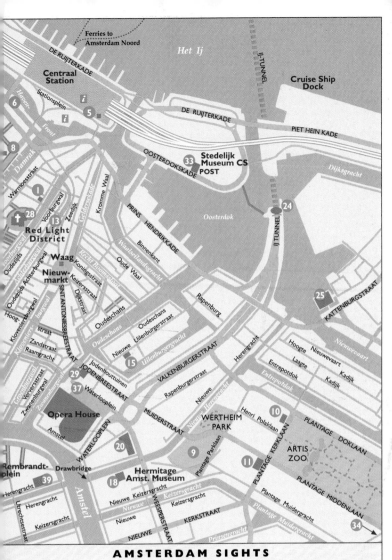

AMSTERDAM SIGHTS

1. Amstelkring Museum
2. Amsterdam History Museum
3. Anne Frank House
4. Begijnhof
5. Bike Rental
6. Canal-Boat Tours (3)
7. Coster Diamonds
8. Damrak Sex Museum
9. De Hortus Botanical Garden
10. Dutch Resistance Museum
11. Dutch Theater Memorial
12. easyInternetcafés (2)
13. Erotic Museum
14. Flower Market
15. Gassan Diamonds
16. Hash, Marijuana & Hemp Museum
17. Heineken Brewery
18. Hermitage Amsterdam Museum
19. Houseboat Museum
20. Jewish Historical Museum
21. Leidseplein
22. Magna Plaza Shopping Center
23. Museumplein
24. NEMO (Science Museum)
25. Netherlands Maritime Museum
26. New Church (Nieuwe Kerk)
27. "Nine Little Streets" (Shops)
28. Old Church (Oude Kerk)
29. Rembrandt's House & Holland Experience
30. Rembrandtplein
31. Rijksmuseum / Philips Wing Entrance
32. Royal Palace
33. Stedelijk Museum CS
34. To Tropical Museum
35. Tuschinski Theater
36. Van Gogh Museum
37. Waterlooplein Flea Market
38. Westerkerk
39. Willet-Holthuysen Museum

North Sea

Wadden Islands

Waddenzee

Emden

Groningen

Leeuwarden

A7

A28

Den Helder

Afsluitdijk

• Hindeloopen

A31

NETHERLANDS

Medemblick •

Open-Air Museum •

A7

Alkmaar •

Enkhuizen

Hoorn •

Zaanse Schans ■

Edam •

Lelystad

Flevoland

Bad Bentheim

Haarlem •

Keukenhof ■

⭐ Amsterdam

Hengelo •

A30

Aalsmeer • ✈ *Schiphol*

A1

Scheveningen •

Leiden •

Utrecht

Kröller-Muller Museum ■

To Harwich, England

The Hague •

A2

A12

Open-Air Museum ■

• Delft

Hoek van Holland

Rotterdam

A15

Arnhem

A16

A27

Waal

A57

Emmerich

Rhine

Nijmegen

A3

Delta Expo ■

Maas

A2

Essen

Middelburg •

Eindhoven

A73

Duisburg •

A58

Venlo

Düsseldorf

To Dover, England

Zeebrugge

A67

A1

Ostende

• Bruges

FLANDERS

• Antwerp

GERMANY

E40

Flanders Fields Museum ■

E313

Köln •

• Ieper

• Ghent ✈

Hasselt

• Maastricht

E17

⭐ Brussels

Leuven

Aachen •

A1

Waterloo ■

E40

Remagen •

LILLE

Tournai •

BELGIUM

Liège

A61

A42

E42

Namur

Meuse

E25

Arras

Cambrai

Mons

WALLONIE

Cochem •

A1

Dinant •

La Roche •

Zell •

FRANCE

Aulnoye

Bastogne ■

ARDENNES

• Vianden

Mosel

St. Quentin

LUXEMBOURG

Laon

Charleville-Mézières

Longwy

• Trier

Soissons

A26

⭐ ✈

Luxembourg City

• Senlis

✈ *Charles de Gaulle* A4

• Reims

Verdun Battlefield

Thionville •

Saarbrücken

A4

A4

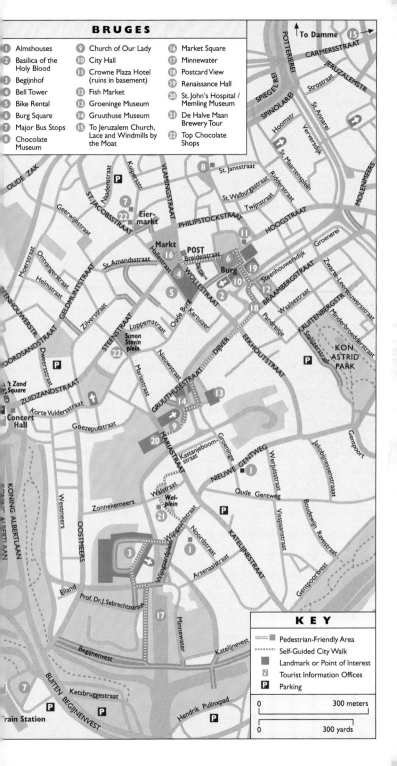

BRUGES

1. Almshouses
2. Basilica of the Holy Blood
3. Begijnhof
4. Bell Tower
5. Bike Rental
6. Burg Square
7. Major Bus Stops
8. Chocolate Museum
9. Church of Our Lady
10. City Hall
11. Crowne Plaza Hotel (ruins in basement)
12. Fish Market
13. Groeninge Museum
14. Gruuthuse Museum
15. To Jeruzalem Church, Lace and Windmills by the Moat
16. Market Square
17. Minnewater
18. Postcard View
19. Renaissance Hall
20. St. John's Hospital / Memling Museum
21. De Halve Maan Brewery Tour
22. Top Chocolate Shops

KEY

Pedestrian-Friendly Area
Self-Guided City Walk
Landmark or Point of Interest
Tourist Information Offices
P Parking

0   300 meters

0   300 yards

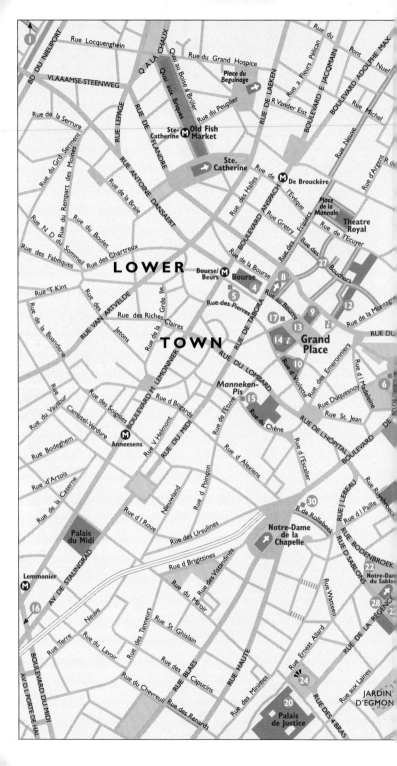

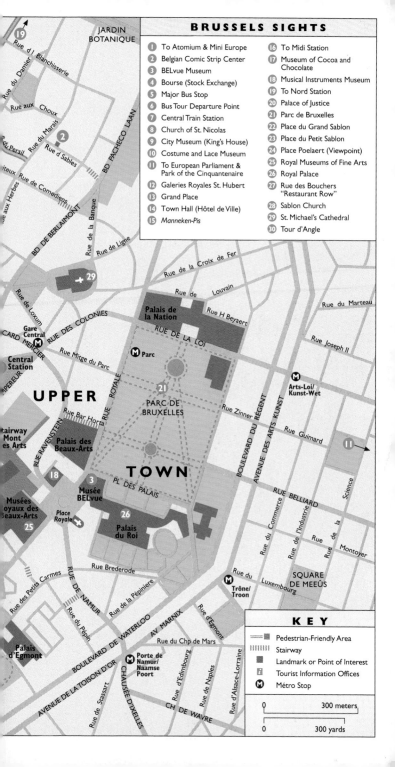

BRUSSELS SIGHTS

1. To Atomium & Mini Europe
2. Belgian Comic Strip Center
3. BELvue Museum
4. Bourse (Stock Exchange)
5. Major Bus Stop
6. Bus Tour Departure Point
7. Central Train Station
8. Church of St. Nicolas
9. City Museum (King's House)
10. Costume and Lace Museum
11. To European Parliament & Park of the Cinquantenaire
12. Galeries Royales St. Hubert
13. Grand Place
14. Town Hall (Hôtel de Ville)
15. *Manneken-Pis*
16. To Midi Station
17. Museum of Cocoa and Chocolate
18. Musical Instruments Museum
19. To Nord Station
20. Palace of Justice
21. Parc de Bruxelles
22. Place du Grand Sablon
23. Place du Petit Sablon
24. Place Poelaert (Viewpoint)
25. Royal Museums of Fine Arts
26. Royal Palace
27. Rue des Bouchers "Restaurant Row"
28. Sablon Church
29. St. Michael's Cathedral
30. Tour d'Angle

KEY

- Pedestrian-Friendly Area
- Stairway
- Landmark or Point of Interest
- Tourist Information Offices
- Métro Stop

0 — 300 meters

0 — 300 yards

AMSTERDAM
BRUGES & BRUSSELS
2006

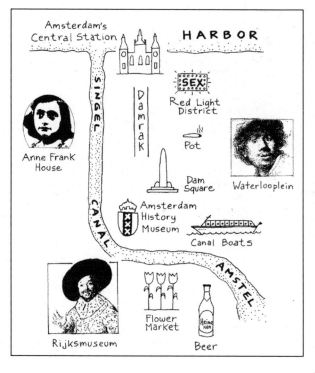

AVALON
TRAVEL

CONTENTS

The Netherlands and Belgium

INTRODUCTION

Amsterdam, Bruges, and Brussels—the three greatest cities of the Low Countries—are a delight to experience. Rattling on your bike over the cobbles, savoring fresh pralines, lingering in flower-carpeted squares, you'll find a slow-down-and-smell-the-tulips world that enchants. Any time of year, you can enjoy the intimate charms of these cities.

Amsterdam is called "the Venice of the North," both for its canals and for its past position as an economic powerhouse. Bruges—once mighty, now mighty cute—comes with fancy beers in fancy glasses, lilting carillons, and lacy Gothic souvenirs of a long-gone greatness. Brussels—the capital of Europe, with a low-rise Parisian ambience—exudes fine living, from its famous cuisine to its love of comic books and chocolate.

Belgium and the Netherlands are called the Low Countries because nearly half their land is below sea level. Surrounded by mega-Europe, it's a region that's easy to overlook. But travel here is a snap, the area is steeped in history, and all the charming icons of the region—whirring windmills, Dutch Masters, dike hikes, one-speed bikes, and ladies tossing bobbins to make fine lace—line up for you to enjoy. If ever an area were a travel cliché come true, it's the Low Countries.

This book covers the predictable biggies in and around Amsterdam, Bruges, and Brussels—and mixes in a healthy dose of Back Door intimacy. In Amsterdam, you can see Vincent van Gogh's *Sunflowers*...and climb through Captain Vincent's tiny houseboat museum. You'll tour Brussels' European Parliament glass skyscraper and enjoy a Michelangelo statue in small-town Bruges. And you'll meet intriguing people: Joos will show you how to swallow pickled herring, Majel will paddle you in a canoe through the *polderland* to her stuck-in-the-mud (and stuck-in-the-past) village, and Frans will pop a taste of his latest chocolate into your mouth.

This book is a tour guide in your pocket—laying out just the best of these three great cities in hopes that you'll enjoy the trip of a lifetime. The best is, of course, only my opinion. But after spending half my adult life researching Europe, I've developed a sixth sense for what travelers enjoy.

This Information Is Accurate and Up-to-Date

This book is updated every year. Most publishers of guidebooks that cover a destination from top to bottom can afford an update only every two or three years (and even then, it's often by e-mail or fax). Since this book is selective, covering only the sights that make the top two weeks in the Low Countries, I can get it updated in person each summer. The telephone numbers, hours, and prices of the places listed in this book are accurate as of mid-2005. Even with annual updates, things change. Still, if you're traveling with the current edition of this book, I guarantee you're using the most up-to-date information available in print. For the latest, visit www.ricksteves.com/update. Also at my Web site, you'll find a valuable list of reports and experiences—good and bad—from fellow travelers who have used this book (www.ricksteves.com/feedback).

Use this year's edition. People who try to save a few bucks by traveling with an old book are not smart. They learn the seriousness of their mistake...in Amsterdam. Your trip costs about $10 per waking hour. Your time is valuable. This guidebook will save you lots of time.

About This Book

Rick Steves' Amsterdam, Bruges & Brussels is a personal tour guide in your pocket. Better yet, it's actually two tour guides in your pocket: The co-author of this book is Gene Openshaw. Since our first "Europe through the gutter" trip together as high-school buddies almost 30 years ago, Gene and I have been exploring the wonders of the Old World. An inquisitive historian and lover of European culture, Gene wrote most of this book's self-guided museum tours and neighborhood walks. Together, Gene and I will keep this book up-to-date and accurate. For simplicity, from this point, "we" will shed our respective egos and become "I."

In the following chapters, you'll find:

An **Orientation** per city that covers tourist information and public transportation. The "Planning Your Time" section offers a suggested schedule with thoughts on how to best use your limited time.

Sights provides a succinct overview of each city's most important sights, arranged by neighborhood, with ratings: ▲▲▲—Don't miss; ▲▲—Try hard to see; ▲—Worthwhile if you can make it; No rating—Worth knowing about.

The **Self-Guided Walks and Tours** take you through the must-see attractions in Amsterdam (Rijksmuseum, Van Gogh Museum, Anne Frank House, a city walk, the Jordaan neighborhood, the Red Light District, and more), nearby Haarlem (the Grote Kerk and the Frans Hals Museum), Bruges (a city walk, Groeninge Museum, and Memling Museum), and Brussels (a city walk, an Upper Town walk, and the Royal Museums of Fine Arts of Belgium).

Sleeping contains detailed descriptions of my favorite good-value hotels.

Eating offers a wide assortment of restaurants ranging from fun, inexpensive eateries to classy splurges.

Smoking covers Amsterdam's best "coffeeshops," which openly sell marijuana.

Shopping gives you tips for shopping painlessly and enjoyably, without letting it overwhelm your vacation or ruin your budget.

Nightlife is your guide to Amsterdam's evening fun, including music, comedy, movies, and cruises.

Day Trips covers small towns and destinations (such as Dutch open-air folk museums) in the Netherlands.

Transportation Connections gives train and bus connections among these cities and to nearby destinations, as well as information on getting to and from the airports.

The **History** chapter gives you a quick overview of Dutch and Belgian history and a timeline of major events.

The **appendix** is a traveler's tool kit, including telephone tips, a climate chart, a list of holidays and festivals, and more.

Throughout this book, when you see a ✪ in a listing, it means that the sight is covered in much more depth in a self-guided walk or one of my museum tours—a page number will tell you just where to look to find more information.

Browse through this book and choose your favorite sights. Then have a great trip! Traveling like a temporary local, you'll get the absolute most out of every mile, minute, and euro. As you travel the route I know and love, I'm happy you'll be meeting some of my favorite Europeans.

PLANNING

Trip Costs

Five components make up your trip costs: airfare, surface transportation, room and board, sightseeing/entertainment, and shopping/miscellany.

Airfare: Don't try to sort through the mess. Find and use a good travel agent. A basic, round-trip, United States–Amsterdam flight costs $600–1,100 (even cheaper in winter), depending on where you fly from and when. While you can often save time in Europe by flying "open jaw" (into one city and out of another), if you're sticking to the Low Countries, you're never more than about three hours from Amsterdam's airport.

Surface Transportation: If you're just touring Amsterdam, Bruges, Brussels, and nearby day-trip destinations, you're best off enjoying the region's excellent and affordable train system. Trains leave at least hourly between each of the cities. It costs about $40 for a ticket from Amsterdam to Brussels or to Bruges. If you plan to venture farther afield, you may want a rental car. Driving in the Low Countries is flat-out easy (figure $750 per person—based on 2 people sharing—for a 3-week car rental, gas, and insurance).

Room and Board: You can thrive in the Low Countries on $90 a day per person for room and board. That allows $10 for lunch, $20 for dinner, and $60 for lodging (based on 2 people splitting the cost of a $120 double room that includes breakfast). To live and sleep more elegantly, I'd propose a budget of $120 per day per person ($10 for lunch, $40 for dinner, and $70 each for a $140 hotel double with breakfast). Students and tightwads do it on $45 a day ($25 per bed, $20 for meals and snacks).

Sightseeing and Entertainment: In big cities, figure $9–11 per major museum (Memling Museum, Van Gogh Museum); $3 for minor ones (climbing church towers or windmills); $10–15 for guided walks, boat tours, and bike rentals; and $30 for splurge experiences such as concerts, special art exhibits, big-bus tours, and guided canoe trips. An overall average of $15 a day works for most. Don't skimp here. After all, this category is the driving force behind your trip—you came to sightsee, enjoy, and experience the Low Countries.

Shopping and Miscellany: Figure $1–2 per postcard, tea, or ice-cream cone, and $4 per beer. Shopping can vary in cost from nearly nothing to a small fortune. Good budget travelers find that this category has little to do with assembling a trip full of lifelong and wonderful memories.

When to Go

Though Bruges and Amsterdam can be plagued by crowds, the long days, lively festivals, and sunny weather make summer a great time to visit. It's rarely too hot for comfort. Brussels' fancy, business-class hotels are deeply discounted in the summer.

Late spring and fall are also pleasant, with generally mild weather and lighter crowds (except during holiday weekends—see page 10). If you're counting on seeing the tulip fields in their full glory, go in the spring.

Winter travel is cold and wet in this region. It's fine for visiting Amsterdam, Bruges, and Brussels, but smaller towns and countryside sights feel dreary and lifeless. Some sights close for lunch, tourist information offices keep shorter hours, and some tourist activities (like English-language windmill tours) vanish altogether.

Sightseeing Priorities

With affordable flights from the United States, minimal culture shock, almost no language barrier, and a well-organized tourist trade, the Low Countries are a good place to start a European trip. Depending on the length of your trip, here are my recommended priorities.

2 days:	Amsterdam, Haarlem
3–4 days, add:	Bruges
5–6 days, add:	Brussels and another day in Amsterdam
7 days, add:	Side-trips from Amsterdam (e.g., Edam, Arnhem, Delft, The Historic Triangle, and more)

Travel Smart

A smart trip is a puzzle—a fun, doable, and worthwhile challenge. Reading this book before you leave, and rereading as you travel, will enhance your enjoyment and save you time and money. The Rijksmuseum is much more entertaining, for instance, if you've boned up on ruffs and Dutch Masters the night before.

Reread entire chapters as you travel, and visit local tourist information offices. Upon arrival in a new town, lay the groundwork for a smooth departure. Buy a phone card and use it for reservations and confirmations. Ask questions. Most locals are eager to point you in their idea of the right direction. Pack along a pocket-size notebook to organize your thoughts. Get a map. Understand and use public transportation. Take advantage of audioguides at sights and local guided tours.

Design an itinerary that enables you to hit the various sights at the best possible times. As you read through this book, note the days when sights are closed. Sundays have pros and cons, as they do for travelers in the U.S. (special events, limited hours, shops and banks closed, limited public transportation, no rush hours). Popular places are even more popular on weekends.

Plan ahead for laundry, Internet stops, and picnics. To maximize rootedness, minimize one-night stands. Mix intense and relaxed periods. Every trip (and every traveler) needs at least a few slack days. Pace yourself. Assume you will return.

RESOURCES

Dutch and Belgian Tourist Information Offices

In the U.S.

National tourist offices are a wealth of information. Before your trip, request any specific information you may want (such as city maps and schedules of upcoming festivals).

Netherlands Board of Tourism: 355 Lexington Ave., 19th floor, New York, NY 10017, tel. 212/557-3500, fax 212/370-9507, www.holland.com, information@holland.com. They no longer distribute printed material; all information is now available only on the Internet.

Belgian National Tourist Office: 220 E. 42nd St. #3402, New York, NY 10017, tel. 212/758-8130, fax 212/355-7675, www .visitbelgium.com, info@visitbelgium.com. Hotel and city guides; brochures for ABC lovers—antiques, beer, and chocolates; map of Brussels; information on WWI and WWII battlefields; and a list of Jewish sights.

In the Netherlands and Belgium

The tourist information office (abbreviated **TI** in this book, and VVV in the Netherlands) is your best first stop in any new city. Throughout the Low Countries, you'll find TIs are usually well-organized and have English-speaking staffers.

Rick Steves' Guidebooks, Public Television Show, and Radio Show

Rick Steves' Europe Through the Back Door gives you budget-travel skills, such as minimizing jet lag, packing light, planning your itinerary, traveling by car or train, finding rooms, changing money, avoiding rip-offs, buying a mobile phone, hurdling the language barrier, staying healthy, taking great photographs, using a bidet, and much more. The book also includes chapters on 38 of my favorite "Back Doors," two of which are in the Netherlands and Belgium.

Country Guides: These annually updated books offer you the latest on the top sights and destinations, with tips on how to make your trip efficient and fun. Here are the titles:

Rick Steves' Best of Europe	*Rick Steves' Great Britain*
Rick Steves' Best of Eastern Europe	*Rick Steves' Ireland*
	Rick Steves' Italy
Rick Steves' England (new in 2006)	*Rick Steves' Portugal*
	Rick Steves' Scandinavia
Rick Steves' France	*Rick Steves' Spain*
Rick Steves' Germany & Austria	*Rick Steves' Switzerland*

City and Regional Guides: Updated every year, these focus on Europe's most compelling destinations. Along with specifics on sights, restaurants, hotels, and nightlife, you'll get self-guided, illustrated tours of the outstanding museums and most character-istic neighborhoods.

*Rick Steves' Amsterdam,
  Bruges & Brussels
Rick Steves' Florence
  & Tuscany
Rick Steves' London
Rick Steves' Paris*

*Rick Steves' Prague
  & the Czech Republic
Rick Steves' Provence
  & the French Riviera
Rick Steves' Rome
Rick Steves' Venice*

Rick Steves' Phrase Books: In much of Europe, a phrase book is as fun as it is necessary. This practical and budget-oriented series covers French, German, Italian, Spanish, Portuguese, and French/Italian/German. You'll be able to make hotel reservations over the phone, chat with your cabbie, and bargain at street markets.

And More Books: *Rick Steves' Europe 101: History and Art for the Traveler* (with Gene Openshaw) gives you the story of Europe's people, history, and art. Written for smart people who were sleep-ing in their history and art classes before they knew they were going to Europe, *101* helps Europe's sights come alive. However, this book has far more coverage of the European continent than of Britain.

Rick Steves' Easy Access Europe, geared for travelers with lim-ited mobility, covers London, Paris, Bruges, Amsterdam, and the Rhine River Valley.

Rick Steves' Postcards from Europe, my autobiographical book, packs 25 years of travel anecdotes and insights into the ultimate 2,000-mile European adventure.

My latest book, *Rick Steves' European Christmas,* covers the joys, history, and quirky traditions of the holiday season in seven European countries.

Public Television Show: My series, *Rick Steves' Europe,* keeps churning out shows (60 at last count), including two featuring the sights in this book.

Radio Show: My new weekly radio show, which combines call-in questions (à la *Car Talk*) and interviews with travel experts, airs on public radio stations. For a schedule of upcoming topics, an archive of past programs, and details on how to call in, see www.ricksteves.com/radio.

Recommended Books and Movies

Guidebooks: This book is all you need. Consider some supple-mental travel information, particularly if you're traveling beyond

Begin Your Trip at www.ricksteves.com

At www.ricksteves.com you'll find a wealth of **free informa-tion** on destinations covered in this book, including fresh European travel and tour news every month and helpful "Graffiti Wall" tips from thousands of fellow travelers.

While you're there, the **online Travel Store** is a great place to save money on travel bags and accessories designed by Rick Steves to help you travel smarter and lighter, plus a wide selection of guidebooks, planning maps, and DVDs.

Traveling through Europe by rail is a breeze, but choosing the right railpass for your trip—amidst hundreds of options—can drive you nutty. At www.ricksteves.com, you'll find **Rick Steves' Annual Guide to European Railpasses**—your best way to convert chaos into pure travel energy. Buy your railpass from Rick, and you'll get a bunch of free extras to boot.

Travel agents will tell you about mainstream tours of Europe, but they won't tell you about **Rick Steves' tours.** Rick Steves' Europe Through the Back Door travel company offers more than two dozen itineraries and 300 departures reaching the best destinations in this book...and beyond. You'll enjoy the services of a great guide, a fun bunch of travel partners (with group sizes in the twenties), and plenty of room to spread out in a big, comfy bus. You'll find trips to fit every vacation size, from weeklong city getaways to longer cross-country adventures. For details, visit www.ricksteves.com or call 425/771-8303 ext 217.

my recommended destinations. Considering the improvements they'll make in your $3,000 vacation, $30 for extra maps and books is money well spent. One simple budget tip can easily justify the price of an extra guidebook.

Historians like the green Michelin guides and the Cadogan series; both have individual books on all three cities—Amsterdam, Bruges, and Brussels. Others go for the well-illustrated Eyewitness guides (titles include *Amsterdam; Holland;* and *Brussels/Bruges/Ghent/Antwerp*). The Lonely Planet series (which has books on Amsterdam, the Netherlands, and Belgium & Luxembourg) is well-researched and geared for a mature audience, but is not updated annually. Students and vagabonds enjoy *Let's Go: Amsterdam* (updated annually) for its coverage of hostelling, night-life, and the student scene.

Nonfiction: For readers interested in the Netherlands, here are several moving books about World War II: *The Diary of a Young Girl* (by Anne Frank), *The Hiding Place* (by Corrie ten Boom), and *A Bridge Too Far* (the story of the battle of Arnhem, by Cornelius

Ryan). *Amsterdam* (by Geert Mak) is an academic but engaging look at centuries of the city's history, while *The Undutchables: An Observation of the Netherlands, Its Culture and Its Inhabitants* (by Colin White and Laurie Boucke) is an irreverent guide to Dutch culture. If you're visiting Belgium and have an interest in World War I, look for Barbara Tuchman's Pulitzer Prize–winning book, *The Guns of August.*

Fiction: Possibilities include *Girl in Hyacinth Blue* (by Susan Vreeland), *Girl With a Pearl Earring* (by Tracy Chevalier), *Tulip Fever* (by Deborah Moggach), *Lust for Life* (by Irving Stone), and *Confessions of an Ugly Stepsister* (by Gregory Maguire). For Belgium, consider the non-fiction *A Tall Man in a Low Land* (by Harry Pearson) and, for fiction, *Resistance* (by Anita Shreve) and *The Adventures of Tintin* (featuring a famous Belgian comic-book character, by Hergé).

Films: *The Diary of Anne Frank* (1959) is a good version of Anne's story, which has been translated into film and theater many times. *Girl with a Pearl Earring* (2003) shows a fictionalized Vermeer in love with his servant in Delft, while *Antonia's Line* (1995) tells the story of five generations of Dutch women. *Ocean's Twelve* (2004) has many scenes set in Amsterdam's Jordaan. *Vincent and Theo* (1990) captures the relationship between the great artist and his brother.

Maps

The black-and-white maps in this book, drawn by Dave Hoerlein, are concise and simple. Dave, who is well-traveled in the Low Countries, has designed the maps to help you quickly orient and painlessly get to where you want to go. For more detail, consider buying a city map at any of the cities' TIs for a euro or two. Before you buy a map, look at it to make sure it has the level of detail you want.

PRACTICALITIES

Red Tape: You need a passport, but no visa or shots, to travel in the Netherlands and Belgium. Some readers report that you may be denied entry into the Netherlands if your passport is due to expire within 90 days—even if you plan to return to the United States long before that date. Check the date, and get it renewed if you'll be cutting it close. Pack a photocopy of your passport in your luggage in case the original is lost or stolen.

Time: In the Low Countries—and in this book—you'll use the 24-hour clock. It's the same through 12:00 noon, then keep going: 13:00, 14:00, and so on. For anything over 12, subtract 12 and add p.m. (14:00 is 2:00 p.m.).

The Netherlands and Belgium are six/nine hours ahead of the East/West Coasts of the U.S.

Holidays: In 2006, these dates can be busy anywhere in Europe: Easter Sunday and Monday (April 16–17), Labor Day (May 1), Ascension (May 25), Pentecost weekend (June 3–4), Assumption (Aug 15), All Saints' Day (Nov 1), Armistice Day (Nov 11), and the winter holidays (late Dec–early Jan). Many sights close on the actual holiday; check with the local tourist offices. In the Netherlands, remember these dates: Queen's Day (April 30, celebrated on April 29 in 2006), Remembrance Day (May 4), and Liberation Day (May 5). Belgium's Independence Day is July 21.

Shopping: Shoppers interested in customs regulations and VAT refunds (the tax refunded on large purchases made by non-EU residents) can refer to page 12.

Discounts: While discounts for sightseeing and transportation are not listed in this book, youths (under 18), students (only with International Student Identity Card; www.isic.org), and seniors can sometimes snare discounts—but only by asking.

Watt's Up? If you're bringing electrical gear, you'll need a two-prong adapter plug and a converter. Travel appliances often have convenient, built-in converters; look for a voltage switch marked 120V (U.S.) and 240V (Europe).

News: Americans keep in touch in Europe with the *International Herald Tribune* (published almost daily via satellite). Every Tuesday, the European editions of *Time* and *Newsweek* hit the stands with articles of particular interest to travelers in Europe. Sports addicts can get their fix from *USA Today*. Good Web sites include www.europeantimes.com and http://news.bbc.co.uk.

MONEY

Banking

Bring plastic (ATM, debit, or credit cards) along with several hundred dollars in hard cash as an emergency backup. Traveler's checks are a waste of time and money.

Before you go, verify with your bank that your card will work, inquire about fees (can be up to $5 per transaction), and alert them that you'll be making withdrawals in Europe; otherwise, the bank may not approve transactions if it perceives unusual spending patterns. Bring an extra card in case one gets demagnetized or gobbled up by a machine.

The best and easiest way to get cash in euros is to use the omnipresent bank machines (always open, low fees, and quick processing). You'll need a PIN code—numbers only, no letters—to use with your Visa or MasterCard. If you end up withdrawing lots of large bills, break some at a bank, especially if you like shopping

---

Exchange Rates

The Netherlands, Belgium, and this book all use the euro currency.

1 euro (€) = about $1.20

Like dollars, one euro (€) is broken down into 100 cents. You'll find coins ranging from one cent to two euros, and bills from five euros to 500 euros. To convert prices in euros to dollars, add 20 percent: €20 is about $24, €45 is about $55, and so on. So, that €65 Delft dinnerware is about $80, and the €90 taxi ride through Brussels is...uh-oh.

---

at mom-and-pop places; they rarely have huge amounts of change.

Just like at home, credit or debit cards work easily at larger hotels, restaurants, and shops. Visa and MasterCard are more commonly accepted than American Express. Smaller businesses prefer payment in local currency. Smart travelers function with hard cash and plastic.

Keep your credit and debit cards and most of your money hidden away in a money belt (a cloth pouch worn around your waist and tucked under your clothes). Thieves target tourists. A money belt provides peace of mind and allows you to carry lots of cash safely. Don't be petty about getting money. Withdraw a week's worth of money, stuff it in your money belt, and travel!

Tips on Tipping

Tipping in Europe isn't as automatic and generous as it is in the U.S.—but for special service, tips are appreciated, if not expected. As in the U.S., the proper amount depends on your resources, tipping philosophy, and the circumstance, but some general guidelines apply.

Restaurants: Tipping is an issue only at restaurants that have waiters and waitresses. If you order your food at a counter, don't tip. At Dutch and Belgian restaurants that have a wait staff, service is included in the menu prices, although it's common to round up the bill about five to 10 percent after a good meal (for an €18.50 meal, pay €20).

Taxis: To tip the cabbie, round up. For a typical ride, round up to the next euro on the fare (to pay a €13 fare, give €14); for a long ride, to the nearest 10 (for a €75 fare, give €80). If the cabbie hauls your bags and zips you to the airport to help you catch your flight, you might want to toss in a little more. But if you feel like you're being driven in circles or otherwise ripped off, skip the tip.

Damage Control for Lost or Stolen Cards

If you lose your credit, debit, or ATM card, you can stop people from using your card by reporting the loss immediately to the respective global customer-assistance centers. Call these 24-hour U.S. numbers collect: Visa (tel. 410/581-9994), MasterCard (tel. 636/722-7111), and American Express (tel. 336/393-1111).

Have, at a minimum, the following information ready: the name of the financial institution that issued you the card, along with the type of card (classic, platinum, or whatever). Ideally, plan ahead and pack photocopies of your cards—front and back—to expedite their replacement. Providing the following information will allow for a quicker cancellation of your missing card: full card number, whether you are the primary or secondary cardholder, the cardholder's name exactly as printed on the card, billing address, home phone number, circumstances of the loss or theft, and identification verification (your birthdate, your mother's maiden name, or your Social Security number—memorize this, don't carry a copy). If you are the secondary cardholder, you'll also need to provide the primary cardholder's identification verification details. You can generally receive a temporary card within two or three business days in Europe.

If you promptly report your card lost or stolen, you typically won't be responsible for any unauthorized transactions on your account, although many banks charge a liability fee of $50.

Hotels: I don't tip at hotels, but if you do, give the porter a euro for carrying bags and leave a couple of euros in your room at the end of your stay for the maid if the room was kept clean.

Special Services: Tour guides at public sites sometimes hold out their hands for tips after they give their spiel; if I've already paid for the tour, I don't tip extra, though some tourists do give a euro or two, particularly for a job well done. In general, if someone in the service industry does a super job for you, a tip of a couple of euros is appropriate...but not required.

When in doubt, ask. If you're not sure whether (or how much) to tip for a service, ask your hotelier or the tourist information office; they'll fill you in on how it's done on their turf.

VAT Refunds for Shoppers

Wrapped into the purchase price of your souvenirs is a Value Added Tax (VAT) of 19 percent in the Netherlands and 21 percent in Belgium. If you make a purchase of more than a certain amount (€137 in the Netherlands, €125.01 in Belgium) at a store that participates in the VAT refund scheme, you're entitled to get most of that tax back. Personally, I've never felt that VAT refunds are worth the hassle, but if you do, here's the scoop.

If you're lucky, the merchant will subtract the tax when you make your purchase (this is more likely to occur if the store ships the goods to your home). Otherwise, you'll need to:

Get the paperwork: Have the merchant completely fill out the necessary refund document, called a "cheque." You'll have to present your passport at the store.

Get your stamp at the border or airport: Process your cheque(s) at your last stop in the EU with the customs agent who deals with VAT refunds. It's best to keep your purchases in your carry-on for viewing, but if they're too large or dangerous (such as knives) to carry on, then track down the proper customs agent to inspect them before you check your bag. You're not supposed to use your purchased goods before you leave. If you show up at customs wearing your new wooden clogs, officials might look the other way—or deny you a refund.

Collect your refund: You'll need to return your stamped documents to the retailer or its representative. Many merchants work with services such as Global Refund or Premier Tax Free, with offices at major airports, ports, or border crossings. These services, which extract a 4 percent fee, can refund your money immediately in your currency of choice or credit your card (within 2 billing cycles). If you have to deal directly with the retailer, mail the store your stamped documents and then wait. It could take months.

Customs Regulations

You can take home $800 in souvenirs per person duty-free. The next $1,000 is taxed at a flat 3 percent. After that, you pay the individual item's duty rate. You can also bring in duty-free a liter of alcohol (slightly more than a standard-size bottle of wine), a carton of cigarettes, and up to 100 cigars. As for food, anything in cans or sealed jars is acceptable. Skip dried meat, cheeses, and fresh fruits and veggies. To check customs rules and duty rates, visit www.customs.gov.

TRANSPORTATION

By Car or Train?

Because of the short distances and excellent public transportation systems in the Low Countries, and the fact that this book covers three big cities, I recommend connecting Amsterdam, Bruges, and Brussels by train, not by car. You absolutely do not want or need a car in any of these cities.

Hourly trains connect each of these towns faster and easier than you could by driving. Just buy tickets as you go. You don't need advance reservations to ride a train between these cities, unless you take the pricey Amsterdam–Brussels Thalys train (it's avoidable; plenty of regular trains make this run). For more extensive travels beyond the Low Countries, you may want to study your railpass options (see www.ricksteves.com/rail).

COMMUNICATING

The Language Barrier

People speak Dutch in Amsterdam, Flemish (virtually identical to Dutch) in Bruges, and French in Brussels. But you'll find almost no language barrier anywhere, as all well-educated folks, nearly all young people, and almost everyone in the tourist trade speak English. Still, it's polite to use some Dutch pleasantries (see page 388).

Telephones

Smart travelers learn the phone system and use it daily for making hotel/restaurant reservations, verifying hours at sights, and phoning home. You can make long-distance calls directly, cheaply, and easily. Amsterdam is a big city. Always use the telephone to confirm tour times or make reservations at fancy restaurants. If you call before heading out, you'll travel more smoothly.

Types of Phones

You'll encounter various kinds of phones in the Low Countries.

Public pay phones, which used to be coin-operated, now almost always take insertable phone cards. A few coin-operated phones still exist; if you use coins to make your calls, have a bunch handy. You can use an international phone card to make calls from pay phones that take coins or insertable cards. For details on the different phone cards, see below.

Hotel room phones are fairly cheap for local calls, but pricey for international calls, unless you use an international phone card (see below).

American mobile phones work in Europe if they're GSM-enabled, tri-band (or quad-band), and on a calling plan that includes international calls. With a T-Mobile service plan, you can roam using your home number, and pay $1–2 per minute for making or receiving calls.

Some travelers buy a **European mobile phone** in Europe. For about $125, you can get a phone that will work in most countries once you pick up the necessary chip (about $30) per country. Or you can buy a cheaper, "locked" phone that only works in the country where you purchased it (about $100, includes $20 worth of calls). If you're interested, stop by any European shop that sells mobile phones; you'll see prominent store window displays. You aren't required to (and shouldn't) buy a monthly contract—buy prepaid calling time instead (as you use it up, buy additional minutes at newsstands or mobile-phone shops). If you're on a budget, skip mobile phones and use phone cards instead.

Paying for Calls

You can spend a fortune making phone calls in Europe...but why would you? Here's the skinny on different ways to pay, including the best deals.

Dutch and Belgian **phone cards** come in two types: phone cards that you insert into a pay phone (best for local calls or quick international calls), and phone cards that come with a dial-up code and can be used from virtually any phone (best for international calls).

Insertable phone cards are a convenient way to pay for calls from public pay phones. You can buy these cards at TIs, tobacco shops, post offices, and train stations. The price of the call (local or international) is automatically deducted while you talk. They are sold in several denominations starting at about €5. Calling the U.S. with one of these phone cards is reasonable (about 2–3 min per euro), but more expensive than using an international phone card (see below). Each European country has its own insertable phone card—so your Dutch card won't work in a Belgian phone.

International phone cards can be used from virtually any phone. These are not inserted into the phone. Instead, you dial the toll-free number listed on the card, reaching an automated operator (English is always available). When prompted, you dial in a code number, also written on the card. A voice tells you how much is left in your account. Then dial your number. Since you don't insert the card in the phone, you can use these to make inexpensive calls from most phones, including the one in your hotel room, avoiding pricey hotel rates. Remember that you don't need the actual card to use a card account, so it's sharable. You can write down the access and code numbers in your notebook and share it with friends.

Calls to the U.S. are very cheap (about 20–25 min per euro). You can use international phone cards to make local and domestic long-distance calls as well. Buy the cards at small newsstand kiosks and hole-in-the-wall long-distance phone shops. Because there are so many brand names, simply ask for an international telephone card and tell the vendor where you'll be making most calls ("to America"), and he'll select the brand with the best deal. Some international phone cards work in multiple countries; if you're traveling to both the Netherlands and Belgium, try to buy a card that will work in both places. Because cards are occasionally duds, avoid the high denominations.

Dialing direct from your hotel room without using an international phone card is usually quite expensive for international calls. (I always ask first how much I'll be charged.) Keep in mind that you might have to pay for local and occasionally even toll-free calls.

Receiving calls in your hotel room is often the cheapest way to keep in touch with the folks back home—especially if your family has an inexpensive way to call you (either a good deal on their long-distance plan, a prepaid calling card with good rates to Europe, or access to an Internet phone service such as Skype—www.skype.com). Give them a list of your hotels' phone numbers before you go. As you travel, send your family an e-mail or make a quick payphone call to set up a time for them to call you, and then wait for the ring.

U.S. calling cards (such as the ones offered by AT&T, MCI, or Sprint) are the worst option. You'll nearly always save a lot of money by paying with a phone card.

How to Dial

Calling from the U.S. to the Netherlands or Belgium, or vice versa, is simple—once you break the code. The European calling chart on page 380 will walk you through it. Remember that Dutch and Belgian time is six/nine hours ahead of the East/West Coasts of the U.S.

Dialing Domestic Calls within the Netherlands: The Netherlands' phone system uses area codes. To make a call within a city, you dial the local number without the area code. To make a long-distance call within the country, include the area code. For example, the number of a recommended hotel in Haarlem is 023/532-4530. To call it within Haarlem, dial 532-4530. To call it from Amsterdam, dial 023/532-4530.

Dialing Domestic Calls within Belgium: Belgium uses a direct-dial system (no area codes). To call anywhere within Belgium, you dial the same nine-digit number.

Dialing International Calls: For a listing of country codes, see the appendix. When making an international call to the Netherlands or Belgium, first dial the international access code of the country you're in (011 from the U.S. or Canada, 00 if you're calling from Europe), then—depending on the country you're calling—dial either the Netherlands' country code (31) or Belgium's country code (32), then drop the first zero of the rest of the number, and dial the remaining digits. For example, to call a recommended Amsterdam hotel from home, you'd dial 011 (the international access code for the U.S. and Canada), 31 (the

Netherlands' country code), 20 (Amsterdam's area code without the initial 0), and 626-9705.

To call my office from anywhere in Europe, I dial 00 (Europe's international access code), 1 (U.S. country code), 425 (Edmonds' area code), and 771-8303.

E-mail and Mail

E-mail: Internet cafés are easy to find in Amsterdam. Many of the Netherlands' marijuana-selling "coffeeshops" also have Internet terminals. The dominant Internet café chain in Amsterdam and Brussels is easyInternetcafé (open long hours, with the best rates and fastest connections in town). Bruges has a fine Internet café.

Many hotels have a dedicated computer for guests' e-mail needs. Small places are accustomed to letting clients (who ask politely) sit at their desk for a few minutes just to check their e-mail.

Mail: To arrange for mail delivery, reserve a few hotels along your route in advance and give their addresses to friends. Allow 10 days for a letter to arrive. Phoning and e-mailing are so easy that I've dispensed with mail stops altogether.

SLEEPING

In the interest of smart use of your time, I favor hotels and restaurants handy to your sightseeing activities. Rather than list hotels scattered throughout a city, I describe two or three favorite neighborhoods and recommend the best accommodations values in each, from $10 bunks to plush $200-plus doubles.

In recommending hotels, I favor small, family-run places that are central, inexpensive, quiet, clean, safe, friendly, English-speaking, and not listed in other guidebooks. I also like local character and simple facilities that don't cater to American "needs." Obviously, a place meeting every criterion is rare, and all of my recommendations fall short of perfection. But I've listed the top values for each price category. The very best values are family-run places with showers down the hall and no elevator.

Any room without a bathroom has access to a bathroom in the corridor (free unless otherwise noted). All rooms have a sink.

Rooms are safe. Still, keep cameras and money out of sight. For environmental reasons, towels are often replaced in hotels only when you leave them on the floor. In cheaper places, they aren't replaced at all, so hang them up to dry and reuse.

The price is usually posted in the room. Before accepting, confirm your understanding of the complete price. I appreciate feedback on your hotel experiences.

Sleep Code

To help you easily sort through the accommodations listed, I've divided the rooms into three categories based on the price for a standard double room with bath.

$$$ **Higher Priced**
$$ **Moderately Priced**
$ **Lower Priced**

To give maximum information with a minimum of space, I use the following code to describe accommodations listed in this book. Prices are listed per room, not per person. When a range of prices is listed for a room, the price fluctuates with room size or season. You can assume a hotel takes credit cards unless you see "cash only" in the listing. Hotel clerks speak at least some English unless otherwise noted.

S = Single room (or price for one person in a double).
D = Double or Twin. Double beds are usually big enough for non-romantic couples.
T = Triple (often a double bed with a single bed moved in).
Q = Quad (an extra child's bed is usually cheaper).
b = Private bathroom with toilet and shower or tub.
s = Private shower or tub only (the toilet is down the hall).

According to this code, a couple staying at a "Db-€90" hotel would pay a total of 90 euros (about $110) for a double room with a private bathroom. The hotel accepts credit cards or cash in payment.

Hotels

In this book, the price for a double room ranges from $60 (very simple, toilet and shower down the hall) to $300 (maximum plumbing and more), with most clustering at about $120. You'll pay more at Amsterdam hotels and less at Bruges B&Bs.

Most hotels have lots of doubles and a few singles, triples, and quads. While groups sleep cheap, traveling alone can be expensive. Singles (except for the rare closet-type rooms that fit only a twin bed) are simply doubles used by one person—so they often cost nearly the same as a double.

A hearty breakfast with cereal, meats, local cheeses, fresh bread, yogurt, juice, and coffee or tea is standard in hotels.

Bed-and-Breakfasts

B&Bs offer double the cultural intimacy and often nicer rooms for a good deal less than most hotel rooms. Hosts usually speak

English and are interesting conversationalists.

In the Low Countries, B&Bs are common in well-touristed areas outside of the big cities. There are plenty to choose from in Haarlem, and especially in Bruges. Amsterdam also has B&Bs, though they tend to be more expensive, less personal, and not as good a value as those in small towns (we've listed the better value B&Bs in Amsterdam). Local TIs have lists of B&Bs and can book a room for you, but you'll save money by booking direct with the B&Bs listed in this book.

Making Reservations

It's possible to travel at any time of year without reservations, but given the high stakes, erratic accommodations values, and the quality of the gems I've found for this book, I'd highly recommend calling for rooms at least several days in advance as you travel.

If tourist crowds are minimal, you might make a habit of calling between 9:00 and 10:00 on the day you plan to arrive, when the hotel knows who'll be checking out and just which rooms will be available. I've taken great pains to list telephone numbers with long-distance instructions (see "Telephones," page 14; also see the appendix). Use the telephone and the convenient telephone cards. Most hotels listed are accustomed to English-only speakers. A hotel receptionist will trust you and hold a room until 16:00 without a deposit, though some will ask for a credit-card number. Honor (or cancel by phone) your reservations. Long distance is cheap and easy from public phone booths. *Trusting people to show up is a hugely stressful issue and a financial risk for B&B owners. Don't let these people down—I promised you'd call and cancel if for some reason you can't show up.* Don't needlessly confirm rooms through the tourist offices; they'll take a commission.

If you know exactly which dates you need and really want a particular place, reserve a room long before you leave home. To reserve from home, call, e-mail, or fax the hotel. E-mail is free, phone and fax costs are reasonable, and simple English is fine. To fax, use the form in the appendix (online at www.ricksteves .com/reservation). A two-night stay in August would be "2 nights, 16/8/06 to 18/8/06." (Europeans write the date day/month/year, and European hotel jargon uses your day of departure.) Hotels often require one night's deposit to hold a room. Usually a credit-card number and expiration date will be accepted as the deposit. Faxing your card number (rather than e-mailing it) keeps it private, safer, and out of cyberspace. If you do reserve with a credit card, you can pay with your card or cash when you arrive; if you don't show up, you'll be billed for the night.

Hotels in larger cities sometimes have strict cancellation policies (you might lose, say, a deposit if you cancel within 2 weeks of your reserved stay, or you might be billed for the entire visit if you leave early); ask about cancellation policies before you book.

On the road, reconfirm your reservations a day or two in advance for safety (or you may be bumped—really). Also, don't just assume you can extend. Take the time to consider in advance how long you'll stay.

Hostels

There are excellent hostels in all three cities covered in this book. Hostels charge about $20 per bed. Travelers of any age are welcome, if they don't mind dorm-style accommodations or meeting other travelers. If you plan to hostel, get a hostel membership card before you go (contact Hostelling International, U.S. tel. 202/783-6161, www.hiayh.org). Travelers without a hostel card can generally spend the night for a small, extra "one-night membership" fee. Cheap meals are sometimes available, and kitchen facilities are usually provided. Expect youth groups in spring, crowds in the summer, and snoring. In official IYHF-member hostels, family rooms are sometimes available on request, but it's basically boys' dorms and girls' dorms. You usually can't check in before 17:00 and must be out by 10:00. There's often a 23:00 curfew. Official hostels are marked with a triangular sign that shows a house and a tree.

The Low Countries have plenty of private hostels, where you'll find no midday lockout, no curfew, no membership requirement, co-ed dorms, simple double rooms, and a more easygoing and rowdy atmosphere.

TRAVELING AS A TEMPORARY LOCAL

We travel all the way to Europe to enjoy differences—to become temporary locals. You'll experience frustrations. There are certain truths that we find God-given and self-evident, such as cold beer, ice in drinks, bottomless cups of coffee, "the customer's always right," easy shower faucets, and driving on the right-hand side of the road. One of the benefits of travel is the eye-opening realization that there are logical, civil, and even better alternatives. A willingness to go local ensures that you'll enjoy a full dose of European hospitality.

If there is a negative aspect to the image Europeans have of Americans, it is that we are big, aggressive, impolite, rich, loud, and a bit naive. Americans tend to be noisy in public places, such as restaurants and trains. Our raised voices can demolish Europe's reserved and elegant ambience. Talk softly.

While Europeans look bemusedly at some of our Yankee excesses—and worriedly at others—they nearly always afford us individual travelers all the warmth we deserve.

Send Me an E-mail, Drop Me a Line

If you enjoy a successful trip with the help of this book and would like to share your discoveries, please fill out the survey at www.ricksteves.com/feedback. I personally read and value all feedback.

Judging from all the happy postcards I receive from travelers who have used this book, it's safe to assume you'll enjoy a great, affordable vacation—with the finesse of an independent, experienced traveler. Thanks, and have a *goede vakantie!*

BACK DOOR TRAVEL PHILOSOPHY
From *Rick Steves' Europe Through the Back Door*

Travel is intensified living—maximum thrills per minute and one of the last great sources of legal adventure. Travel is freedom. It's recess, and we need it.

Experiencing the real Europe requires catching it by surprise, going casual..."Through the Back Door."

Affording travel is a matter of priorities. (Make do with the old car.) You can travel—simply, safely, and comfortably—anywhere in Europe for $100 a day plus transportation costs (allow more for Amsterdam). In many ways, spending more money only builds a thicker wall between you and what you came to see. Europe is a cultural carnival, and, time after time, you'll find that its best acts are free and the best seats are the cheap ones.

A tight budget forces you to travel close to the ground, meeting and communicating with the people, not relying on service with a purchased smile. Never sacrifice sleep, nutrition, safety, or cleanliness in the name of budget. Simply enjoy the local-style alternatives to expensive hotels and restaurants.

Extroverts have more fun. If your trip is low on magic moments, kick yourself and make things happen. If you don't enjoy a place, maybe you don't know enough about it. Seek the truth. Recognize tourist traps. Give a culture the benefit of your open mind. See things as different but not better or worse. Any culture has much to share.

Of course, travel, like the world, is a series of hills and valleys. Be fanatically positive and militantly optimistic. If something's not to your liking, change your liking. Travel is addictive. It can make you a happier American as well as a citizen of the world. Our Earth is home to six billion equally important people. It's humbling to travel and find that people don't envy Americans. They like us, but, with all due respect, they wouldn't trade passports.

Globe-trotting destroys ethnocentricity. It helps you understand and appreciate different cultures. Regrettably, there are forces in our society that want you dumbed down for their convenience. Don't let it happen. Thoughtful travel engages you with the world—more important than ever these days. Travel changes people. It broadens perspectives and teaches new ways to measure quality of life. Many travelers toss aside their hometown blinders. Their prized souvenirs are the strands of different cultures they decide to knit into their own character. The world is a cultural yarn shop. And Back Door travelers are weaving the ultimate tapestry. Come on, join in!

THE NETHERLANDS

Holland: windmills, wooden shoes, cheese, tulips, and tranquility. In its 17th-century glory days, tiny Holland was a world power— politically, economically, and culturally—with more great artists per square mile than any other country.

Today, the Netherlands is Europe's most densely populated country, and also one of its wealthiest and best organized. In 1944, the neighboring countries of Belgium, the Netherlands, and Luxembourg formed the nucleus of a united Europe when they joined economically to form Benelux.

Efficiency is a Dutch custom. The average income is higher than in the United States. Though only 8 percent of the labor force is made up of farmers, 70 percent of the land is cultivated, and you'll travel through vast fields of barley, wheat, sugar beets, potatoes, and flowers.

"Holland" is just a nickname for the Netherlands. North Holland and South Holland are the largest of the 12 provinces that make up the Netherlands. The word Netherlands means "lowlands," and the country is so named because half of it is below sea level, reclaimed from the sea (or rivers). That's why the locals say, "God made the Earth, but the Dutch made Holland." Modern technology and plenty of Dutch elbow grease have turned much of the sea into fertile farmland. Though a new province—Flevoland,

---

How Big, How Many, How Much

- 13,000 square miles, a little larger than Maryland
- 16.4 million people (1,250 people per square mile; 15 times the population density of the U.S.)
- €1 = about $1.20

The Netherlands

near Amsterdam—has been drained, dried, and populated in the last 100 years, Dutch reclamation projects are essentially finished. In the era of global warming and rising sea levels, the Dutch have continued to innovate, building floatable homes and industrial greenhouses that rise with the tides.

All the flat, reclaimed land makes Holland a biker's dream. The Dutch, who average four bikes per family, have put small bike roads (with their own traffic lights) beside nearly every major highway. You can rent bikes at most train stations and drop them off at most others. And you can take bikes on trains, outside of rush hour, for €6 per day.

The Dutch can generally speak English, they pride themselves on their frankness, and they like to split the bill. Traditionally, Dutch cities have been open-minded, loose, and liberal (to attract sailors in the days of Henry Hudson). And today, Amsterdam is a capital of alternative lifestyles—a city where nothing's illegal as long as nobody gets hurt. While freewheeling Amsterdam does have a quiet side (particularly in the pleasant Jordaan neighborhood), travelers who prefer more small-town Dutch evenings sleep in a small town nearby, such as Haarlem, and side-trip into the big city.

AMSTERDAM

ORIENTATION

Amsterdam is a progressive way of life housed in Europe's most 17th-century city. Physically, it's built upon millions of pilings. But more than that, it's built on good living, cozy cafés, great art, street-corner jazz, stately history, and a spirit of live-and-let-live. It has 739,000 people and almost as many bikes. It also has more canals than Venice...and about as many tourists.

During its Golden Age in the 1600s, Amsterdam was the world's richest city, an international sea-trading port, and the cradle of capitalism. Wealthy, democratic burghers built a planned city of canals lined with trees and townhouses topped with fancy gables. Immigrants, Jews, outcasts, and political rebels were drawn here by its tolerant atmosphere, while painters such as young Rembrandt captured that atmosphere on canvas.

In 2006, Amsterdam will turn into Party Central to celebrate Rembrandt's 400th birthday. Expect some exciting Rembrandt-related exhibits. The most important will be in the Van Gogh Museum exhibition hall (Feb 24–June 8; see sidebar on page 41). For Rembrandt's birthday-party details, visit www.rembrandt400.com.

The Dutch are unique. They may be the world's most handsome people—tall, healthy, and with good posture—and the most open, honest, and refreshingly blunt. They like to laugh. As connoisseurs of world culture, they appreciate Rembrandt paintings, Indonesian food, and the latest French film—but with an unsnooty, blue-jeans attitude.

Approach Amsterdam as an ethnologist observing a strange culture. Stroll through any neighborhood and see things that are commonplace here, but rarely found elsewhere. Carillons chime quaintly in neighborhoods selling sex, as young professionals smoke pot with impunity next to old ladies in bonnets selling flowers. Observe the neighborhood's "social control," where an elderly man feels safe in his home knowing he's being watched by the prostitutes next door.

Be warned: Amsterdam, a bold experiment in freedom, may box your Puritan ears. Take it all in, then pause to watch the sunset—at 10:00 p.m. during summer—and see the Golden Age reflected in a quiet canal.

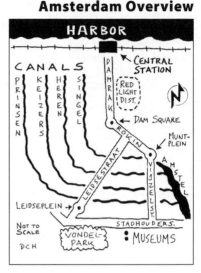

Planning Your Time

Amsterdam is worth a full day of sightseeing on even the busiest itinerary. While the city has a couple of must-see museums, its best attraction is its own breezy ambience. The city's a joy on foot—and a breezier and faster joy by bike.

Amsterdam in One Day

9:00   Follow my self-guided Amsterdam City Walk, which takes you from the train station to the Rijksmuseum, with stops at the peaceful Begijnhof, Amsterdam History Museum, and flower market. Break the walk in the middle with a relaxing hour-long canal cruise (departs from Spui dock or from near Leidseplein).

14:00   Visit Amsterdam's two great art museums, located side by side: the Van Gogh and the Rijksmuseum.

18:30   Tour the Anne Frank House. Visiting after 18:00 in summer saves an hour in line. Arrive earlier off-season (Sept–March) when the sight closes at 19:00.

19:30   Wander the Jordaan neighborhood, finding dinner in this idyllic side of town.

21:30   Stroll the Red Light District for some of Europe's most fascinating window-shopping.

Amsterdam in Two or More Days
Day 1

9:00   Follow my self-guided Amsterdam City Walk, leading from the train station to the Rijksmuseum, via the quiet

Daily Reminder

The biggest Amsterdam sights—the Rijksmuseum, the Van Gogh Museum, and the Anne Frank House—are open daily year-round. The city's naughty sights, as you might expect, stay open late every day (Erotic Museum until 24:00, Damrak Sex Museum until 23:30, and the Hash, Marijuana, and Hemp Museum until 22:00).

Sunday: These sights have limited, afternoon-only hours today: the Amsterkring Museum (13:00–17:00), New Church (13:00–18:00), and Old Church (13:00–17:00). The Westerkerk church and tower are closed, and the Waterlooplein flea market is shut down.

Monday: These are closed today—the Heineken Brewery and Houseboat Museum (also closed Tue–Thu Nov–Feb). The Netherlands Maritime Museum is closed on Mondays in winter (mid-Sept–mid-June).

Tuesday–Thursday: All recommended sights are open.

Friday: These are open late—the Rijksmuseum and Van Gogh Museum (both until 22:00), plus Rembrandt's House (until 21:00).

Saturday: All recommended sights are open.

       Begijnhof, Amsterdam History Museum (make time to tour this), and flower market.

12:00   Stop for lunch in the Spui neighborhood before completing the walk.

14:00   Visit Amsterdam's two outstanding art museums, located next to each other: the Van Gogh and the Rijksmuseum.

18:00   Dinner.

21:00   Stroll the Red Light District for some memorable window-shopping.

Day 2

10:00   Start your day with a one-hour canal boat tour (boats leave across from train station).

11:00   Visit the sights that interest you around Rembrandtplein (Rembrandt's House, Waterlooplein flea market, Gassan Diamonds polishing demo, Dutch Resistance Museum), breaking for lunch at the recommended restaurant adjacent to the Dutch Resistance Museum.

14:30   Free time to shop and explore.

17:00   Tour the Anne Frank House. (If lines are long, come back later. The museum closes at 21:00 April–Aug and at 19:00 Sept–March.)

18:30   Take my self-guided Jordaan Walk.
20:00   Dinner in the Jordaan.

Day 3
Visit the nearby town of Haarlem (see page 183).

Day 4
Side-trip by train to an open-air folk museum (either Arnhem's Open-Air Folk Museum, Zaanse Schans, or Enkhuizen's Zuiderzee), and visit Edam or Delft.

OVERVIEW

(area code: 020)
Amsterdam's Central Train Station, on the north edge of the city, is your starting point, with the TI, bike rental, and trams fanning out to all points. Damrak is the main north–south street axis, connecting Central Station with Dam Square (people-watching and hangout center) and its Royal Palace. From this spine, the city spreads out like a fan, with 90 islands, hundreds of bridges, and a series of concentric canals—named Herengracht (Gentleman's Canal), Keizersgracht (Emperor's Canal), and Prinsengracht (Prince's Canal)—that were laid out in the 17th century, Holland's Golden Age. Amsterdam's major sights are within walking distance of Dam Square.

To the east of Damrak is the oldest part of the city (today's Red Light District), and to the west is the newer part, where you'll find the Anne Frank House and the Jordaan neighborhood. Museums and Leidseplein nightlife cluster at the southern edge of the city center.

Tourist Information
There are four VVV offices. "VVV," pronounced "vay vay vay," is Dutch for "TI," a tourist information office. These are inside of Central Station at track 2b (Mon–Sat 8:00–20:00, Sun 9:00–17:00), in front of Central Station (daily 9:00–17:00, most crowded), on Leidsestraat (less crowded, daily 9:00–19:00), and at the airport (daily 7:00–22:00).

Avoid Amsterdam's crowded, inefficient tourist offices if you can. For €0.60 a minute, you can save yourself a trip by calling the TI toll line at 0900-400-4040 (Mon–Fri 9:00–17:00). If you're staying in nearby Haarlem, ask your Amsterdam questions and pick up the brochures at the helpful, friendly, and rarely crowded Haarlem TI (see page 184).

At Amsterdam's TIs, consider buying a city map (€2) and any of the walking-tour brochures (€1.50 each, including *Discovery Tour*

Dutch Landmarks

Dam (pronounced dahm)	Amsterdam's main square
Damrak (DAHM-rock)	Main street between Central Station and Dam Square
Spui (spow, rhymes with cow)	Both a street and square
Rokin (roh-KEEN)	Street connecting Dam Square and Spui
Kalverstraat (KAL-ver-strot)	Pedestrian street
Leidseplein (LIDE-zuh-pline)	Lively square
Jordaan (yor-DAHN)	Neighborhood in southwest Amsterdam
Museumplein (myoo-ZAY-um-pline)	Square with Rijks and Van Gogh museums
gracht (khrockt, guttural)	canal
straat (straht)	street
plein (pline)	public square
huis (house)	house
kerk (kerk)	church

Through the Center, The Former Jewish Quarter, and *Walks Through Jordaan*). For entertainment, pick up the *Day by Day* calendar (€1.75), call the Last Minute Ticket Shop (tickets for theater, classical music, and major rock shows, tel. 0900-0191, www.lastminuteticketshop .nl), and check out this book's Nightlife chapter.

At Amsterdam's Central Station, GWK Change has hotel reservation windows whose clerks sell local and international phone cards and cheaper city maps (€1.60) and can answer basic tourist questions, with shorter lines (in west tunnel, at right end of station as you leave platform, tel. 020/627-2731).

Don't use the TI or GWK to book a room; you'll pay €5 per person and your host loses 13 percent—meaning you'll likely be charged a higher rate. The phone system is easy, everyone speaks English, and the listings in this book are a better value than the potluck booking you'd get from the TI.

I amsterdam **Card:** This card includes free entry to most city sights, discounts on other sights and attractions, two free canal boat tours, and unlimited use of the trams, buses, and metro (€33/24 hrs, €43/48 hrs, €53/72 hrs, sold at TIs, www.iamsterdamcard.com). The pass covers most major Amsterdam museums, including the Van Gogh and the Rijksmuseum (but not the Anne Frank House). If you'll be doing a lot of sightseeing—say, visiting the Van Gogh, the Rijksmuseum, and Amsterdam History Museum, plus taking a canal boat tour in one day—this pass will save you a little money (€2.50). While they are sold at the TI, avoid the line by buying it at the adjacent GVB transit office (across from the station).

Tourist Information Online: Try www.visitamsterdam.nl (Amsterdam Tourism Board), www.amsterdam.nl (City of Amsterdam), and www.holland.com (Netherlands Board of Tourism).

Arrival in Amsterdam

By Train: Amsterdam swings, and the hinge that connects it to the world is its perfectly central Central Station. Expect a chaotic construction zone—the station is being renovated through 2010. The international ticket office should be at track 2, and luggage lockers are at the far east end of the building (from €5.70/24 hrs, daily 7:00–23:00, ID required).

Walk out the door of the station, and you're in the heart of the city. You'll nearly trip over trams ready to take you anywhere your feet won't. Straight ahead is Damrak street, leading to Dam Square. With your back to the entrance of the station, the TI and GVB public-transit offices are just ahead and to your left. And on your right is a vast, multistory bike garage.

By Plane: For details on getting from Schiphol Airport into downtown Amsterdam, see page 240.

Helpful Hints

Theft Alert: Tourists are considered green and rich, and the city has more than its share of hungry thieves—especially on trams and at the many hostels. Wear your money belt.

Emergency Telephone Number: Throughout the Netherlands, dial 112.

Street Smarts: Most canals are lined by streets with the same name. When walking around town, beware of the silent transportation—trams and bicycles. (Don't walk on tram tracks or pink bicycle paths.)

Shop Hours: Most shops are open Tuesday through Saturday from 10:00 to 18:00, and Sunday and Monday from 12:00 to 18:00. Some shops stay open later (21:00) on Thursdays. Supermarkets are generally open Monday through Saturday from 8:00 to 20:00, and closed on Sundays.

Internet Access: It's easy at cafés all over town. Two huge **easy-Internetcafés** offer hundreds of terminals with fast, cheap (€2.50/hr) access: there's one a block in front of the train station at **Damrak 33** (daily 10:00–20:00) and another between Mint Tower and Rembrandtplein at **Reguliersbreestraat 22** (daily 9:00–21:00). "Coffeeshops," which sell marijuana, usually also offer Internet access—letting you surf the Net with a special bravado.

English Bookstore: For fiction and guidebooks—including mine—try the **American Book Center** at Kalverstraat 125 (Mon–Sat 10:00–20:00, Sun 11:00–18:30) or the huge and helpful **Scheltema,** near the Leidsestraat at Koningsplein 20 (included in Amsterdam City Walk—see page 59, store open Mon–Sat 10:00–18:00, Thu until 21:00, Sun 12:00–18:00; lots of English novels, guidebooks, and maps).

Maps: The free and cheap tourist maps can be confusing. Consider paying a bit more (about €2) for a top-notch map. I like the *Carto Studio Centrumkaart Amsterdam* or, better yet, the *Amsterdam: Go Where the Locals Go* map by Amsterdam Anything.

Queen's Day: On Queen's Day (usually celebrated on April 30), Amsterdam turns into a gigantic garage sale/street market. Note that in 2006, Queen's Day will be celebrated on April 29, a Saturday.

Getting Around Amsterdam

The helpful GVB public-transit information office is in front of the train station (next to TI, daily 8:00–21:00). Its free, multilingual *Public Transport Amsterdam Tourist Guide* includes a transit map and explains ticket options and tram connections to all the sights. In keeping with the Dutch mission to automate life, they'll tack on a €0.50 penalty if you buy your transit tickets from a human ticket seller, rather than from a machine.

By Bus, Tram, and Metro: Trams #2 and #5 travel the north–south axis from Central Station to Dam Square to Leidseplein to Museumplein. Tram #14 goes east–west (Westerkerk–Dam Square–Muntplein–Waterlooplein–Plantage). If you get lost in Amsterdam, 10 of the city's 17 trams take you back to Central Station. The metro (underground train) is used mostly for commuting to the suburbs, but it does connect Central Station with some sights east of Damrak (Nieuwmarkt–Waterlooplein–Weesperplein).

You have various ticket options:

- **Individual tickets** cost €1.60 and give you an hour on the buses, trams, and metro system (pay as you board on trams and buses; for the metro, buy tickets from machines).
- The **24-hour** (€6.30), **48-hour** (€10), or **72-hour** (€13) **tickets** give you unlimited transportation on Amsterdam's (and the Netherlands') public transit network. Buy them at the GVB public-transit office (all versions available) or as you board (24-hr version only, costs €0.50 extra).
- **Strip tickets** *(strippenkaart)*, cheaper than individual tickets, are good on buses, trams, and the metro in Amsterdam and

Bike Theft

Bike thieves are bold and brazen in Amsterdam. Bikes come with two locks and stern instructions to use them both. The wimpy ones go through the spokes, and the industrial-strength chains are meant to be wrapped around the actual body of the bike and connected to something stronger than any human. Do this diligently. On my last trip, I used both locks, but my chain wasn't around the main bar of my bike's body. In the morning, I found only my front tire (still safely chained to the metal fence). If you're sloppy, it's an expensive mistake, and one that any "included" theft insurance won't cover.

anywhere in the Netherlands. The further you go, the more strips you'll use: Any downtown ride in Amsterdam costs two strips (good for 1 hr of transfers). A card with 15 strips costs €6.50 (you can share them with your partner). Shorter strip tickets (2, 3, and 8 strips) are sold on some buses and trams, but the per-strip cost is about double. It's cheapest to buy the 15-strip tickets at the GVB public-transit office, machines at the train station, bookstores, post offices, airport, or tobacco shops throughout the country. You can also buy them (for a little more) directly from the driver.

Armed with your *strippenkaart*, board the tram (you may have to press a button to open the doors) and have your strip ticket stamped by a conductor/driver or a machine. For the machine, fold over the number of strips you need (2 for rides in central Amsterdam), stick that end in the slot, and it will stamp the time. To transfer (good for 1 hr), just show the conductor/driver your stamped *strippenkaart*.

• Along with its sightseeing perks, the *I amsterdam* **Card** offers unlimited use of the tram, bus, and metro for its duration (1, 2, or 3 days, see above).

By Foot: The longest walk a tourist would take is an hour from the station to the Rijksmuseum. Watch out for silent but potentially painful bikes, trams, and crotch-high curb posts.

By Bike: Everyone—bank managers, students, pizza delivery boys, and police—uses this mode of transport. It's *the* smart way to travel in a city where 40 percent of all traffic rolls on two wheels. You'll get around town by bike faster than you can by taxi. On my last visit, I rented a bike for five days, chained it up outside my hotel, and enjoyed wonderful mobility. I highly encourage this for anyone who wants to get maximum fun per hour in Amsterdam. One-speed bikes, with *"brrringing"* bells, rent for about €7–10 per day (cheaper for longer periods) at any number of places. Hotels can send you to the nearest spot.

MacBike, with 900 bikes, is the bike-rental powerhouse, with a huge and efficient out-let at Central Station (daily 9:00–17:45, €6/3 hrs, €8.50/24 hrs, more for 3 gears, no helmets, €50 deposit plus passport or credit-card imprint, at east end of station—on the left as you're leaving, by the buses, tel. 020/624-8391, can reserve online, www.macbike.nl). Mac-Bike sells several booklets outlining bike tours in and around Amsterdam for €1.

Frederic Rent-a-Bike, near the Anne Frank House, is also good, with quality bikes and a helpful staff (€10/24 hrs, daily 9:00–18:00, Brouwersgracht 78, tel. 020/624-5509, www.frederic.nl).

No one wears helmets. For safety: Use arm signals, follow the bike-only traffic signals, stay in the obvious and omnipresent bike lanes, yield to traffic on the right, and fear tram tracks. Cross tram tracks at a perpendicular angle to avoid catching your tire in the rut. Warning: Police ticket bikers as drivers. Obey all traffic signals, and walk your bike through pedestrian zones. Fines for biking through pedestrian zones are reportedly €300.

By Boat: While the city is great on foot or bike, another option is the **Museum Boat,** which shuttles tourists from sight to sight on an all-day ticket. Tickets cost €14 (includes sight discounts worth about €2.25). The sales booths in front of the Central Station (and the boats) offer handy, free brochures with museum times and admission prices. The narrated ride takes two hours if you don't get off (about hourly, 12 stops, recorded narration, departures daily 10:00–17:00, discounted after 13:00 to €12.50, tel. 020/530-1090).

The nearby and similar **Canal Bus** offers 14 stops on three different routes (€16, ticket is valid until 12:00 the following day, departures daily 10:00–18:00, longer hours in summer, tel. 020/623-9886, www.canal.nl).

If you're looking for a floating nonstop tour, the regular canal tour boats (without the stops) give more information, cover more ground, and cost less (see "Tours," below). For do-it-yourself canal tours and lots of exercise, Canal Boat also rents "canal bikes" (a.k.a.

paddleboats) near the Anne Frank House and Rijksmuseum (€8/hr per person, daily July–Aug 10:00–21:30, Sept–June 10:00–18:00).

By Taxi: Amsterdam's taxis are expensive (€3.50 drop, €2 per kilometer). You can wave them down, find a rare taxi stand, or call one (tel. 020/677-7777). Given the fine tram system, taxis are rarely a good value. You'll also see **bike taxis,** particularly near Dam Square and Leidseplein. Negotiate a rate for the trip before you board (no meter) and they'll wheel you wherever you want to go (€10/30 min, no surcharge for baggage or extra weight, sample fare from Leidseplein to Anne Frank House: about €6).

By Car: Forget it—all you'll find are frustrating one-way streets, terrible parking, and meter maids with a passion for booting cars wrongly parked.

TOURS

▲▲Canal Boat Tours—These long, low, tourist-laden boats leave continually from several docks around the town for a relax-
ing, if uninspiring, one-hour introduction to the city (with recorded headphone commentary). The only reason to choose one over the others is for convenience based on the starting point, or if that particular one is free and included with your *I amsterdam* Card (it covers Rederij Noord-Zuid

and Holland International boats). Choose from one of these three companies:

Rondvaart Kooij is cheapest, and has the boats I prefer—all the seats face forward (€7, 2/hr in summer 10:00–22:00, 2/hr in winter 10:00–17:00, at corner of Spui and Rokin streets, about 5 min from Dam Square, tel. 020/623-3810, www.rederijkooij.nl).

Rederij Noord-Zuid departs from near Leidseplein (€9, 2/hr April–Oct 10:00–18:00, 1/hr Nov–March 10:00–17:00, tel. 020/679-1370, www.canal-cruises.nl).

Holland International offers the standard one-hour trip and a variety of longer tours (€8.50, 3/hr mid-March–Oct 9:00–22:00, 2/hr Nov–mid-March 10:00–18:00, blue boats depart from in front of Central Station, tel. 020/622-7788).

No fishing allowed—but bring your camera. Some prefer to cruise at night, when the bridges are illuminated.

Red Light District Tours—You have two walking-tour options for seeing Amsterdam's most infamous neighborhood with a guide (also consider my self-guided Red Light District Walk, page 78).

Randy Roy's Red Light Tours consists of one expat American women, Kimberly. She lived in the Red Light District for years, and she gives fun, casual, yet informative 90-minute walks through this fascinating and eye-popping neighborhood. While the actual information is light, you'll walk through various porn and drug shops and have an expert to answer your questions (€12.50 includes a drink in a colorful bar at the end, nightly at 20:00, occasional Fri and Sat 22:00 tours, meet in front of Victoria Hotel—in front of the station, mobile 06-4185-3288, call to confirm).

Zoom Amsterdam Citywalk starts at a café in the Tower of Tears (located across from Central Station, to the southwest), where you listen to an initial 30-minute spiel about the history of the city. Then you'll hit the streets for another two hours to find out the complicated story behind the Red Light District, including some fascinating, locals-only info (such as the scams that unscrupulous bar owners use on the many young, male Brits who flock here). If you're curious about the area but would rather explore with a group, Zoom Amsterdam is a good way to go (€12.50, daily at 17:00; book ahead at VVV, through hotel, or by calling 020/623-6302; www.zoomamsterdam.com).

Bike Tours—The **Yellow Bike Guided Tours** company offers a three-hour city tour (€19, April–Oct Sun–Fri at 9:30 and 13:00, Sat at 9:30 and 14:00) and a six-hour, 22-mile tour of the countryside (€25, April–Oct daily at 11:00, €100 deposit or credit-card imprint; both tours leave from Nieuwezijds Kolk 29, 3 blocks from Central Station, tel. 020/620-6940, www.yellowbike.nl). If you take their tour, you can rent the bike for the rest of the day at a discount. **MacBike** also runs city bike tours (€12.50, Thu–Sun at 14:00, listed above).

Wetlands Safari, Nature Canoe Tours near Amsterdam—If you'd like to get some exercise and a dose of the *polder* country and village life, consider this tour. Majel Tromp, a friendly villager who speaks great English, takes groups limited to 15 people. The program: Meet at the VVV tourist information office outside Central Station at 9:30, catch a public bus, stop for coffee, take a 3.5-hour canoe trip (2–3 people per canoe) with several stops, tour a village by canoe, munch a rural canalside picnic lunch (included), then canoe and bus back into the big city by 14:30 (€33, 10 percent off with this book through 2006, May–mid-Sept Mon–Fri, reservations required, tel. 020/686-3445, mobile 06-5355-2669, www.wetlandssafari.nl, info@wetlandssafari.nl).

Adam's Apple Tours—This walking tour offers a two-hour, English-only look at the historic roots of Amsterdam. You'll have a small group and a caring guide, starting off at Central Station and ending up at the Dam Square (€22.50; Fri–Sun at 10:00, 12:30, and 15:00; call 020/616-7867 to confirm times and book, www.adamsapple.nl, Frank).

Private Guide—Ab Walet is a likeable, hardworking, and knowledgeable local guide who enjoys personalizing tours for Americans interested in knowing his city better. He specializes in history and architecture and exudes a passion for Amsterdam (€40/2 hrs, €80/4 hrs, for small groups of up to 4 people, on foot or by bike, tel. 020/671-2588, mobile 06-2069-7882, abwalet@yahoo.com). Ab also can take travelers to nearby towns.

Do-It-Yourself Bike Tour of Amsterdam—A day enjoying the bridges, bike lanes, and sleepy, off-the-beaten-path canals on your own one-speed is an essential Amsterdam experience. The real joys of Europe's best-preserved 17th-century city are the countless intimate glimpses it offers: the laid-back locals sunning on their porches under elegant gables, rusted bikes that look as if they've been lashed to the same lamppost since the 1960s, wasted hedonists planted on canalside benches, and happy sailors permanently moored, but still manning the deck.

For a good day, rent a bike at Central Station (see "By Bike" on page 33). Head west down Haarlemmerstraat, working your wide-eyed way down the Prinsengracht (drop into Café 't Papeneiland at Prinsengracht 2) and detouring through the gentrified small streets of the Jordaan neighborhood before popping out at Westerkerk under the tallest spire in the city.

Pedal out to the lush and peaceful Vondelpark, then cut back through the center of town (Leidseplein to the Mint Tower, down Rokin street to Dam Square). From there, cruise the Red Light District, following Oudezijds Voorburgwal past the Old Church (Oude Kerk) to Zeedijk street, and return to the train station.

From Central Station, you can escape into the countryside by hopping on the free ferry behind the station. In five minutes, Amsterdam will be gone, and you'll be rolling through your very own Dutch painting (get free *Great Waterland Bicycle Tour* brochure from MacBike rental shop, described on page 34).

Prinsengracht Via de Opstapper—For a do-it-yourself public-bus tour along the scenic Prince's Canal (Prinsengracht), catch Amsterdam's cute little mini-bus Opstapper service. It arcs along the city's longest canal, offering clever budget travelers a very cheap and fun 20-minute experience. The scenic bus ride goes where normal big buses can't fit (along the bumpy and cobbled canalside lanes), giving you a delightful look at the workaday city—without a tourist in sight. The high ride and big windows show you

Amsterdam well, and it's much faster than a touristy canal tour. Get on at the train station, and you'll have comfortable seats (those in back have the best view) the entire way.

From the train station, you pass my two favorite brown cafés in the Jordaan district, countless houseboats, and the whole gamut of gables (under a parade of leaning, Golden Age buildings complete with all the hooks and pulleys). Rolling along the Prinsengracht, you'll see the long line at the Anne Frank House just before the towering Westerkerk. You pass within a block of the thriving Leidseplein and Rijksmuseum before crossing the Amstel River to finish at the Waterlooplein flea market (near Rembrandt's House, Gassan Diamonds, and the metro station).

There are no stops. People just wave it down. The white mini-buses go on the outside of the canal counterclockwise and return clockwise along the inside. Any individual ticket is good for an hour. If you see something fun, just jump out. There's another bus in 10 minutes (€1.60 or 2 strips, 6/hr, 9 seats, Mon–Sat 7:30–18:30, not Sun, can be muggy on hot days). Buses depart from a tiny lot in front of Victoria Hotel, across from Central Station, and finish at the Waterlooplein metro station (with subway trains coming every 2 min, returning you to Central Station in 3 min).

SIGHTS

One of Amsterdam's delights is that it has perhaps more small specialty museums than any other city its size. From houseboats to sex, from cannabis to costumes, you can find a museum to suit your interests. Buying the *I amsterdam* Card, which is good at most of the museums below (see page 30), can make even lesser sights interesting enough to justify the entry price (i.e., free). Note that most museums require baggage check (usually free, often in coin-op lockers where you get your coin back).

The following sights are arranged by neighborhood for handy sightseeing. When you see a ✪ in a listing, it means the sight is covered in much more depth in my self-guided walks or one of the museum tours.

Southwest Amsterdam

▲▲▲**Rijksmuseum**—Built to house the nation's great art, the Rijksmuseum owns several thousand paintings, including an incomparable collection of Dutch Masters: Rembrandt, Vermeer, Hals, and Steen. The museum has made it easy for you to focus on the highlights, because that's all that is on display while most of the building undergoes several years of renovation (due to reopen in the summer of 2008). Wander through the Rijksmuseum's Philips Wing for a wonderful, concentrated dose of 17th-century Dutch masterpieces (€10, covered by *I amsterdam* Card, audio-guide-€4, daily 9:00–18:00, Friday until 22:00, tram #2 or #5 from train station to Hobbemastraat, tel. 020/674-7047, www.rijksmuseum.com). The Philips Wing entrance is near the corner of Hobbemastraat and Jan Luijkenstraat on the south side of the Rijks—the part of the huge building nearest the Van Gogh Museum. ✪ See Rijksmuseum Tour, page 101. Because 2006 is the anniversary of Rembrandt's 400th birthday, expect lots of special

Southwest Amsterdam

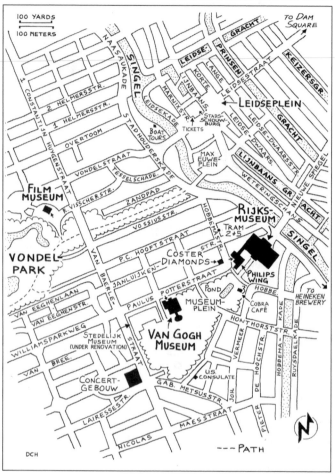

attractions and crowds at Rembrandt-related sights (see sidebar).

▲▲▲**Van Gogh Museum**—Near the Rijksmuseum, this remark-able museum features works by the troubled Dutch artist whose art seemed to mirror his life. During the first half of 2006, the museum hosts a special Rembrandt/Caravaggio exhibition in its exhibit hall (go down the escalator from the ground floor lobby); see the sidebar on page 41.

Vincent, who killed himself in 1890 at age 37, is best known for sunny, Impressionist canvases that vibrate and pulse with life. The museum's 200 paintings, a stroll through the artist's work and life, were owned by Theo, Vincent's younger, art-dealer brother. Highlights include *Sunflowers*, *The Bedroom*, *The Potato Eaters*, and

Happy 400th, Rembrandt!

Rembrandt van Rijn, who lived from 1606 to 1669, is the greatest Dutch artist and perhaps history's finest painter of self-portraits. In 2006, Amsterdam will turn into Party Central to celebrate his 400th birthday.

The most important event is the Rembrandt Exhibition, highlighting paintings by Rembrandt and Caravaggio, the Italian predecessor who pioneered the light/dark style Rembrandt perfected. The exhibit runs from February 24 through June 18 at the Van Gogh Museum and costs €20. Note that any art-loving tourist will do better by getting the big €25 combo-ticket for the Rijksmuseum, Van Gogh Museum, and special Rembrandt Exhibition.

The Rijksmuseum will showcase its entire Rembrandt collection, plus several special exhibits throughout the year. Rembrandt's House celebrates the milestone with 50 of Rembrandt's paintings hung in his actual house, plus many of his etchings (April–June 2006, see listing on page 49). Several other museums (including the Amstelkring Museum, Amsterdam History Museum, and Jewish Museum) and galleries will also mount special exhibits. For Rembrandt's birthday-party details, see www .rembrandt400.com.

many brooding self-portraits. The third floor shows works that influenced Vincent, from Monet and Pissarro to Gauguin, Cézanne, and Toulouse-Lautrec. The worthwhile audioguide includes insightful commentaries and quotes from Vincent himself (€10, covered by *I amsterdam* Card, audioguide-€4, daily 10:00–18:00, Fri until 22:00, Paulus Potterstraat 7, tel. 020/570-5200, www .vangoghmuseum.nl). ✪ See Van Gogh Museum Tour, page 119.

▲**Museumplein**—Bordered by the Rijks, Van Gogh, and the Concertgebouw (classical music hall), this square is interesting even to art-haters. Amsterdam's best acoustics are found underneath the Rijksmuseum, where street musicians perform everything from chamber music to Mongolian throat singing. Mimes, human statues, and crafts booths dot the square. Skateboarders careen across a concrete tube, while locals enjoy a park bench or a coffee at the Cobra Café.

Nearby is **Coster Diamonds**, a handy place to see a diamond-cutting and polishing demo (free and interesting 30-min tours

Amsterdam

on request followed by sales pitch, popular for decades with tour groups, prices marked up to include tour guide kickbacks, daily 9:00–17:00, 2 Paulus Potterstraat). The tour at Gassan Diamonds is better (see "Southeast Amsterdam," below), but Coster is convenient to the Museumplein scene.

▲Heineken Brewery—The leading Dutch beer is no longer brewed here, but this old brewery now welcomes visitors to a slick and entertaining beer-appreciation experience. It's the most enjoyable brewery tour I've encountered in Europe. You'll learn as much as you want, marvel at the huge vats and towering ceilings, see videos, and go on rides. "What's it like to be a Heineken bottle and be filled with one of the best beers in the world? Try it for yourself." An important section recognizes a budding problem of our age, vital to people as well as beer: this planet's scarcity of clean water. With globalization, corporations are well on their way to owning the world's water supplies (€10 for self-guided, 75-minute tour and 3 beers or soft drinks; must be over age 18, Tue–Sun 10:00–18:00, last entry 17:00, closed Mon, tram #16 or #24 to Heinekenplein, an easy walk from Rijksmuseum, tel. 020/523-9666).

▲**Leidseplein**—Brimming with cafés, this people-watching mecca is an impromptu stage for street artists, accordionists, jugglers, and unicyclists. Sunny afternoons are liveliest. The Boom Chicago theater fronts this square (see page 181). Stroll nearby Lange Leidsedwarsstraat (1 block north) for a taste-bud tour of ethnic eateries, from Greek to Indonesian.

▲▲**Vondelpark**—This huge and lively city park is popular with the Dutch—families with little kids, romantic couples, strolling seniors, and hippies sharing blankets and beers. It's a favored venue for free summer concerts. On a sunny afternoon, it's a hedonistic scene that seems to say, "Parents... relax."

Amsterdam Film Museum—This is actually not a museum, but a movie theater. In its three 80-seat theaters, it shows several films a day, from small foreign productions to 70-mm classics drawn from its massive archives (€8, always in the original language, often English subtitles, Vondelpark 3, tel. 020/589-1400, www.filmmuseum.nl).

Rembrandtplein and Tuschinski Theater—One of the city's premier nightlife spots is the leafy **Rembrandtplein** (the artist's modest statue stands here) and the adjoining Thorbeckeplein. Several late-night dance clubs (such as IT, a half block east down Amstelstraat) keep the area lively into the wee hours. Utrechtsestraat is lined with upscale shops and restaurants.

The **Tuschinski Theater**, a movie palace from the 1920s (a half block from Rembrandtplein down Reguliersbreestraat) glitters inside and out. Still a working theater, it's a

Amsterdam at a Glance

▲▲▲**Rijksmuseum** Best collection anywhere of the Dutch Masters: Rembrandt, Hals, Vermeer, and Steen. **Hours:** Daily 9:00–18:00, Friday until 22:00.

▲▲▲**Van Gogh Museum** 200 paintings by the angst-ridden artist. **Hours:** Daily 10:00–18:00, Fri until 22:00.

▲▲▲**Anne Frank House** Young Anne's hideaway during the Nazi occupation. **Hours:** Daily April–Aug 9:00–21:00, Sept–March 9:00–19:00.

▲▲**Vondelpark** City park and concert venue. **Hours:** Always open.

▲▲**Dutch Resistance Museum** History of the Dutch struggle against the Nazis. **Hours:** Tue–Fri 10:00–17:00, Sat–Mon 12:00–17:00.

▲▲**Amstelkring Museum** Catholic church hidden in the attic of a 17th-century merchant's house. **Hours:** Mon–Sat 10:00–17:00, Sun 13:00–17:00.

▲▲**Red Light District** Women of the world's oldest profession on the job. **Hours:** Best between noon and night—avoid late night.

▲**Museumplein** Square with art museums, street musicians, crafts, and nearby diamond demos. **Hours:** Always open.

▲**Heineken Brewery** Best beer tour in Europe. **Hours:** Tue–Sun 10:00–18:00, closed Mon.

delightful old place to see first-run movies. The exterior is an interesting hybrid of styles, forcing the round peg of Art Nouveau into the square hole of Art Deco. The stone-and-tile facade features stripped down, functional Art Deco squares and rectangles, but is ornamented with Art Nouveau elements—Tiffany-style windows, garlands, curvy iron lamps, Egyptian pharaohs, and exotic gold lettering over the door. Inside (lobby is free), the sumptuous decor features red carpets, nymphs on the walls, and semi-abstract designs. Grab a seat in the lobby and watch the ceiling morph (Reguliersbreestraat 26–28).

▲**Leidseplein** Lively square with cafés and street musicians. **Hours:** Always open, best on sunny afternoons.

▲**Begijnhof** Quiet courtyard lined with picturesque houses. **Hours:** Daily 8:00–17:00.

▲**Amsterdam History Museum** Shows city's growth from fishing village to trading capital to today, including some Rembrandts and a playable carillon. **Hours:** Mon–Fri 10:00–17:00, Sat–Sun 11:00–17:00.

▲**Rembrandt's House** The master's reconstructed house, displaying his etchings. **Hours:** Sat–Thu 10:00–17:00, Fri 10:00–21:00.

▲**Diamonds** Tours at shops throughout the city. **Hours:** Generally daily 9:00–17:00.

▲**Willet-Holthuysen Museum (a.k.a. Herengracht Canal Mansion)** Elegant 17th-century house. **Hours:** Mon–Fri 10:00–17:00, Sat–Sun 11:00–17:00.

▲**Hermitage Amsterdam Museum** Russia's Tsarist treasures on loan from St. Petersburg **Hours:** Daily 10:00–17:00.

▲**Dutch Theater** Moving memorial in former Jewish detention center. **Hours:** Daily 11:00–16:00.

▲**Tropical Museum** Re-creations of tropical-life scenes. **Hours:** Daily 10:00–17:00.

▲**Hash, Marijuana, and Hemp Museum** All the dope, from history and science to memorabilia. **Hours:** Daily 11:00–22:00.

Houseboat Museum (Woonbootmuseum)—In the 1930s, modern cargo ships came into widespread use—making small, sail-powered cargo boats obsolete. In danger of extinction, these little vessels found new life as houseboats lining the canals of Amsterdam. Today, 2,500 such boats—their cargo holds turned into classy, comfortable living rooms—are called home by locals. For a peek into this *gezellig* (cozy) world, visit this tiny museum. Captain Vincent enjoys showing visitors around the houseboat, which feels lived-in because, until 1997, it was (€3, covered by *I amsterdam* Card, March–Oct Tue–Sun 11:00–17:00, closed Mon; Nov–Feb Fri–Sun 11:00–17:00, closed Mon–Thu; on Prinsengracht,

opposite #296 facing Elandsgracht, tel. 020/427-0750, www
.houseboatmuseum.nl).

Central Amsterdam, near Dam Square

▲▲▲**Anne Frank House**—A pilgrimage for many, this house
offers a fascinating look at the hideaway of young Anne during the
Nazi occupation of the Netherlands. Anne, her parents, an older
sister, and four others spent a little more than two years in a "Secret
Annex" behind her father's business. While in hiding, 13-year-
old Anne kept a diary chronicling her extraordinary experience.
Acting on a tip, the Nazis arrested them in August 1944 and sent
the group to concentration camps in Poland and Germany. Anne
and her sister died of typhus in March 1945, only weeks before
their camp was liberated. Of the eight inhabitants of the Secret
Annex, only Anne's father, Otto Frank, survived. He returned to
Amsterdam and arranged for his daughter's diary to be published
in 1947. It was followed by many translations, a play, and a movie.

Pick up the English pamphlet at the door. The exhibit offers
thorough coverage of the Frank family, the diary, the stories of
others who hid, and the Holocaust. In summer, skip the hour-long
daytime lines by arriving after 18:00 (last entry is 20:30) and visit
after dinner (€7.50, daily April–Aug 9:00–21:00, Sept–March
9:00–19:00, closed for Yom Kippur—Oct 2 in 2006, last entry 30
min before closing, strict and required baggage check for large
bags, Prinsengracht 267, near Westerkerk, tel. 020/556-7100, www
.annefrank.org). ✪ See Anne Frank House Tour, page 131.

For an interesting glimpse of Holland under the Nazis, rent
the powerful movie *Soldier of Orange* before you leave home.

Westerkerk—Near the Anne Frank House, this landmark church
(free, generally open April–Sept Mon–Sat 10:00–15:00, closed
Sun) has a barren interior, Rembrandt's body buried somewhere
under the pews, and Amsterdam's tallest steeple.

The tower is open by tour only and offers a grand city view.
The tour guide, who speaks in English and Dutch, tells of the
church and its carillon. Only five people are allowed at a time, so
lines can be long (€5, 30 min, departures on the half hour, April–
Sept Mon–Sat 10:00–17:30, last tour leaves at 17:30, closed Sun
and Oct–March, call 020/689-2565 for info and to arrange private
tour).

Royal Palace (Koninklijk Huis)—The palace, which will be closed
for renovation through 2008, is right on Dam Square. It was built
as a lavish City Hall for Amsterdam, when the country was a proud
new republic and Amsterdam was the richest city on the planet—
awash in profit from trade. When constructed in 1648, this building
was one of Europe's finest, with a sumptuous interior. Today, it's the
official (but not actual) residence of the queen (tel. 020/620-4060,

Central Amsterdam

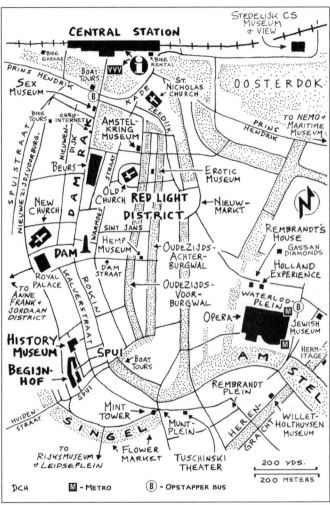

CENTRAL STATION

STEDELIJK CS MUSEUM & VIEW

BIKE GARAGE · BOAT TOURS · VVV · i · BIKE RENTAL

PRINS HENDRIK

SEX MUSEUM

OOSTERDOK

ST. NICHOLAS CHURCH

ZEEDIJK

BIKE TOURS · EASY INTERNET

AMSTEL-KRING MUSEUM

TO NEMO & MARITIME MUSEUM

PRINS HENDRIK

BEURS

NIEUWENDIJK

DAMRAK

NIEUWE ZIJDSVOORBURG.

SPUISTRAAT

NEW CHURCH

OLD CHURCH

EROTIC MUSEUM

RED LIGHT DISTRICT

NIEUW-MARKT

DAM

SINT JANS

WARMOES

HEMP MUSEUM

OUDEZIJDS-ACHTER-BURGWAL

REMBRANDT'S HOUSE

GASSAN DIAMONDS

HOLLAND EXPERIENCE

ROYAL PALACE

DAM STRAAT

OUDEZIJDS-VOOR-BURGWAL

WATERLOO-PLEIN · M · B

TO ANNE FRANK & JORDAAN DISTRICT

KALVERSTRAAT

ROKIN

OPERA

JEWISH MUSEUM

HISTORY MUSEUM

SPUI

BOAT TOURS

M

HERM-ITAGE

BEGIJN-HOF

SPUI

REMBRANDT PLEIN

AMSTEL

HUIDEN-STRAAT

MINT TOWER

MUNT-PLEIN

HEREN-GRACHT

WILLET-HOLTHUYSEN MUSEUM

SINGEL

TO RIJKSMUSEUM & LEIDSEPLEIN

FLOWER MARKET

TUSCHINSKI THEATER

200 YDS.

200 METERS

DCH · ☐ - METRO · Ⓑ - OPSTAPPER BUS

www.koninklijkhuis.nl; for more info, see page 63).

New Church (Nieuwe Kerk)—Barely newer than the "Old" Church (located in the Red Light District), this 15th-century church has an intentionally dull interior, after the decoration was removed by 16th-century iconoclastic Protestants seeking to unclutter their communion with God. This is where many Dutch royal weddings and all coronations take place, and it hosts temporary exhibits. While there's a steep €8 entrance fee to see the various exhibitions (covered by *I amsterdam* Card), anyone can pop in free for a look at the vast interior (Mon–Sat 10:00–18:00,

Sun 13:00–18:00, on Dam Square, tel. 020/638-6909, www
.nieuwekerk.nl; also see page 65).

▲**Begijnhof**—Stepping into this tiny, idyllic courtyard in the
city center, you escape into the charm of old Amsterdam. Notice
house #34, a 500-year-old wooden structure (rare, since repeated
fires taught city fathers a trick called brick). Peek into the hidden
Catholic church, dating from the time when post-Reformation
Dutch Catholics couldn't worship in public. It's opposite the
English Reformed church, where the Pilgrims worshipped while
waiting for their voyage to the New World (marked by a plaque
near the door). Be considerate of the people who live around the
courtyard (free, daily 8:00–17:00, on Begijnensteeg lane, just off
Kalverstraat between #130 and #132, pick up flier at office near
entrance, for more details, see page 69).

▲**Amsterdam History Museum (Amsterdams Historisch
Museum)**—Follow the city's growth from fishing village to
world trader to hippie haven. Housed in a 500-year-old former
orphanage, this creative and hardworking museum features
Rembrandt's paintings, fine English descriptions, and a carillon
loft. The loft comes with push-button recordings of the town bell
tower's greatest hits, and a self-serve carillon "keyboard" that lets
you ring a few bells yourself (€6.50, covered by I amsterdam Card,
Mon–Fri 10:00–17:00, Sat–Sun 11:00–17:00, pleasant restaurant,
next to Begijnhof, Kalverstraat 92, tel. 020/523-1822, www.ahm
.nl). The museum's free pedestrian corridor—lined with old-time
group portraits—is a powerful teaser. ✪ See Amsterdam History
Museum Tour, page 146.

Southeast Amsterdam

To reach the following sights from the train station, take tram #9
or #14. All of these sights except the last two (Tropical Museum
and Maritime Museum) are close to each other and can easily
be connected into an interesting walk, or better yet, a bike ride.
Several of the sights in southeast Amsterdam cluster near the large
square, Waterlooplein, dominated by the modern opera house.
Most sights are covered by the I amsterdam Card.

For an orientation, survey the neighborhood from the lamp-
lined **Blauwbrug** ("Blue Bridge")—a modest, modern version of
Paris' Pont Alexandre III. The bridge crosses the **Amstel River**.
From this point, the river is channeled to form the city's canals.

Pan clockwise. The big, curved modern facade belongs to
the opera house (commonly called the "Stopera," after a public outcry wanting to stop its construction). Behind the Stopera
are these sights (not visible from here, but described below):
the Waterlooplein flea market, Rembrandt's House, Holland
Experience, and Gassan Diamonds. To the right of the Stopera are

Southeast Amsterdam

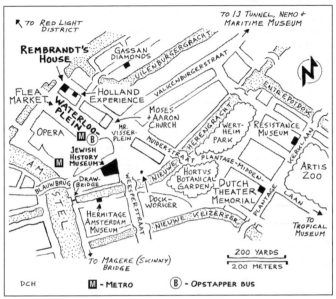

the twin gray steeples of the Moses and Aaron Church, which sits roughly in the center of the former Jewish Quarter.

Several Jewish sights cluster to the right of the Moses and Aaron Church: the Jewish Historical Museum, the Portuguese Synagogue, and the dockworker memorial. Just east of those is the De Hortus Botanical Garden.

The modern drawbridge in the foreground, though not famous, is photogenic. Beyond that is the Hermitage Amsterdam Museum (see below). Crossing the Amstel upstream is one of the city's romantic spots, the Magere Brug ("Skinny Bridge"). And a block away is the city's best look at a Golden Age mansion, the Willet-Holthuysen Museum (a.k.a. Herengracht Canal Mansion).

Waterlooplein Flea Market—For more than a hundred years, the Jewish Quarter flea market has raged daily except Sunday (at the Waterlooplein metro station, behind the Rembrandt House). The long, narrow park is filled with stalls selling cheap clothes, hippie stuff, old records, tourist knickknacks, and garage-sale junk.

▲**Rembrandt's House (Rembrandthuis Museum)**—A middle-aged Rembrandt lived here after his wife's death, as his popularity and wealth dwindled down to obscurity and bankruptcy (1639–1658). Tour the place this way: See the 10-minute introductory video (Dutch and English showings alternate); explore Rembrandt's reconstructed house (filled with exactly what his bankruptcy inventory of 1656 said he owned); imagine him at work in his reconstructed studio; marvel at his personal collection of exotic objects, many of which he included in paintings; ask the printer to explain the etching process (drawing in soft wax on a metal plate that's then dipped in acid, inked up, and printed); then, for the finale, enjoy several rooms of original, marvelous, and well-described Rembrandt etchings. I came away wanting to know more about the man and his art (€7.50, covered by *I amsterdam* Card, €13.50 combo-ticket includes *Holland Experience*—see below, Sat–Thu 10:00–17:00, Fri 10:00–21:00, Jodenbreestraat 4, tel. 020/520-0400, www.rembrandthuis.nl).

Special Exhibit at Rembrandt's House: In 2006, Rembrandt is 400 years old, and Amsterdam will celebrate the event with gusto. While the permanent collection at Rembrandt's House includes only two of the artist's paintings, a special exhibit (April–June) will push the total up to 50! (€5 extra, includes audioguide, see sidebar on page 41 for more Rembrandt events.)

Holland Experience—Bragging "Experience Holland in 30 minutes," this 3-D movie takes you traveling through an idealized montage of Dutch clichés. There are no words, but lots of images (€8.50, €2 discount with this book through 2006, €13.50 combo-ticket includes Rembrandt's House, daily 10:00–18:00, several shows a day, alternating in 2006 with a Rembrandt video, adjacent to Rembrandt's House at Jodenbreestraat 8, tel. 020/422-2233, www.holland-experience.nl). While it's a cheesy presentation (and the schedule, with showings only every couple of hours, can be frustrating), the *Experience* is relaxing, and puts you in a Dutch frame of mind. The men's urinal is a trip to the beach. Plan for it. There's also a goofy chance to pose in a fake Red Light District window.

▲**Diamonds**—Many shops in the "city of diamonds" offer tours. These tours come with two parts: a chance to see experts behind magnifying glasses polishing the facets of precious diamonds, followed by a visit to an intimate sales room to see (and perhaps buy) a mighty shiny yet very tiny souvenir.

The handy and professional **Gassan Diamonds** facility fills a huge warehouse a block from Rembrandt's House. A visit here plops you in the big-tour-group fray (notice how each tour group has a color-coded sticker so they know which guide gets the commission on what they buy). You'll get a sticker, join a tour to see a polisher at work, and hear a general explanation of the process (free, 15 min). Then you'll have an opportunity to sit down and have color and clarity described and illustrated with diamonds ranging in value from $100 to $30,000. Before or after, you can have a free cup of coffee in the waiting room across the parking lot (daily 9:00–17:00, Nieuwe Uilenburgerstraat 173, tel. 020/622-5333, www.gassandiamonds.com). Another company, Coster, also offers diamond demos, not as good as Gassan's, but handy if you're near the Rijksmuseum (see page 41).

▲**Willet-Holthuysen Museum (a.k.a. Herengracht Canal Mansion)**—This 1687 townhouse is a must for devotees of Hummel-topped sugar bowls and Louis XVI–style wainscoting. For others, it's a pleasant look inside a typical (rich) home with much of the original furniture and decor. Forget the history and just browse through a dozen rooms of beautiful and saccharine objects from the 19th century.

Upon entering, see photos of the owners during the house's heyday in the 1860s. The 15-minute video explains how the wealthy heiress Louise Holthuysen and the art-collecting bon vivant, Abraham Willet, got married and became joined at the hyphen, then set out to make their home the social hub of Amsterdam.

Picture the couple's servants in the kitchen—before electricity and running water—turning meat on the spit at the fireplace or filtering rainwater. Upstairs, where the Willet-Holthuysens entertained, wall paintings introduce you to Abraham's artistic tastes, showing scenes of happy French peasants and nobles frolicking in the countryside. Several rooms are done in the Louis XVI style, featuring chairs with straight, tapering legs (not the heavy, curving, animal-claw feet of earlier styles); blue, yellow, and purple-themed rooms; wainscoting ("wallpaper" covering only the lower part of walls); and mythological paintings on the ceiling.

The impressive ballroom contains a painting showing the room in its prime—and how little it's changed. Imagine Abraham, Louise, and 22 guests retiring to the Dining Room, dining off the 275-piece Meissen porcelain set; or chatting with friends in the Blue Room by the canal; or sipping tea in the Garden Room, gazing out at symmetrically curved hedges and classical statues. Up another flight is the bedroom, with a canopy bed and matching oak washstand and makeup table (and a chamber pot tucked under the bed).

When the widow Louise died in 1895, she bequeathed the house to the city, along with its collection of candelabras, snuff boxes, and puppy paintings (€4, covered by *I amsterdam* Card, Mon–Fri 10:00–17:00, Sat–Sun 11:00–17:00, tram #4 or #9 to

Herengracht 605, 1 block southeast of Rembrandtplein, tel. 020/523-1870, www.willetholthuysen.nl).

▲**Hermitage Amsterdam Museum**—The famous Hermitage Museum in St. Petersburg, Russia, loans art to Amsterdam for display in the Amstelhof, a 17th-century former nursing home on the Amstel River. The exhibit changes twice a year. The highlights in 2006 include a look at the icons and precious religious hardware from Byzantium (through March 2006), and, later, "Silver Wonders from the East"—objects from China, India, and Indonesia collected by the tsar (April–mid-Sept).

Why all this Russian-owned art in Amsterdam? The Hermitage collection in St. Petersburg is so vast that they can only show about five percent of it at any one time. Therefore, the Hermitage is establishing satellite collections around the world. The one here in Amsterdam is the biggest, and will be growing considerably as the museum takes over more of the Amstelhof. By law, the great Russian collection can only be out of the country for six months at a time, so the collection will always be rotating. Curators in Amsterdam make a point to display art that complements—rather than just repeats—what the city's other museums show so well (€6, covered by *I amsterdam* Card, daily 10:00–17:00, Nieuwe Herengracht 14, tram #4 to Rembrandtplein or #9 to Waterlooplein, tel. 020/531-8751, www.hermitage.nl).

De Hortus Botanical Garden—This is a unique oasis of tranquility within the city (no mobile phones are allowed, because "our collection of plants is a precious community—treat it with respect"). One of the oldest botanical gardens in the world, it dates from 1638, when medicinal herbs were grown here. Today, among its 6,000 different kinds of plants—most of which were collected by the Dutch East India Company in the 17th and 18th centuries—you'll find medicinal herbs, cacti, several greenhouses (one with a fluttery butterfly house—a hit with kids), and a tropical palm house. Much of it is described in English: "A Dutch merchant snuck a coffee plant out of Ethiopia, which ended up in this garden in 1706. This first coffee plant in Europe was the literal granddaddy of the coffee cultures of Brazil—long the world's biggest coffee producer" (€6, covered by *I amsterdam* Card, Mon–Fri 9:00–17:00, Sat–Sun 10:00–17:00, until 16:00 in winter, Plantage Middenlaan 2A, tel. 020/625-9021, www.hortus-botanicus.nl).

Jewish Historical Museum (Joods Historisch Museum)—Four historic buildings have been joined by steel and glass to make one modern complex that tells the story of Amsterdam's Jews through the centuries, while serving as a good introduction to Judaism in general. There are several sections ("Jews in Amsterdam," children's museum, and temporary exhibits), but the highlight is the Great Synagogue, restored in 1981.

Jews in Amsterdam

In 1940, one in 10 Amsterdammers was Jewish, and most lived in the neighborhood behind Waterlooplein. Jewish traders had long been welcome in a city that cared more about business than religion. In the late 1500s, many Sephardic Jews from Spain and Portugal immigrated, fleeing persecution. (The philosopher Baruch Spinoza's ancestors were among them.) In the 1630s, Yiddish-speaking Eastern European Jews (Ashkenazi) poured in. By 1700, the Jewish Quarter was a bustling, exotic, multicultural world, with more people speaking Portuguese, German, and Yiddish than Dutch.

Jews were not first-class citizens. They needed the city's permission to settle there, and they couldn't hold public office (but then, neither could Catholics under Calvinist rule). Still, the Jewish Quarter was not a ghetto (enforced segregation), there were no special taxes, and cosmopolitan Amsterdam was well-acquainted with all types of beliefs and customs.

In 1796, Jews were given full citizenship. In exchange, they were required to learn the Dutch language and submit to the city's legal system...and the Jewish culture began assimilating into the Dutch.

In 1940, Nazi Germany occupied the Netherlands. On February 22, 1941, the Nazis began rounding up Jews and shipping them to extermination camps in Eastern Europe. By war's end, more than 100,000 of the city's 130,000 Jews had died.

Today, about 25,000 Jews live in Amsterdam, and the Jewish Quarter has blended in with the modern city.

Sit in the high-ceilinged synagogue, surrounded by religious objects, and picture it in its prime (1671–1943). The hall would be full for a service—men downstairs, women above in the gallery. On the east wall (the symbolic direction of Jerusalem) is the Ark, where they keep the scrolls of the Torah (the Jewish scriptures, including the first 5 books of the Christian Bible). The rabbi and other men, wearing thigh-length prayer shawls, would approach the Ark and carry the Torah to the raised platform in the center of the room. After unwrapping it from its drapery and silver cap, one would use a *yad* (ceremonial pointer) to follow along while singing the text aloud.

Video displays around the room explain Jewish customs, from birth (circumcision) to puberty (the bar/bat mitzvah, celebrating the entry into adulthood) to marriage—culminating in the groom stomping on a glass while everyone shouts "Mazel tov!" (€6.50, covered by *I amsterdam* Card, daily 11:00–17:00, free audioguide but displays all have English explanations, good kosher café, Jonas

Daniel Meijerplein 2, tel. 020/626-9945, www.jhm.nl.)

▲**Dutch Theater (Hollandsche Schouwburg)**—Once a lively theater in the Jewish neighborhood, and today a moving memorial, this building was used as an assembly hall for local Jews destined for Nazi concentration camps. On the wall, 6,700 family names pay tribute to the 104,000 Jews deported and killed by the Nazis. Some 70,000 victims spent time here, awaiting transfer to concentration camps. Upstairs is a small history exhibit with photos and memorabilia of some victims, putting a human face on the staggering numbers. Press the buttons on a model of the neighborhood to see round-up spots from the Nazi occupation. The ruined theater actually offers little to see but plenty to think about. Back on the ground floor, notice the hopeful messages that visiting school groups attach to the wooden tulips (free, daily 11:00–16:00, Plantage Middenlaan 24, tel. 020/626-9945, www.hollandscheschouwburg.nl).

▲▲**Dutch Resistance Museum (Verzetsmuseum)**—This is an impressive look at how the Dutch resisted their Nazi occupiers from 1940 to 1945. You'll see propaganda movie clips, study forged ID cards under a magnifying glass, and read about ingenious and courageous efforts—big and small—to hide local Jews from the Germans and undermine the Nazi regime.

The first dozen displays set the stage, showing peaceful, upright Dutch people of the 1930s, living oblivious to the rise of fascism. Then—bam—it's May 1940 and the Germans invade the Netherlands, pummel Rotterdam, send Queen Wilhelmina into exile, and—in four short days of fighting—hammer home the message that resistance is futile. The Germans install local Dutch Nazis in power (the "NSB"), led by Anton Mussert.

Next, in the corner of the exhibition area, push a button to see photos of the event that first mobilized organized resistance. In February, 1941, Nazis started rounding up Jews from the neighborhood, killing nine protesters. Amsterdammers responded by shutting down the trams, schools, and businesses in a massive two-day strike. (This heroic gesture is honored today with a statue of a striking dockworker on the square called Jonas Daniel Meyerplein, where Jews were rounded up). The next display makes it clear that this brave strike still did little to save 100,000 Jews from extermination.

Turning the corner into the main room, you'll see numerous exhibits on Nazi rule and the many ways the Dutch resisted it: schoolkids telling "Kraut jokes," vandals turning Nazi V-for-Victory posters into W-for-Wilhelmina, preachers giving pointed sermons, printers distributing underground newspapers (such as *Het Parool*, which became a major daily paper), counterfeiters forging documents, and ordinary people hiding radios under floorboards and Jews inside closets. As the war progressed, the armed Dutch Resistance became bolder and more violent, killing German occupiers and Dutch collaborators. In September 1944, the Allies liberate Antwerp, and the Netherlands starts celebrating...too soon. The Nazis dig in and punish the country by cutting off rations, plunging West Holland into the "Hunger Winter" of 1944–1945 in which 20,000 die. Finally, it's springtime. The Allies liberate the country, and at war's end, Nazi helmets are turned into Dutch bedpans.

Besides the history lesson, this thought-provoking exhibit examines the moral dilemmas of life under oppressive rule: Is it right to give money to poor people if the charity is run by Nazis? Should I quit my government job when the Nazis take control, or stay on to do what good I can? If I disagree with my government, is it okay to lie? To vandalize? To kill? (€5, covered by *I amsterdam* Card, Tue–Fri 10:00–17:00, Sat–Mon 12:00–17:00, well-described in English, no flash photos, tram #9 from station, Plantage Kerklaan 61, tel. 020/620-2535, www.verzetsmuseum.org.)

The recommended Restaurant Plancius is adjacent to the museum (see page 170) and Amsterdam's famous zoo is just across the street.

▲**Tropical Museum (Tropenmuseum)**—As close to the Third World as you'll get without lots of vaccinations, this imaginative museum offers wonderful re-creations of tropical-life scenes and explanations of Third World problems (partly created by Dutch colonialism). Ride the elevator to the top floor, and circle your way down through this immense collection opened in 1926 to give the Dutch a peek at their vast colonial holdings. Don't miss the display case allowing you to see and hear the world's most exotic musical instruments. The Ekeko cafeteria serves tropical food (€7.50, covered by *I amsterdam* Card, daily 10:00–17:00, tram #9 to Linnaeusstraat 2, tel. 020/568-8215, www.tropenmuseum.nl).

Northeast Amsterdam

Stedelijk Museum CS—The modern-art museum, temporarily located on the second and third floors of the towering post office building, features art that would normally be displayed at the main Stedelijk Museum building (near the Rijksmuseum), but it's under renovation until 2008. The fun, far-out, refreshing collection consists of post-1945 experimental and conceptual art. The Stedelijk's famous masterpieces (works by Picasso, Chagall, Cézanne, Kandinsky,

and Mondrian) will not be on display until the museum moves back into its regular home (€9, covered by *I amsterdam* Card, daily 10:00–18:00, just east of Central Station—to the left as you exit—look for *Post CS* tower at Oosterdokskade 5, tel. 020/573-2911, www.stedelijk.nl).

Best Amsterdam Viewpoint: Along with the Westerkerk's tower, the best viewpoint of the city is from the 11th floor of the Post building (near the train station, which temporarily houses the Stedelijk Museum). Café 11 is a trendy nightspot that doubles as an eatery during the day. Riding the elevator to the 11th floor to see the view for free.

Netherlands Maritime Museum (Nederlands Scheepvaart-museum)—This huge collection of model ships, maps, and sea-battle paintings fills the 300-year-old Dutch Navy Arsenal. Given Dutch seafaring heritage, I expected a more interesting museum. Sailors may disagree, but—even with its re-creation of an 18th-century Dutch East India Company ship manned by characters in old costumes—I found the place pretty lifeless (€9, covered by *I amsterdam* Card; mid-June–mid-Sept daily 10:00–17:00; mid-Sept–mid-June Tue–Sun 10:00–17:00, closed Mon; English explanations, don't waste your time with 30-min movie, bus #22 or #42 to Kattenburgerplein 1, tel. 020/523-2222, www.scheepvaartmuseum .nl). The museum is closing in 2007 for a major renovation.

NEMO (National Center for Science and Technology)—This kid-friendly science museum is also a landmark. Its distinctive copper-green building, jutting up from the water like a sinking ship, has prompted critics to nickname it the *Titanic*. Designed by Italian architect Renzo Piano (known for Paris' Pompidou Center and Berlin's Potsdamer Platz complex), the building's shape reflects its nautical surroundings as well as the curve of the underwater tunnel it straddles. Several floors feature permanent and rotating exhibits that allow kids (and adults) to explore topics such as light, sound, and gravity, and play with bubbles, topple giant dominoes, and draw with lasers. English explanations are available. Up top is a restaurant with a great city view, as well as a sloping terrace that becomes a "beach" in summer, complete with lounge chairs, sandbox, and lively bar.

Cost: €11, not covered by *I amsterdam* Card, includes rooftop beach in July–Aug, €2.50—beach only. The roof terrace is generally free and open to the public September through June.

Hours: Tue–Sun 10:00–17:00, generally closed Mon, but open daily in July–Aug. Beach open later in summer.

Getting There: It's a 15-minute walk from Central Station or bus #22 to Kadijksplein stop (Oosterdok 2, above entrance to IJ tunnel, tel. 0900-919-1100—€0.35/min, www.e-nemo.nl).

Red Light District

▲▲**Amstelkring Museum (Our Lord in the Attic)**—While Amsterdam has long been known for its tolerant attitudes, 16th-century politics forced Dutch Catholics to worship discreetly. Near the train station in the Red Light District, you'll find a fascinating hidden Catholic church filling the attic of three 17th-century merchants' houses. Don't miss the silver collection and other exhibits of daily life from 300 years ago (€7, covered by *I amsterdam* Card, Mon–Sat 10:00–17:00, Sun and holidays 13:00–17:00, closed Jan 1 and April 29, Oudezijds Voorburgwal 40, tel. 020/624-6604, www.museumamstelkring.nl). ✪ See Amstelkring Museum Tour, page 138.

▲▲**Red Light District**—Europe's most touristed ladies of the night tease and tempt, as they have for centuries here, in 450 display-case windows around Oudezijds Achterburgwal and Oudezijds Voorburgwal, surrounding the Old Church (Oude Kerk, see below). Drunks and druggies make the streets uncomfortable late at night after the gawking tour groups leave (about 23:00), but it's a fascinating walk between noon and nightfall.

The neighborhood, one of Amsterdam's oldest, has had prostitutes since 1200. Prostitution is entirely legal here, and the prostitutes are generally entrepreneurs, renting space and running their own businesses. Popular prostitutes net about €500 a day (for what's called S&F in its abbreviated, printable form, costing €25–50 per customer), fill out tax returns, and even pay union dues. ✪ See Red Light District Walk, page 78.

The **Prostitution Information Center,** open to the public, offers a small €1.50 booklet that answers most of the questions tourists have about the Red Light District (free, Tue–Sat 12:00–17:00, closed Sun–Mon, facing Old Church at Enge Kerksteeg 3, www.pic-amsterdam.com).

Sex Museums—Amsterdam has two sex museums: one in the Red Light District, and another a block in front of the train station on Damrak. While visiting one can be called sightseeing, visiting both is hard to explain. Here's a comparison:

The **Erotic Museum** in the Red Light District is less offensive. Its five floors rely heavily on badly dressed dummies of prostitutes in various acts. It also has a lot of uninspired paintings, videos, phone sex, old photos, and sculpture (€5, daily 11:00–24:00, along the canal at Oudezijds Achterburgwal 54, tel. 020/624-7303; see page 88).

The **Damrak Sex Museum** goes farther, telling the story of pornography from Roman times through 1960. Every sexual deviation is revealed in various displays, and the nude and pornographic art is a cut above that of the other sex museum. Also interesting are the early French pornographic photos and memorabilia from

Europe, India, and Asia. You'll find a Marilyn Monroe tribute and some S&M displays, too (€2.50, daily 10:00–23:30, Damrak 18, a block in front of station).

Old Church (Oude Kerk)—This 14th-century landmark—the needle around which the Red Light District spins—has served as a reassuring welcome-home symbol to sailors, a refuge to the downtrodden, an ideological battlefield of the Counter-Reformation, and today, a tourist sight with a dull interior (€4, covered by *I amsterdam* Card, Mon–Sat 11:00–17:00, Sun 13:00–17:00, www.oudekerk.nl; see page 82).

▲Hash, Marijuana, and Hemp Museum—This is a collection of dope facts, history, science, and memorabilia (€5.70, daily 11:00–22:00, Oudezijds Achterburgwal 148, tel. 020/623-5961, www.hashmuseum.com). While small, it has a shocking finale: the high-tech grow room, in which dozens of varieties of marijuana are cultivated in optimal hydroponic (among other) environments. Some plants stand five feet tall and shine under the intense grow lamps. The view is actually through glass walls into the neighboring Sensi Seed Bank Grow Shop, which sells carefully cultivated seeds and all the gear needed to grow them (Seed Bank may move 50 yards north in 2006).

The **Cannabis College**, "dedicated to ending the global war against the cannabis plant through public education," is a half block away at #124 (free, daily 11:00–19:00, tel. 020/423-4420, www.cannabiscollege.com). For more, see the ✪ Red Light District Walk (page 78) and Smoking (page 172).

AMSTERDAM CITY WALK

From Central Station to the Rijksmuseum

Amsterdam today looks much as it did in its Golden Age, the 1600s. It's a retired sea captain of a city, still in love with life, with a broad outlook and a salty story to tell.

Take a Dutch sampler walk from one end of the old center to the other, tasting all that Amsterdam has to offer along the way. It's your best single stroll through Dutch clichés, hidden churches, surprising shops, thriving happy-hour hangouts, and eight centuries of history.

ORIENTATION

Length of This Walk: Allow three hours.

Bike Rental: If you'd like to make this "walk" a much faster "roll," there's a handy bike-rental place in Central Station (MacBike, daily 9:00–17:45, at left side of station as you leave it, on right side if you're facing it, tel. 020/624-8391, www.macbike.nl).

Tips: You can find public toilets at fast-food places (generally €0.30) and near the entrance to the Amsterdam History Museum. Beware of silent transport—trams and bikes. Stay off the tram tracks and bike paths, and yield to bell-ringing bikers.

New Church (Nieuwe Kerk): €8, covered by *I amsterdam* Card, Mon–Sat 10:00–18:00, Sun 13:00–18:00, Dam Square, tel. 020/638-6909, www.nieuwekerk.nl.

Amsterdam Diamond Center: Free, Mon–Sat 10:00–18:00, Sun 11:00–18:00, Rokin 1, tel. 020/624-5787, www.amsterdamdiamondcenter.com.

De Papegaai Catholic Church: Free, daily 10:00–16:00, on Kalverstraat.

Amsterdam History Museum: €6.50, covered by *I amsterdam* Card, Mon–Fri 10:00–17:00, Sat–Sun 11:00–17:00, Kalverstraat 92, tel. 020/523-1822.

Begijnhof: Free, daily 8:00–17:00 for "tourist visits" (groups and guided tours). At other times, be quiet and stick to the area near the churches. Don't photograph homes or their residents, and remember that these are private dwellings (on Begijnensteeg lane, just off Kalverstraat between #130 and #132). The English Church is sometimes open for tourists (free, open about 4 days a week 10:00–14:00 and always for English-speaking worshippers at Sun service at 10:30).

Rijksmuseum: €10, covered by *I amsterdam* Card, daily 9:00–18:00, tel. 020/674-7047, www.rijksmuseum.com.

Van Gogh Museum: €9, covered by *I amsterdam* Card, €4 audioguide, Sat–Thu 10:00–18:00, Fri 10:00–22:00, Paulus Potterstraat 7, tel. 020/570-5200, www.vangoghmuseum.nl.

OVERVIEW

The walk starts at the central-as-can-be train station. You'll walk about three miles, heading down Damrak to Dam Square, continuing south down Kalverstraat to the Mint Tower, then wafting through the Bloemenmarkt (flower market), before continuing south to Leidseplein and jogging left to the Rijksmuseum. To return to Central Station, catch tram #2 or #5 from the southwest corner of the Rijksmuseum.

THE WALK BEGINS

Central Station

Here where today's train travelers enter the city, sailors of yore disembarked from seagoing ships to be met by street musicians, pickpockets, hotel-runners, and ladies carrying red lanterns. When the station was built (on reclaimed land) at the former harbor mouth, Amsterdam lost some of its harbor feel, but it's still a bustling port of entry.

Central Station, with warm red brick and prickly spires, is the first of several neo-Gothic buildings we'll see from the late 1800s, built during Amsterdam's economic revival. One of the towers has a clock dial; the other tower's dial is a weathervane. Watch the hand twitch as the wind gusts.

Amsterdam City Walk

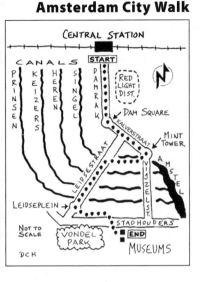

As you emerge from the train station, you'll immediately see a mess. All the construction is for the new cultural center and library (left of station as you leave it) and subway line (in front of station). The new north–south metro line (to open in 2011) will complement the existing east–west one. While it sounds like a fine idea, the billion euros being spent on it is considered riddled with corruption. The big, ugly building in the canal directly in front of the train station will eventually be sunk underground and become part of the subway station.

Beyond the construction, the city spreads out before you in a series of concentric canals. Ahead of you stretches the street called Damrak, leading to Dam Square, a half mile away. To the left of Damrak is the city's old *(oude)* side, to the right is the new *(nieuwe)*.

The big church towering above the old side (at about 10 o'clock) is St. Nicholas Church, built in the 1880s when Catholics—after about three centuries of oppression—were finally free to worship in public. The church marks the beginning of the Red Light District. The city's biggest bike garage, a multistory wonder, is on your right (in front of the Ibis Hotel).

• *We'll basically walk south from here to the Rijksmuseum. The art museum and the station—designed by the same architect—stand like bookends holding the old town together. Follow the crowds south on Damrak, walking along the right side of the street.*

Damrak

Stroll past every Dutch cliché at the tourist shops: wooden shoes, plastic tulips, Heineken fridge magnets, and windmill saltshakers. Listen to a hand-cranked barrel organ. Order french fries (called *Vlaamse frites,* or Flemish fries, since they were invented in the Low Countries) and dip them in mayonnaise, not ketchup. Eating international cuisine (Indonesian *rijsttafel,* Argentine steak, Middle Eastern *shoarma*—pronounced SHWAHR-mah) is like going local in cosmopolitan Amsterdam. And you'll find the city's most notorious commodity displayed at the Damrak Sex Museum (see page 57).

The street was once a riverbed, where the Amstel River flowed north into the IJ (eye) river behind today's train station. Both rivers then emptied into a vast inlet of the North Sea (the Zuiderzee), making Amsterdam a major seaport. Today, the Amstel is channeled into canals, its former mouth has been covered by Central Station, the North Sea inlet has been diked off to make an inland lake, and 100,000 ships a year reach the open waters by sailing west through the North Sea Canal.

Local landowners are concerned that the tunneling for the new subway line will cause their buildings to settle. The snoopy-looking white cameras mounted on various building corners (such as the Beurs) are monitoring buildings to check for settling.

• *The long brick building with the square clock tower, along the left side of Damrak, is the...*

Stock Exchange (Beurs)

Built with nine million bricks on about 5,000 tree trunks hammered into the marshy soil, the Beurs stands as a symbol of the city's long tradition as a trading town.

Back when "stock" meant whatever could be loaded and unloaded onto a boat, Amsterdammers gathered to trade. Soon, rather than trading goats, chickens, and kegs of beer, they were exchanging slips of paper and "futures" at one of the world's first stock exchanges. Traders needed moneychangers, who needed bankers, who made money by lending money...and Amsterdam of the 1600s became one of the world's first great capitalist cities, loaning money to free-spending kings, dukes, and bishops.

This impressive building, built in 1903 in a geometric, minimal, no-frills style, is one of the world's first "modern" (i.e., 20th century–style) buildings, emphasizing function over looks. In 1984, the stock exchange moved next door (see the stock prices readout) to the Euronext complex—a joint, if overly optimistic, attempt by France, Belgium, and the Netherlands to compete with the power of Britain's stock exchange. The old Beurs building now hosts concerts and a museum for temporary exhibits.

Amsterdam still thrives as the center of Dutch businesses, such as Heineken, Shell Oil, Philips Electronics, KLM Airlines, and Unilever. Amsterdammers have always had a reputation for putting business above ideological differences, staying neutral while trading with both sides.

• *Damrak opens into...*

Dam Square

The city got its start right here in about 1250, when fishermen in this marshy delta settled along the built-up banks of the Amstel River. They blocked the river with a *damme,* and created a small village called "Amstel-damme." Soon the fishermen were trading with German riverboats traveling downstream and with seafaring boats from Stockholm, Hamburg, and London. Dam Square was the center of it all.

The dam on the Amstel divided the *damrak* (meaning "outer harbor"—for sea traffic) from the *rokin* ("inner harbor"—for river traffic). Land trade routes converged here as well, and a customs house stood here. Today, the Damrak and Rokin (roh-KEEN) are major roads, and the city's palace and major department stores face the square, where mimes, jugglers, and human statues mingle with locals and tourists. This is the historic heart of the city. As the symbolic center of the Netherlands, it's where political demonstrations begin and end.

Pan the square clockwise to see the following: the Royal Palace (the large domed building on the west side), the New Church (Nieuwe Kerk), an ABN Amro bank, Damrak, the proud old De Bijenkorf (literally, "The Beehive") department store, the Krasnapolsky Hotel, the white phallic obelisk of the National Monument, the Rokin, touristy Madame Tussaud's, and the entrance to pedestrian-only Kalverstraat (look for *Rabobank* sign).

Royal Palace

The name is misleading, since Amsterdam is one of the cradles of modern democracy. For centuries, this was the Town Hall of a self-governing community that prided itself on its independence and thumbed its nose at royalty. The current building, built in 1648, is appropriately classical (like the democratic Greeks), with a triangular pediment featuring—fittingly for Amster-

dam—denizens of the sea cavorting with Neptune (with his green copper trident.)

After the city was conquered by the French, Napoleon imposed a monarchy on Holland, making his brother Louis the king of the Netherlands (1808). Louis used the city hall as his "royal palace," giving the building its current name. When Napoleon was defeated, the victorious powers dictated that the Netherlands remain a monarchy, under a noble Dutch family called the House of Orange. If the current Queen Beatrix is in town, this is, technically, her

Amsterdam City Walk—First Half

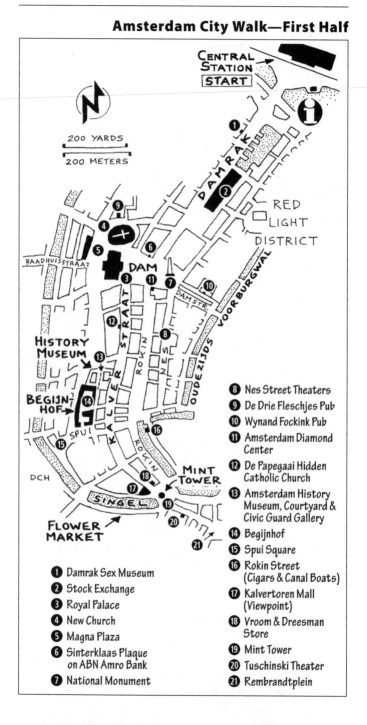

CENTRAL STATION START

200 YARDS
200 METERS

RED LIGHT DISTRICT

DAMRAK

VOORBURGWAL

RAADHUISSTRAAT

DAM

DAMSTR

OUDEZIJDS

HISTORY MUSEUM

KALVER STRAAT

ROKIN

NES

BEGIJN HOF

SPUI

MINT TOWER

ROKIN

DCH

SINGEL

FLOWER MARKET

8 Nes Street Theaters
9 De Drie Fleschjes Pub
10 Wynand Fockink Pub
11 Amsterdam Diamond Center
12 De Papegaai Hidden Catholic Church
13 Amsterdam History Museum, Courtyard & Civic Guard Gallery
14 Begijnhof
15 Spui Square
16 Rokin Street (Cigars & Canal Boats)
17 Kalvertoren Mall (Viewpoint)
18 Vroom & Dreesman Store
19 Mint Tower
20 Tuschinski Theater
21 Rembrandtplein

1 Damrak Sex Museum
2 Stock Exchange
3 Royal Palace
4 New Church
5 Magna Plaza
6 Sinterklaas Plaque on ABN Amro Bank
7 National Monument

residence (thought it's currently under renovation, and closed to visitors through 2008). Amsterdam is the nominal capital of the Netherlands, but all governing activity—and the Queen's actual permanent home—are in The Hague (a city 30 miles southwest).

New Church (Nieuwe Kerk)

The "New" Church is 600 years old (newer than the 700-year-old "Old" Church in the Red Light District). The sundial above the entrance once served as the city's official timepiece.

The church's bare, spacious, well-lit interior (often occupied by temporary art exhibits) looks quite different from the Baroque-encrusted churches found in the rest of Europe. In 1566, clear-eyed Protestant extremists throughout Holland marched into Catholic churches (like this once was), lopped off the heads of holy statues, stripped gold-leaf angels from the walls, urinated on Virgin Marys, and shattered stained glass windows in a wave of anti-Catholic vandalism.

This iconoclasm (icon-breaking) of 1566 started an 80-year war against Spain and the Hapsburgs, leading finally to Dutch independence in 1648. Catholic churches like this one were converted to the new dominant religion, Calvinist Protestantism (today's Dutch Reformed Church). From then on, Dutch churches downplayed the "graven images" and "idols" of ornate religious art.

From just inside the door, you can get a free look at the 1655 organ (far left end, often encased in its painted wooden cupboard); the stained-glass window (opposite entrance) showing Count William IV giving the city its "XXX" coat of arms (symbolism described on page 68); and the window (over entrance) showing the inauguration of Queen Wilhelmina. She grew to become the steadfast center of Dutch Resistance during World War II.

This church is where many of the Netherlands' monarchs are married and all are crowned. In 1980, Queen Beatrix—Wilhelmina's granddaughter—said "I do" in the New Church. When Beatrix dies or retires, her son, Crown Prince Willem Alexander, will parade to the center of the church, sit in front of the golden choir screen, and—with TV lights glaring and flashbulbs popping—be crowned the next sovereign.

• *Looking between the Royal Palace and the New Church, you'll see the fanciful brick facade of the Magna Plaza shopping center. Back in Dam Square, on the wall of the ABN Amro bank, find the colorful little stone plaque of...*

Sinterklaas—St. Nicholas

Jolly old St. Nicholas (Nicolaas in Dutch) is the patron saint of seafarers (see the 3 men in a tub) and of Amsterdam, and is also the model for Sinterklaas—the guy we call Santa Claus. Every year in late November, Holland's Santa Claus arrives by boat near Central Station (from his legendary home in Spain), rides a white horse up Damrak with Peter, his servant in blackface, and arrives triumphant in this square while thousands of kids cheer.

December 5, the feast day of St. Nicholas, is when the Dutch exchange presents and Sinterklaas leaves goodies in good kids' wooden shoes. (Smart kids maximize capacity by putting out big boots.) Many Dutch celebrate Christmas on December 25, as well.

Around the corner on Damrak, the bank has an ATM and a chip-loader *(Oplaadpunt)*. The ATM is familiar, but what's that small keypad next to it? It's for loading up the Dutch cash card—an attempt to eliminate the need for small change. With the keypad, the Dutch transfer money from their accounts onto a card with a computer chip. Then they can make purchases at stores by inserting the card into a pay-point, the way Americans buy gas from the pump.

National Monument

The obelisk, which depicts a crucified Christ, men in chains, and howling dogs, was built in 1956 as a WWII memorial. Now it's considered a monument for peace.

The Nazis occupied Holland from 1940 to 1945. They deported 100,000 Amsterdam Jews, driving many—including young Anne Frank and her family—into hiding. Near the end of the war, the "Hunger Winter" of 1944–1945 killed thousands and forced many to survive on tulip bulbs. Today, Dutch people in their 70s—whose growth-spurt years coincided with the Hunger Winter—are easy to identify, because they are uniformly short.

Circling the Square

You're at the center of Amsterdam. A few blocks to the east is the top of the Red Light District. Amsterdam is a world center for experimental theater, and several edgy theaters line the street called the Nes (stretching south from Hotel Krasnapolsky).

Office workers do afternoon happy hours at crowded bars that stock *jenevers* and liqueurs in wooden kegs. De Drie Fleschjes, a

City on a Sandbar

Amsterdam is built upon millions of wooden pilings. The city was founded on unstable mud, which sits on stable sand. In the Middle Ages, buildings were made of wood, which rests lightly and easily on mud. But devastating fires repeatedly wiped out entire neighborhoods, so stone became the building material of choice. Stone is fire-resistant, but was too heavy for a mud foundation. For more support, pilings were driven 30 feet through the mud and into the sand. The Royal Palace sits upon 13,000 such pilings—still solid after 350 years. (The wood survives fine if kept wet and out of the air.) Since World War II, concrete, rather than wood, has been used for the pilings, with foundations driven 60 feet deep through the first layer of sand, through more mud, and into a second layer of sand. And today's biggest buildings have foundations sinking as much as 120 feet deep.

particularly casual pub, is tucked right behind the New Church. The more upscale Wynand Fockink (100 yards down the alley along the right side of Hotel Krasnapolsky) serves fruit brandies produced in its adjoining distillery (which you can visit). Though the brew is bottled and distributed all over Holland, what you get here in the home-office bar is some of the best Fockink liqueur in the entire world.

At the Amsterdam Diamond Center (where Rokin street meets Dam Square), see cutters and jewelry-setters handling diamonds, plus some small educational displays and fake versions of big, famous stones. Since the 1500s, the city has been one of the world's diamond capitals. Eighty percent of industrial diamonds (for making drills and such) pass through here, as do many cut and polished jewels, like the Koh-i-Noor diamond.

• *From Dam Square, head south (at* Rabobank *sign) on...*

Kalverstraat

This pedestrian-only street is lined with many familiar franchise stores and record shops. (If you're on a bike, you must dismount and walk it.) This has been a shopping street for centuries, and today it's notorious among locals as *the* place for cheesy, crass materialism. For smaller and more elegant stores, try the adjacent district called De

Negen Straatjes (literally "The Nine Little Streets"), where 190 shops mingle by the canals (about 4 blocks west of Kalverstraat).
• *About 120 yards along (across from the McDonald's), pop into...*

De Papegaai Hidden Catholic Church (Petrus en Paulus Kerk)

This Catholic church, while not exactly hidden (you found it), keeps a low profile, even now that Catholicism has been legalized in Amsterdam. In the late 1500s, with Protestants fighting Catholics and the Dutch fighting Spanish invaders, Amsterdam tried to stay neutral, doing business with all parties. Finally, in 1578 Protestant extremists (following the teachings of Reformer John Calvin) took political control of the city. They expelled Catholic leaders and bishops, outlawed the religion, and allied Amsterdam with anti-Spanish forces in an action known to historians as the Alteration.

For the next two centuries, Amsterdam's Catholics were driven underground. Catholicism was illegal but tolerated, as long as it was practiced not in public, but in humble, unadvertised places like this. (The stuffed parrot—*papegaai*—hanging in the nave refers to the house formerly on this site, which had a carving of a parrot in its gable stone.)

Today, the church, which asks for a mere "15 minutes for God" *(een kwartier voor God)*, stands as a metaphor for how marginal religion has long been in highly commercial and secular Amsterdam.
• *Farther along (about 75 yards) at #92, where Kalverstraat crosses Wijde Kapel Steeg, look to the right at an archway leading to the...*

Courtyard of the Amsterdam History Museum

On the arch is Amsterdam's coat of arms—a red shield with three Xs and a crown. Not a reference to the city's sex trade, the X-shaped crosses (which appear everywhere in the city) represent

the crucifixion of St. Andrew, the patron saint of fishermen, and symbolize heroism, determination, and mercy. The crown dates to 1489, when Maximilian I (the Low Countries' first Hapsburg ruler and later Holy Roman Emperor) paid off a big loan from city bankers and, as thanks for the cash, gave the city permission to use his prestigious trademark, the Hapsburg crown, atop its shield. The relief above the door (see photo), dated 1581, shows boys around a dove, reminding all who pass that this was an orphanage and asking for charity. Go inside.

The pleasant David & Goliath café (with a shady courtyard) is watched over by a giant statue of Goliath and a knee-high David (from 1650). In the courtyard are the lockers for the orphan's uniforms and a pay toilet.

• *The courtyard leads to another courtyard with the best city history museum in town, the* ✪ *Amsterdam History Museum (see page 146). In between the two courtyards (on the left) is a free, glassed-in passageway lined with paintings, called the...*

Civic Guard Gallery (Schuttersgalerij)

In these group portraits from Amsterdam's Golden Age (early 1600s), look into the eyes of the frank, dignified men (and occasionally women) with ruffs and lace collars, who made Amsterdam the most prosperous city in Europe, sending trading ships to distant colonies and pocketing interest from loans. The weapons they carry are mostly symbolic, since these "Civic Guards," who once protected the town (fighting the Spanish), had become more like fraternal organizations of business bigwigs.

Many paintings look the same in this highly stylized genre. Military companies often sit in two rows. Someone holds the company flag. Rank is indicated by the weapons they hold: Captains wield pikes (axe-like weapons topped with spearhead-shaped tips); lieutenants hold partisans (pikes with sword-like tips); and relative grunts wield hatchet-headed halberds or muskets. Later group portraits showed "captains" of industry going about their work, dressed in suits, along with the tools of their trade—ledger books, quill pens, and money.

Everyone looks straight out, and every face is lit perfectly. Each paid for his own portrait and wanted it right. It took masters like Rembrandt and Frans Hals to take the starch out of the collars and compose more natural scenes.

• *The gallery offers a shortcut to the Begijnhof, 75 yards farther south. But if the gallery is closed, backtrack to Kalverstraat, continue south, then turn right on Begijnensteeg. Either route leads to the entrance of the walled courtyard called the...*

Begijnhof

This quiet courtyard (pronounced gutturally: buh-HHHINE-hof), lined with houses around a church, has sheltered women since 1346. This was for centuries the home of Beguines—women who removed themselves from the world at large to dedicate their

lives to God. It literally was a "woman's island"—a circle of houses facing a peaceful courtyard, surrounded by water. (To ensure a pleasant visit, see "Begijnhof" in the Orientation on page 60.)

The Beguines' ranks swelled during the Crusades, when so many men took off, never to return, leaving society with an abundance of single women. Later, women widowed by the hazards of overseas trade lived out their days as Beguines. Poor and rich women alike turned their backs on materialism and marriage to live here in Christian poverty. While obedient to a mother superior, the lay order of Beguines were not nuns. The Beguines were very popular in their communities for the unpretentious, simple, and Christ-like lives they led. They spent their days deep in prayer and busy with daily tasks—spinning wool, making lace, teaching, and caring for the sick and poor. In quiet seclusion, they inspired each other as well as their neighbors.

In 1578, when Catholicism was outlawed, the Dutch Reformed Church (and the city) took over many Catholic charities like this place. The last Beguine died in 1971, but this Begijnhof still provides subsidized housing to about a hundred needy single women (mostly Catholic seniors and students). The Begijnhof is just one of about 75 *hofjes* (housing projects surrounding courtyards) that dot Amsterdam.

Begin your visit at the statue of one of these charitable sisters. She faces the **wooden house** *(houten huys)* at #34. The city's old-est, it dates from 1477. Originally, the whole city consisted of wooden houses like this one. To the left of the house is a display of carved gable stones that once adorned housefronts and served as street numbers (and still do at #19 and #26, the former mother superior's house). Inside the covered passageway at the south end of the square (near the oldest house), find images of things forbidden in this all-female enclave—roosters (male), dogs (dirty), and male humans over age three (dangerous).

The brick-faced **English Church** (Engelse Kerk, from 1420) was the Beguine church until 1607, when it became Anglican. The Pilgrims (strict Protestants), fleeing persecution in England, stopped here in tolerant Amsterdam and prayed in this church before the *Mayflower* carried them to religious freedom at

Plymouth Rock in America. If the church is open (its hours are sporadic), step inside to see a stained-glass window of the Pilgrims praying before boarding the *Mayflower* (far end), an old pew they may have sat on (right wall), and a 1763 Bible (on the altar) with lot*f* of old-*f*tyle *ff*'s.

The "hidden" **Catholic Church** (notice the painted-out windows, 2nd and 3rd floors) faces the English Church. Amsterdam's oppressed 17th-century Catholics, who refused to worship as Protestants, must have eagerly awaited the day when, in the 19th century, they were legally allowed to say Mass. Step inside (through the low-profile doorway), pick up an English brochure near the entry, and rap softly on a "marble" column.

Today, Holland is still divided religiously, but without the bitterness. Roughly a third of the population is Catholic, a third Protestant...and a third list themselves as "unchurched."

• *Backtrack to busy Kalverstraat, turn right, and continue south. Pause at the intersection with Spuistraat and look to the right.*

Spui and the Rokin

A block to the right is the square called **Spui** (spow, rhymes with "cow"). Lined with cafés and bars, it's one of the city's more popular spots for nightlife and sunny afternoon people-watching.

A block to the left is the busy street called **Rokin** (ro-KEEN). A statue of Queen Wilhelmina (1880–1962) on the Rokin shows her riding daintily sidesaddle. Remember that in real life, she was the iron-willed inspiration for the Dutch Resistance against the Nazis.

Canal cruises depart from the Rondvaart Kooij dock (€7, 2/ hr in summer 10:00–22:00, 2/ hr in winter 10:00–17:00, yellow canal house). These are the cheapest game in town, but if you have an *I amsterdam* Card, you'll go free on the Rederij Noord-Zuid boats that leave from near Leidseplein (coming up later on this walk; or see page 34).

The **House of Hajenius,** at Rokin 92 (50 yards left of the canal dock, toward the train station), is a temple of cigars, a "paradise for the connoisseur" showing "175 years of tradition and good taste." To enter this sumptuous Art Nouveau building with painted leather ceilings is to step back into 1910 (free, Tue–Sat 9:30–18:00, Sun 12:00–17:00, Mon 12:00–18:00). Don't be shy—the place is as much a free museum for visitors as it is a store for paying customers. The brown-capped canisters are for smelling fine pipe tobacco.

Take a whiff. The personal humidifiers (read the explanation) allow locals (famous local names are on the cupboard doors) to call in an order and have their cigars waiting for them at just the right humidity. Look up at the humidifier pipes pumping moisture into the room. Upstairs in back is a small, free museum.

Head back toward the pedestrian street, Kalverstraat, and turn left when you get there. You'll pass various department stores with cafeterias. At the end of Kalverstraat, the **Kalvertoren** shopping complex offers a top-floor viewpoint and café (walk straight into the glass atrium and go past the escalators to ride the slanting glass elevator; Mon 11:00–18:30, Tue–Fri 10:00–18:30, Thu until 21:00, Sat 10:00–18:00, Sun 12:00–18:00). Across Kalverstraat, the **Vroom & Dreesman** department store (at #200) is one of Holland's oldest chains. Inside, La Place is a sprawling self-service cafeteria—handy for a quick and healthy lunch (Mon–Sat 10:00–20:00, Thu until 21:00, Sun 12:00–20:00).

• *Continue on Kalverstraat, which dead-ends at the...*

Mint Tower (Munttoren)

This tower, which marked the limit of the medieval walled city, served as one of the original gates (the steeple was added later,

in 1620). The city walls were girdled by a moat—the Singel canal. Until about 1500, the area beyond here was nothing but marshy fields and a few farms on reclaimed land.

From the busy intersection at Muntplein, look left (at about 10 o'clock) down Reguliersbreestraat. A long block east of here (where you see trees) is Rembrandtplein, another major center for nightlife. Halfway down the block (past the massive easyInternetcafé—daily 9:00–21:00, Reguliersbreestraat 33), the twin green domes mark the exotic Tuschinski Theater, where you can see current movies in a sumptuous Art Deco setting (see page 43). Take a seat in the lobby and stare at the ever-changing ceiling, imagining this place during the Roaring '20s.

• *Just past the Mint Tower, turn right and walk west along the south bank of the Singel, which is lined with the greenhouse shops of the...*

Flower Market (Bloemenmarkt)

This busy block of cut flowers, plants, bulbs, seeds, and garden supplies attests to Holland's reputation for growing flowers. Tulips, imported from Turkey in the 1600s, grew well in the sandy soil of

Amsterdam City Walk—Second Half

200 YARDS
200 METERS

FLOWER MARKET
START
SINGEL
KEIZERS STRAAT
HERENGRACHT
REGULIERS
MINT TOWER
PRINSEN
KORTE
LEIDSE GRACHT
MARNIX STRAAT
LEIDSEKADE
LEIDSEPLEIN
LEIDSE DWARSSTRAAT
LEIDSE GRACHT
'T LIJNBAANSGRACHT
VONDEL-PARK
SINGELGRACHT
STADHOUDERSKADE
HOBBEMA STR.
P.C. HOOFT
JAN LUIJKEN
END
RIJKS-MUSEUM

21 Flower Market
22 Koningsplein
23 Metz & Co. (view)
24 Smartshop
25 The Delft Shop
26 Stadsschouwburg
27 Last Minute Ticket Shop
28 Melkweg
29 Boom Chicago Nightclub
30 "Restaurant Row"
31 Bulldog Café
32 Rederij Noord-Zuid canal boats
33 Max Euweplein
34 Paradiso
35 Rijksmuseum
36 Trams #2 & #5

the dunes and reclaimed land. By the 1630s, the country was in the grip of a full-blown tulip mania, when a single bulb sold for as much as a house, and fortunes were won and lost. Finally, in 1637, the market plummeted, and the tulip became just one of many beauties in the country's flower arsenal. Today, Holland is a major exporter of flowers. Certain seeds are certified and OK to bring back into the United States (merchants have the details).

• *The long Flower Market ends at the next bridge, where you'll see a square named...*

Koningsplein

Choke down a raw herring—the commodity that first put Amsterdam on the trading map—with locals who flock to this popular outdoor herring stand. (*Hollandse nieuwe* means the herring are in season.)

• *From Koningsplein, we'll turn left, heading straight to Leidseplein. At first, the street southward is just labeled Koningsplein (Scheltema, Amsterdam's leading bookstore, is at Koningsplein 20). Soon, Koningsplein becomes...*

Leidsestraat

Between here and Leidseplein, you'll cross several grand canals, following a street lined with fashion and tourist shops, and

crowded with shoppers, tourists, bicycles, and trams. Trams must wait their turn to share a single track as the street narrows.

The once grand, now frumpy **Metz & Co.** department store (where Leidsestraat crosses Herengracht) offers a rare above-the-rooftops panorama of the city from its sixth-floor café.

Looking left down Herengracht, you'll see the **"Golden Curve"** of the canal, lined with grand, classical-style gables.

• *Past the posh stores of Laura Ashley, DKNY, and Lush, find a humble establishment where Leidsestraat crosses the Keizersgracht (at Keizersgracht 508, daily 10:00–22:00)...*

When Nature Calls Smartshop

"Smartshops" like this one are clean, well-lighted, fully professional retail outlets that sell powerful drugs, many of which are illegal in America. Their "natural" drugs include harmless nutrition boosters (royal jelly), harmful but familiar tobacco, herbal

versions of popular dance-club drugs (herbal Ecstasy), and powerful psychoactive plants (psilocybin mushrooms). The big item: marijuana seeds.

Prices are clearly marked, with brief descriptions of the drugs, their ingredients, and effects. The knowledgeable salespeople can give more information on their "100 percent natural products that play with the human senses."

Still, my fellow Americans, *caveat emptor!* We've grown used to thinking, "If it's legal, it must be safe. If it's not, I'll sue." While perfectly legal and aboveboard, some of these substances can cause powerful, often unpleasant reactions.

• *Where Leidsestraat crosses the Prinsengracht, just over the bridge on the right (at Prinsengracht 440), you'll find...*

The Delft Shop

The distinctive blue-and-white design characterizes glazed ceramics made in Delft (30 miles southwest of here). Dutch traders learned the technique from the Chinese of the Ming dynasty, and many pieces have an Oriental look. The doodads with arms branching off a trunk are popular "flower pagodas," vases for displaying tulips.

• *Leidsestraat empties into the square called...*

Leidseplein

Filled with outdoor tables under trees, ringed with cafés, theaters, and nightclubs, bustling with tourists, diners, trams, mimes, and

fire-eaters, and lit by sun- or lantern-light, Leidseplein is Amsterdam's liveliest square.

Do a 360-degree spin: Leidseplein's south side is bordered by the city's main serious theater, the **Stadsschouwburg**, which dates back to the 17th-century Golden Age (present building from 1890). Tucked into a corner of the theater is the Last Minute Ticket Shop, which sells tickets to all the shows in town, including half-price, same-day tickets (after 12:00) to select shows (Leidseplein 26, tel. 0900-0191). To the right of the Stadsschouwburg, down a lane behind the big theater, stands the **Melkweg** (literally "Milky Way"), the once revolutionary, now institutional entertainment complex housing all things youth-oriented under one roof (Lijnbaansgracht 234a); step into the lobby or check out posters plastered on the walls to find out who's playing tonight. On Leidseplein's west side, at #12, is the **Boom Chicago** nightclub theater, presenting English-language spoofs of politics, Amsterdam, and tourists (see page 181; pick up their free, informative intro-to-Amsterdam magazine at the door). The neighborhood beyond Häagen-Dazs and Burger King is the "**Restaurant Row**," featuring countless Thai, Brazilian, Indian, Italian, Indonesian, and even a few Dutch eateries. Next, on the east end of Leidseplein, is the **Bulldog Café and Coffeeshop,** the

flagship of several café/bar/coffeeshops in town with that name. (Notice the sign above the door: It once housed the police bureau.) A small green-and-white decal in the window indicates that it's a city-licensed "coffeeshop," where marijuana is sold and smoked legally. Nearby are Rederij Noord-Zuid **canal boats**, offering one-hour tours (€9, free with *I amsterdam* Card, 2/hr April–Oct 10:00–18:00, 1/hr Nov–March 10:00–17:00).

• *From Leidseplein, turn left and head along the taxi stand down the broad, busy, tram-filled boulevard called Kleine-Gartman Plantsoen, which becomes Weteringschans. At the triangular garden filled with iguanas, cross the street and pass under a row of tall, gray, Greek-style columns, entering...*

Max Euweplein

The Latin inscription above the colonnade—*Homo Sapiens non urinat in ventum*—means "Don't pee into the wind." Pass between the columns and through a passageway to reach a pleasant interior courtyard with cafés and a large chessboard with knee-high kings. (Max Euwe was a Dutch world chess champion.) The square gives you access to the Casino, and just over the small bridge is the entrance to **Vondelpark.**

• *Return to Weteringschans street. Turn right and continue 75 yards east to a squat, red-brick building called...*

Paradiso

Back when rock-and-roll was a religion, this former church staged intimate concerts by big-name acts such as the Rolling Stones. In the late 1960s, when city fathers were trying hard to tolerate hordes of young pot-smokers, this building was redecorated with psychedelic colors and opened up as the first place where marijuana could be smoked—not legally yet, but it was tolerated. Today, the club hosts live bands and DJs and sells pot legally (for current shows, see www.paradiso.nl).

• *Continue down Weteringschans to the first bridge, where you'll see the Rijksmuseum across the canal.*

The Rijksmuseum and Beyond

The best visual chronicle of the Golden Age is found in the Rijksmuseum's portraits and slice-of-life scenes. ✪ For a tour of the Rembrandts, Vermeers, and others, see the Rijksmuseum Tour, page 101.

Canals

Amsterdam's canals tamed the flow of the Amstel River, creating pockets of dry land to build on. The city's 100 canals are  about 10 feet deep, crossed by some 1,200 bridges, fringed with 100,000 Dutch elm and lime trees, and bedecked with 2,500 houseboats. A system of locks (back near Central Station) controls the flow outward to (eventually) the North Sea and inward to the Amstel River. The locks are opened periodically to flush out the system.

Some of the boats in the canals look pretty funky by day, but Amsterdam is an unpretentious, anti-status city. When the sun goes down and the lights come on, people cruise the sparkling canals with an on-board hibachi and a bottle of wine, and even scows can become chick magnets.

On this walk, we've seen landmarks built during the city's late-19th-century revival: Central Station, the Stadsschouwburg, and now the Rijksmuseum. They're all similar, with red-brick and Gothic-style motifs (clock towers, steeples, prickly spires, and stained glass). Petrus Cuypers (1827–1921), who designed the train station and the Rijksmuseum, was extremely influential. Mainly a builder of Catholic churches, he made the Rijksmuseum, with its stained glass windows, a temple to art. The building is currently closed for renovation, with the highlights of the collection beautifully displayed in its Philips Wing (around back, on the right). Next to the Philips Wing, a small, free exhibit describes the exciting renovation project.

Behind the Rijksmuseum are the Museumplein (always entertaining) and the Van Gogh Museum (✪ see tour on page 119). The Heineken Brewery museum is a half mile east of the Rijks on Stadhouderskade (see page 42), and the Albert Kuyp street market is a block south of the brewery.

To return to Central Station (or to nearly anyplace along this walk), catch tram #2 or #5 from the southwest corner of the Rijks. Trams #6, #7, and #10 (catch them on Weteringschans) can take you farther south, east, or west. Or walk north on Nieuwe Spiegelstraat, which leads (with a little detour) back to the Mint Tower.

RED LIGHT DISTRICT WALK

Amsterdam's oldest neighborhood has hosted the world's oldest profession since 1200. The district lies between Damrak and Nieuwmarkt. Amsterdammers call it De Wallen, or "The Walls," after the old city walls that once stood here. On our walk, we'll see history, sleaze, and cheese—chickens in Chinatown windows, drunks in doorways, cruising packs of foreign twentysomethings, cannabis in windows, and sex for sale.

The sex trade runs the gamut from sex shops selling porn and accessories to blue video arcades, from glitzy nightclub sex shows featuring strippers and sex acts to the real deal—prostitutes in bras, thongs, and high heels, standing in window displays, offering their bodies. Amsterdam keeps several thousand prostitutes employed—and it's all legal.

Not for Everyone: The Red Light District has something offensive for everyone. Whether it's in-your-face images of graphic sex, exploited immigrant women, whips-and-chains, passed-out drug addicts, the pungent smells of pot smoke and urine, or just the shameless commercialism of it all, it's not everyone's cup of tea. While I encourage people to expand their horizons—that's a great thing about travel—it's perfectly OK to say "No, thank you."

ORIENTATION

Length of This Walk: Allow two hours.

Photography: Consider leaving your camera in your bag. Absolutely avoid taking photos of ladies in windows—even with a nobody-will-notice camera phone—or a snarling bouncer may appear from out of nowhere to forcibly rip it from your hands. Taking even seemingly harmless pictures of ordinary people is frowned upon by privacy-loving locals.

Photos of landmarks like the Old Church (Oude Kerk) and wide shots of distant red lights from the bridges are certainly OK, but remember that cameras are a prime target in this high-theft area.

When to Go: Mornings are quiet, but that's also when you see more passed-out-drunk-in-a-doorway scenes. Afternoons bring out more prostitutes, and evenings (starting at about 20:00) are actually quite festive, with many tourists and out-of-towners. Avoid late nights (after about 22:30), when the tourists disappear.

Safety: Coming here is asking for trouble, but if you're on the ball and smart, it's perfectly safe. While there are plenty of police on horseback keeping things orderly, there are also plenty of rowdy drunks, drug-pushing lowlifes, con artists, and pickpockets (not to mention extremely persuasive women in windows). Assume any fight or commotion in the streets is a ploy to distract innocent victims who are about to lose their wallets. As always, wear your money belt and keep a low profile.

Tours: This walk is enough for most visitors, but if you want a more in-depth visit with a guide and a group, consider Randy Roy's Red Light Tours or Zoom Amsterdam Citywalks (both described on page 36).

Condomerie: Mon–Sat 11:00–18:00, closed Sun, Warmoesstraat 141.

Old Church (Oude Kerk): €4, covered by *I amsterdam* Card, Mon–Sat 11:00–17:00, Sun 13:00–17:00, www.oudekerk.nl.

Prostitution Information Center: Free, Tue–Sat 12:00–17:00, closed Sun–Mon, facing the Old Church at Enge Kerksteeg 3, www.pic-amsterdam.com.

Amstelkring Museum (Our Lord in the Attic): €7, covered by *I amsterdam* Card, Mon–Sat 10:00–17:00, Sun 13:00–17:00, Oudezijds Voorburgwal 40, tel. 020/624-6604, www.museumamstelkring.nl.

Lotus Flower Chinese Buddhist Temple: Free, daily 12:00–17:00, Zeedijk street.

Banana Bar (Bananenbar): Nightly, Ouedezijds Achterburgwal 37, tel. 020/622-4670.

Erotic Museum: €5, daily 11:00–24:00, O.Z. Achterburgwal 54, tel. 020/624-7303.

Casa Rosso: Nightly until 2:00, O.Z. Achterburgwal 106–108, tel. 020/627-8954.

Cannabis College: Daily 11:00–19:00, O.Z. Achterburgwal 124, tel. 020/423-4420, www.cannabiscollege.com.

Hash, Marijuana, and Hemp Museum: €5.70, daily 11:00–22:00, O.Z. Achterburgwal 148, tel. 020/623-5961, www.hashmuseum.com.

Sensi Seed Bank Grow Shop: Free, Sun–Wed 11:00–18:00, Thu–Sat 11:00–21:00, O.Z. Achterburgwal 150 (may move 50 yards north in 2006).

OVERVIEW

The walk starts at the centrally located Dam Square. Two parallel streets with similar names—Oudezijds Voorburgwal and Oudezijds Achterburgwal—run north–south through the heart of De Wallen. We'll walk a big, long loop: north on Voorburgwal ("Voor") street past the Old Church, hook around on Zeedijk street, and return on Achterburgwal ("Achter"), ending two blocks from Dam Square.

THE WALK BEGINS

• *From Dam Square, head down Warmoesstraat (left facing the big, fancy Hotel Krasnapolsky). At the first interection, you'll see a small shop on the right...*

Condomerie

This condom shop has a knack for entertainment. Inside is a small glass case displaying a condom museum. On the counter is a three-ring notebook displaying all of the inventory.

• *From here, pass the two little phallic street barricades with cute red lights around them and enter the traffic-free world of...*

De Wallen

Dildos, dirty playing cards, penis-headed lipstick, S&M starter kits, kinky magazines, and blue videos—welcome to De Wallen. While the Red Light District is notorious throughout the Netherlands, even small rural towns often have a sex shop like this to satisfy their citizens' needs. Browsers are welcome inside the sex shops. Video arcades—giving access to dozens of porn films—charge by the minute.

According to legend, Quentin Tarantino holed up at the **Winston Hotel** for three months in 1993 to write *Pulp Fiction*. Farther down, you come to an intersection with the Old Church down the street on the right. Note the gay rainbow flags and the S&M flags (black and blue with a heart). Also notice the security cameras and modern lighting. While freedom reigns here, everything is kept under a watchful eye by the two neighborhood police departments.

Red Light District Walk

1 Condomerie & Museum

2 Sex Shops, S&M Flags & Mr. B's

3 Old Church

4 Prostitutes in Narrow Alleyways

5 Cheaper Prostitutes

6 Prostitution Info Center & Room-Rental Office

7 Princess Juliana School

8 Pill Bridge

9 Amstelkring Museum

10 Historic Building (1580)

11 View of Little Venice

12 Old Wooden House

13 Zeedijk Street & Locks

14 Police Station

15 Buddhist Temple & Chinatown

16 The Waag & Nieuwmarkt

17 S.M. Sign

18 Banana Bar

19 Erotic Museum

20 Absolute Danny Shop

21 Theatre Casa Rosso

22 Cannabis College

23 Hash, Marijuana & Hemp Museum

24 Sensi Seed Bank Store

At #97 is the **Elements of Nature Smartshop,** a little grocery store of mind-bending natural ingredients. Hallucinogenic mushrooms are in the fridge.

At #89, **Mr. B's Leather and Rubber Land**, marked by the S&M flag, takes macho to painful and what seems like anatomically impossible extremes. Downstairs you'll find great deals on whips and masks.

• *A block farther north is the impressive...*

Old Church (Oude Kerk)

Returning from a long sea voyage, sailors of yore would spy the steeple of the Old Church on the horizon, and know they were home. They thanked St. Nicholas—the patron of this church, seafarers, and Amsterdam—for their safe return.

Begun in about 1300 (some of the tower is original) and dedicated to St. Nicholas, the gangly church was built in fits and starts during the next 300 years. Even when the rival New Church (Nieuwe Kerk) was built on Dam Square, Amsterdam's oldest church still had the tallest spire, biggest organ, and most side-altars, and remained the neighborhood's center of activity, bustling inside and out with merchants and street markets.

The tower (290 feet high), with an octagonal steeple atop a bell tower, is an 18th-century update of the original 1300 tower, which was the model for many other Dutch churches. The carillon's 47 bells chime mechanically or can be played by one of Amsterdam's three official carillonneurs.

Today, there's not much to see inside. Of the 2,500 gravestones in the floor, the most famous is opposite the entrance: "Saskia 19 Juni 1642," the grave of Rembrandt's wife. The church is spacious and stripped-down, due to iconoclastic vandals. In the 16th century, rioting anti-Spanish Protestants gutted the church, smashed windows, and removed politically incorrect "graven images" (religious statues). One renowned girl threw her shoe at the Virgin statue. (Strict Calvinists at one point even removed the organ as a senseless luxury, until they found they couldn't stay on key singing hymns without it.) Atop the brass choir screen, an inscription *('t misbruyk in Godes...)* commemorates the iconoclasm: "The false practices introduced into God's church were undone here in 1578."

The church, permanently stripped of "pope-ish" decoration, was transformed from Catholic to Dutch Reformed, the name St. Nicholas' Church was dropped, and it became known by the nickname everyone called it anyway—the Old Church.

Around the Old Church

The church is surrounded by prostitution, yes, but there are other things as well—namely, everyday life. Attached to the Old Church like barnacles are small buildings, originally homes for priests, church offices, or rental units. The house to the right of the entrance (#25), inhabited by an elderly woman, is very tiny—32 feet by eight feet. Remember, someone lives here—be discreet.

Though the Red Light District is considered prime real estate, the ugly, 1970s-style apartments (near the church tower) offer a few lucky residents cheap subsidized housing. Along the canal is a green metal urinal that gets a lot of use. And, a few steps to the left of the Old Church's entrance, look down to find boobs in the pavement.

• *From the Old Church, backtrack a half block south on Voor street to just before the Bulldog Café and turn right at a narrow alleyway. Take a deep breath and squeeze into this tight opening.*

Prostitutes in Narrow Alleyways

You're right in the thick of high-density sleaze. Several narrow streets are lined with panty-and-bra-clad women in the windows

winking at horny men, rapping on the window to attract attention, or looking disdainfully at sightseers. You may notice that different zones feature prostitutes from different lands—Asia, Africa, Eastern Europe. This is to cater to customer tastes, as regulars know what they want.

The area sure looks rough, but, aside from tricky pickpockets, these streets are actually very safe. The entire Red Light District is dotted with teeny-tiny video surveillance cameras, located above doorways and in narrow alleys. If prostitutes have or notice any trouble, they press a buzzer that swiftly unleashes a burly, angry bouncer or the police.

There are other pockets of prostitution around, but this is one of the most concentrated. Explore.

• *Now circle the church clockwise. Around the back you'll see older, plumper (and cheaper) prostitutes.*

While many women choose prostitution as a lucrative career, many others are forced into it by circumstance—poverty, drug addiction, abusive men, and immigration scams. Since the fall of the Iron Curtain, many Eastern Europeans have flocked here for the high wages. The line between victim and entrepreneur grows finer and less clear.

• *On Enge Kerk Steeg, around the back of the Old Church, is the...*

Prostitution Information Center (#3)

Doling out information, books, condoms, and souvenir T-shirts, the PIC welcomes visitors. They have a map showing exactly where

Prostitution

Prostitution has been legal here since the 1980s. The women are often entrepreneurs, renting space and running their own businesses. Women usually rent their space for eight-hour shifts. A good spot costs €75 for a day shift and €150 for an evening. The rooms look tiny from the street ("Do they have to do it standing up?"), but most are just display windows, opening onto a room behind or upstairs with a bed, a sink, and little else.

Prostitutes have to keep their premises hygienic, use condoms, and avoid minors. Most prostitutes opposed legalization, not wanting taxes and bureaucratic regulations.

Popular prostitutes charge €25–50 for a 20-minute visit and make about €500 a day. They fill out tax returns, and many belong to a loose union called the Red Thread. The law, not pimps, protects prostitutes. If a prostitute is diagnosed with AIDS, she gets a subsidized apartment to encourage her to quit the business. Shocking as this may seem to some, it's a good example of a pragmatic Dutch solution to a problem—getting the most dangerous prostitutes off the streets to combat the spread of AIDS.

prostitution is legal and offer a small, frank €1.50 booklet answering the most common questions tourists have about Amsterdam's Red Light District.
• *Next door is a...*

Room-Rental Office (Kamerverhuurbedrijf)

Women come here to rent window-space and bedrooms to use for prostitution. Several of the available rooms are just next door. In return for their eight-, 12-, or 24-hour rental, they get security—the man at the desk keeps an eye on them via video surveillance. (See the monitors inside, and the small cameras and orange alarm lights above the doors.) The office also sells supplies (condoms by the case, lubricants, Coca-Cola).

This man does not arrange sex. The women who rent space from this business are self-employed. Customers negotiate directly with a woman at her door.

How does it work? A customer browses around. A prostitute catches his eye. If the prostitute is interested in his business (they are selective for their own safety), she winks him over. They talk at the door as she explains her price. Many are very aggressive at getting the man inside, where the temptation game revs up. A price is agreed and paid in advance.

Are there male prostitutes? Certainly, anything you might want is available somewhere in the Red Light District, but an experiment in the 1990s to put male prostitutes in windows didn't stand up. There are, however, "reconstructed women"—gorgeous transvestites who may (or may not) warn customers, to ward off any rude surprises.

• *Continue circling the church. At the back side of the church, amid prostitutes in windows, you'll pass the...*

Princess Juliana School

Life goes on, and locals need someplace to send their kids. This school was built in the 1970s, when the idea was to mix all dimensions of society together, absorbing the seedy into the decent. The location of this preschool (for kids from newborn to 4 years old) would be a tough sell where I come from.

• *Turn left at the canal and continue north on Voor street to the end of the canal. Along the way, you'll pass...*

Pill Bridge and Little Venice

The first bridge you pass is nicknamed "Pill Bridge" for the retail items sold by the seedy guys who hang out here. Beyond that is the fascinating Amstelkring Museum, in the Our Lord in the Attic church (at #40, one of the city's most visit-worthy museums—see Amstelkring Museum Tour, page 138).

Where Voor street intersects Oudezijds Armsteeg street (at #14) is a historic building from 1580 (two years after Amsterdam's Protestants booted out their Spanish rulers, and two decades before the Dutch East India Company formed, but built during a time of increasing overseas trade). Notice the small gap between this building and the neighboring building—these tiny alleys were for water drainage during rainstorms.

On the right, a view of "Little Venice" shows houses rising directly from the water (no quays or streets). Like Venice, the city was built in a marshy delta area, on millions of pilings. And, like Venice, it grew rich on sea trade.

• *From here, Voor street climbs slightly uphill (passing a collection of fine gable stones embedded in the wall on the right) to Zeedijk street. Turn left and walk along Zeedijk street to where it dead-ends at a viewpoint overlooking the marina, Damrak, and Central Station. On the corner, at Zeedijk #1, you'll find an...*

Old Wooden House

Picture the scene in the 1600s, when this café was a tavern, sitting right at what was then the water's edge. (Central Station sits on reclaimed land at the former mouth of the harbor.) Sailors tied up in today's marina, arriving from, say, a two-year voyage to Bali, bringing home fabulous wealth. They spilled into Zeedijk street, were greeted by swinging ladies swinging red lanterns, and stopped by St. Olaf's chapel to say a prayer of thanks, then anchored in this tavern for a good Dutch beer.

• *Turn around and head up Zeedijk street, to the crest of a bridge, to see...*

The Zeedijk and the Locks

The street called Zeedijk runs along the top of the "sea dike" that historically protected sea-level Amsterdam from North Sea tides. Once a day, a city worker unlocks the green box (by the railing) and presses a button, the locks open, and the tides flush out the city's canals. If the gate is open, you may see water flowing in or out.

In the 1970s and 1980s, this street was unbelievably sleazy (I live to tell)—a no-man's-land of junkies fighting amongst themselves. Today, it's increasingly trendy and upscale, fast becoming a *Sesame Street* neighborhood of urban diversity.

The street is a mix of ethnic restaurants (Thai and Portuguese) and bars, like the gay-oriented Queen's Head (#20). The new building at #30, built in "MIIM" (1998), offers apartments for rent and sale to the neighborhood's new, upscale inhabitants.

The former Café 't Mandje (#63) was perhaps Europe's first gay bar (opened in 1927 and closed in 1985). It stands as a memorial to owner Bet van Beeren (1907–1967), "Queen of the Zeedijk." The original Zee-dyke, Bet cruised the street in leather on her motorcycle. The café's interior has been rebuilt as an exhibit in the Amsterdam History Museum (see page 146).

Amsterdam's Chinatown is just around the corner, featuring chickens in windows, some of the city's best Chinese restaurants (such as Nam Kee at #113), and Asian gift shops.

It's easy to miss the police station (#80), which is deliberately

Social Control

The buzzword in Holland is "social control," meaning that neighborhood security comes not from iron shutters, heavily armed cops, and gated communities, but from neighbors looking out for each other. Everyone knows everyone in this tight-knit neighborhood. If Magreet doesn't buy bread for two days, the baker asks around. Unlike in many big cities, there's no chance that anyone here could lie dead in his house unnoticed for weeks. Video surveillance cameras watch prostitutes, while prostitutes survey the streets, buzzing for help if they spot trouble. Watch the men who watch the women who watch out for their neighbors across the street who watch the flower shop on the corner—"social control."

low-profile. In addition to patrolmen on foot, the neighborhood is peppered with plainclothes cops.

• *From the police station, this walk turns right on Korte Stormsteeg street, back to the canalside red lights. But first, you may wish to venture a block or two farther south, where you'll find a temple and a prison...*

The Lotus Flower Chinese Buddhist Temple

Enter this colorful, red-and-yellow, open-air temple by climbing the stairs, passing through one of the three entry arches representing the Buddhist Threefold Path (clean living, meditation, and wisdom). Under the roof, on lotus flowers, sits a statue of Guan Yin, whose thousand hands are always busy helping Buddha.

Three nuns (who live in the convent) and Chinatown's faithful kneel before the goddess, burn incense, and offer her fruit and flowers. The walls hold terra-cotta panels bearing the names of donors to this new addition to the neighborhood.

The Waag and Nieuwmarkt

In 1488, this octagonal tower was the main gate of the city's eastern wall. Later, it became a weighing house *(Waag)*, then a prison. In the 1600s, the tower was an operating theater for med students, where Rembrandt sat, sketchpad in hand, to see a criminal's body dissected. The painting that resulted *(The Anatomy Lesson of Dr. Deijman)* now hangs in the Amsterdam History Museum (see page 149).

Today, the Waag is a café, sitting in the middle of Nieuwmarkt Square (which sports a modern public urinal)—a scene that is somewhat seedy, but hip, bar-filled, and very local.

• *From Zeedijk street (at the police station), head west on Korte Stormsteeg, then left on Oudezijds Achterburgwal street.*

Oudezijds Achterburgwal

This beautiful, tree-lined canal is the heart of Red Light District nightlife, playing host to most of the main nightclubs. The majority of the sights we'll see are along the right-hand side of the street.

• *But first, on the left-hand side, find...*

S.M. Sign (#11)

The *S.M.* signs in the windows advertise prostitutes specializing in sadomasochistic sex. Formerly, the international code for rough sex was "Russian Massage." ("French" meant oral, "Greek" meant anal, and "British," I believe, meant sharing tea.)

Banana Bar (Bananenbar, at #37)

The facade of this nightclub is decorated with Art Nouveau eroticism classier than what's offered inside. For €40, you get admission for an hour, with drinks included. Undressed ladies serve the drinks, perched atop the bar. Touching is not allowed, but you can order a banana, and the lady will serve it to you any way you like.... For a full description, step into the lobby.

• *On side streets around here, you'll notice blue lights—these mark the transvestites. On the right side of Oudezijds Achterburgwal is the...*

Erotic Museum (#54)

"Wot a rip-off!" said a drunk British lout to his mates as he emerged from the Erotic Museum. If it's graphic sex you seek, this is not the place (perhaps try the Damrak Sex Museum—see page 57).

What you will see, besides the self-pleasuring bicycle girl in the lobby, is erotic statuettes from Asian cultures and some mildly risqué John Lennon sketches of him and Yoko Ono (on the 1st floor); a collection of racy comic books, photos, and old French literature (on the 2nd floor); reconstructions of what you see in today's Red Light District, including a prostitute's chambers, sex-shop window displays, and videos of nightclub sex shows (on the 3rd floor); and finally, the S&M room, where you're greeted by a mannequin urinating on you (on the top floor). S-mannequins torment M-mannequins for their mutual pleasure, and there are photos of America's raunchy 1950s pinup girl, Betty Page, in black hair, stockings, garters, and high heels.

Absolute Danny (#76)

This shop "for all your sensual clothing" sells leather and rubber outfits with dog collars suggesting bondage scenarios, in a full array of colors from red to black to...well, that's about it.

• *If you missed the Waag café, look east across the Achter canal and down Bloedstraat (lined with prostitutes) for a view. Continuing south on Achter street, you'll find...*

Theatre Casa Rosso

The area's best-known nightclub for live sex shows is fronted by a continuously ejaculating penis fountain with rotating testicles. Unlike some sex shows that draw you in to rip you off with hidden charges, the Casa Rosso is a legitimate operation. Fixed-price tickets offer evening performances featuring strippers and live sex acts, some simulated, some real.

• *Along the right side of the next block, you'll find three cannabis sights, starting with the...*

Cannabis College

This free public study center explains the positive industrial, medicinal, and recreational uses of cannabis. Books and newspaper clippings tell about practical hemp products, the medical uses of marijuana, and police prosecution/persecution of cannabis users. The pride and joy of the college is downstairs—the organic flowering cannabis garden, "where you can admire the plant in all her beauty." The garden—access by donation—happens to fit the Dutch legal limit of three plants per person or five per household.

The Hash, Marijuana, and Hemp Museum (#148)

Though informative, this earnest museum is small and somewhat overpriced, educational but not very entertaining. If you patiently read the displays, however, you'll learn plenty about cannabis and its various uses through history.

The leafy, green cannabis plant was grown by (among others) Golden Age Dutch merchants on large plantations. They turned the fibrous stalks (hemp) into rope and canvas for ships, and used it to make clothing and lace.

Some cannabis plants—particularly mature females of the *sativa* and *indica* species—contain the psychoactive alkaloid tetra-hydrocannabinol (THC) that makes you high. The buds, flowers, and leaves of the plant (marijuana) and the brown sap/resin/pitch that oozes out of the leaves (hashish, or hash) can be dried and smoked to produce effects ranging from euphoria to paranoia to the munchies.

Some peoples, from ancient Scythians and Hindus to modern Nepalis and Afghanis, have used cannabis as a sacred ritual drug. Modern Rastafarians, following a Bible-based religion centered in Jamaica, smoke cannabis, bob to reggae music, and praise God for creating "every herb" and calling them all "good" (Genesis 1:11–12).

The museum's highlight is the grow room, where you look through windows at real live cannabis plants in various stages of growth, some as tall as my mom. Grown hydroponically (in water, no soil) under grow lights, at a certain stage they're "sexed" to weed out the boring males and "selected" to produce the most powerful strains.

Sensi Seed Bank Store

Also known as the Cannabis Connoisseurs Club, this shop—likely to move 50 yards north in 2006—is geared toward cannabis growers. They sell seeds, grow lights, climate-control devices, bug sprays, how-to books, and CDs of music to grow dope by.

• *Where Achter street intersects Oude Doelen street, look to the right to see the Royal Palace on Dam Square, two blocks away.*

TOUR OVER

You've peeked at locals—from prostitutes to drug pushers to Buddhists to politically active heads with green thumbs—and survived. Congratulations. Now, go back to your hotel and take a shower.

JORDAAN WALK

This walk takes you from Dam Square—the "Times Square" of Amsterdam—to Anne Frank's House, and then deep into the characteristic Jordaan neighborhood. It's a cultural scavenger hunt, offering you a chance to appreciate the laid-back Dutch lifestyle and catch a few intimate details that most busy tourists never appreciate.

In the Jordaan (yor-DON), you'll see things that are commonplace in Amsterdam, but which you won't find in any other city in the world.

This is a short and easygoing walk—nice in the sleepy morning or en route to a Jordaan dinner in the evening. Bring your camera, as you'll enjoy some of Amsterdam's most charming canal scenes.

ORIENTATION

Length of This Walk: Allow 1.5 hours.

St. Andrew's Hof: Free, Mon–Sat 9:00–18:00, closed Sun, Egelantiersgracht 107.

Electric Ladyland: €5, Tue–Sat 13:00–18:00, closed Sun–Mon, Tweede Leliedwarsstraat 5-HS, tel. 020/420-3776, www.electric-lady-land.com.

OVERVIEW

The walk begins at Dam Square and ends at the center of the Jordaan by Egelantiers canal. To return to Dam Square, it seems quicker to hike (10–15 min) than take a tram (walk 4 blocks south to Rozengracht and catch tram #13, #14, or #17).

THE WALK BEGINS

• *From Dam Square, leave the McDonald's, the mimes, and the tourists behind, and head to the place where real Amsterdammers live. Face the palace. Slip (to the right) between the palace and the New Church (Nieuwe Kerk), and you'll see the facade of the redbrick...*

Magna Plaza Shopping Center

Built in 1899 on top of 4,560 pilings, this "modern"-looking building symbolized the city's economic revival after two centuries of

decline. The revival was brought on by the opening of the North Sea Canal and increased industrialization, capped by a World's Fair in 1883. The shopping center, originally the main post office, now houses 40 stores. On the ground floor (on the left), a cheery cheese lady would love you to try her Gouda (free and generous samples of 3 or 4 kinds, with an explanation).

• *Exiting Magna Plaza, take two lefts—walking 50 yards on busy Nieuwezijds Voorburgwal, then left on tiny Molsteeg.*

(The pink pavement alerts you that this stretch of street is actually a bike path—keep to the sides.) From here, it's a straight shot west (though the street changes names along the way) to the Anne Frank House and into the Jordaan.

Bicycles

At the intersection with Spuistraat, with its pink-paved bike path (indicating that you must yield to bikes), see the rows of bicycles parked along the street. Amsterdam's 739,000 residents own nearly that many bikes. Holland's 16.3 million people own 16.3 million bikes, with many people owning two—a long-distance racing bike and an in-city bike, often deliberately kept in poor maintenance, so it's less enticing to the many bike thieves. Locals are diligent about locking their bikes twice: They lock the spokes and then use a heavy chain to attach the bike to something immovable.

The Dutch appreciate the efficiency of a self-propelled machine that travels five times faster than walking, without pollution, noise, parking problems, or high fuel costs. On a *fiets* (bicycle), a speedy local can traverse the historic center in 10 minutes. As you explore, enjoy the quiet of a people-friendly town where bikes outnumber cars.

• *After another block, the street opens onto a small square straddling the Singel canal.*

Jordaan Walk

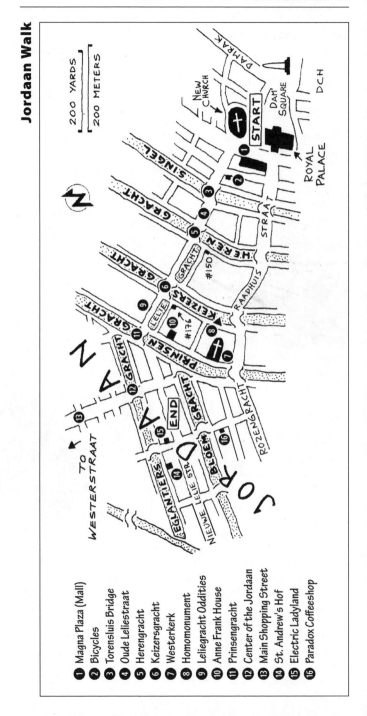

1. Magna Plaza (Mall)
2. Bicycles
3. Torensluis Bridge
4. Oude Leliestraat
5. Herengracht
6. Keizersgracht
7. Westerkerk
8. Homomonument
9. Leliegracht Oddities
10. Anne Frank House
11. Prinsengracht
12. Center of the Jordaan
13. Main Shopping Street
14. St. Andrew's Hof
15. Electric Ladyland
16. Paradox Coffeeshop

Torensluis Bridge

With cafés and art galleries, this quiet neighborhood seems farther than just three blocks from busy Dam Square. The canal today looks much as it might have during the Golden Age of the 1600s, when the city quickly became a major urban center. Pan 360 degrees and take in the variety of buildings.

The so-called **skinniest house in Amsterdam** is the red house at #166. In fact, it's just the entryway to a normal house that opens up farther back. Most Amsterdam buildings extend far back, with interiors looking quite different from what you might expect from the facade. Real estate has always been expensive on this canal, and owners were taxed by the amount of street frontage. A local saying at the time was, "Only the wealthy can live on the inside of a canal's curve" (where they would have maximum taxable frontage with a minimum of usable space).

The houses crowd together, shoulder to shoulder. Built on top of thousands of logs hammered vertically into the marshy soil, they've shifted with the tides over the years, some leaning to the sides. Houses that lean out over the street are often built that way to maximize interior space. Many brick houses have iron rods strapped onto the sides, binding the bricks to an inner skeleton of wood. Most have big, tall windows to admit as much light as possible. Mingled among the old houses are a few modern buildings—sleek, gray-metal apartments—that try to match the humble, functional spirit of the older ones.

Two **characteristic bars** spill out onto the bridge. Van Zuylen is famous for its variety of beers. Villa Zeezicht is popular for its sandwiches and apple pie. Both are great for their canal setting.

The statue of **Multatuli** (1820–1887) honors the "Dutch Rudyard Kipling," whose autobiographical novel *Max Havelaar* (1860) follows a progressive bureaucrat's fight to improve the lives of Javanese natives slaving away on Dutch-owned plantations. He was the first to criticize Dutch colonial practices—very bold back then.

Amsterdam's **canals** (roughly 50 miles of them) are about 10 feet deep, and are flushed daily by opening the locks as the North

Gables

Along the rooftops, Amsterdam's famous gables are false fronts to enhance roofs that are, generally, sharply pitched. Gables come in all shapes and sizes, sometimes decorated with animal and human heads, garlands, urns, scrolls, and curlicues. Despite the infinite variety, you can recognize several generic types.

A simple point gable just follows the triangular shape of a normal pitched roof. A bell gable—there's one two doors to the right of the skinny house—is shaped like (duh) a bell. Step gables, triangular in shape and lined with steps, are especially popular in Belgium. Spout gables have a rectangular protrusion at the peak. Neck gables rise up vertically from a pair of sloping "shoulders." Cornice gables make pointed roofs look classically horizontal. (There's probably even a clark gable, but frankly, I don't give a damn.)

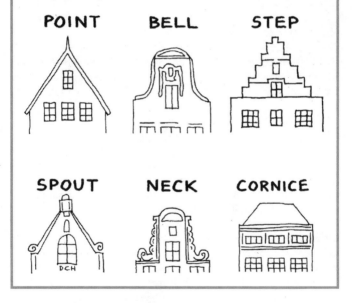

Sea tides come in and out. You can glimpse the locks in the distance at the north end of the Singel canal—the white flagpole thingies sprouting at 45-degree angles (beyond the dome) are part of the apparatus to open and shut the gates. The Dutch are credited with inventing locks in the 1300s. This single greatest invention in canal-building allows ships to pass from higher to lower water levels.

The historic Singel canal was originally the moat running around the medieval walled city. The green copper dome in the distance marks the Lutheran church. Left of that is the new city—

reclaimed in the 1600s and destined to be the high-rent district. To the right is the old town.

• *Continue west on...*

Oude Leliestraat

Consumers will find plenty to consume on this block of shops and cafés that runs Amsterdam's gamut—Puccini's bonbons, Grey Area's marijuana, Foodism's vegetarian fare, De Lelie's Surinamese chicken *rotis,* Zool's traditional café fare, and Cafeteria's lamb *shoarmas.*

Grey Area bucks the trend of typical coffeeshops. While most cultivate a dark, exotic, opium-den atmosphere, this is small, clean, and well-lit. The green-and-white decal in the window identifies it as #092 in the city's licensing program. This esteemed coffeeshop was the winner of Amsterdam's 2001 Cannabis Cup, a high honor.

• *The next canal is the...*

Herengracht

The house that's kitty-corner across the bridge (Herengracht 150) fronts the canal, giving us a cutaway of its entire depth—the long white side. Most Amsterdam buildings are much bigger than they appear from the front. On the roof, rods support the false-front gable.

Parking is a problem in a city designed for boats, not cars. Parking signs (there's one along Herengracht—on the left) warn you to put money in the meter at the end of the block, or have your wheels shackled with "the boot," which stays on until you pay your fine. Parking in the center runs €6 an hour, and parking fees and fines fund a substantial portion of the city's transportation budget.

• *Continue west, walking along...*

Leliegracht

This is one of the city's prettiest small canals, lined with trees and crossed by a series of arched bridges (some of the city's 400). Notice that some of the buildings—furniture stores and bookstores—have staircases leading down below the street level to residences.

Many buildings have a beam jutting out from the top with a hook on the end. Attach a pulley to that, and you can lift up a sofa and send it through a big upper-story window—much easier than lugging it up a narrow staircase.

• *The next canal you cross is...*

Keizersgracht

The **Westerkerk** tower rises above the rooftops, capped with a golden crown and the Amsterdam coat of arms. The crown shape was a gift of the Hapsburg Maximilian I, as thanks for a big loan. Rembrandt is buried under the floor of this "Western Church," which dates from 1631. Its carillons toll every 15 minutes, a sound that reminded Anne Frank—who hid out just down the street—that there was, indeed, an outside world.

Kitty-corner across the bridge (Keizersgracht 176) is a building that recalls the modern style known as the Amsterdam School (c. 1910). The overall look is squarish and modern, but small towers, mosaics, and curvy bay windows relieve the minimalism.

Detour a hundred yards left (south) along the Keizers canal, a triangular pink dock juts into the canal—the **Homomonument.** There are often flowers on it, remembering another AIDS victim. The pink triangle design co-opts the Nazi concentration-camp symbol for gays. Amsterdam often hosts international conventions on AIDS and gay awareness.

The green metal structure near the Homomonument is a public urinal (called a *pissoir*) that offers only minimal privacy. But for Dutch men ignored by worldly Dutch women, it's no problem.

The busy street just beyond the Homomonument is Raadhuis Straat, where there's a taxi stand, the handy east–west trams #13, #14, and #17, and a french-fry stand featuring art with the lowly fried potato worked into some famous paintings.

• *Backtrack to Leliegracht and continue west...*

More on Leliegracht

Some things are commonplace in Amsterdam, but odd elsewhere in the world. The mail slots on several doors have stickers saying *Nee* or *Ja* (no or yes), telling the postman what types of junk mail they'll accept or refuse. At #52, a handy bike ramp slants down the steps to a home below street level. And at #62, glance up to the first story to see a

rear-view mirror. Why go way down steep stairs to see who's at the door when you can just check the well-aimed mirror?

• *At the Prinsengracht, the Anne Frank House (❂ see Anne Frank House Tour, page 131) is 100 yards to the left, and the Westerkerk is another 100 yards beyond that.*

Prinsengracht

One of the most livable canals in town is lined with several of the city's estimated 2,500 houseboats. When small sail-powered cargo ships became uneconomical with the advent of modern cargo boats in the 1930s, they found a new use—as houseboats lining the canals of Amsterdam, where land was so limited and pricey. Today, their cargo holds are fashioned into elegant, cozy living rooms. Moorage spots are prized and grandfathered in, making some of the junky old boats worth more than you'd think. Along this canal, boaters can plug hoses and cables into outlets along the canal side to get water and electricity. (To learn more about houseboats, visit the charming Houseboat Museum, described on page 45.)

Notice the canal traffic. The speed limit on canals is four miles per hour. At night, boats must have running lights on the top, side, and stern. Most boats are small and low to glide under the city's bridges. The Prinsengracht bridge is average size, with less than seven feet of headroom (it varies with the water level); some bridges have less than six feet. Good maps indicate the critical height of the bridges.

Just across the bridge are several typical cafés. The relaxed Café de Prins serves food and drink both day and night. The old-timey De 2 Zwaantjes occasionally features the mournful songs of the late local legend Johnny Jordaan. And the Café 't Smalle (not visible from here, a half block to the right) has a deck where you can drink outside along a quiet canal (for details, see "Hungry?" on page 99).

• *Once you cross the Prinsengracht, you enter the Jordaan. Facing west (toward Café de Prins), cross the bridge and veer left at 11 o'clock (using a hypothetical clock as a compass) down...*

Nieuwe Leliestraat

The buildings are smaller, the ground-level apartments are remarkably open to the street, signs warn speeding drivers to *Let op!* (Watch out!) for the speed bumps *(drempels)*, and the mail slots sport more *Nee*s than *Ja*s (no junk mail, please). Welcome to quiet Jordaan. Built in the 1600s as a working-class housing area, it's now home to artists and yuppies. Though many apartments have windows right on the street, the neighbors don't stare and the residents don't care. They even invite their friends for candlelit dinners right by the front window. The name Jordaan probably wasn't derived from the French *jardin*—but given the neighborhood's garden-like ambience, it seems like it should have been.

• *At the first intersection, Eerste Leliedwarsstraat, chess players may wish to detour left one block to the smoky but intensely cerebral Schaak Café (Bloemengracht 20). If chess isn't your game, turn right on Eerste Leliedwarsstraat and go one block to Egelantiers canal. The bridge over the canal is what I think of as...*

The Center of the Jordaan

This place—with its bookstores, small cafés full of rickety tables, art galleries, and working artists' studios—sums up the Jordaan.

Look down the quiet Egelantiers canal, lined with trees and old, narrow, gabled buildings, and scattered with funky scows by day that become cruising *Love Boat*s by night.

Look south at the Westerkerk, and see a completely differ-ent view than the tourists at the Anne Frank House get. Framed

by narrow streets, crossed with streetlamp wires, and looming over shoppers on bicycles, this is the church in its best light.

With your back to the church, look north down the street called Tweede Egelantiers Dwarsstraat, the laid-back neighborhood's main shopping and people street, lined with boutiques, antiques, hair salons, restaurants, and cafés. A few blocks down (but don't go there now), the street intersects Westerstraat, a wide, east–west boulevard with more everyday businesses and a weekend street market.

• *Just past the next bridge west on Egelantiers canal at #107 is the entrance to...*

St. Andrew's Hof (Sint-Andrieshof)

Enter—quietly—through the black door marked *Sint-Andrieshof 107 t/m 145* (open until 18:00, push hard on door) and encounter a slice of Vermeer—a tiny courtyard surrounded by a dozen or so residences. Take a seat on a bench and immerse yourself in this still world. This small-scale version of the Begijnhof is one of scores of *hofjes* (subsidized residences built around a courtyard), funded by churches, charities, and the city for low-income widows and pensioners.

Hungry?

There are several recommended restau-rants in the area. Especially good are **Café**

Restaurant de Reiger (daily 18:00–22:30, Nieuwe Leliestraat 34, tel. 020/624-7426) and **Café 't Smalle** (lunch 12:00–17:00; eat or drink canalside, inside at the bar, or in an upstairs room; at Egelantiersgracht 12 where it hits Prinsengracht, tel. 020/623-9617). For full descriptions, see Amsterdam's Eating chapter, page 161.

• *Your tour's over. To get back to Dam Square, you can walk (10–15 min) or catch a tram (walk 4 blocks south to Rozengracht, then take tram #13, #14, or #17).*

But old hippies have two more stops: Heading back toward the center of town along Egelantiers canal, make a right turn on Tweede Leliedwarsstraat, where you'll find...

Hippie Highlights

A small shop with a flowery window display, **Electric Ladyland: The First Museum of Fluorescent Art,** hides a fluorescent won-

derland. It's the creation of Nick Padalino...one cool cat who really found his black-light niche in life. Downstairs, under Nick's shop, is a unique and tiny museum featuring fluorescent black-light art. Nick lovingly guides you, demonstrating fluorescent minerals from all over the world and fluorescence in everyday objects (stamps, candy, and so on). He seems to get a bigger kick out of it than even his customers. You can see the historic first fluorescent crayon from San Francisco in the 1950s. Wow. The label says, "Use with black light for church groups." Wow. (€5, Tue–Sat 13:00–18:00, closed Sun–Mon, Tweede Leliedwarsstraat 5-HS, tel. 020/420-3776, www.electric-lady-land.com.)

The nearby **Paradox Coffeeshop** is the perfect coffeeshop for the nervous American who wants a mellow place to go local (light meals, fresh juice, easy music, daily 10:00–20:00, Eerste Bloemdwarsstraat 2).

RIJKSMUSEUM TOUR

At the Rijksmuseum ("Rijks" sounds like "hikes"), Holland's Golden Age shines with the best collection anywhere of the Dutch Masters—from Vermeer's quiet domestic scenes to Steen's raucous family meals to Hals' snapshot portraits to Rembrandt's moody brilliance.

The 17th century saw the Netherlands at the pinnacle of its power. The Dutch had won their independence from Spain, trade

and shipping boomed, the wealth poured in, and the arts flourished. For the Dutch, this was their Golden Age. With no local church or royalty to commission big canvases in the Protestant Dutch republic, artists had to find different patrons—the upper-middle-class businessmen who fueled Holland's capitalist economy. Artists painted their portraits, and decorated their homes with pretty still lifes and non-preachy, slice-of-life art.

The main core of the Rijksmuseum is closed until 2008 for a massive renovation. Thankfully, the most famous masterpieces—nearly everything on the typical tourist's hit list—are on display in the wonderful Philips Wing (southwest corner of the Rijks, the part of the building nearest the Van Gogh Museum).

ORIENTATION

Cost: €10, covered by *I amsterdam* Card, tickets good all day. The year 2006 marks the 400th birthday of Rembrandt, and the Rijksmuseum has co-sponsored a special exhibition—with the Van Gogh Museum—in his honor. If you're visiting the Rijks between February 24 through June 18 and planning to also see the Van Gogh Museum (where the special exhibit is being held), buy the €25 combo-ticket for entry to all three: Rijks, Van Gogh Museum, and the special exhibit. For more on the 2006 Rembrandt events, see page 41.

Hours: Daily 9:00–18:00, Friday until 22:00, closed only on Jan 1.

Getting There: The entrance to the Philips Wing is clearly marked near the corner of Jan Luijkenstraat and Hobbemastraat. From the train station, catch tram #2 or #5 (get out at Hobbemastraat, directly at the Philips Wing).

Information: The helpful information booth inside the museum has free maps and a good guidebook, *The Masterpieces* (€7.50). A new information center outside in the garden explains the renovation (on Jan Luijkenstraat, to the left as you enter). Tel. 020/674-7047, www.rijksmuseum.com.

Audioguide Tour: The €4 tour covers many paintings with dial-a-number convenience and provides a blitz visit for those interested in only the highlights.

Length of This Tour: Allow one hour.

Checkrooms: Leave your bag at the free checkrooms.

Cuisine Art: Vondelpark (picnic-perfect park with the delightful Café Vertigo, daily 11:00–24:00, beneath Film Museum at Vondelpark 3) and Leidseplein (a lively square with cafés) are each a short walk away. The Cobra Café is on Museumplein (towards the Van Gogh Museum). For good pancakes, try the untouristy Le Soleil (€4–8, daily 10:00–18:00, share a big table with other guests, Nieuwe Spiegelstraat 56).

Photography: Permitted without a flash.

Starring: Frans Hals, Rembrandt van Rijn, Johannes Vermeer, Jan Steen.

THE TOUR BEGINS

Dutch Art

Dutch art is meant to be enjoyed, not studied. It's straightforward, meat-and-potatoes art for the common man. The Dutch love the beauty of everyday things painted realistically and with exquisite detail. So, set your cerebral cortex on "low" and let this art pass straight from the eyes to the heart, with minimal detours.

Museumplein

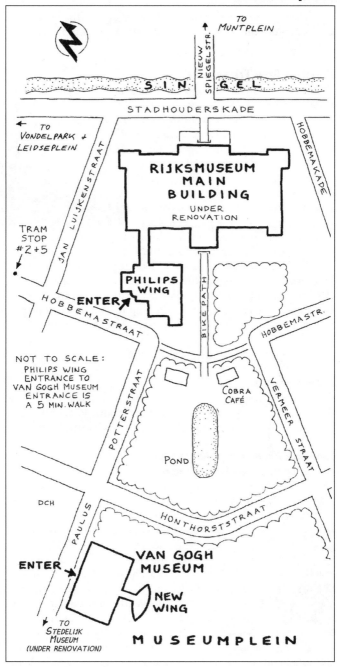

• *Enter the large Room 1, dominated by the large, colorful painting of a group of men eating, drinking, and staring at you,* The Banquet in Celebration of the Treaty of Münster *(1648), by Bartholomeus van der Helst.*

Golden Age Treasures

Welcome to the Golden Age. Gaze into the eyes of the men who made Amsterdam the richest city on earth in the 1600s. Though shown in their military uniforms, these men were really captains of industry—shipbuilders, seamen, salesmen, spice-tasters, bankers, and venture capitalists—all part of the complex economic web that planned and financed overseas trade. Also in Room 1, find a ship's cannon and a big

wooden model of a 74-gun Dutch man-of-war that escorted convoys of merchant ships loaded with wealth.

The five rooms on the ground floor display objects that bring Holland's Golden Age to life, including weapons, dolls' houses (Room 3), and precious objects (especially Delftware, inspired by Chinese porcelain, Room 5). Soak up the ambience to prepare for the paintings that the Golden Age generation produced and enjoyed.

• *Ride the spacey elevator upstairs to Room 6.*

New Genres

Rather than religious art, Dutch painters portrayed small-scale, down-home, happy subjects, such as portraits, landscapes, still lifes, and so-called "genre scenes" (snapshots of everyday life).

Hendrick Avercamp (1585–1634)—
Winter Landscape with Ice Skaters

The village stream has frozen over, and the people all come out to play. (Even today, tiny Holland's speed-skating teams routinely beat the superpowers.) In the center, a guy falls flat on his face.

A couple makes out in the hay-tower silo. There's a "bad moon on the rise" in the broken-down outhouse at left, and another nearby. We see the scene from above (the horizon line is high), making it seem as if the fun goes on forever.

A song or a play is revealed to the audience at the writer's pace. But in a painting, we set the tempo, choosing where to look and

The Golden Age
(1600s)

Who bought this art? Look around at the Rijksmuseum's many portraits, and you'll see ordinary middle-class people, merchants, and traders. Even in their Sunday best, you can see that these are hardworking, businesslike, friendly, simple people (with a penchant for ruffled lace collars).

Dutch fishermen sold their surplus catch in distant areas of Europe, importing goods from these far lands. In time, fishermen became traders, and by 1600, Holland's merchant fleets ruled the waves with colonies as far away as India, Indonesia, and America (New York was originally "New Amsterdam"). The Dutch slave trade—selling Africans to Americans—generated a lot of profit for luxuries such as the art you're looking at. Back home, these traders were financed by shrewd Amsterdam businessmen on the new frontiers of capitalism.

Look around again. Is there even one crucifixion? One saint? One Madonna? OK, maybe one. But this is people art, not church art. In most countries, Catholic bishops and rich kings supported the arts. But the Republic of the Netherlands, recently free of Spanish rule and Vatican domination, was independent, democratic, and largely Protestant, with no taste for saints and Madonnas.

Instead, Dutch burghers bought portraits of themselves, and pretty, unpreachy, unpretentious works for their homes. Even poor people bought smaller canvases by "no-name" artists designed to fit the budgets and lifestyles of this less-than-rich-and-famous crowd. We'll see examples of their four favorite subjects—still lifes (of food and everyday objects), landscapes, portraits (often of groups), and scenes from everyday life.

how long to linger. Exercise your right to loiter. Avercamp, who was deaf and mute, presents a visual symphony of small scenes. Just skate among these Dutch people—rich, poor, lovers hand in hand, kids, and moms—and appreciate the silent beauty of this intimate look at old Holland.
• *Enter Room 7.*

Frans Hals (c. 1581–1666)—*The Merry Drinker* (1627)
You're greeted by a jovial man in a black hat, capturing the earthy, exuberant spirit of the Golden Age. Notice the details—the happy red face of the man offering us a glass of wine, the sparkle in his eyes, the lacy collar, the decorative belt buckle, and so on.

Now move in closer. All these meticulous details are accomplished with a few quick, thick, and messy brushstrokes. The beard

Rijksmuseum—The Philips Wing

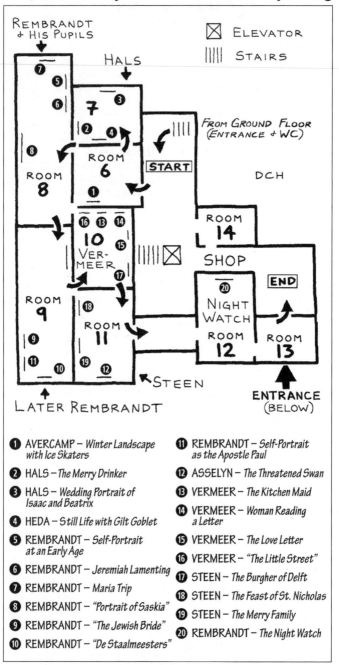

1 AVERCAMP – *Winter Landscape with Ice Skaters*

2 HALS – *The Merry Drinker*

3 HALS – *Wedding Portrait of Isaac and Beatrix*

4 HEDA – *Still Life with Gilt Goblet*

5 REMBRANDT – *Self-Portrait at an Early Age*

6 REMBRANDT – *Jeremiah Lamenting*

7 REMBRANDT – *Maria Trip*

8 REMBRANDT – *"Portrait of Saskia"*

9 REMBRANDT – *"The Jewish Bride"*

10 REMBRANDT – *"De Staalmeesters"*

11 REMBRANDT – *Self-Portrait as the Apostle Paul*

12 ASSELYN – *The Threatened Swan*

13 VERMEER – *The Kitchen Maid*

14 VERMEER – *Woman Reading a Letter*

15 VERMEER – *The Love Letter*

16 VERMEER – *"The Little Street"*

17 STEEN – *The Burgher of Delft*

18 STEEN – *The Feast of St. Nicholas*

19 STEEN – *The Merry Family*

20 REMBRANDT – *The Night Watch*

is a tangle of brown worms, the belt buckle a yellow blur. His hand is a study in smudges. Even the expressive face is done with a few well-chosen patches of color. Unlike the still-life scenes, this canvas is meant to be viewed from a distance, where the colors and brushstrokes blend together.

Frans Hals was the premier Golden Age portrait painter. Merchants hired him the way we'd hire a wedding photographer. With a few quick strokes, Hals captured not only the features, but the personality.

Rather than posing his subject, making him stand for hours saying "cheese," Hals tried to catch him at a candid moment. He often painted common people, fishermen, and barflies, such as this one. He had to work quickly to capture the serendipity of the moment. Hals uses a stop-action technique, freezing the man in mid-gesture, where the rough brushwork creates a blur that suggests the man is still moving.

Two centuries later, the Impressionists learned from Hals' messy brushwork. In the Van Gogh Museum, you'll see how van Gogh painted, say, a brown beard by using thick dabs of green, yellow, and red that blend at a distance to make brown.

Frans Hals—*Wedding Portrait of Isaac Abrahamsz Massa and Beatrix van der Laen* (1622)

This wedding portrait of a chubby, pleasant merchant and his bride sums up the story of the Golden Age. This overseas trader was away from home for years at a time on business. So Hals makes a special effort to point out his patron's commitment to marriage. Isaac pledges allegiance to his wife, putting his hand on his heart. Beatrix's wedding ring is prominently displayed dead center between them (on her right-hand forefinger, Protestant-style). The vine clinging to a tree is a symbol of man's support and woman's dependence. And in the distance at right, in the classical love garden, are other happy couples strolling arm in arm amid peacocks, a symbol of fertility.

In earlier times, marriage portraits put the man and wife in separate canvases, staring out grimly. Hals' jolly couple reflects a societal shift from marriage as business partnership to an arrangement that's more friendly and intimate.

Hals didn't need symbolism to tell us that these two are prepared for their long-distance relationship—they seem relaxed together, but they each look at us directly, with a strong, individual identity. Good as gold, these are the type of people who propelled this soggy little country into its glorious Golden Age.

Various Still Lifes (c. 1630)

Savor the fruits of Holland's rich overseas trade—lemons from the south, pitchers from Germany, and spices from Asia, including those most exotic of spices...salt and pepper. These carefully composed, photo-realistic still lifes reflect the same sense of pride the Dutch have for their homes, cultivating them like gardens until they're immaculate, decorative, and well-ordered.

Pick one, such as *Still Life with Gilt Goblet* (by Willem Heda). Get so close that the guard joins you. Linger over the little things: the pewterware, the seafood, the lemon peels, the rolls, and the glowing goblets that cast a warm reflection on the tablecloth. You'd swear you can see yourself reflected in the pewter vessels. At least, you can see the faint reflections of the food and even of surrounding windows. The closer you get, the better it looks.

• *Enter Room 8.*

Rembrandt van Rijn (1606–1669)—Early Works

Rembrandt van Rijn is the greatest Dutch painter. Whereas most painters specialized in one field—portraits, landscapes, still lifes—Rembrandt excelled in them all.

Rembrandt—*Self-Portrait at an Early Age*

Here we see the young, small-town boy about to launch himself into whatever life has to offer. Rembrandt was a precocious kid.

His father, a miller, insisted he be a lawyer. His mother hoped he'd be a preacher (look for a portrait of her reading the Bible, nearby). Rembrandt combined the secular and religious worlds by becoming an artist, someone who can hint at the spiritual by showing us the beauty of the created world.

He moved to Amsterdam and entered the highly competitive art world. Amsterdam was a booming town and, like today, a hip and cosmopolitan city. Rembrandt portrays himself at age 22 as being divided—half in light, half hidden by hair and shadows—open-eyed, but wary of an uncertain future. As we'll see, Rembrandt's paintings are often light-and-dark, both in color and in subject, exploring the "darker" side of human experience.

Rembrandt—
Jeremiah Lamenting the Destruction of Jerusalem **(1630)**

The Babylonians have sacked and burned Jerusalem. But

Rembrandt leaves the pyrotechnics (in the murky background at left) to Spielberg and the big screen. Instead, he tells the story of Israel's destruction in the face of the prophet who predicted the disaster. Jeremiah slumps in defeat, deep in thought, confused and despondent, trying to understand why this evil had to happen. Rembrandt turns his floodlight of truth on the prophet's deeply lined forehead.

Rembrandt wasn't satisfied to crank out portraits of fat merchants in frilly bibs, no matter what they paid him. He wanted to experiment, trying new techniques and more probing subjects. Many of his paintings weren't commissioned and were never even intended for sale. His subjects could be brooding and melancholy, a bit dark for the public's taste. So was his technique.

You can recognize a Rembrandt canvas by his play of light and dark. Most of his paintings are a deep brown tone, with only a few bright spots glowing from the darkness. This allows Rembrandt to highlight the details he thinks are most important, and express moody emotions.

Light has a primal appeal to humans. (Dig deep into your DNA and remember the time when fire was not tamed. Light! In the middle of the night! This miracle separated us from our fellow animals.) Rembrandt strikes at that instinctive level.

Rembrandt—*Maria Trip* **(1639)**

This debutante daughter of a wealthy citizen is shy and reserved—maybe a bit awkward in her new dress and adult role, but still self-

assured. When he chose to, Rembrandt could dash off a commissioned portrait like nobody's business. The details are immaculate—the lace and shiny satin, the pearls behind the veil, the subtle face and hands. But Rembrandt gives us not just a person, but a personality.

Look at the red rings around her eyes, a detail a lesser painter would have airbrushed out. Rembrandt takes this feature, unique to her, and uses it as a setting for her luminous, jewel-like eyes. Without being prettified, she's beautiful.

Rembrandt—*A Young Woman* (a.k.a *The Portrait of Saskia,* 1633)

It didn't take long for Amsterdam to recognize Rembrandt's great talent. Everyone wanted a portrait done by the young master.

He became wealthy and famous. He fell in love with and married the rich, beautiful, and cultured Saskia. By all accounts, the two were enormously happy, entertaining friends, decorating their house with fine furniture, raising a family, and living the high life. In this wedding portrait, thought to be of Saskia, the bride's face literally glows. A dash of white paint puts a sparkle in her eye. Barely 30 years old, Rembrandt was the most successful painter in Holland. He had it all.

Other "Rembrandts"

The Rijksmuseum displays real Rembrandts, paintings by others that look like his, portraits of Rembrandt by his students, and one or two "Rembrandts" that may not be his. A century ago, there were 1,000 so-called Rembrandt paintings in existence. Since then, a five-man panel of art scholars has declared most of those to be by someone else, winnowing the number of authentic Rembrandts to 300, with some 50 more that may one day be "audited" by the Internal Rembrandt Service. Most of the fakes are not out-and-out forgeries, but works by admirers of his distinctive style. Be careful the next time you plunk down $15 million for a "Rembrandt."

• *In Room 9, you'll find...*

Rembrandt's Later Works

Enjoying fame, wealth, and happiness, Rembrandt may have had it all, but not for long. His wife, Saskia, died. The commissions came more slowly. The money ran out. His mother died. One by one, his sons died. He had to auction off his paintings and furniture to pay debts. He moved out of his fine house to a cheaper place. His bitter losses added a new wisdom to his work.

Rembrandt—*Isaac and Rebecca* (a.k.a *The Jewish Bride,* 1667)

The man gently draws the woman toward him. She's comfortable enough with him to sink into thought, and she reaches up unconsciously to return the gentle touch. They're young but wizened. This uncommissioned portrait (known as *The Jewish Bride,* though the subject is unknown) is a truly human look at the relationship between two people in love. They form a protective pyramid of love

Rembrandt van Rijn
(1606–1669)

The son of a Leiden miller (who owned a waterwheel on the Rhine—"van Rijn"), Rembrandt took Amsterdam by storm with his famous painting of *The Anatomy Lesson* (1632, currently in the Mauritshuis museum in The Hague). The commissions poured in for official portraits, and he was soon wealthy and married (1634) to Saskia van Uylenburgh. They moved to an expensive home in the Jewish Quarter (today's Rembrandt's House museum), and decorated it with their collection of art and exotic furniture. His portraits were dutifully detailed, but other paintings explored strong contrasts of light and dark, with dramatic composition.

In 1642, Saskia died, and his fortunes changed, as the public's taste shifted and commissions dried up. In 1649, he hired an 18-year-old model named Hendrickje Stoffels, and she soon moved in with him and gave birth to their illegitimate daughter. Holland's war with England (1652–1654) devastated the art market, and Rembrandt's free-spending ways forced him to declare bankruptcy (1656)—the ultimate humiliation in success-oriented Amsterdam. He moved to more humble lodgings on Rozengracht Straat.

In his last years, his greatest works were his self-portraits, showing a tired, wrinkled man stoically enduring life's misfortunes. Rembrandt piled on layers of paint and glaze to capture increasingly subtle effects.

In 1668, his lone surviving son, Titus, died, and Rembrandt passed away the next year. His death effectively marked the end of the Dutch Golden Age.

amid a gloomy background. The touching hands form the center of this somewhat sad but peaceful work. Van Gogh said, "Rembrandt alone has that tenderness—the heartbroken tenderness."

Rembrandt was a master of oil painting. In his later years, he rendered details with a messier, more Impressionistic style. The red-brown-gold of their clothes is a patchwork of oil laid on thick with a palette knife.

Rembrandt—*The Syndics of the Amsterdam Drapers' Guild* (*De Staalmeesters*, 1662)

While commissions were rarer, Rembrandt could still paint an official group portrait better than anyone. In the painting made famous by Dutch Masters cigars, he catches the Drapers Guild in a natural but dignified pose (dignified, at least, until the guy on the left sits down in his friend's lap).

It's a business meeting, and they're all dressed in black with black hats—the standard power suit of the Golden Age. They gather around a table examining the company's books. Suddenly, someone walks in (us), and they look up. It's as natural as a snapshot, though X-rays show Rembrandt made many changes in posing them perfectly.

The figures are "framed" by the table beneath them and the top of the wood paneling above their heads, making a three-part composition that brings this band of colleagues together. Even in this simple portrait, we feel we can read the guild members' personalities in their faces. (If the table in the painting looks like it's sloping a bit unnaturally, lie on the floor to view it at Rembrandt's intended angle.)

Rembrandt—*Self-Portrait as the Apostle Paul* (1661)

Rembrandt's many self-portraits show us the evolution of a great painter's style, as well as the progress of a genius' life.

For Rembrandt, the two were intertwined.

Compare this later self-portrait (he's 55, but looks 70) with the youthful, curious Rembrandt of age 22 we saw earlier. With lined forehead, bulbous nose, and messy hair, he peers out from under several coats of glazing, holding old, wrinkled pages. His look is... skeptical? Weary? Resigned to life's misfortunes? Or amused? (He's looking at us, but remember that a self-portrait is done staring into a mirror.)

This man has seen it all—success, love, money, fatherhood, loss, poverty, death. He took these experiences and wove them into his art. Rembrandt died poor and misunderstood, but he remained very much his own man to the end.

• *Enter Room 10.*

Johannes Vermeer (1632–1675)

Vermeer is the master of tranquility and stillness. He creates a clear and silent pool that is a world in itself. Most canvases show

Shhh...Dutch Art

You're sitting at home late one night, and it's perfectly quiet. Not a sound, very peaceful. And then...the refrigerator motor turns off, and it's really quiet.

Dutch art is quiet art. It silences our busy world, so that every sound, every motion stands out. You can hear cows tearing off grass 50 yards away. Dutch art is still. It slows our fast-lane world, so we notice the motion of birds. We observe how the cold night air makes the stars sharp. We notice that the undersides of leaves and cats are always a lighter shade than the tops. Dutch art stills the world so we can hear our own heartbeat and reflect upon that most noble muscle that

without thinking gives us life.

To see how subtle Dutch art is, realize that one of the museum's most exciting, dramatic, emotional, and extravagant Dutch paintings is probably *The Threatened Swan* (in Room 11). Quite a contrast to the rape scenes and visions of heaven of Italian Baroque from the same time period.

interiors of Dutch homes, where Dutch women engage in everyday activities, lit by a side window.

Vermeer's father, an art dealer, gave Johannes a passion for painting. Late in the artist's career, with Holland fighting draining wars against England, the demand for art and luxuries went sour in the Netherlands, forcing Vermeer to downsize—he sold his big home, packed up his wife and 14 children, and moved in with his mother-in-law. He died two years later, and his works fell into centuries of obscurity.

The Rijksmuseum has the best collection of Vermeers in the world—all four of them. (There are only some 30 in captivity.) But each is a small jewel worth lingering over.

Vermeer—*The Kitchen Maid* (c. 1658)

Shhh...you can practically hear the milk pouring into the bowl.

Vermeer brings out the beauty in everyday things. The subject is ordinary—a kitchen maid—but you could look for hours at the tiny details and rich color tones. These are everyday objects, but they glow in a diffused light: the crunchy crust, the hanging basket, even the rusty nail in the wall with its tiny shadow. Vermeer had a unique ability with surface texture, to show how things feel when you touch them.

The maid is alive with Vermeer's distinctive yellow and blue—the colors of many traditional Dutch homes—against a white backdrop. She is content, solid, and sturdy, performing this simple task like it's the most important thing in the world. Her full arms are built with patches of reflected light. Vermeer squares off a little world in itself (framed by the table in the foreground, the wall in back, the window to the left, and the footstool at right), then fills this space with objects for our perusal.

Vermeer—*Woman Reading a Letter* (c. 1662–1663)

Vermeer's placid scenes often have an air of mystery. The woman is reading a letter. From whom? A lover? A father on a two-year business trip to Indonesia? Not even taking time to sit down, she reads it intently, with parted lips and a bowed head. It must be important. (She looks pregnant, adding to the mystery, but that may just be the cut of her clothes.)

Again, Vermeer has framed off a moment of everyday life. But within this small world are hints of a wider, wilder world. The light coming from the left is obviously from a large window, giving us a whiff of a much broader world outside. The map hangs prominently, reminding us of travel, and perhaps of where the letter is from.

Vermeer—*The Love Letter* (c. 1669–1670)

There's a similar theme here. The curtain parts, and we see through

the doorway into a dollhouse world, then through the seascape on the back wall to the wide ocean. A woman is playing a lute when she's interrupted by a servant bringing a letter. The mysterious letter stops the music, intruding like a pebble dropped into the pool of Vermeer's quiet world. The floor tiles create a strong 3-D perspective that sucks us straight into the center of the painting—the woman's heart.

Vermeer—*View of Houses in Delft* (a.k.a. *The Little Street,* c. 1658)

Vermeer was born in the picturesque town of Delft, grew up near

its Market Square, and set a number of his paintings there. This may be the view from his front door.

In *The Little Street*, the details actually aren't very detailed—the cobblestone street doesn't have a single individual stone in it. But Vermeer shows the beautiful inter-play of colored rectangles on the buildings. Our eye moves back and forth from shutter to gable to win-dow...and then from front to back, as we notice the woman deep in the alleyway.

Jan Steen—*The Burgher of Delft* (1655)

This painting is the latest major acquisition of the Rijksmuseum and a new star in its lineup. In August of 2004, they paid $15 mil-lion for it...and figure they got a great deal. While the rest of the Steen collection is in the next room (see below), they're displaying this one with Vermeer's works because it's pristine and peaceful—more like an exquisite Vermeer than a raucous Steen.

Steen's well-dressed burgher sits on his front porch, when a poor woman and child approach to beg, putting him squarely between the horns of a moral dilemma. On the one hand, we see his rich home, well-dressed daughter, and a vase of flowers—a symbol that his money came from morally suspect capitalism (that produced the folly of 1637's "tulipmania"). On the other hand, there are his poor fellow citizens and the church steeple, remind-ing him of his Christian duty. The man's daughter avoids the con-frontation. Will the burgher set the right Christian example? The moral dilemma perplexed many nouveau riche Dutch Calvinists of Steen's day.

This early painting by Steen demonstrates his mastery of several popular genres: portrait, still life (the flowers and fabrics), cityscape, and moral instruction.

Jan Steen (1626–1679)

Not everyone could afford a masterpiece, but even poorer people wanted works of art for their own homes (like a landscape from Sears for over the sofa). Jan Steen, the Norman Rockwell of his day, painted humorous scenes from the lives of the lower classes. As a tavern owner, he observed society firsthand.

Ruffs

I cannot tell you why Dutch men and women of the Golden Age found these ruffled, fanlike collars attractive, but they

were the rage here and elsewhere in Europe. Ruffled collars and sleeves were first popular in Spain in the 1540s, but the style really took off with a marvelous discovery in 1565—starch. Within decades, Europe's wealthy merchant class was wearing nine-inch collars made from 18 yards of material.

The ruffs were detachable, made from a long, pleated strip of linen set into a neck (or wrist) band. You tied it in front with strings. Big ones required that you wear a wire frame underneath for support. There were various types—the "cartwheel" was the biggest, a "double ruff" had two layers of pleats, and a "cabbage" was somewhat asymmetrical.

Ruffs required elaborate maintenance. You washed and starched the linen. While the cloth was still wet, hot metal pokers were inserted into the folds to form the characteristic figure-eight pattern. Ruffs were stored in special round boxes to hold their shape.

By 1630, Holland had come to its senses, and the fad faded.

Jan Steen—*The Feast of St. Nicholas*

It's Christmas time, and the kids have been given their gifts. A little girl got a doll. The mother says, "Let me see it," but the girl turns away playfully.

Everyone is happy except...the boy who's crying. His Christmas present is only a branch in his shoe—like coal in your

stocking, the gift for bad boys. His sister gloats and passes it around. The kids laugh at him. But wait—it turns out the family is just playing a trick. In the background, the grandmother beckons to him, saying, "Look, I have your real present in here." Out of the limelight, but smack in the middle, sits the father providing ballast to this family scene and clearly enjoying his children's pleasure.

Steen has frozen the moment, sliced off a piece, and laid it on a canvas. He's told a story with a past, present, and future. These are real people in a real scene.

Steen's fun art reminds us that museums aren't mausoleums.

Jan Steen—*The Merry Family* (1668)

This family—three generations living happily under one roof—is eating, drinking, and singing like there's no tomorrow. The broken

eggshells and scattered cookware symbolize waste and extravagance. The neglected proverb tacked to the fireplace reminds us that children will follow the footsteps of their parents. The father in this jolly scene is very drunk—ready to topple over—while in the foreground his mischievous daughter is feeding her brother wine straight from the flask. Mom and grandma join the artist himself (playing the bagpipes) in a lively sing-along, but the child learning to smoke would rather follow dad's lead.

Golden Age Dutch families were notoriously lenient with their kids. Even today, the Dutch describe a rowdy family as a "Jan Steen household."

• *Room 12 is dominated by...*

Rembrandt—*The Night Watch*

• *The best viewing spot is to the right of center—the angle Rembrandt had in mind when he designed it for its original location.*

This is Rembrandt's most famous—though not necessarily greatest—painting. Done in 1642 when he was 36, it was one of his most important commissions: a group portrait of a company of Amsterdam's civic guards to hang in their meeting hall.

It's an action shot. With flags waving and drums beating, the guardsmen (who, by the 1640s, were really only an honorary militia

of rich bigwigs) spill into the street from under an arch in the back. It's "all for one and one for all" as they rush to the rescue of Amsterdam. The soldiers grab lances and load their muskets. In the center, the commander (in black, with a red sash)

strides forward energetically with a hand gesture that seems to say, "What are we waiting for? Let's move out!" His lieutenant focuses on his every order.

Rembrandt caught the optimistic spirit of Holland in the 1600s. Their war of independence from Spain was heading to victory and their economy was booming. These guardsmen on the move epitomize the proud, independent, upwardly mobile Dutch.

Why is *The Night Watch* so famous? Compare it with other, less famous group portraits, where every face is visible, and everyone is well-lit, flat, and flashbulb-perfect. These people paid good money to have their mugs preserved for posterity, and they wanted it right up front. Other group portraits may be colorful, dignified, works by a master...but not quite masterpieces.

By contrast, Rembrandt rousted the civic guards off their fat duffs. By adding movement and depth to an otherwise static scene, he took posers and turned them into warriors. He turned a simple portrait into great art.

OK, some *Night Watch* scuttlebutt: First off, "Night Watch" is a misnomer. It's a daytime scene, but over the years, as the preserving varnish darkened and layers of dirt built up, the sun set on this painting, and it got its popular title. When the painting was moved to a smaller room, the sides were lopped off (and the pieces lost), putting the two main characters in the center and causing the work to become more static than intended. During World War II, the painting was rolled up and hidden for five years. More recently, a madman attacked the painting, slicing the captain's legs (now skillfully repaired).

The Night Watch, contrary to popular myth, was a smashing success in its day. However, there are elements in it that show why Rembrandt soon fell out of favor as a portrait painter. He seemed to spend as much time painting the dwarf and the mysterious glowing girl with a chicken (the very appropriate mascot of this "militia" of shopkeepers) as he did the faces of his employers.

Rembrandt's life darkened long before his *Night Watch* did. This work marks the peak of Rembrandt's popularity...and the beginning of his fall from grace. He continued to paint masterpieces. Free from the dictates of employers whose taste was in their mouths, he painted what he wanted, how he wanted it. Rembrandt goes beyond mere craftsmanship to probe into, and draw life from, the deepest wells of the human soul.

VAN GOGH MUSEUM TOUR

The Van Gogh Museum (we say "van GO," the Dutch say "van HOCK") is a cultural high even for those not into art. Located near the Rijksmuseum, the museum houses the 200 paintings owned by Vincent's younger brother, Theo. It's a user-friendly stroll through the work and life of one enigmatic man. If you like bright-colored landscapes in the Impressionist style, you'll like this museum. If you enjoy finding deeper meaning in works of art, you'll really love it. The mix of van Gogh's creative genius, his tumultuous life, and the traveler's determination to connect to it makes this museum as much a walk with Vincent as with his art.

ORIENTATION

Cost: €10, covered by *I amsterdam* Card, free for those under 12 and for those with one ear.

Special Exhibitions: The museum regularly hosts temporary exhibits. In 2006, the Van Gogh Museum celebrates the 400th birthday of that other Dutch painter—Rembrandt—by filling its exhibition hall with Rembrandts (and Caravaggios). The special show runs from February 24 through June 18, and costs €20. Note that any tourist will do better by getting the big €25 combo-ticket for the Rijksmuseum, Van Gogh Museum, and special Rembrandt exhibition.

Hours: Daily 10:00–18:00, Fri until 22:00, closed only on Jan 1.

Crowd Control: There can be long lines to get into the crowded museum. But with three cashiers, the line moves quickly, and the wait is rarely more than 15 minutes. *I amsterdam* Card holders still have to wait in line, but if you buy a ticket online (and print it out), you can skip ahead.

Van Gogh Museum—First Floor

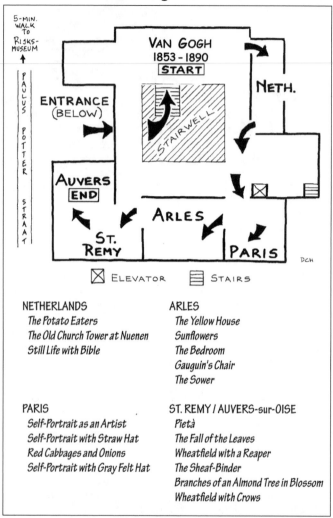

NETHERLANDS
The Potato Eaters
The Old Church Tower at Nuenen
Still Life with Bible

ARLES
The Yellow House
Sunflowers
The Bedroom
Gauguin's Chair
The Sower

PARIS
Self-Portrait as an Artist
Self-Portrait with Straw Hat
Red Cabbages and Onions
Self-Portrait with Gray Felt Hat

ST. REMY / AUVERS-sur-OISE
Pietà
The Fall of the Leaves
Wheatfield with a Reaper
The Sheaf-Binder
Branches of an Almond Tree in Blossom
Wheatfield with Crows

Getting There: It's the big, mod, grey-and-beige place behind the Rijksmuseum at Paulus Potterstraat 7. From Central Station, catch tram #2 or #5 to Hobbemastraat.

Information: At the information desk, pick up a free floor plan (containing a brief history of the artist's brief life). The bookstore is understandably popular, with several good basic "Vincent" guidebooks and lots of posters (with tubes). Tel. 020/570-5200, www.vangoghmuseum.nl.

Audioguide Tour: The €4 audioguide includes 90 creatively produced minutes of insightful commentaries about van Gogh's paintings, along with related quotations from Vincent himself.

Length of This Tour: Allow one hour.

Checkroom: Free and mandatory.

Cuisine Art: The terrace cafeteria (soup, salads, sandwiches) is OK. You could also consider the Cobra Café on Museumplein; the many cafés at Leidseplein (a 15-min walk to the northwest); or the picnic-friendly Vondelpark and Café Vertigo (Vondelpark 3).

Photography: No photos allowed, but you can send a free "video postcard" from the terminals with cameras near the exit.

OVERVIEW

The core of the museum and this entire tour is on the first floor (one flight up from the ground floor). The bookstore and cafeteria are on the ground floor. Also on the ground floor are paintings by artists who preceded and influenced van Gogh's generation. The second floor has a study area and more paintings (including van Gogh's smaller-scale works). The third floor shows works by his friends and colleagues, from smooth-surfaced Academy art to Impressionists Claude Monet and Camille Pissarro to fellow post-Impressionists Paul Gauguin, Paul Cézanne, and Henri de Toulouse-Lautrec. These are painters who influenced and were influenced by van Gogh. The exhibition wing (accessed from the ground floor by going down the escalator) showcases temporary exhibitions (see previous page).

The main collection of van Gogh paintings on the first floor is arranged chronologically, taking us through the changes in Vincent van Gogh's life and styles. The paintings are divided into five periods of Vincent's life—Netherlands, Paris, Arles, St. Rémy, and Auvers-sur-Oise—proceeding clockwise around the floor. (Although the busy curators frequently move the paintings around, they *usually* keep them within the same room, so look around; some may even be upstairs.) Some background on Vincent's star-crossed life makes the museum even better, so I've included doses of biographical material for each painting.

THE TOUR BEGINS

• *Climb the stairs to the first floor. The first room—often displaying self-portraits—introduces you to the artist.*

Vincent van Gogh (1853–1890)

"I am a man of passions..."

You can see Vincent van Gogh's canvases as a series of suicide notes—or as the record of a life full of beauty...too full of beauty. He attacked life with a passion, experiencing highs and lows more intensely than the average person. The beauty of the world overwhelmed him, and its ugliness struck him as only another dimension of beauty. He tried to absorb all of life, good and bad, and channel it onto a canvas. The frustration of this overwhelming task drove him to madness. If all this is a bit overstated—and I guess it is—it's an attempt to show the emotional impact van Gogh's works have had on many people, myself included.

Vincent, a pastor's son from a small Dutch town, started working at age 16 as a clerk for an art dealership. But his two interests, art and religion, distracted him from his dreary work and, after several years, he was finally fired.

The next 10 years were a collage of dead ends as he traveled northern Europe pursuing one path after another. He launched into each project with incredible energy, then became disillusioned and moved on to something else: teacher at a boarding school, assistant preacher, bookstore apprentice, preacher again, theology student, English student, literature student, art student. He bounced around England, France, Belgium, and the Netherlands. He fell in love, but was rejected for someone more respectable. He quarreled with his family and was estranged. He lived with a prostitute and her daughter, offending the few friends he had. Finally, in his late 20s, worn out, flat broke, and in poor health, he returned to his family in Nuenen and made peace. He started to paint.

• *For his stark early work, enter the next room.*

The Netherlands (1880–1885): Poverty and Religion

These dark gray canvases show us the hard, plain existence of the people and town of Nuenen, in the rural southern Netherlands. We see simple buildings, bare or autumnal trees, and overcast skies—a world where it seems spring will never arrive. What warmth there is comes from the sturdy, gentle people themselves.

The style is crude—van Gogh couldn't draw very well, nor would he ever be a great technician. The paint is laid on thick, as though painted with Nuenen mud. The main subject is almost always dead center, with little or no background, so there's

a claustrophobic feeling. We are unable to see anything but the immediate surroundings.

The Potato Eaters (1885)

"Those that prefer to see the peasants in their Sunday-best may do as they like. I personally am convinced I get better results by painting them in their roughness.... If a peasant picture smells of bacon, smoke, potato steam—all right, that's healthy."

—Vincent van Gogh

In a dark, cramped room lit only by a dim lamp, poor workers help themselves to a steaming plate of potatoes. They've earned

it. Vincent deliberately wanted the canvas to be potato-colored.

Vincent had dabbled as an artist during his wandering years, sketching things around him and taking a few art classes, but it wasn't until age 29 that he painted his first oil canvas. He soon threw himself into it with abandon.

He painted the poor working peasants. He worked as a lay minister among the poorest of the poor, peasants and miners. He joined them at work in the mines, taught their children, and even gave away his own few possessions to help them. The church authorities finally dismissed him for "excessive zeal," but he came away understanding the poor's harsh existence and the dignity with which they bore it.

The Old Church Tower at Nuenen (1885)

The crows circle above the local cemetery of Nuenen. Soon after his

father's death, Vincent—in poor health and depressed—moved briefly to Antwerp. He then decided to visit his brother Theo, an art dealer living in Paris, the art capital of the world. Theo's support—financial and emotional—allowed Vincent to spend the rest of his short life painting.

Still Life with Bible (1885)

"I have a terrible need of—shall I say the word?—religion. Then I go out and paint the stars."

—Vincent van Gogh

The Bible and Emile Zola's *La Joie de Vivre*—these two books dominated van Gogh's life. In his art, he tried to fuse his religious upbringing with his love of the world's beauty. He lusted after life with a religious fervor. The burned-out candle tells us of the recent death of his father. The Bible is open to Isaiah 53: "He was despised and rejected of men, a man of sorrows...."

Vincent moved from rural, religious, poor Holland to Paris, the City of Light. Vincent van Gone.

• *Continue to...*

Paris (March 1886–Feb 1888): Impressionism

The sun begins to break through, lighting up everything he paints. His canvases are more colorful, and the landscapes more spacious, with plenty of open sky, giving a feeling of exhilaration after the closed, dark world of Nuenen.

In the cafés and bars of Paris' bohemian Montmartre district, Vincent met the revolutionary Impressionists. He roomed with Theo and became friends with other struggling young painters, such as Paul Gauguin and Henri de Toulouse-Lautrec. His health improved, he became more sociable, had an affair with an older woman, and was generally happy.

He signed up to study under a well-known classical teacher, but quit after only a few classes. He couldn't afford to hire models, so he roamed the streets with sketch pad in hand and learned from his Impressionist friends.

The Impressionists emphasized getting out of the stuffy studio and setting up canvases outside on the street or in the countryside to paint the play of sunlight off the trees, buildings, and water.

As you see in this room, at first, Vincent copied from the Impressionist masters. He painted garden scenes like Claude Monet, café snapshots like Edgar Degas, "block prints" like the Japanese masters, and self-portraits...like nobody else.

Self-Portrait as an Artist (1888)

"I am now living with my brother Vincent, who is studying the art of painting with indefatigable zeal."

—Theo van Gogh to a friend

Here, the budding young artist proudly displays his new palette full of bright new colors, trying his hand at the Impressionist technique of building a scene using dabs of different-colored paint. A whole new world of art—and life—opened up to him in Paris.

Self-Portrait with Straw Hat (1887)

> *"You wouldn't recognize Vincent, he has changed so much.... The doctor says that he is now perfectly fit again. He is making tremendous strides with his work....He is also far livelier than he used to be and is popular with people."*
>
> —Theo van Gogh to their mother

In Paris, Vincent learned the Impressionist painting technique. The shimmering effect comes from placing dabs of different colors side by side on the canvas. At a distance, the two colors blend in the eye of the viewer to become a third color. Here, Vincent uses separate strokes of blue, yellow, green, and red to create a brown beard—but a brown that throbs with excitement.

Still Lifes, such as Red Cabbages and Onions (1887)

Vincent quickly developed his own style—thicker paint, broad, swirling brushstrokes, and brighter, clashing colors that make even inanimate objects seem to pulsate with life. The many different colors are supposed to blend together, but you'd have to back up to Belgium before these colors resolve into focus.

Self-Portrait with Gray Felt Hat (1887–1888)

> *"He has painted one or two portraits which have turned out well, but he insists on working for nothing. It is a pity that he*

> *shows no desire to earn some money because he could easily do so here. But you can't change people."*
>
> —Theo van Gogh to their mother

Despite his new sociability, Vincent never quite fit in with his Impressionist friends. As he developed into a good painter, he became anxious to strike out on his own. Also, he thought the social life of the big city was distracting him from serious work. In this painting, his face screams out from a swirling background of molecular activity. He wanted peace and quiet, a place where he could throw himself into his work completely. He headed for the sunny south of France.

• *Travel to the next room to reach...*

Arles (Feb 1888–May 1889): Sunlight, Beauty, and Madness

Winter was just turning to spring when Vincent arrived in Arles, near the French Riviera. After the dreary Paris winter, the colors of springtime overwhelmed him. The blossoming trees inspired him to paint canvas after canvas, drenched in sunlight.

The Yellow House (a.k.a. The Street, 1888)

"It is my intention...to go temporarily to the South, where there is even more color, even more sun."

—Vincent van Gogh

Vincent rented this house with the green shutters. (He ate at the pink café next door.) Look at that blue sky! He painted in a frenzy, working feverishly to try and take it all in. For the next nine months, he produced an explosion of canvases, working very quickly when the mood possessed him. His unique style evolved beyond the Impressionists'—thicker paint, stronger outlines, brighter colors (often applied right from the paint tube), and swirling brushwork that makes even inanimate objects pulse and vibrate with life.

Sunflowers (1889)

"The worse I get along with people, the more I learn to have faith in Nature and concentrate on her."

—Vincent van Gogh

Vincent saw sunflowers as his signature subject, and he painted a half dozen versions of them, each a study in intense yellow. If he signed the work (see the "V. G." on the vase), it means he was proud of it.

Even a simple work like these *Sunflowers* bursts with life. Different people see different things in *Sunflowers*. Is it a happy painting, or is it a melancholy one? Take your own emotional temperature and see.

The Bedroom (1888)

"I am a man of passions, capable of and subject to doing more or less foolish things—which I happen to regret, more or less, afterwards."

—Vincent van Gogh

Vincent was alone, a Dutchman in Provence. And that had its downside. Vincent swung from flurries of ecstatic activity to bouts

of great loneliness. Like anyone traveling alone, he experienced those high highs and low lows. This narrow, trapezoid-shaped, single-room apartment (less than 200 square feet) must have seemed like a prison cell at times. (Psychologists point out that most everything in this painting comes in pairs—two chairs, two paintings,

a double bed squeezed down to a single—indicating his desire for a mate. Hmm.)

He invited his friend Paul Gauguin to join him, envisioning a sort of artists' colony in Arles. He spent months preparing a room upstairs for Gauguin's arrival.

Gauguin's Chair (1888)

"Empty chairs—there are many of them, there will be even more, and sooner or later, there will be nothing but empty chairs."

—Vincent van Gogh

Gauguin arrived. At first, they got along great, painting and carousing. But then things went bad. They clashed over art, life, and personalities. On Christmas Eve 1888, Vincent went ballistic. Enraged during an alcohol-fueled argument, he pulled out a knife and waved it in Gauguin's face. Gauguin took the hint and quickly left

town. Vincent was horrified at himself. In a fit of remorse and madness, he mutilated his own ear and presented it to a prostitute.

The Sower (1888)

A dark, silhouetted figure sows seeds in the burning sun. It's late in the day. The heat from the sun, the source of all life, radiates out in thick swirls of paint. The sower must be a hopeful man, because the field looks slanted and barren. Someday, he thinks, the seeds he's planting will grow into something great, like the tree that slashes diagonally across the scene—tough and craggy, but with small, optimistic blossoms.

In his younger years, Vincent had worked in Belgium sowing the Christian gospel in a harsh environment (see Mark 4:1–9). Now in Arles, ignited by the sun, he cast his artistic seeds to the wind, hoping.

• *Continue into the next room.*

St. Rémy (May 1889–1890): The Mental Hospital

The people of Arles realized they had a madman on their hands. A doctor diagnosed "acute mania with hallucinations," and the local vicar talked Vincent into admitting himself to a mental hospital. Vincent wrote to Theo: "Temporarily I wish to remain shut up, as much for my own peace of mind as for other people's."

In the mental hospital, Vincent continued to paint whenever he was well enough. He often couldn't go out, so he copied from books, making his own distinctive versions of works by Rembrandt, Delacroix, Millet, and others.

We see a change from bright, happy landscapes to more introspective subjects. The colors are less bright and more surreal, the brushwork even more furious. The strong outlines of figures are twisted and tortured.

Pietà, after Delacroix (1889)

It's evening after a thunderstorm. Jesus has been crucified, and the corpse lies at the mouth of a tomb. Mary, whipped by the cold wind, holds her empty arms out in despair and confusion. She is the tender mother who receives us all in death, as though saying, "My child, you've been away so long—rest in my arms." Christ has a Vincent-esque red beard.

At first, the peace and quiet of the asylum did Vincent good, and his health improved. Occasionally, he was allowed outside to paint the gardens and landscapes. Meanwhile, the paintings he had sent to Theo began to attract attention in Paris for the first time. A woman in Brussels bought one of his canvases—the only painting he ever sold during his lifetime. Nowadays, a *Sunflowers* sells for $40 million.

The Garden of Saint Paul's Hospital (a.k.a. The Fall of the Leaves, 1889)

> "...a traveler going to a destination that does not exist...."
> —Vincent van Gogh

The stark brown trees are blown by the wind. A solitary figure (Vincent?) winds along a narrow, snaky path as the wind blows leaves on him. The colors are surreal—blue, green, and red tree trunks with heavy black outlines. A road runs away from us, heading nowhere.

Wheatfield with a Reaper (1889)

"I have been working hard and fast in the last few days. This is how I try to express how desperately fast things pass in modern life."

—Vincent van Gogh

The harvest is here. The time is short. There's much work to be done. A lone reaper works uphill, scything through a swirling wheat field, cutting slender paths of calm.

The Sheaf-Binder, after Millet (1889)

"I want to paint men and women with that something of the eternal which the halo used to symbolize...."

—Vincent van Gogh

Vincent's compassion for honest laborers remained constant following his work with Belgian miners. These sturdy folk, with their curving bodies, wrestle as one with their curving wheat. The world Vincent sees is charged from within by spiritual fires, twisting and turning, matter turning into energy and vice versa.

The fits of madness returned. During these spells, he lost all sense of his own actions. He couldn't paint, the one thing he felt driven to do. He wrote to Theo, "My surroundings here begin to weigh on me more than I can say—I need air. I feel overwhelmed by boredom and grief."

Auvers-sur-Oise (May–July 1890): Flying Away

"The bird looks through the bars at the overcast sky where a thunderstorm is gathering, and inwardly he rebels against his fate. 'I am caged, I am caged, and you tell me I have everything I need! Oh! I beg you, give me liberty, that I may be a bird like other birds.' A certain idle man resembles this idle bird...."

—Vincent van Gogh

Branches of an Almond Tree in Blossom (1890)

Vincent moved north to Auvers, a small town near Paris where he could stay at a hotel under a doctor friend's supervision. On the way

there, he visited Theo. Theo's wife had just had a baby, whom they named Vincent. Brother Vincent showed up with this painting under his arm as a birthday gift. Theo's wife later recalled, "I had expected a sick man, but here was a sturdy, broad-shouldered man with a healthy color, a smile on his face, and a very resolute appearance."

In his new surroundings, he continued painting, averaging a canvas a day, but was interrupted by spells that swung from boredom to madness. His letters to Theo were generally optimistic, but he worried that he'd soon succumb completely to insanity and never paint again. The final landscapes are walls of bright, thick paint.

Wheatfield with Crows (1890)

> *"This new attack...came on me in the fields, on a windy day, when I was busy painting."*
>
> —Vincent van Gogh

On July 27, 1890, Vincent left his hotel, walked out to a nearby field and put a bullet through his chest.

This is the last painting Vincent finished. We can try to search the wreckage of his life for the black box explaining what happened, but there's not much there. His life was sad and tragic, but the record he

left is one not of sadness, but of beauty. Intense beauty.

The windblown wheat field is a nest of restless energy. Scenes like this must have overwhelmed Vincent with their incredible beauty—too much, too fast, with no release. The sky is stormy and dark blue, almost nighttime, barely lit by two suns boiling through the deep ocean of blue. The road starts nowhere, leads nowhere, disappearing into the burning wheat field. Above all of this swirling beauty fly the crows, the dark ghosts that had hovered over his life since the cemetery in Nuenen.

ANNE FRANK HOUSE TOUR

ANNE FRANK
TAGEBUCH

On May 10, 1940, Germany's Luftwaffe began bombing Schiphol Airport, preparing to invade the Netherlands. The Dutch army fought back, and the Nazis responded by leveling Rotterdam. Within a week, the Netherlands surrendered, Queen Wilhelmina fled to Britain, and Nazi soldiers goose-stepped past the Westerkerk church and into Dam Square, where they draped huge swastikas on the Royal Palace. A five-year occupation began. The Netherlands had been neutral in World War I, and Amsterdam—progressive and modern, but a bit naive—was in for a rude shock.

The Anne Frank House immerses you, in a very immediate way, in the struggles and pains of the war years. Walk through rooms where, for two years, eight Amsterdam Jews hid from Nazi persecution. Though they were eventually discovered, and seven of the eight died in concentration camps, their story has an uplifting twist—the diary of Anne Frank, preserving the human spirit that cannot be crushed.

ORIENTATION

Cost: €7.50, not covered by *I amsterdam* Card.

Hours: Daily April–Aug 9:00–21:00, Sept–March 9:00–19:00, last entry 30 min before closing. Closed on Yom Kippur (Oct 2 in 2006).

Crowd Control: Why do thousands endure hour-long daytime lines in summer, when they can walk right in by arriving after 18:00? Avoid summertime crowds by visiting after dinner (last entry April–Aug is 20:30).

Getting There: It's at Prinsengracht 267, near Westerkerk and about a 20-minute walk from Central Station. Or take tram #13, #14, or #17 or bus #21, #170, #171, or #172 to the Westermarkt stop, about a block from the museum's entrance.

Information: The museum has excellent information in English—a pamphlet at the door, and fine descriptions with quotes from the diary throughout. Use this chapter as background, and then let the displays and videos tell you more. Tel. 020/556-7100, www.annefrank.org. Note that the house has many steep, narrow stairways.

For more on Anne Frank, visit the Amsterdam History Museum's special exhibit, "Anne Frank—Her Life in Letters" (April 12–Sept 3; see page 146).

Baggage Check: The museum enforces a strict, required bag check for large bags.

Length of This Tour: Allow one hour.

OVERVIEW

We'll walk through the rooms where Anne Frank's family and four other Jews hid for 25 months. The front half of the building, facing the canal, remained the offices and warehouses of an operating business. The back half, where the Franks and others lived, was the Secret Annex, its entrance concealed by a bookcase.

THE TOUR BEGINS

• *Buy your ticket and enter the ground-floor exhibit.*

Models of the Secret Annex

Two models—of the two floors where Anne's family lived with the rest—use doll-house furniture to help you envision life in the now bare living quarters. In the first model, find the swinging bookcase that hid the secret entrance leading to Anne's parents' room (with wood stove). Anne's room is next to it, with a blue bed, a brown sofa, a table/chair/bookcase ensemble, and photos on the wall. On the upper floor (the next model) was the living room and the van Pels' rooms. All told, eight people lived in a tiny apartment smaller than 1,000 square feet.

• *After viewing the important five-minute video, go upstairs to the offices/warehouses of the front half of the building.*

First Floor: Offices

From these offices, Otto Frank ran a successful business called Opekta, selling spices and pectin for making jelly. When the Nazis gained power in Germany in 1933, Otto had moved his family from Frankfurt to tolerant Amsterdam, hoping for a better life.

Photos and displays show Otto with some of his colleagues. During the Nazi occupation, while the Frank family hid in the back of the building, these brave people kept Otto's business running, while secretly bringing supplies to the Franks. Miep Gies, Otto's secretary (see her in the video), brought food every few days, while bookkeeper Victor Kugler cheered up Anne with the latest movie magazines.

• *Go upstairs to the...*

Second Floor: Warehouse

At first, the Nazi overlords were tolerant of, and even friendly with, the vanquished Dutch. But soon they imposed restrictions that affected one in 10 Amsterdammers—that is, Jews. Jews had to wear yellow-star patches and register with the police. They were forbidden in movie theaters and on trams, and even forbidden to ride bikes.

In February 1941, the Nazis started rounding up Jews, shipping them by train to "work camps," which, in reality, were transit stations on the way to death camps in the east. Outraged, the people of Amsterdam called a general strike that shut down the city for two days...but the Nazis responded with even harsher laws.

In July 1942, Anne's sister Margot got her **call-up notice** for a "work-force project." Otto handed over the keys to the business to his Aryan colleagues, sent a final postcard to relatives, gave the family cat to a neighbor, spread rumors they were fleeing to Switzerland, and prepared his family to "dive under" (*onderduik,* as it was called) into hiding.

Photos of *The People in Hiding* put faces on the eight people—all Jewish—who eventually inhabited the Secret Annex. First was the Frank family—Otto and Edith and their daughters, 13-year-old Anne and 16-year-old Margot. A week later, they were joined by the van Pels (called the "van Daans" in the *Diary*), with their teenage son, Peter. A few months later, Fritz Pfeffer (called "Mr. Dussel" in the *Diary*) was invited in.

• *At the back of the third floor warehouse is...*

Life in the Annex

By day, it's enforced silence, so no one can hear them in the offices. They whisper, tiptoe, and step around squeaky places in the floor. The windows are blacked out, so they can't even look outside. They read or study, and Anne writes in her diary.

At night and on weekends, when the offices close, one or two might sneak downstairs to listen to Winston Churchill's BBC broadcasts on the office radio. Everyone's spirits rise and sink with news of Allied victories and setbacks.

Anne's diaries make clear the tensions, petty quarrels, and domestic politics of eight people living under pressure. Mr. van Pels annoys Anne, but he gets along well with Margot. Anne never gets used to Mr. Pfeffer, who is literally invading her space. And, most of all, pubescent Anne is often striking sparks with her German mom (Anne's angriest comments about her mom were deleted from early editions).

Despite their hardships, the group feels guilty—they have shelter, while so many other Jews are rounded up and sent off.

As the war progresses, they endure long nights when the house shakes from Allied air raids, and Anne cuddles up in her dad's bed.

Boredom tinged with fear—existentialist hell.

The Bookcase Entrance

On a rainy Monday morning, July 6, 1942, the Frank family—wearing extra clothes to avoid carrying suspicious suitcases—breathed their last fresh air, took a long look at the Prinsengracht canal, and disappeared into the back part of the building, where they spent the next two years. Victor Kugler concealed the entrance to the annex with this swinging bookcase, stacked with business files.

Though not exactly a secret (since it's hard to hide an entire building), the annex was just one of thousands of back-houses (*achterhuis*), a common feature in Amsterdam, and the Nazis had no reason to suspect anything on the premises of the legitimate Opekta business.

• *Pass through the bookcase entrance into the Secret Annex into...*

Otto, Edith, and Margot's Room

The family carried on life as usual. Otto read Dickens' *Sketches by Boz*, Edith read from a **prayer book** in their native German, and the children continued their studies, with Margot taking **Latin lessons** by correspondence course. They avidly followed the course of the war by radio broadcasts and news from their helpers. As the tides of war slowly turned and it appeared they might one day be saved from the Nazis, Otto tracked the Allied advance on a **map** of Normandy.

The room is very small, even without the furniture. Imagine yourself and two fellow tourists confined here for two years....

Pencil lines on the wall track Margot's and Anne's heights, marking the point at which these growing lives were cut short.

Anne Frank's Room

Pan the room clockwise to see some of the young girl's idols in photos and clippings she pasted there herself: American actor Robert Stack, the future Queen Elizabeth II as a child, matinee idol Rudy Vallee, figure-skating actress Sonja Henie, and on the other wall, actress Greta Garbo, actor Ray Milland, Renaissance man Leonardo da Vinci, and actress Ginger Rogers.

Out the window (which had to be blacked out) is the back courtyard—a chestnut tree and a few buildings. These things, along with the Westerkerk bell chiming every 15 minutes, represented the borders of Anne's "outside world."

Picture Anne at her small desk, writing in her diary.

In November 1942, they invited a Jewish neighbor to join them, and Anne was forced to share the tiny room. Fritz Pfeffer (known in the *Diary* as "Mr. Dussel") was a middle-aged dentist with whom Anne didn't get along. Pfeffer wrote a farewell letter to his non-Jewish fiancée, who continued to live nearby and receive news of him from Miep Gies without knowing his whereabouts.

The Bathroom

The eight inhabitants shared this bathroom. During the day, they didn't dare flush the toilet.

• *Ascend the steep staircase—silently—to the...*

Common Living Room

This was also the kitchen and dining room. Otto Frank was well off, and early on, the annex was well-stocked with food. Miep Gies would dutifully take their shopping list, buy food for her "family" of eight, and secretly lug it up to them. Buying such large quantities in a coupon-rationed economy was highly suspect, but she knew a sympathetic grocer (a block away in Leliegracht) who was part of a ring of Amsterdammers risking their lives to help the Jews.

The **menu** for a special dinner lists soup, roast beef, salad, potatoes, rice, dessert, and coffee. Later, as war and German restrictions plunged Holland into poverty and famine, they survived on canned foods and dried kidney beans.

At night, the living room became sleeping quarters for Hermann and Auguste van Pels.

Peter van Pels' Room

On Peter's 16th birthday, he got a Monopoly-like board game called "The Broker" as a present.

Initially, Anne was cool toward Peter, but after two years together, a courtship developed, and their flirtation culminated in a kiss.

The staircase (no visitor access) leads up to where they stored their food. Anne loved to steal away here for a bit of privacy. At night, they'd open a hatch to let in fresh air.

One hot August day, Otto was in this room helping Peter learn English, when they looked up to see a man with a gun. The hiding was over.

• *From here, we leave the Secret Annex, returning to the Opekta storeroom and offices in the front house. As you work your way downstairs, you'll see a number of exhibits on the aftermath of this story.*

Front House: The Arrest, Deportation, and Auschwitz Exhibits

They went quietly. On August 4, 1944, a German policeman accompanied by three Dutch Nazis pulled up in a car, politely entered the Opekta office, and went straight to the bookcase entrance. No one knows who tipped them off. The police gave the surprised hiders time to pack. They demanded their valuables, and stuffed them into Anne's briefcase...after dumping her diaries onto the floor.

Taken in a van to Gestapo headquarters, the eight were processed in an efficient, bureaucratic manner, then placed on a train to Westerbork, a concentration camp northeast of the city (see their 3-inch by 5-inch **registration cards**).

From there, they were locked in a car on a normal passenger train and sent to Auschwitz , a Nazi extermination camp in Poland (see the **transport list**, which includes "Anneliese Frank"). On the platform at Auschwitz, they were "forcibly separated from each other" (as Otto later reported) and sent to different camps. Anne and Margot were sent to Bergen-Belsen.

Don't miss the **video** of one of Anne's former neighbors who, by chance, ended up at Bergen-Belsen with Anne. In English, she describes their reunion as they talked through a barbed wire fence shortly before Anne died. She says of Anne, "She didn't have any more tears."

Anne and Margot both died of typhus in March of 1945, only weeks before the camp was liberated. Five of the other original eight were either gassed or died of disease. Only Otto survived.

The Franks' story was that of Holland's Jews. The seven who died were among 100,000 Dutch Jews (out of a total of 130,000) who did not survive the war. Of Anne's school class of 87 Jews, only 20 survived.

• *In the next room is an exhibit of...*

The Diaries

See Anne's three diaries, which were discovered and published after the war. Anne got the first diary as a birthday present when she turned 13, shortly before they went into hiding. She wrote it in the form of a letter to an imaginary friend named Kitty.

• *Go downstairs to view the...*

Videos and the Published Diaries

The video of Miep Gies describes how she found Anne's diaries in the Secret Annex after the arrest and gave them to Otto when he returned. Another video shows Otto's reaction. Though the annex's furniture had been ransacked during the arrest, afterward the rooms remained virtually untouched, and we see them today much as they were.

Otto decided to have the diaries published, and in 1947, *De Achterhuis (The Back-House)* appeared in Dutch, soon followed by many translations, a play, and a movie. While she was alive, Anne herself had recognized the uniqueness of her situation and had been in the process of revising her diaries, preparing them to one day be published.

• *Continue downstairs to the ground floor and enter the video room.*

Exhibits

The thinking that made the Holocaust possible survives. Even today, some groups promote the notion that the Holocaust never occurred, and contend that stories like Anne Frank's are only a hoax. In this room, the curators offer temporary exhibits and videos on such themes as racism. They hope that the souvenir you'll take away from this visit is a heightened awareness of this evil, yet persistent, human trait.

AMSTELKRING MUSEUM TOUR

Our Lord in the Attic—
A Hidden Catholic Church

For two centuries (1578–1795), Catholicism in Amsterdam was illegal, but tolerated (like pot in the 1970s). When hardline Protestants took power in 1578, Catholic churches were vandalized and shut down, priests and monks were rounded up and kicked out of town, and Catholic kids were razzed on their way to school. The city's Catholics were forbidden to worship openly, so they gathered secretly to say Mass in homes and offices. In 1663, a wealthy merchant built Our Lord in the Attic (Ons' Lieve Heer op Solder), one of a handful of places in Amsterdam to serve as a secret parish church until Catholics were once again allowed to worship in public. This unique church—embedded within a townhouse in the middle of the Red Light District—comes with a little bonus: a rare glimpse inside a historic Amsterdam home straight out of a Vermeer painting.

ORIENTATION

Cost: €7, covered by *I amsterdam* Card.

Hours: Mon–Sat 10:00–17:00, Sun and holidays 13:00–17:00, closed Jan 1 and April 29 in 2006.

Getting There: It's at Oudezijds Voorburgwal 40, a seven-minute walk from either Central Station or Dam Square.

Information: Tel. 020/624-6604, www.museumamstelkring.nl. Note that the museum has several steep, narrow staircases.

Length of This Tour: Allow one hour.

THE TOUR BEGINS

Exterior

Behind the attic windows of this narrow townhouse sits a 150-seat, three-story church the size of a four-lane bowling alley. Below it is the home of the wealthy businessman who built the church. This 17th-century townhouse, like many in the city, also has a back-house *(achterhuis)* that was rented out to another family. On this tour, we'll visit the front house, then the church, then the back-house. Before entering, notice the emergency-exit door in the alley. This was once the hidden church's main entrance.

• *Step inside. Buy your ticket and climb the stairs to the first floor, where we begin touring the front house. The first stop is a room with a big fireplace, the...*

Parlor

By humble Dutch standards, this is an enormous, highly ornate room. Here, in the largest room of the house, the family received guests and hosted parties. The decor is the Dutch version of classical, where everything comes in symmetrical pairs—corkscrew columns flank the fireplace, the coffered ceiling mirrors the patterned black-and-white marble floor, and a fake exit door balances the real entrance door.

Over the fireplace is the coat of arms of Jan Hartman (1619–1668), a rich Catholic businessman who built this house for his family and the church for his fellow Catholics in the neighborhood. The family symbol, the crouching hart (deer), became the nickname of the church—*Het Hert.*

The painting over the fireplace *(The Presentation in the Temple)* has hung here since Hartman's time, and shows his taste for Italian, Catholic, Baroque-style beauty. On the wall opposite the windows, the family portrait is right out of the Dutch Golden Age, showing a rich Catholic businessman and his family of four... but it's not Hartman.

• *Now ascend the small spiral staircase that leads to a room facing the canal, called the...*

Canal Room

Unlike the rather formal parlor, this was where the family just hung out, staring out the windows or warming themselves at the stove. The furnishings are typical of a wealthy merchant's home of the time. The wood stove and the textiles on the walls are re-creations, but look like the originals. The Delftware vase would have been filled with tulips, back then still an exotic and expensive transplant from the East. In the Dutch custom (still occasionally seen today), the family covered tables with exotic Turkish rugs imported by traders of the Dutch East India Company. The tall ceramic doo-dad is a multi-armed tulip vase. Its pagoda shape reminds us that Delftware originally came from China.

Despite the family's wealth, space was tight. In the 1600s, entire families would often sleep together in small bed cabinets. They sat up to sleep, because they believed if they lay down, the blood would pool in their heads and kill them.

The black ebony knickknack cabinet is painted with a scene right out of the 1600s Red Light District. On the right door, the Prodigal Son spends his inheritance, making merry with bare-breasted, scarlet-clothed courtesans—high-rent prostitutes who could also entertain educated, cello-loving clients. On the left door, the Prodigal Son has spent it all. He can't pay his bill, and is kicked out of a cheap tavern—still half-dressed—by a pair of short-changed prostitutes.

• *As you climb the staircase up to the church, you can look through a window into the small...*

Chaplain's Room

Originally the maid's room, this humble bedroom is now furnished to look as it did in the 1800s, when the church chaplain lived here. See the tiny bed cabinet decorated with a tiny skull—a reminder of mortality—and a pipe on the table. Next to the room is the font used by worshippers to wet their fingers and cross themselves upon entering the church.

• *Continue up to the church.*

Our Lord in the Attic Church—Nave and Altar

The church is long and narrow, with an altar at one end, an organ at the other, and two balconies overhead to maximize the seating in this relatively small space. Compared with Amsterdam's whitewashed Protestant churches, this Catholic church has touches of elaborate Baroque decor, with statues of saints, garlands, and baby angels. The balconies are suspended from the ceiling and held in place by metal rods.

This attic church is certainly hidden, but everyone knew it was here. In tolerant (and largely Catholic) Amsterdam, it was rare for Catholics to actually be arrested or punished (after the Protestants' initial anger of 1578), but they were socially unacceptable. Hartman was a respected businessman who used his wealth and influence to convince the city fathers to look the other way as the church was built. Imagine the jubilation when the church opened its doors in

Anti-Catholic = Anti-Spanish

The anti-Catholic laws imposed by Protestants were partly retribution for the Catholics' own oppressive rule, partly a desire to reform what was seen as a corrupted religion...and largely political. By a quirk of royal marriage, Holland was ruled from afar by Spain—Europe's most militantly Catholic country, home of the Inquisition, the Jesuits, and the pope's own Counter-Reformation army.

In 1578, Amsterdam's hard-line Protestants staged the "Alteration"—a coup kicking out their Spanish oppressors and allying the city with the Prince of Orange's rebels. Catholics in the city—probably a majority of the population—were considered guilty by association. They were potential enemies, suspected as puppets of the pope, spies for Spanish kings, or subverters of the social order. In addition, Catholics were considered immoral worshippers of false idols, bowing down to graven images of saints and the Virgin Mary.

Catholic churches were seized and looted, and prominent Catholics were dragged to Dam Square by a lynch mob, before being freed unharmed outside the city gates. Laws were passed prohibiting open Catholic worship. For two centuries, Protestant extremists gave Catholics a taste of their own repressive medicine. However, Amsterdam's long tradition of tolerance meant that Catholics were not actually arrested or prosecuted under these laws. Still, many families over many generations were torn apart by the religious and political strife of the Reformation.

1663, and Catholics could finally gather together and worship in this fine space without feeling like two-bit criminals.

The altar is flanked by classical columns and topped with an arch featuring a stucco God the Father, a dove of the Holy Spirit, and trumpeting angels.

The **base of the left column**—made of wood painted to look like marble—is hollow. Inside is a fold-out wooden pulpit that could be pulled out for the priest to preach from—as explained with photos on the wall opposite.

The altarpiece painting (Jacob de Wit's *Baptism of Jesus*) is one of three that could be rotated with the feast days. Step into the room behind the altar to see the two spares. In a glass case on the back side of the altar, squint at the ship-in-a-bottle miniature home devotionals.

• *Behind the altar is a room called the...*

Lady Chapel

An altar dedicated to Our Lady—the Virgin Mary, the mother of Christ—contains more of the images that so offended and outraged hard-line Protestants. See her statue with baby Jesus and find her symbols, the rose and crown, in the blue damask altar cloth.

Catholics have traditionally honored Mary, addressing prayers to her or to other saints, asking them to intercede with God on their behalf. To Calvinist extremists, this was like bowing down to a false goddess. They considered statues of the Virgin to be among the "graven images" forbidden by the Ten Commandments (Exodus 20:4).

The **collection box** (*voor St. Pieter*, on the wall by the staircase down) was for donations sent to fund that most Catholic of monuments, the pope's own church, the Basilica of St. Peter in Rome—to Calvinists, the center of corruption, the "whore of Babylon."

• *Later, we'll head down the stairs here, but first climb the stairs to the first balcony above the church.*

Lower Balcony

The window to the left of the altar (as you face it) looks south, across ramshackle rooftops (note the complex townhouse-with-back-house design of so many Amsterdam buildings) to the steeple of the Old Church (Oude Kerk). The Old Church was the main Catholic church until 1578, when it was rededicated as Dutch Reformed (Protestant), the new official religion of the Netherlands. For the next hundred years, Catholics had no large venue to gather in until Our Lord in the Attic opened in 1663.

The 1749 organ is small, but more than adequate. These days, music-lovers flock here on special evenings for a *Vondelkonzert*

(wandering concert). They listen to a few tunes here, have a drink, then move on to hear more music at, say, the Old Church or the Royal Palace.

Next to the organ, the painting *Evangelist Matthew with an Angel* (*De Evangelist Mattheus,* c. 1625, by Jan Lievens) features the wrinkled forehead and high-contrast shadings used by Lievens' more famous colleague, Rembrandt.

• *Stairs next to the organ lead to the...*

Calvinism

Holland's Protestant movement followed the stern reformer John Calvin more than the beer-drinking German Martin Luther. Calvin's French followers, called Huguenots, fled religious persecution in the 1500s, finding refuge in tolerant Amsterdam. When Catholic Spain began persecuting them in Holland, they entered politics and fought back.

Calvin wanted to reform the Catholic faith by condemning corruption, simplifying rituals, and returning the faith to its biblical roots. Like other Protestants, Calvinists emphasized that only God's grace—and not our good works—can get us to heaven.

He went so far as to say that God predestined some for heaven, some for hell. Later, some overly pious Calvinists even claimed to be able to pick out the lucky winners from the unlucky, sinful losers. Today, the Dutch Reformed Church (and some other Reformed and Presbyterian churches) carries on Calvin's brand of Christianity.

Upper Balcony

Looking down from this angle, the small church really looks small. It could accommodate 150 seated worshippers. From here, the tapering roofline creates the "attic" feel that gives the church its nickname.

• *At the back of the upper balcony is the...*

Canalside Room—Religious Art

This kind of religious hardware is standard in Catholic church services—elaborate silver and gold monstrances (ornamental holders in which the Communion wafer is displayed), chalices (for the Communion wine), ciboria (chalices with lids for holding consecrated wafers), pyxes (for storing unconsecrated wafers), candlesticks, and incense burners. "Holy earth boxes" were used for Catholics denied burial in consecrated ground. Instead, they put a little consecrated dirt in the box, and placed it in the coffin.

Admiring these beautiful pieces, remember that it was this kind of luxury, ostentation, and Catholic mumbo-jumbo that drove thrifty Calvinists nuts.

Looking out the window, you can see that you're literally in the attic. Straight across the canal is a house with an ornate gable featuring dolphins. This street was once the city's best address.

• *Back down on the lower balcony, circle around to the window just to the right of the altar for a...*

Northern View

Look north across modern junk on rooftops to the impressive dome and twin steeples of St. Nicholas' Church, near Central Station. This is the third Amsterdam church to be dedicated to the patron saint of seafarers and of the city. The first was the Old Church (until 1578), then Our Lord in the Attic (1663). Finally, after the last anti-Catholic laws were repealed (1821), St. Nicholas was built as a symbol of the faith's revival.

When St. Nicholas was dedicated in 1887, Our Lord in the Attic closed up shop. The next year, wealthy Catholics saved it from the wrecking ball, turning it into one of Amsterdam's first museums.

• *Head back downstairs, passing through the room behind the altar with the Lady Chapel and taking the stairs (past the offering box) down to the...*

Confessional

The confessional dates from 1740. The priest sat in the left half, while parishioners knelt in the right to confess their sins through a grilled window. Catholic priests have church authority to forgive sins, while Protestants take their troubles directly to God.

(The sociologist Max Weber theorized that frequently-forgiven Catholics more easily accept the status quo, while guilt-ridden Protestants are driven to prove their worth by making money. Hence, northern Protestant countries—like the Netherlands—became capitalist powerhouses, while southern Catholic countries remained feudal and backward. Hmm.)

• *Go down another flight and turn right, into the...*

Jaap Leeuwenberg Room (Room 10)

We've now left the church premises and moved to the back-house rooms that were rented out to other families. This room's colors are seen in countless old homes—white walls, ochre-yellow beamed ceiling, oxblood-red landing, and black floor tiles. The simple colors, lit here by a light shaft, make small rooms seem bright and spacious.

• *Some very steep stairs lead down to the...*

17th-Century Kitchen

This reconstructed room was inhabited as-is up until 1952. Blue-tiled walls show playful scenes of kids and animals. Step into the small pantry, then open a door to see the toilet.

• *Climb the rope back up the stairs and turn left to find exhibits on Amsterdam's other Catholic churches and the "Miracle of Amsterdam." Then descend a different set of stairs into the...*

19th-Century Kitchen

This looks just so Dutch, with blue tiles, yellow walls, and Vermeer lighting from a skylight. The portrait opposite the fireplace depicts the last resident of this house on her First Communion day. When she died in 1953, her house became part of this museum.

Think of how her age overlaps our age...of all the change since she was born. Consider the contrast of this serene space with the wild world that awaits just outside the door of this hidden church. And plunge back into today's Amsterdam.

AMSTERDAM HISTORY MUSEUM TOUR

(Amsterdam Historisch Museum)

Dozens of rooms (with great English explanations) take you creatively through Amsterdam's story, from fishing village to sea-trading superpower to hippie haven to city of immigrants. Simply follow the *Grand Tour Route* signs, and you'll see every room on your hike through 1,000 years of Amsterdam history. I've highlighted a few stops worth checking out.

ORIENTATION

Cost: €6.50, covered by *I amsterdam* Card.

Special Exhibit: The museum hosts "Anne Frank—Her Life in Letters" (April 12–Sept 3), giving us a new look at Anne's remarkable powers of observation and her growth as a writer from 1936 to 1944.

Hours: Mon–Fri 10:00–17:00, Sat–Sun 11:00–17:00.

Getting There: It's on Kalverstraat 92, next to the Begijnhof, in downtown Amsterdam.

Information: Tel. 020/523-1822, www.ahm.nl.

Length of This Tour: Allow one hour.

Cuisine Art: The museum has the classy David & Goliath café and restaurant—peek inside to see the huge 17th-century Goliath statue (€8–9 salads and sandwiches, daily 9:30–18:00, until 17:00 in winter).

THE TOUR BEGINS

Ground Floor Entrance Hall: Growth of the City

Take time to watch the entire sequence as the computer-generated growth screen ("The Growth of Amsterdam," at the far end of the room) takes you through time. Watch the population go from zero to 739,000 in a thousand years. Witness the birth of the city—the damming of the Amstel, which created Dam Square, the commercial zone where the Damrak's sea harbor met the Rokin's river port. Then follow the subsequent canalization as the city fills in its fortified center and continues to expand outward in rings.

Rooms 2–7: From a City of Monasteries to a Trading Power

Rooms 2–3 show how Amsterdam was once a Catholic city rich with monasteries. Then (Room 5, filled with globes) it's 1650, and it's clear that Holland has become a great trading power. Press a button on the world map to watch the 1609 voyage of Henry Hudson, an Englishman sailing for Holland, as he searched for a Western Passage to Asia, but kept bumping into New York. Room 6 shows the growth of Dam Square, with models of the Royal Palace/Town Hall and the tower of the New Church (Nieuwe Kerk).

• *Climb the stairs to the first floor.*

Room 8: Amsterdam's Harbor

Look for the interesting model (in the stairwell) showing how ships got in and out of the city's shallow harbor. Ingenious 150-foot wooden pontoons, pumped full of air, were attached to the sides of ships to float them high over sandbars. The next room (Room 9) displays instruments of medieval-style justice and paintings of great faces, from the big shots to the orphans who used to inhabit this building.

• *In Room 10, find a staircase up to...*

Carillon Lessons

Invented by Dutch bellmakers in the 1400s and perfected in the 1600s, this musical instrument is a Flemish specialty. The carillon player (called a "carillonneur"), seated at his keyboard up in the tower, presses keys with his fists and feet, jerking wires that swing clappers against tuned bells. The bells range in size from 20-pound high notes to eight-ton low notes, struck by hundred-pound clappers. These days, some carillons have electric actions to make it easier, plus player-piano mechanisms to automate the playing.

Mozart, Vivaldi, Handel, and Bach—all of whom lived during the carillon's heyday—wrote Baroque music that sounds beautiful on bells.

Amsterdam's Story

Visualize the physical layout of this man-made city: built on trees, protected by dikes, and laced with canals in the marshy delta at the mouth of the Amstel River. Location, location, location. Boats could arrive here from Germany by riverboat down the Rhine, from England across the Channel and down the IJ River, and from Denmark by entering the Zuiderzee inlet of the North Sea. St. Nicholas, protector of water travelers, was the city's patron.

As early as 1300, Amsterdam was already an international trade center of German beer, locally caught herring, cloth, bacon, salt, and wine. Having dammed and canalized the Amstel and diked out the sea tides, the Dutch drained land, sunk pilings, and built a city from scratch. When the region's leading bishop granted the town a charter (1300), Amsterdammers could then set up their own law courts, judge their own matters, and be essentially autonomous. The town thrived.

By 1500, Amsterdam was a walled city of 12,000, with the Singel canal serving as the moat. Midcentury, the city got a growth spurt when its trading rival Antwerp fell to Spanish troops and a flood of fellow Flemish headed north, fleeing chaos and religious persecution.

In 1602, hardy Dutch sailors (and the Englishman Henry Hudson) tried their hand at trade with the Far East. When they returned, they brought with them valuable spices, jewels, luxury goods...and the Golden Age.

The Dutch East India Company (abbreviated as "V.O.C." in Dutch), a state-subsidized import/export business, combined nautical skills with capitalist investing. With 500 or so 150-foot ships cruising in and out of Amsterdam's harbor, it was the first great multinational corporation. Amsterdam's Golden Age (c. 1600–1650) rode the wave of hard work and good fortune. Over the next two centuries, the V.O.C. would send a half million Dutch people on business trips to Asia, broadening their horizons.

The city of the Golden Age was perhaps the wealthiest on earth, thriving as the "warehouse of the world." Goods came from everywhere. The V.O.C.'s specialties were spices (pepper

Sit down and pound your fists on the keys (that's why they're there). Hitting the red-marked keys, play a chromatic scale (successive keys) as fast as you can. Hit 'em hard (try to pound out "Louie Louie"). Then push the buttons on the walls to hear recordings of actual Amsterdam carillons in action—and imagine the fists flying.

• Cross the skybridge (over the Civic Guard's Gallery) into Room 11, where you'll find...

and cinnamon), coffee and tea, Chinese porcelain (Delftware's Eastern inspiration), and silk. Meanwhile, the Dutch West India Company concentrated on the New World, trading African slaves for South American sugar. With its wealth, Amsterdam built in grand style, erecting the gabled townhouses we see today. The city expanded west and south, adding new neighborhoods.

But by 1650, Amsterdam's overseas trade was being eclipsed by new superpowers England and France. Inconclusive wars with Louis XIV and England drained the economy, destroyed the trading fleet, and demoralized the people. Throughout the 1700s, Amsterdam was a city of backwater bankers rather than international traders, although it remained the cultural center of Holland.

In 1795, the city was beached at low tide. Napoleon's French troops occupied the country and the economy was dismal.

A revival in the 1800s was spurred by technological achievements. The Dutch built a canal reconnecting Amsterdam directly with the North Sea (1824–1876), railroads laced the small country, and the city was expanded southward by draining new land. The Rijksmuseum, Central Station, and Magna Plaza were built as proud monuments to the economic upswing.

The 1930s Depression hit hard, followed by four years of occupation under the Nazis, aided by pro-Nazi Dutch. The city's large Jewish population was decimated by Nazi deportations and extermination (falling from 130,000 Jews in 1940 to 30,000 in 1945).

With postwar prosperity, 1960s Amsterdam again became a world cultural capital as the center for Europe's hippies, who came here to smoke marijuana. Grassroots campaigns by young, artistic, politically active people promoted free sex and free bikes.

Today, Amsterdam is a city of 739,000 people jammed into small apartments (often with the same floor plan as their neighbors'). Since the 1970s, many immigrants have become locals. One in 10 Amsterdammers is Surinamese, and one in 10 bows toward Mecca.

Rembrandt's *The Anatomy Lesson of Dr. Jan Deijman*

His famous *Anatomy Lesson of Dr. Tulp* (1632, now in The Hague's Mauritshuis) put young Rembrandt on Amsterdam's artistic map two decades earlier. Now, in 1656, Rembrandt returned to the dissection room for another anatomy lesson—this time from Dr. Jan Deijman.

A fire in 1732 damaged this group portrait, incinerating the surrounding spectators and leaving us with just the stars of the scene—Dr. Deijman and the corpse. The body of this recently hanged thief ("Black Jack" Fonteijn) was donated to the surgery theater in the Waag (today's Red Light District), where Dr. D. held a dissecting demonstration for med students and the paying public. Rembrandt attended, sketch pad in hand.

The corpse's feet are right in our face (similar to Mantegna's famous *Dead Christ*), a masterpiece of foreshortening. We stare into the gaping hole of his disemboweled stomach. The doctor (head burned off in the fire) does the work, opening the head and exposing the brain, while the assistant looks on calmly, hand on hip.

• *Return to Room 10 and continue through Rooms 13–16 until you reach Room 17. Hop on the bike—that's what it's there for—and take a ride through Amsterdam in the 1920s. The next few rooms, "Modern City" (Rooms 17–21), give you a sense of...*

20th-Century Sociology

Room 19 shows housing in contemporary Amsterdam. Many residents are crammed into small apartments, either in historic buildings or in developments of city-built housing. Recently, many Indonesian and Surinamese have immigrated here. Tracing the evolution of housing in Amsterdam in the 20th century, you study typical apartments from aerial views and dollhouses. The big blue board of doorbells (Room 19) represents the residents who live in a suburban apartment complex (in a district called Fleerde, which has probably never seen a tourist). Hit the red buzzers to meet the residents and tour their homes.

• *Head upstairs to the second floor.*

Room 22: World War II

This section includes black-and-white photos and color footage of Liberation Day in 1945. A touch-screen computer lets you witness a terrible event on Dam Square, the Grote Club Massacre. Just a few days after the war ended (May 7), German troops who were holed up in a club overlooking Dam Square opened fire on celebrating locals, killing 19 and injuring 117.

Room 23 & Room 24: Hippie Age

In the 1960s, hippies from around the world were drawn to free-wheeling Amsterdam. The socialist group called the Provos provoked the Establishment by publishing an outrageous magazine (the first issue contained a page of smokable paper made from marijuana), staging pro-pot events, and promoting innovative (but ultimately unsuccessful) campaigns to provide free white bicycles and white electric-powered cars to city commuters. You can trace the evolution of Amsterdam's "no war on drugs," and even listen to a Ted Koppel interview of former New York mayor Ed Koch and his Dutch counterparts on the pros and cons of legalizing marijuana.

In Room 24, you enter a reconstruction of the famous Café 't Mandje from 1967, a gay bar on Zeedijk street. See a photo of owner Bet van Beeren and her motorcycle in the window, then step inside to see her hanging collection of neckties, which she cut off delighted customers with a butcher knife. For more details on the café, see page 86).

• *As you leave the museum, don't miss the room opposite the ticket desk (between the WC and the exit door)...*

Former Orphanage and Regents' Room

The first small room tells of the orphanage here. Originally a cloister, it became an orphanage in 1570, and took in kids until the 1960s.

Finally, you enter a stately Regents' Room (for the orphanage's board of directors), where you'll see grand, ego-elevating paintings honoring big shots. Many of the Dutch Masters' paintings you'll see in the Netherlands' museums were commissioned to decorate rooms like this.

SLEEPING

Greeting a new day by descending steep stairs and stepping into a leafy canalside scene—graceful bridges, historic gables, and bikes clattering on cobbles—is a fun part of experiencing Amsterdam. But Amsterdam is a tough city for budget accommodations, and any room under €140 will have rough edges. Still, you can sleep well and safely in a great location for €80 per double.

Amsterdam is jammed during convention periods, Queen's Day (normally observed on April 30, but celebrated on April 29 in 2006), and on summer weekends. Many hotels will not take weekend bookings for people staying fewer than three nights.

Parking in Amsterdam is even worse than driving. You'll pay €32 a day to park safely in a garage—and then hike to your hotel.

If you'd rather trade big-city action for small-town coziness, consider sleeping in Haarlem, 15 minutes away by train (see page 212).

Near the Train Station

$$ Ibis Amsterdam Hotel is a modern and efficient, 187-room place towering over the station and a multistory bicycle garage. It offers a central location, comfort, and good value, without a hint of charm (Db-€137, Qb-€189, €10 extra Fri–Sat, skip breakfast and save €13 per person, check Web site for deals, book long in advance, air-con, smoke-free floor, Stationsplein 49, tel. 020/638-9999, fax 020/620-0156, www.ibishotel.com, h1556@accor-hotels.com). When business is slow, they often rent rooms to same-day drop-ins for €105.

$$ Amstel Botel, the city's only remaining "boat hotel," is a shipshape, bright, and clean floating hotel with 175 rooms (Sb/Db-€87, Tb-€117, worth the extra €5 per room for canal view, breakfast-€10, elevator, 400 yards from train station, on your left

Sleep Code

(€1 = about $1.20, country code: 31, area code: 020)
S = Single, **D** = Double/Twin, **T** = Triple, **Q** = Quad, **b** = bathroom,
s = shower only. Nearly everyone speaks English in the Netherlands. Credit cards are accepted, and prices include breakfast and tax unless otherwise noted.

To help you easily sort through these listings, I've divided the rooms into three categories, based on the price for a standard double room with bath:

$$$ Higher Priced—Most rooms €140 or more.
$$ Moderately Priced—Most rooms between €80–140.
$ Lower Priced—Most rooms €80 or less.

as you leave station, you'll see the sign and the big white boat at Oosterdokskade 2–4, tel. 020/626-4247, fax 020/639-1952, www .amstelbotel.nl). The boat may chug to a new location in 2006 to steer clear of the major construction project around the station.

Between Dam Square and the Anne Frank House
$$$ Hotel Toren is a chandeliered, historic mansion in a pleasant, quiet, canalside setting in downtown Amsterdam. This splurge, run by Eric and Petra Toren, is classy yet friendly, and two blocks northeast of the Anne Frank House. It's the least expensive four-star in town and a great value (Sb-€135, Ds-€150, Db-€195, deluxe Db-€240, Tb-€225, prices decrease in winter, 10 percent discount with this book through 2006 if mentioned when booking, 5 percent tax, breakfast buffet-€12, air-con, Keizersgracht 164, tel. 020/622-6352, fax 020/626-9705, www.hoteltoren.nl, info@hoteltoren.nl). The capable and friendly staff is a great source of local advice.

$$$ Canal House Hotel, a few doors down, offers a plush 17th-century atmosphere rich with history. Above generous and elegant public spaces, tangled, antique-filled halls lead to 26 tastefully appointed rooms. Evenings come with candlelight and soft music (Db-€150–190, prices depend on room size, 8 percent discount with this book in 2006—but only if claimed at time of booking, elevator, Keizersgracht 148, tel. 020/622-5182, fax 020/624-1317, www.canalhouse.nl, info@canalhouse.nl).

$$$ Hotel Ambassade, lacing together 60 rooms in 10 houses, is amazingly elegant and fresh, sitting aristocratically on the Herengracht. Its public rooms are palatial, with a library, antique furnishings, and modern art (Sb-€165, Db-€195, Db suite-€270, Tb-€227, extra bed-€35, 5 percent tax, breakfast-€16—and actually worth it, elevator, free Internet access in lobby,

Amsterdam Hotels

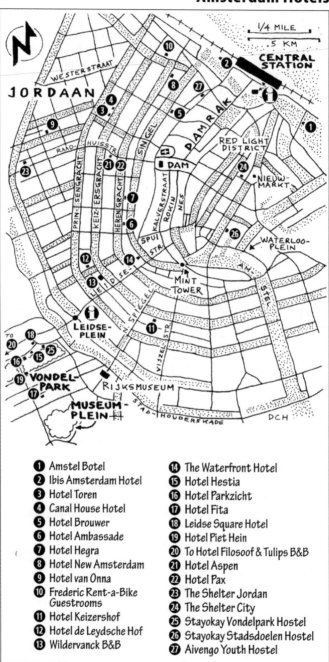

1 Amstel Botel
2 Ibis Amsterdam Hotel
3 Hotel Toren
4 Canal House Hotel
5 Hotel Brouwer
6 Hotel Ambassade
7 Hotel Hegra
8 Hotel New Amsterdam
9 Hotel van Onna
10 Frederic Rent-a-Bike Guestrooms
11 Hotel Keizershof
12 Hotel de Leydsche Hof
13 Wildervanck B&B
14 The Waterfront Hotel
15 Hotel Hestia
16 Hotel Parkzicht
17 Hotel Fita
18 Leidse Square Hotel
19 Hotel Piet Hein
20 To Hotel Filosoof & Tulips B&B
21 Hotel Aspen
22 Hotel Pax
23 The Shelter Jordan
24 The Shelter City
25 Stayokay Vondelpark Hostel
26 Stayokay Stadsdoelen Hostel
27 Aivengo Youth Hostel

Herengracht 341, tel. 020/555-0222, www.ambassade-hotel.nl, info@ambassade-hotel.nl).

$$ Hotel New Amsterdam is the perfect mix of comfort, value, and good management. It's conveniently located near the train station, but just far enough away for you to enjoy idyllic, romantic Amsterdam. The rooms are clean and comfy, with new carpet, modern baths, and solid-wood furniture. Manager Ronald is very hands-on—he's slept in all 26 of his rooms (Db-€100, €20 more Fri–Sat, prices promised with this book in 2006, always free coffee, fans on request, tangled floorplan connecting 3 canalside buildings, garage parking-€20, Herengracht 13, tel. 020/522-2345, fax 020/522-2389, www.hotelnewamsterdam.nl, info@hotelnewamsterdam.nl).

$$ Hotel Brouwer, a woody and homey old-time place situated tranquilly but centrally on the Singel canal, rents eight rooms up lots of very steep stairs (Sb-€55, Db-€90, Tb-€105, small elevator, located between train station and Dam Square, near Lijnbaanssteeg at Singel 83, tel. 020/624-6358, fax 020/520-6264, www.hotelbrouwer.nl, akita@hotelbrouwer.nl).

$$ Hotel Hegra is a rare, basic yet comfy, sedate, and cat-friendly 11-room place, run by Robert de Vries. It's well-worn and a bit humid, but feels safe and peaceful (D-€65, Ds-€80, Db-€90, Herengracht 269, tel. 020/623-7877, fax 020/623-8159).

In and near the Jordaan

$$ Hotel van Onna, smoke-free and professional-feeling, has 41 simple, industrial-strength rooms. While the beds can feel like springy cots and the lights are dim, the price is right, and the location makes you want to crack out your easel. Loek van Onna, who has slept in the building—probably on a cot—all his life, runs the hotel (Sb-€45, Db-€90, Tb-€135, cash only, reserve only by phone, in the Jordaan at Bloemgracht 104, tel. 020/626-5801, www.hotelvanonna.com).

$ Frederic Rent-a-Bike Guestrooms, with a bike rental shop as the reception, is a collection of private rooms on a gorgeous canal just outside the Jordaan, a five-minute walk from the train station. Frederic has amassed about 100 beds, ranging from dumpy €70 doubles to spacious and elegant apartments (from €46 per person). Some places are ideal for families and groups of up to six. He also rents houseboat apartments. All are displayed on his Web site (book with credit card but pay with cash, 2-night minimum, no breakfast, Brouwersgracht 78, tel. 020/624-5509, www.frederic.nl). His excellent bike shop is open daily 9:00–18:00 (€10/24 hrs).

Leidseplein Neighborhood

The area around Amsterdam's rip-roaring nightlife center (Leidseplein) is colorful, comfortable, and convenient. These canalside places are within a five-minute walk of Leidseplein, but in generally quiet and characteristic settings.

$$ Hotel de Leydsche Hof is a hidden gem located on a canal. Its two large, well-designed rooms are a symphony in white (1 room overlooks the canal, the other a tree-filled backyard), while its attic apartment comes with a full kitchen (Db-€90–100, apartment-€130, breakfast-€10, cash only, Leidsegracht 14—don't confuse it with noisy shopping street Leidsestraat a block south, tel. 020/638-2327, mobile 065-125-8588 or 065-347-9812, loespiller@planet.nl, gentleman Frits, diva Loes, and yappy Api).

$$ Wildervanck B&B, run by Helene and Sjoerd Wildervanck, offers two rooms in an elegant, 17th-century canal house (big Db on 1st floor-€125, Db with twin beds on ground floor-€105, extra bed-€25, family deals, breakfast in their pleasant dining room, family has 3 little girls, Keizersgracht 498, on Keizersgracht canal just west of Leidsestraat, tel. 020/623-3846, fax 020/421-6575, www.wildervanck.com, info@wildervanck .com). As it's in a busy area, you may get some bar noise at night.

$$ Hotel Keizershof, which requires a four-night minimum stay, is wonderfully Dutch, with six bright, airy rooms in a 17th-century canal house. A steep spiral staircase leads to rooms named after old-time Hollywood stars. The enthusiastic hospitality of the de Vries family gives this place a friendly, almost small-town charm (S-€55, D-€75–80, Ds-€90, Db-€110, strictly non-smoking; tram #16, #24, or #25 from train station; Keizersgracht 618, where Keizers canal crosses Nieuwe Spiegelstraat, tel. 020/622-2855, fax 020/624-8412, www.hotelkeizershof.nl).

$$ The Waterfront Hotel, farther north up Leidsestraat and just west of Koningsplein, has 10 rustic yet cozy rooms and lots of steep stairs (Sb-€95, Db-€110, view Db-€135, Tb-€150, Singel 458, tel. & fax 020/421-6621, www.waterfront.demon.nl, info@hotelwaterfront.nl).

Near Vondelpark

These options cluster around Vondelpark in a safe neighborhood. While they don't have a hint of Old Dutch or romantic canalside flavor, they're reasonable values and only a short walk from the action. Many are in a pleasant nook between the rollicking Leidseplein and the park. They are easily connected with the train station by trams #1, #2, and #5.

$$$ Leidse Square Hotel is an 89-room, American-style hotel well-situated on a quiet street, just across the bridge from the Leidseplein (Sb-€99, Db-€119, Tb-€139, some rooms with air-con,

Hotels and Restaurants near Museumplein

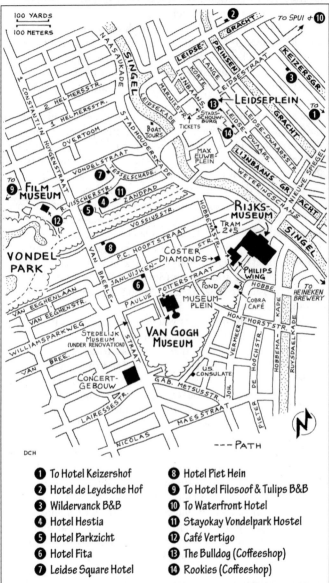

1 To Hotel Keizershof
2 Hotel de Leydsche Hof
3 Wildervanck B&B
4 Hotel Hestia
5 Hotel Parkzicht
6 Hotel Fita
7 Leidse Square Hotel
8 Hotel Piet Hein
9 To Hotel Filosoof & Tulips B&B
10 To Waterfront Hotel
11 Stayokay Vondelpark Hostel
12 Café Vertigo
13 The Bulldog (Coffeeshop)
14 Rookies (Coffeeshop)

elevator, Tesselschadestraat 23, tel. 020/612-6876, fax 020/683-8313, www.amsterdamcityhotels.nl).

$$$ Hotel Fita has 16 bright, fresh rooms located 100 yards from the Van Gogh Museum (Sb-€90, 2 small basement Db-€120, Db-€135–145, Tb-€175, discounts for multiple nights—ask when you book, free laundry service, elevator, Jan Lykenstraat 37, tel. 020/679-0976, fax 020/664-3969, www.fita.nl, info@fita.nl, joking and affable owner Hans).

$$ Hotel Hestia, on a safe and sane street, is efficient and family-run, with 18 clean, airy, and generally spacious rooms (Sb-€80, very small Db-€95, standard Db-€110–135, Tb-€160, Qb-€188, elevator, Roemer Visscherstraat 7, tel. 020/618-0801, fax 020/685-1382, www.hotel-hestia.nl, info@hotel-hestia.nl).

$$ Hotel Parkzicht, an old-fashioned place with extremely steep stairs, rents 13 big, plain rooms on a quiet street bordering Vondelpark (S-€39, Sb-€49, Db-€78–90, Tb-€110–120, Qb-€120-130, closed Nov–March, Roemer Visscherstraat 33, tel. 020/618-1954, fax 020/618-0897, www.parkzicht.nl, hotel@parkzicht.nl).

$$$ Hotel Piet Hein offers comfortable, renovated rooms with a swanky, nautical atmosphere (Sb-€95–105, Db-€145–165, extra bed-€30, Vossiusstraat 52–53, tel. 020/6627205, www.hotelpiethein.nl, info@hotelpiethein.nl).

$$ Hotel Filosoof greets you with Aristotle and Plato in the foyer and classical music in its generous lobby. Its 38 rooms are decorated with themes; the Egyptian room has a frieze of hieroglyphics. Philosophers' sayings hang on the walls, and thoughtful travelers wander down the halls or sit in the garden, rooted in deep discussion. The rooms are small, but the hotel is endearing (Db-€128–150, Tb-€175, elevator, 3-min walk from tram line #1, get off at Jan Pieter Heijestraat, Anna Vondelstraat 6, tel. 020/683-3013, fax 020/685-3750, www.hotelfilosoof.nl, reservations@hotelfilosoof.nl).

$$ Tulips B&B, with a bunch of cozy rooms in several neighbors' homes, is run by a friendly Englishwoman, Karen, and her Dutch husband, Paul. Rooms are clean, white, and bright, with red carpeting and green plants (D-€55–75, Db-€100, suite-€130, family deals, includes milk and cereal breakfast, cash only, 2-night minimum, non-smoking, south end of Vondelpark at Sloterkade 65, they send directions when you book, tel. 020/679-2753, fax 020/408-3028, www.bedandbreakfastamsterdam.net).

Cheap Hotels in the Center

Inexpensive, well-worn hotels line the convenient but noisy main drag between City Hall and the Anne Frank House. Expect a long, steep, and depressing stairway, noisy rooms in the front, and quieter rooms in the back.

$ Hotel Aspen, a good value for a budget hotel, is tidy, stark, and well-maintained (8 rooms, S-€38, tiny D-€50, Db-€68, Tb-€85, Qb-€95, no breakfast, Raadhuisstraat 31, tel. 020/626-6714, fax 020/620-0866, www.hotelaspen.nl, info@hotelaspen.nl, run by Esam and his family).

$ Hotel Pax, a few doors away, has large and plain, but airy rooms (S-€35–40, D-€60, Db-€75, T-€75, Tb-€95, Q-€100, no breakfast, 2 showers and 2 toilets shared by 6 rooms, Raadhuisstraat 37, tel. 020/624-9735, run by 2 young brothers named Philip and Pieter).

Hostels in the Center
Amsterdam has a world of good, cheap hostels. Most are designed for the party crowd, but here are a few quieter options.

In the Jordaan: **The Shelter Jordan** is a scruffy, friendly, Christian-run, 100-bed place in a great neighborhood. While most of Amsterdam's hostels are pretty wild, this place is drug-free and alcohol-free, with boys on one floor and girls on another. These are Amsterdam's best budget beds, in 14- to 20-bed dorms (€18 per bed, €3 extra Fri–Sat, includes sheets, maximum age 35, Internet access in lobby, non-smoking, 2:00 curfew, near Anne Frank House, Bloemstraat 179, tel. 020/624-4717, www.shelter.nl, jordan@shelter.nl). The Shelter serves hot meals, runs a snack bar in its big, relaxing lounge, offers lockers, and leads nightly Bible studies.

In the Red Light District: **The Shelter City** is Shelter Jordan's sister—similar, but definitely not preaching to the choir (€19 per bed, includes sheets, maximum age 35, curfew, Barndesteeg 21, tel. 020/625-3230, fax 020/623-2282, www.shelter.nl, city@shelter.nl).

In Vondelpark: **Stayokay Vondelpark (IYHF)** is one of Amsterdam's top hostels (€19.50–27 per bed, D-€68–80, higher prices are for March–Oct, nonmembers pay €2.50 extra, cash only, family rooms, lots of school groups, 4–20 beds per room, lockers, right on Vondelpark at Zandpad 5, tel. 020/589-8996, fax 020/589-8955, www.stayokay.com). While Stayokay Vondelpark and Stayokay Stadsdoelen (listed below) are generally booked long in advance, a few beds open up each day at 11:00.

Near Waterlooplein: **Stayokay Stadsdoelen (IYHF)**, smaller and simpler than its Vondelpark sister (listed above), has only large dorms and no private bathrooms, but is free from big school groups (€19.50–23.50 per bed, nonmembers pay €2.50 extra, cash only, Kloveniersburgwal 97, tel. 020/624-6832, fax 020/639-1035, www.stayokay.com).

Near Central Station: **Aivengo Youth Hostel** has 32 beds in two Moroccan-themed rooms (1 for males, 1 for females). It's clean, new-feeling, and bare-bones, with no common room or lunch counter—but it's well-located, just a five-minute walk from Central Station (€20–22 per bed, includes sheets, maximum age 35, non-smoking, free Internet at its 1 terminal, Spuistraat 6 at Kattegat, tel. 020/421-3670).

EATING

Traditional Dutch food is basic and hearty, with lots of bread, cheese, soup, and fish. Lunch and dinner are served at American times (roughly 12:00–14:00 and 18:00–21:00).

Dutch treats include cheese, pancakes *(pannenkoeken)*, gin *(jenever)*, light, pilsner-type beer, and "syrup waffles" *(stroopwafels)*.

Experiences you owe your tongue in Holland: trying a raw herring at an outdoor herring stand, lingering over coffee in a "brown café," sipping an old *jenever* with a new friend, and consuming an Indonesian feast—a *rijsttafel*.

Budget Tips: Get a sandwich to go, and grab a park bench on a canal. Sandwiches *(broodjes)* of delicious cheese on fresh bread are cheap at snack bars, delis, and *broodjes* restaurants. Ethnic fast-food stands abound, offering a variety of meats wrapped in pita bread. Easy to buy at grocery stores, yogurt in the Netherlands (and throughout Northern Europe) is delicious and often drinkable right out of its plastic container.

Types of Eateries

Any place labeled "restaurant" will serve full, sit-down meals for lunch or dinner. But there are other places to fill the tank.

An *eetcafé* is a simple restaurant serving basic soups, salads, sandwiches, and traditional meat-and-potatoes meals in a generally comfortable but no-nonsense setting.

A *salon de thé* serves tea and coffee, yes, but also croissants, pastries, and sandwiches for a light brunch, lunch, or afternoon snack.

Cafés are all-purpose establishments, serving light meals at mealtimes and coffee, drinks, and snacks the rest of the day and night. *Bruin* cafés ("brown cafés," named for their nicotine-stained walls) are usually a little more bar-like, with dimmer lighting, wood paneling, and more tobacco smoke.

A *proeflokaal* is a bar (with snacks) for tasting wine, spirits, or beer. *Coffeeshop* is the code word for an establishment where marijuana is sold and consumed, though most also offer drinks and munchies, too (for details, see Smoking chapter on page 172).

There's no shortage of stand-up, take-out places serving fast food, sandwiches, and all kinds of quick ethnic fare.

No matter what the type of establishment you choose, expect it to be *gezellig*—a much-prized Dutch virtue, meaning an atmosphere of relaxed coziness.

Etiquette and Tipping

The Dutch are easygoing. Pay as you go or pay after? Usually it's your choice. Wait for table service or order at the bar? Whatever you do, you won't be scolded for your faux pas, as you might be in France or Italy. Dutch establishments are *gezellig*. Still, here are some guidelines:

- Tipping is not necessary in restaurants (15 percent service is usually already included in the menu price), but a tip of about five to 10 percent is a nice reward for good service. In bars, rounding up to the next euro ("keep the change") is appropriate if you get table service, rather than order at the bar.
- When ordering drinks in a café or bar, you can just pay as you go (especially if the bar is crowded), or wait until the end to settle up, as many locals do. If you get table service, take the cue from your waiter.
- Cafés with outdoor tables generally do not charge more if you sit outside (unlike in France or Italy).
- Expect tobacco smoke in any establishment.
- Waiters constantly say *"Alstublieft"* (AHL-stoo-bleeft). It's a catch-all polite word, meaning "please," "here's your order," "enjoy," and "you're welcome." You can respond with a thank you by saying, "Dank u wel" (dahnk oo vehl).

Typical Meals

Breakfast: Breakfasts are big by continental standards—bread, meat, cheese, and maybe an egg or omelet. Hotels generally put out a buffet spread, including juice and cereal.

Lunch: Simple sandwiches are called *broodjes* (most commonly made with cheese and/or ham). An open-face sandwich of ham and cheese topped with two fried eggs is an *uitsmijter* (OUTS-mi-ter). Soup is popular for lunch.

Snacks and Take-out Food: Small stands sell french fries *(frites)* with mayonnaise; raw or marinated herring; falafels (fried chick-pea balls in pita bread); *shoarmas* (lamb tucked in pita bread); and

Birgit Jons' Diary

9:00   Had coffee with small breakfast of bread, cheese, ham, and a boiled egg.

11:00 Stopped at a *salon de thé* for an *uitsmijter* sandwich.

12:30 Cold out, so warmed up with *erwtensoep* at an *eetcafé*. Also had more bread, cheese, and ham, and a small salad.

15:00 Dirk bought me a *shoarma* with fries and mayonnaise. Topped it off at a stand selling—mmm!—*poffertjes*.

16:30 Work's done! Sat in the sun along a canal outside a *proeflokaal* and sipped...was it fruit brandy? Got courage to swallow whole raw herring from kiosk—mistake!

17:30 Cappuccino and *appelgebak*.

19:00 Finally, dinner! I've been starving myself all day. First, fresh Zeeland oysters. Next, the main course: meat, potatoes, and white asparagus, all heaped on one plate. For dessert, *pannenkoeken* topped with strawberries and whipped cream, with coffee and a weird liqueur.

21:00 Party! We met at De Prins for a *pils* and an *oude jenever*. Smoked six cigarettes (no artificial preservatives).

23:00 Need grease—inhaled two *frikandellen* at late-night deli. Fortified for tomorrow—another busy day!

doner kebabs (Turkish version of a *shoarma*). Delis have deep-fried croquettes *(kroketten)*.

Dinner: It's the biggest meal of the day, consisting of meat or seafood with boiled potatoes, cooked vegetables, and a salad. Hearty stews are served in winter. These days, many people eat more vegetarian fare.

Sweets: Try *poffertjes* (small, sugared doughnuts without holes), *pannenkoeken* (pancakes with fruit and cream), *stroopwafels* (syrup waffles), and *appelgebak* (apple pie).

Local Specialties

Cheeses: Edam (covered with red wax) or Gouda (HOW-dah). Gouda can be young or old—*jong* is mellow, and *oude* is salty, crumbly, and strong, sometimes seasoned with cumin or cloves.

French Fries: Commonly served with mayonnaise (ketchup and curry sauce are often available) on a paper tray or in a newspaper cone. Flemish *(Vlaamse) frites* are made from whole potatoes, not pulp.

Haring (herring): Fresh, raw herring, marinated or salted, often served with onions or pickles, sometimes with sour cream, on a thick, soft, white bun.

Hutspot: Hearty meat stew with mashed potatoes, onions, and carrots, especially popular on winter days.

Kroketten (croquettes): Log-shaped rolls of meats and vegetables (kind of like corn dogs) breaded and deep-fried, such as *bitterballen* (meatballs), *frikandelen* (sausage), or *vlammetjes* (spring rolls).

Pannenkoeken: Either sweet dessert pancakes or crêpe-like dinner pancakes.

Ethnic Foods

If you're not in the mood for meat and potatoes, sample some of Amsterdam's abundant ethnic offerings.

Indonesian (Indisch): The tastiest "Dutch" food is Indonesian, from the former colony. Find any Indisch restaurant and experience a *rijsttafel* (rice table). With as many as 30 spicy dishes and a big bowl of rice (or noodles), a *rijsttafel* can be split and still fill two hungry tourists. *Nasi rames* is a cheaper, smaller version of a *rijsttafel*. Another popular dish is *bami goreng*—stir-fried noodles served with meat, vegetables, and *rijsttafel* items. *Nasi goreng* is like *bami*, but comes with fried rice. *Saté* is skewered meat, and *gado-gado* consists of steamed vegetables and hard-boiled eggs with peanut sauce. Among the most common sauces are peanut, red chili *(sambal)*, and dark soy.

Middle Eastern: Try a *shoarma* (roasted lamb with garlic in pita bread, served with bowls of different sauces), falafel, gyros, or a *doner kebab*.

Surinamese (Surinaamse): Surinamese cuisine is a mix of Caribbean and Indonesian influences, featuring *roti* (spiced chicken wrapped in a tortilla) and rice (white or fried) served with meats in sauces (curry and spices). Why Surinamese food in Amsterdam? In 1667, Holland traded New York City ("New Amsterdam") to Britain in exchange for the small country of Suriname (which borders Guyana on the northeast coast of South America). For the next three centuries, Suriname (renamed Dutch Guyana) was a Dutch colony, which is why it has indigenous Indians, Creoles, and Indonesian immigrants who all speak Dutch. When Suriname gained independence in 1975, 100,000 Surinamese emigrated to Amsterdam, sparking a rash of Surinamese fast-food outlets.

Drinks

Beer: Order "a beer," and you'll get a *pils,* a light lager/pilsner-type beer in a 10-ounce glass with a thick head leveled off with a stick. (Typical brands are Heineken, Grolsch, Oranjeboom, and Amstel.) A common tap beer is Palm Speciale, an amber ale served in a stemmed, wide-mouth glass. Belgian beers are popular, always available in bottles and sometimes on tap. *Witte* (white) beer is light-colored and summery, sometimes served with a lemon slice (it's like American Hefeweizen, but yeastier).

Jenever: This is Dutch gin made from juniper berries. *Jong* (young) is sharper; *oude* (old) is mellow. Served chilled, *jenever* (yah-NAY-ver) is meant to be chugged with a *pils* chaser (this combination is called a *kopstoot*—head-butt). While cheese gets harder and sharper with age, *jenever* grows smooth and soft. Old *jenever* is best.

Liqueur: You'll find a variety of local fruit brandies and cognacs.

Wine: Dutch people drink a lot of fine wine, but it's almost all imported.

Coffee: The Dutch love their coffee, enjoying many of the same drinks (espresso, cappuccino) served in American or Italian coffee shops. Coffee usually comes with a small spice cookie. A *koffie verkeerd* (fer-KEERT, "coffee wrong") is an espresso with a lot of steamed milk.

Soft Drinks: You'll find the full array.

Orange Juice: Many cafés/bars have a juicer for making fresh-squeezed orange juice.

Water: The Dutch (unlike many Europeans) drink tap water with meals, but many prefer mineral water, still or sparkling (Spa brand is popular).

RESTAURANTS

Of Amsterdam's thousand-plus restaurants, no one knows which are best. I'd pick an area and wander. The rowdy food ghetto thrives around Leidseplein; wander along Leidsedwarsstraat, Restaurant Row. The area around Spui canal and that end of Spuistraat is also trendy and not as noisy. For fewer crowds and more charm, find something in the Jordaan district. Most hoteliers keep a reliable eating list for their neighborhood and know which places keep their travelers happy.

Here are some handy places to consider.

Near Spui, in the Center

The first four places cluster along the colorful, student-filled Grimburgwal lane, near the intersection of Spui and Rokin (midway between Dam Square and the Mint Tower).

Restaurants and Coffeeshops

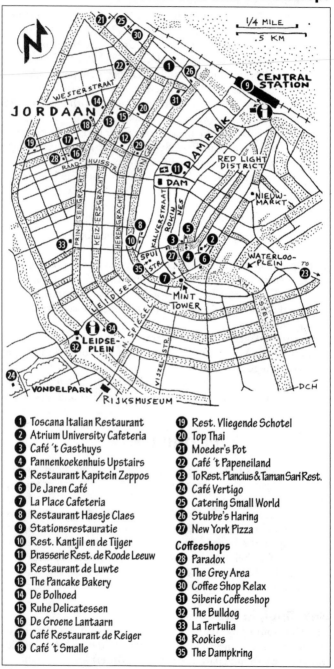

1 Toscana Italian Restaurant
2 Atrium University Cafeteria
3 Café 't Gasthuys
4 Pannenkoekenhuis Upstairs
5 Restaurant Kapitein Zeppos
6 De Jaren Café
7 La Place Cafeteria
8 Restaurant Haesje Claes
9 Stationsrestauratie
10 Rest. Kantjil en de Tijger
11 Brasserie Rest. de Roode Leeuw
12 Restaurant de Luwte
13 The Pancake Bakery
14 De Bolhoed
15 Ruhe Delicatessen
16 De Groene Lantaarn
17 Café Restaurant de Reiger
18 Café 't Smalle

19 Rest. Vliegende Schotel
20 Top Thai
21 Moeder's Pot
22 Café 't Papeneiland
23 To Rest. Plancius & Taman Sari Rest.
24 Café Vertigo
25 Catering Small World
26 Stubbe's Haring
27 New York Pizza

Coffeeshops
28 Paradox
29 The Grey Area
30 Coffee Shop Relax
31 Siberie Coffeeshop
32 The Bulldog
33 La Tertulia
34 Rookies
35 The Dampkring

Atrium University Cafeteria feeds students and travelers well at great prices. Enjoy the budget eats among all the Amsterdam University students (€6 meals, Mon–Fri 11:00–15:00 & 17:00–19:30, closed Sat–Sun, from Spui, walk west down Landebrug Steeg past canalside Café 't Gasthuys 3 blocks to Oudezijds Achterburgwal 237, go through arched doorway on the right; tel. 020/525-3999).

Café 't Gasthuys, one of Amsterdam's many brown cafés (so called for their smoke-stained walls), has a busy dumbwaiter cranking out light lunches, good sandwiches, and reasonably priced dinners. It offers a long bar, a fine secluded back room, peaceful canalside seating, and sometimes slow service (€11 dinner specials, daily 12:00–16:30 & 17:30–22:00, Grimburgwal 7, tel. 020/624-8230).

Pannenkoekenhuis Upstairs is a tiny and characteristic perch up some extremely steep stairs, where Arno Jakobs cooks and serves delicious €7 pancakes to four tables (daily 12:00–19:00, Grimburgwal 2, tel. 020/626-5603).

Restaurant Kapitein Zeppos, named for an old-time Belgian TV star, serves French-Dutch food amid dressy yet unpretentious 1940s ambiénce. The light lunch specials—soups and sandwiches—cost €5–10. Dinners go for about €20 (€30 *menu*, daily 11:00–15:30 & 17:30–23:00, good Belgian beer on tap, just off Grimburgwal at Gebed Zonder End 5, tel. 020/624-2057).

De Jaren Café (literally "The Years Café") is a chic yet inviting place—clearly a favorite with locals. Upstairs is the minimalist restaurant with a top-notch salad bar and a canal-view deck (serving €12–15 dinners after 17:30, including fish, meat, and veggie dishes, and salad bar). Downstairs is a modern Amsterdam café, great for light lunches (soups, salads, and sandwiches, served all day and evening), or just coffee over a newspaper. On a sunny day, the café's canalside patio is a fine spot to nurse a drink (daily 10:00–24:00, Nieuwe Doelenstraat 20–22, a long block up from Muntplein, tel. 020/625-5771).

La Place, on the ground floor of the Vroom & Dreesman department store, has an abundant, colorful array of fresh, appealing food served cafeteria-style. It has a non-smoking section and a small outdoor terrace upstairs. This bustling place has a lively market feel and lots of great vegetables (Mon–Sat 10:00–20:00, Thu until 21:00, Sun 12:00–20:00, at the end of Kalverstraat, near Mint Tower, tel. 020/622-0171). For fast and healthy take-out food (sandwiches, yogurt, fruit cups, and more), try the bakery on the department store's ground floor.

Restaurant Haesje Claes, popular with tour groups, offers traditional Dutch cooking in the center. It's the Dutch equivalent of TGI Friday's: big, with fast service, edible food, and reasonable prices (€20 *menu*, daily 12:00–22:00, Spuistraat 275, tel. 020/624-9998). The area around it is a huge and festive bar scene.

Restaurant Kantjil en de Tijger is a plain yet thriving place, full of happy eaters who know a good value. The food is purely Indonesian; the waiters are happy to explain your many enticing options. Their three *rijsttafels* (traditional "rice tables" with 11 dishes) range from €20–30 per person (ask for a description of each). While they are designed for two people, there's plenty food for more; three people can make a meal by getting a *rijsttafel* for two, and for good form, ordering a bowl of soup or light dish for the third person (daily 16:30–22:30, reserve on weekends, mostly indoor with a little outdoor seating, non-smoking section, Spuistraat 291, tel. 020/620-0994).

Kantjil To Go is a tiny take-out bar serving up inexpensive Indonesian fare (€4–6 meals, vegetarian specials, daily 12:00–21:00, storefront at Nieuwezijds Voorburgwal 342, connected through a back hallway to main sit-down restaurant listed directly above, tel. 020/620-3074).

In the Train Station

Stationsrestauratie is a surprisingly good budget, self-service option inside the station on platform 2 (daily 8:00–20:00). The entire platform 2 is lined with eateries, including the tall, venerable, 1920s-style First Class Grand Café.

Near Dam Square

Brasserie Restaurant de Roode Leeuw offers a respite from the crush of Damrak. Choose the restaurant in back (finer service and tablecloths, higher prices) or the brasserie in front (casual, simpler menu from same kitchen, better people-watching on Damrak). Either way, you'll get a menu filled with traditional Dutch food, good service, and the company of plenty of tourists (restaurant: €18–23 entrées, €30 for a 3-course *menu* with lots of intriguing choices; brasserie: €10–13 entrées; daily 12:00–22:00, Damrak 93–94, tel. 020/555-0666).

Near the Anne Frank House and in the Jordaan District

Nearly all of these places are within a few scenic blocks of the Anne Frank House, providing handy lunches and atmospheric dinners in Amsterdam's most characteristic neighborhood.

Restaurant de Luwte is romantic, located on a picturesque street overlooking a canal, with lots of candles, a muted but fresh modern interior, a few cool outdoor canalside tables, and French Mediterranean cuisine (€20 entrées, €32 for a 3-course *menu*, big dinner salads for €16, non-smoking section, daily 18:00–22:00,

Leliegracht 26–28, tel. 020/625-8548, Marko).

The Pancake Bakery serves good pancakes in a nothing-special, family atmosphere. The menu features a fun selection of ethnic-themed pancakes—including Indonesian, for those who want two experiences in one (€8–12 pancakes, splitting is OK, 25 percent discount with *I amsterdam* Card, daily 12:00–21:30, Prinsengracht 191, tel. 020/625-1333).

De Bolhoed serves serious vegetarian and vegan food in a colorful setting that Buddha would dig (€15 meals, light lunches, daily 12:00–22:00, serious dinners from 17:00, Prinsengracht 60, tel. 020/626-1803).

De Groene Lantaarn (literally "The Green Lantern") is fun for fondue. The menu offers fish, meat, and cheese (Dutch and Swiss) with salad and fruit for €17–25 (Thu–Sun from 18:00, closed Mon–Wed, a few blocks into the Jordaan at Bloemgracht 47, tel. 020/620-2088).

Café Restaurant de Reiger must offer the best cooking of any *eetcafé* in the Jordaan. It's famous for its fresh ingredients and delightful bistro ambience. In addition to an English menu, ask for a translation of the €15–18 daily specials on the chalkboard. They're proud of their fresh fish. The café, which is crowded late and on weekends, takes no reservations, but you're welcome to have a drink at the bar while you wait (glass of house wine-€2.50). While there's a non-smoking section in front, the energy is with the smokers in the back room (daily 18:00–22:30, veggie options, Nieuwe Leliestraat 34, tel. 020/624-7426).

Café 't Smalle is extremely charming, with three zones where you can enjoy a light lunch or a drink: canalside, inside around the bar, and up some steep stairs in a quaint little loft. While the café is open daily until midnight, simple meals (salads, soup, and fresh sandwiches) are served only from 12:00 to 17:00 (plenty of fine Belgian beers on tap and interesting wines by the glass posted, at Egelantiersgracht 12 where it hits Prinsengracht, tel. 020/623-9617).

Restaurant Vliegende Schotel is a folksy, unvarnished little Jordaan eatery decorated with children's crayon art. Its cheap and fun menu features fish and vegetarian fare. Choose a table (I'd avoid the empty non-smoking section and eat with the regulars), and then order at the counter. Nothing trendy about this place—just locals who like vegetarian food and don't want to cook. The €8 *Vliegende Schotel* salad is a vegetarian extravaganza (€8–11 entrées, wine by the glass, daily 17:00–23:00, Nieuwe Leliestraat 162, tel. 020/625-2041).

Moeder's Pot, a six-table neighborhood eatery with great character and charm, is gruff, with the smell of fried food and cigarettes. Hearty main courses come with fried potatoes and vegetables, applesauce, and salad. The place is not central, but puts you in a charming little neighborhood at the seaside edge of the Jordaan (€7–15 entrées, Mon–Sat 17:00–22:00, closed Sun and holidays, Vinkenstraat 119, tel. 020/623-7643).

Catering Small World is a cozy sandwich bar with good coffee, the best muffins in town, and only a few seats (€4–10 items, Mon–Sat 10:30–20:00, Sun 12:00–20:00, Binnen Oranjestraat 14).

Ruhe Delicatessen, run for decades by Mr. Ruhe, is the perfect late-night deli for a quick, cheap picnic dinner (a block from recommended Hotel Toren at Prinsenstraat 13, daily 12:00–22:00, tel. 020/626-7438).

Top Thai, a block from Hotel Toren, offers top-quality meals for under €20, either to enjoy at their restaurant or take out (daily 16:30–22:30, Herenstraat 22, tel. 020/6234633, delivery tel. 020/6881305, www.topthai.nl).

Toscana Italian Restaurant is the Jordaan's favorite place for good, inexpensive Italian cuisine, including pizza, in a woody Dutch-beer-hall setting (pizza-€4–8, pastas-€7, daily 16:00–24:00, Haarlemmerstraat 130, tel. 020/622-0353).

Drinks Only: **Café 't Papeneiland,** a classic brown café with Delft tiles, an evocative old stove, and a stay-awhile perch overlooking a canal with welcoming benches, has been the neighborhood hangout since the 17th century (drinks but no food, overlooking northwest end of Prinsengracht at #2, tel. 020/624-1989). It feels a little exclusive; patrons who come here to drink and chat aren't eager to see it overrun by tourists. The café's name literally means "Papists' Island," since this was once a refuge for Catholics; there used to be an escape tunnel here for priests on the run.

Near the Botanical Garden and Dutch Resistance Museum

Restaurant Plancius, adjacent to the Dutch Resistance Museum, is a mod, handy spot for lunch. Its good indoor and outdoor seating make it popular with the broadcasters from the nearby local TV studios (creative breakfasts, light €4–8 lunches and €15–18 dinners, daily 10:00–22:00, Plantage Kerklaan 61a, tel. 020/330-9469).

Taman Sari Restaurant is the local choice for Indonesian, serving hearty, quality €9.50 dinners and *rijsttafel* dinners for €16–22.50 (daily 17:00–23:00, Plantage Kerklaan 32, tel. 020/623-7130).

Near Vondelpark

Café Vertigo offers a fun selection of excellent soups and sandwiches. The service can be slow, but if you grab an outdoor table, you can watch the world spin by (daily 11:00–24:00, beneath Film Museum, Vondelpark 3, tel. 020/612-3021).

Munching Cheap

Traditional fish stands sell €3 herring sandwiches and other salty treats, usually from easy-to-understand photo menus. **Stubbe's Haring**, where the Stubbe family has been selling herring for 100 years, is handy and well-established (Tue–Sat 10:00–18:00, closed Sun–Mon, at the locks where Singel canal arrives at the train station). Grab a sandwich and have a picnic canalside. There's another stand at the Westerkerk next to the Anne Frank House.

New York Pizza serves hearty €2.50 pizza slices that are much-loved by local students (same price munched on a stool or to go; at Spui 2 just across from the end of Rokin Canal). Another New York Pizza is at Leidsestraat 23.

SMOKING

Tobacco

A third of Dutch people smoke tobacco. You don't have to like it, but expect it—in restaurants, bars, bus stops, almost everywhere. Holland has a long tradition as a smoking culture, being among the first to import the tobacco plant from the New World. Tobacco shops, such as the House of Hajenius, glorify the habit (see page 71), yet the Dutch people are among the healthiest in the world. Tanned, trim, firm, 60-something Dutch people sip their beer, take a drag, and ask me why Americans murder themselves with Big Macs.

Still, their version of the Surgeon General is finally waking up to the drug's many potential health problems. Since 2002, warning stickers bigger than America's are required on cigarette packs, and some of them are almost comically blunt, such as: Smoking will make you impotent...and then you die. (The warnings prompted gag stickers like, "If you can read this, you're healthy enough," and "Life can kill you.")

Smoking was recently prohibited on trains. It's unclear how much this will be obeyed or enforced.

Marijuana (a.k.a. Cannabis)

Amsterdam, Europe's counterculture mecca, thinks the concept of a "victimless crime" is a contradiction in terms. Heroin and cocaine are strictly illegal in the Netherlands, and the police stringently enforce laws prohibiting their sale and use. But, while hard drugs are definitely out, marijuana causes about as much excitement as a bottle of beer. If tourists call an ambulance after smoking too much pot, medics just say, "Drink something sweet and walk it off."

Throughout the Netherlands, you'll see "coffeeshops"— pubs selling marijuana. The minimum age for purchase is 18.

Coffeeshops can sell up to five grams of marijuana per person per day. Locals buy marijuana by asking, "Can I see the cannabis menu?" The menu looks like the inventory of a drug bust. Display cases show various joints or baggies for sale.

The Dutch usually include a little tobacco in their prerolled joints (though a few coffeeshops sell joints of pure marijuana). To avoid the tobacco, smokers roll their own (cigarette papers are free with the purchase, dispensed like toothpicks) or borrow a pipe or bong. Baggies of marijuana usually cost €10–15, and a smaller amount means better quality. As long as you're a paying customer (e.g., buy a cup of coffee), you can pop into any coffeeshop and light up, even if you didn't buy your pot there.

Pot should never be bought on the street in Amsterdam. Well-established coffeeshops are considered much safer. Coffeeshop owners have an interest in keeping their trade safe and healthy. They warn Americans—unused to the strength of the local stuff—to try a lighter leaf. In fact, they are generally very patient in explaining the varieties available.

Several forms of the cannabis plant are sold. Locals smoke more hashish (the sap of the cannabis plant) than the leaf of the plant (which they call "marijuana" or "grass"). White varieties (called "White Widow" or "Amsterdam White") are popular, featuring marijuana with white, fiber-like strands.

So what am I? Pro-marijuana? Let's put it this way: I agree with the Dutch people, who remind me that a society either has to allow alternative lifestyles...or build more prisons. Last year alone, more than 700,000 Americans were arrested for marijuana use; only Russia incarcerates more of its citizens. The Dutch are not necessarily pro-marijuana, but they do believe that a prohibition on marijuana would cause more problems than it solves. Statistics support the Dutch belief that their system works. They have fewer hard drug problems than other countries. And they believe America's policy—like so many other touchy issues in the news lately—is based on electoral politics, rather than rationality.

To learn more about marijuana, drop by Amsterdam's Cannabis College or the Hash, Marijuana, and Hemp Museum. To see where cannabis growers buy their seeds, stop by the Sensi Seed Bank Store. These three places are located on Oudezijds Achterburgwal street (see page 88). Back home, if you'd like to support an outfit dedicated to taking the crime out of pot, read up on the National Organization for the Reform of Marijuana Laws (www.norml.org).

Coffeeshops

Most of downtown Amsterdam's coffeeshops feel grungy and foreboding to anyone over 30. The neighborhood places (and those in small towns around the countryside) are much more inviting to people without piercings, tattoos, and favorite techno artists. I've listed a few places with a more pub-like ambience for Americans wanting to go local, but within reason. For locations, see the map on page 166.

Paradox is the most *gezellig* (cozy) coffeeshop I found—a mellow, graceful place. The managers, Ludo and Jan, are patient with descriptions and happy to walk you through all your options. This is a rare coffeeshop that serves light meals. The juice is fresh, the music is easy, and the neighborhood is charming. Colorful murals with bright blue skies are all over the walls, creating a fresh and open feeling (loaner bongs, games, daily 10:00–20:00, 2 blocks from Anne Frank House at Eerste Bloemdwarsstraat 2, tel. 020/623-5639, www.paradoxamsterdam.demon.nl).

The Grey Area coffeeshop is a cool, welcoming, and smoky hole-in-the-wall appreciated among local aficionados as winner of Amsterdam's Cannabis Cup awards. Judging by the proud autographed photos on the wall, many famous Americans have dropped in. You're welcome to just nurse a bottomless cup of coffee (open Tue–Sun high noon to 20:00, closed Mon, between Dam Square and Anne Frank House at Oude Leliestraat 2, tel. 020/420-4301, www.greyarea.nl, run by 2 friendly Americans, Steven and Jon—who know the value of a bottomless cup of coffee).

Coffee Shop Relax is simply the neighborhood pub serving a different drug. It's relaxed and has a helpful staff and homey atmosphere, with plants, couches, and bar seating. The great, straightforward menu chalked onto the board details what it has to offer (daily 10:00–24:00, a bit out of the way, but a pleasant Jordaan walk to Binnen Orangestraat 9).

Siberie Coffeeshop is central, but feels cozy, with a friendly canal-side ambience (daily 11:00–23:00, Internet access, helpful staff, fun English menu that explains the personality of each item, Brouwersgracht 11, www.siberie.net).

Coffeeshop Interlude

A tourist walks into a coffeeshop and asks the bartender, "Can I see the cannabis menu?"

"Yes, of course," says the bartender, and directs her to a desk near the door, where the list of marijuana products is displayed. The woman is no cannabis connoisseur, and she's a bit dazzled by the exotic names on the menu and the sheer variety of substances produced from the same plant. But soon, her eye zeroes in on some familiar words:

Hash

Thai baby	1 gram	€13
Jungle stick	1 gram	€15
Etc.		

Marihuana

Black Widow	2.1 g	€13
Amsterdam White	1.9 g	€12
Etc.		

Joints

With tobacco	4 joints	€15
Pure marihuana	4 joints	€15
Etc.		

Not wanting to appear unsophisticated, she thinks quickly: "I don't want hash (the waxy resin), because I'd have to mix it with tobacco to smoke it. I just want the leafy stuff, but I don't have a pipe, and I couldn't roll a joint (cigarette of marijuana leaves) to save my life."

"Four joints of marijuana, please," she tells the man at the desk. She pays the man, takes the joints to an empty table, borrows a lighter from a fellow patron, and smokes. Chiding herself for being so timid, she marvels at how legal it all is. She buys an orange juice at the bar, then goes back outside and orders three pastries from a bakery.

La Tertulia is a sweet little mother-and-daughter-run place with pastel decor and a cheery terrarium ambience (Tue–Sat 11:00–19:00, closed Sun–Mon, sandwiches, brownies, games, Prinsengracht 312, www.coffeeshopamsterdam.com).

The Bulldog is the high-profile, leading touristy chain of coffeeshops. These establishments are young but welcoming, with

reliable selections. They're pretty comfortable for green tourists wanting to just hang out for a while. The flagship branch, in a former police station right on Leidseplein, is very handy, offering fun outdoor seating where you can watch the world skateboard by (daily 9:00–1:00 in the morning, Leidseplein 17, tel. 020/625-6278, www.bulldog.nl). They opened up their first café (on the canal near the Old Church in the Red Light District) in 1975.

Rookies, a block east of Leidseplein along "Restaurant Row," is one of the rare coffeeshops that sells individual, prerolled, decent-quality joints of pure marijuana—with no tobacco (€5.50, daily 10:00–1:00 in the morning, Fri–Sat until 3:00 in the morning, Korte Leidsedwarsstraat 14).

The Dampkring is one of very few coffeeshops that also serve alcohol. It's a high profile and busy place, filled with a young clientele, but the owners still take the time to explain what they offer. Scenes from the movie *Ocean's Twelve* were filmed here (daily 11:00–1:00 in the morning, close to Spui at Handboogstraat 29).

Smartshops

These business establishments (one is listed on page 74) sell "natural" drugs that are legal. Many are harmless nutritional supplements, but they also sell hallucinogenic mushrooms, stimulants similar to Ecstasy, and strange drug cocktails rolled into joints. It's all perfectly legal, but if you've never taken drugs recreationally, don't start here.

SHOPPING

Amsterdam brings out the browser even in those who were not born to shop. Ten general markets, open six days a week (closed Sun), keep folks who brake for garage sales pulling U-turns. Markets include Waterlooplein (the flea market); the huge Albert Cuyp street market; and various flower markets (such as the Singel canal Flower Market near Mint Tower, which is open daily).

When you need to buy something but don't know where to go, two chain stores—Hema and Vroom & Dreesmann—are handy for everything from inexpensive clothes and notebooks to food and cosmetics. Hema is at Kalverstraat 212, in Kalvertoren (Mon–Sat 9:30–18:30, Thu until 21:00, Sun 12:00–18:00), and Vroom & Dreesman is at Kalverstraat 200 (Mon–Sat 10:00–20:00, Thu until 21:00, Sun 12:00–20:00; great La Place cafeteria on ground floor). Two other department stores are De Bijenkorf (old-time fancy) and Metz & Co. (decent but getting dowdy). The most expensive shopping street is P.C. Hooftstraat, between Museumplein and Vondelpark.

For more information, pick up the TI's *Shopping in Amsterdam* brochure. To find out how to get a VAT (Value Added Tax) refund on your purchases, see page 12.

Most shops in the center are open 10:00–18:00 (Thu until 21:00); the businesslike Dutch know no siesta, but many shopkeepers take Sunday and Monday mornings off. Supermarkets are open Monday–Saturday 8:00–20:00 (closed Sun).

Amsterdam's Top Shopping Zones

Jordaan—The colorful, old, working-class district of the Jordaan and its main drag, Westerstraat, are a wonderland of funky, artsy shops. On Mondays, you'll find busy markets at the end of Westerstraat (Noordermarkt) and the neighboring street, Lindengracht.

Leidsestraat—This bustling shopping street has elegant and trendy shops, along with the department store, Metz & Co.

The Nine Little Streets—De Negen Straatjes is home to 190 diverse shops mixing festive, creative, nostalgic, practical, and artistic items. The cross streets make a tic-tac-toe with a couple of canals and bicycle-friendly canalside streets just west of Kalverstraat. (Look for the zone where Hartenstraat, Wolvenstraat, and Huidenstraat cross the Keizersgracht and Herengracht canals.)

Kalverstraat–Heiligeweg–Spui—This is the busiest shopping corridor in town. Kalverstraat, a pedestrian street, is a human traffic jam of low-end shoppers. It feels soulless, but if you explore the fringes, there are some interesting places.

Spiegelkwartier—Located between the Rijksmuseum and the city center, this is *the* place for art and antiques. You'll find 70 dealers offering 17th-century furniture, old Delftware, Oriental art, clocks, jewelry, and Art Nouveau doodads. Wander down Spiegelgracht and Nieuwe Spiegelstraat.

Prinsheerlijk—Along Herenstraat and Prinsenstraat, you'll find top-end fashion, interior design, and gift shops. If you're looking for jewelry, accessories, trendy clothing, and fancy delicatessens, this may be an expensive but rewarding stroll.

Magna Plaza Shopping Center—Formerly the main post office, this grand 19th-century building has been transformed into a stylish mall with 40 boutiques. You'll find fashion, luxury goods, and gift shops galore. It's just behind the Royal Palace a block off Dam Square (see page 92).

Albert Cuyp Market—Amsterdam's biggest open-air market, stretching for several blocks along Albert Cuypstraat, bustles daily (roughly 9:00–17:00) except Sunday. You'll find fish, exotic vegetables, bolts of fabric, pantyhose, bargain clothes, ethnic food stands (especially Surinamese *rotis*), and great people-watching. It's located a 10-minute walk east of Museumplein, and a block south of the Heineken Brewery (tram #16 or #24).

Popular Souvenirs

Amsterdam has lots of one-of-a-kind specialty stores. Poke around and see what you can find. If you want to bring home edibles and drinkables, check "Custom Regulations" first (page 13).

Wooden Shoes—Originally key for navigating soggy Amsterdam, now something to clomp around in.

Delftware—Ceramic plates, vases, and tiles decorated with a fake Chinese blue-and-white design popularized in the 1600s. Only a few licensed places sell the real stuff (expensive) and antiques (very expensive). You can find fireplace tiles (cheap) at most gift shops.

Diamonds—Cut or uncut, expensive or really expensive. Diamond dealers offer free cutting and polishing demos at their shops. Gassan Diamonds, near Rembrandt's House, is best (page 50); Coster is on Potterstraat, behind the Rijksmuseum (page 41); and the Amsterdam Diamond Center is on Dam Square.

Beers—A yeasty, frothy souvenir.

Jenever—Dutch gin (made from juniper berries) sold in traditional stone bottles.

Marijuana Pipes—Need to be clean and unused, because even a little residue can get you busted at U.S. Customs. Note that, these days, American laws are written in a way that—technically—even importing an unused pipe could get you arrested.

Chocolate—Belgian or Dutch Verkade or Droste cocoa in tins.

Flower Seeds and Bulbs—Packed with a seal that promises they are U.S. Customs–friendly.

Posters and Art Postcards—Good selection at the Van Gogh Museum bookshop (which sells mailing tubes to protect posters).

Old Maps—Capturing the Golden Age.

Old Books—Treasures found in musty bookshelves.

NIGHTLIFE

Amsterdam hotels serve breakfast until 11:00 because so many people—visitors and locals—live for nighttime in Amsterdam.

On summer evenings, people flock to the main squares for drinks at outdoor tables. Leidseplein is the glitziest, surrounded by theaters, restaurants, and nightclubs. The slightly quieter Rembrandtplein (with adjoining Thorbeckeplein) is the center of gay discos. Spui features a full city block of bars. And Nieuwmarkt, on the east edge of the Red Light District, is a bit rough, but is probably the most local.

The Red Light District (particularly Oudezijds Achterburgwal) is less sleazy at night, almost carnival-like, as the neon comes on and the streets fill with Japanese tour groups (✪ see Red Light District Walk, page 78).

Information

Boom! and *Uitkrant* are two free publications (available at TIs and many bars) that list festivals and performances of theater, film, dance, cabaret, and live rock, pop, jazz, and classical music. The irreverent *Boom!*, which has the best lowdown on the youth and nightlife scene, is packed with practical tips and countercultural insights (includes €3 discount on the Boom Chicago R-rated comedy theater act described below). *Uitkrant* is in Dutch, but it's just a calendar of events, and anyone can figure out the name of the event and its date, time, and location.

There's also *What's On in Amsterdam*, *Time Out Amsterdam*, the Thursday edition of many Dutch papers, and the *International Herald Tribune*'s special Netherlands inserts (all sold at newsstands).

The Last Minute Ticket Shop at Stadsschouwburg Theater (Leidseplein 26, tel. 0900-0191, www.lastminuteticketshop.nl) is the best one-stop-shopping box office for theater, classical music, and major rock shows. They also sell half-price, same-day (after 12:00) tickets to certain shows.

Music
You'll find classical music at the Concertgebouw (free 12:30 lunch concerts on Wed, at far south end of Museumplein, tel. 020/671-8345, www.concertgebouw.nl) and at the former Beurs (on Damrak). For opera and dance, try the opera house on Waterlooplein (tel. 020/551-8100). In the summer, Vondelpark hosts open-air concerts.

Two rock music (and hip-hop) clubs near Leidseplein are Melkweg (Lijnbaansgracht 234a, tel. 020/531-8181, www.melkweg .nl) and Paradiso (Weteringschans 6, tel. 020/626-4521, www .paradiso.nl; see page 76). They present big-name acts that you might recognize if you're younger than I am.

Jazz has a long tradition at the Bimhuis nightclub, east of the Red Light District (concerts Thu–Sat, Oude Schans 73–77, www .bimhuis.nl).

The nearby town of Haarlem offers free pipe organ concerts on Tuesdays in summer at its 15th-century church, the Grote Kerk (at 20:15 mid-May–mid Oct, see page 193).

Comedy
Boom Chicago, an R-rated comedy improv act, was started 10 years ago by a group of Americans on a graduation tour. They have been entertaining tourists and locals alike ever since. The show is a series of rude, clever, and high-powered improvisational skits offering a raucous look at Dutch culture and local tourism (€18– 20, 25 percent discount with *I amsterdam* Card, Sun–Fri at 20:15, Fri also at 23:30, Sat at 19:30 and 22:45, in 300-seat Leidseplein Theater, Leidseplein 12, tel. 020/423-0101, www.boomchicago.nl). They do various shows: *Best of Boom* (a collection of their greatest hits over the years) as well as new shows for locals and return customers. You'll sit in a 300-seat theater with optional meal and drink service.

Theater
Amsterdam is one of the world centers for experimental live theater (much of it in English). Many theaters cluster around the street called the Nes, which stretches south from Dam Square.

Movies
Catch modern movies in the 1920s setting of the classic Tuschinski Theater (between Muntplein and Rembrandtplein, described on page 43). The Amsterdam Film Museum, which has

some evening showings, is also worth checking out (Vondelstraat 69, near Vondelpark, tel. 020/589-1400, www.filmmuseum.nl, see page 43). It's not unusual for movies at many cinemas to be sold out—consider buying tickets during the day.

Museums

Several of Amsterdam's museums stay open late. The Anne Frank House is open daily until 21:00 in summmmer (April–Aug) and until 19:00 the rest of the year. The Rijksmuseum and Van Gogh Museum are open on Fridays until 22:00. The Hash, Marijuana, and Hemp Museum is open daily until 22:00. And there are the sex museums (Erotic Museum daily until 24:00, Damrak Sex Museum daily until 23:30).

Skating After Dark

While there hasn't been a good canal freeze since 1996, Amsterdammers still get their skating fix on wheels every Friday night in summer. Huge groups don inline skates and meet at the Film Museum in Vondelpark (at 20:00 or 20:30). Tourists can roll along; there's a skate-rental shop at the far end of the park (Vondel Tuin Rental, €5/hr, daily 11:00–24:00, tel. 020/664-5091).

HAARLEM

ORIENTATION AND SIGHTS

Cute and cozy, yet authentic and handy to the airport, Haarlem is a fine home base, giving you small-town warmth overnight, with easy access (15 min by train) to wild and crazy Amsterdam during the day.

Bustling Haarlem gave America's Harlem its name back when New York was New Amsterdam, a Dutch colony. For centuries, Haarlem has been a market town, buzzing with shoppers heading home with fresh bouquets, nowadays by bike.

Enjoy the market on Monday (clothing) or Saturday (general), when the square bustles like a Brueghel painting, with cheese, fish, flowers, and families. Make yourself at home; buy some flowers to brighten your hotel room.

OVERVIEW

(area code: 023)
Tourist Information
Haarlem's TI (VVV), at the train station, is friendlier, more helpful, and less crowded than Amsterdam's. Ask your Amsterdam questions here. They also offer train-travel advice and sell tickets for destinations in the Netherlands, Belgium, and Germany (April–Sept Mon–Fri 9:00–17:30, Sat 10:00–16:00, closed Sun; Oct–March Mon–Fri 9:30–17:00, Sat 10:00–15:00, closed Sun; tel. 0900-616-1600, €0.50/min, helpful parking brochure). The €1 *Holiday Magazine* is not necessary, but it's free if you buy the fine €2 town map. The TI also sells a €2 self-guided walking-tour map for overachievers. The little yellow computer terminal on the curb outside the TI prints out free maps anytime. (It's fun...just dial the street and hit "print." Drivers will also find these terminals stationed at roads coming into town.)

Haarlem

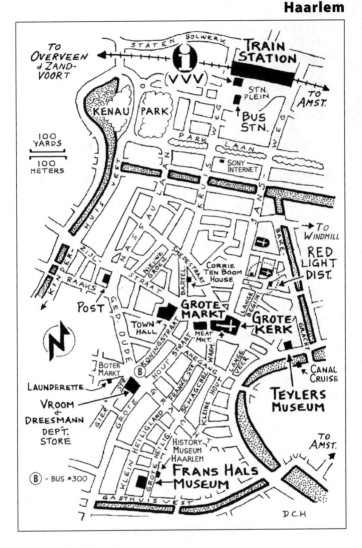

Arrival in Haarlem

By Train: As you walk out of Haarlem's train station (lockers available), the TI is on your right and the bus station is across the street. Two parallel streets flank the train station (Kruisweg and Jansweg). Head up either street, and you'll reach the town square and church within 10 minutes. If you need help, ask a local person to point you toward the Grote Markt (Market Square).

By Car: Parking is expensive on the streets (€2.50/hr) and cheaper in several central garages (€1.50/hr). Two main garages let you park overnight for €2 (at the train station and near the recommended Die Raeckse Hotel).

By Plane: For details on getting from Schiphol Airport into Haarlem, see page 242.

Helpful Hints

Blue Monday: Most sights are closed on Monday, except the church.

Money: The handy GWK currency exchange office at the train station offers fair rates (Mon–Fri 8:00–20:00, Sat 9:00–17:00, Sun 10:00–17:00).

Internet Access: Try **Internet Café Amadeus** (in Hotel Amadeus overlooking Market Square, €1.20/15 min, 25 percent discount with this book through 2006) or nearly any **coffeeshop** (if you don't mind marijuana smoke). Perhaps the cheapest place in town is **Sony Teletechniques** (€2/hr, daily 10:00–24:00, near train station at Lange Herenstraat 4).

Post Office: It's at Gedempte Oude Gracht 2 (Mon–Fri 9:00–18:00, Sat 10:00–13:30, closed Sun, has ATM).

Laundry: My Beautiful Launderette is handy and cheap (€6 self-service wash and dry, daily 8:30–20:30, €9 full service available Mon–Fri 9:00–17:00, near Vroom & Dreesmann department store at Boter Markt 20).

Bike Rental: You can rent bikes at the train station (€7.50/day, €50 deposit and passport number, Mon–Sat 6:00–24:00, Sun 7:30–24:00).

Local Guide: For a historical look at Haarlem, consider hiring Walter Schelfhout (€75/2-hr walk, tel. 023/535-5715, schelfhout@dutch.nl).

Bulb Flower Parade: On Saturday, April 22, 2006, an all-day Bulb Flower Parade of floats, decorated with real blossoms, wafts through eight towns, including Haarlem. The floats are parked in Haarlem at Gedempte Oude Gracht overnight, when they're illuminated, and through the next day.

SELF-GUIDED WALK

Welcome to Haarlem's Market Square

Haarlem's market square (Grote Markt), where 10 streets converge, is a ▲▲ sight and the town's delightful centerpiece...as it has been for 700 years. To enjoy a coffee or beer here, simmering in Dutch good living, is a quintessential European experience. In a recent study, the Dutch were found to be the most content people in Europe. In another study, the people of Haarlem were found to be the most content in the Netherlands. Observe. Sit and gaze at

Haarlem of the Golden Age

Parts of Haarlem still look like they did four centuries ago, when the city was a bustling commercial center rivaling Amsterdam. It's easy to imagine local merchants and their wives dressed in black with ruff collars, promenading the Market Square.

Back then, the town was a port on the large Haarlemmer Lake, with the North Sea only about five miles away. As well as being the tulip capital of the country, Haarlem was a manufacturing center, producing wool, silk, lace, damask cloth, furniture, smoking pipes (along with cheap, locally grown tobacco), and mass quantities of beer. Haarlemmers were notorious consumers of beer. It was a popular breakfast drink, and the average person drank six pints a day.

In 1585, the city got an influx of wealthy merchants when Spanish troops invaded the culturally rich city of Antwerp, driving Protestants and Jews north. Even when hard-line, moralistic Calvinists dominated Haarlem's politics, the city remained culturally and religiously diverse.

In the 1700s, Haarlem's economy declined, along with that of the Netherlands. In the succeeding centuries, industry—printing, textiles, ship building—once again made the city an economic force.

the church, appreciating the same scene Dutch artists captured in oil paintings that now hang in museums.

Just a few years ago, trolleys ran through the square, and cars were parked everywhere. But today, it's a people zone, with market stalls filling the square on Mondays and Saturdays and café tables on other days.

This is a great place to build a picnic with Haarlem finger foods—raw herring, local cheese (Gouda and Edam), a *frikandel* (little corn-dog sausage), french fries with mayonnaise, *stroopwafels* (waffles with syrup), *poffertjes* (little sugar doughnuts), or one of many different ethnic foods (falafel, *shoarma*, Indonesian dishes).

• *Overseeing the square is the...*

L. J. Coster Statue: Forty years before Gutenberg invented movable type, this man carved the letter *A* out of wood, dropped it

into some wet sand, and saw the imprint it left. He got the idea of making movable type out of wood (and later, he may have tried using lead). For Haarlemers, that was good enough, and they credit their man, Coster, with inventing modern printing. In the statue, Coster (c. 1370–1440) holds up a block of movable type and points to himself, saying, "I made this." How much Coster did is uncertain, but Gutenberg trumped him by building a printing press, casting type in metal, and pounding out the Bible.

• *Coster is facing the...*

Town Hall: While most of medieval Europe was ruled by kings, dukes, and barons, Haarlem has been largely self-governing since 1425. The town hall—built from a royal hunting lodge in the mid-1200s, then rebuilt after a 1351 fire—has served as Haarlem's town hall since about 1400. The facade dates from 1630.

The town drunk used to hang out on the bench in front of the town hall, where he'd expose himself to newlyweds coming down the stairs. The Dutch, rather than arresting the man, moved the bench.

• *Next to the church is the...*

Meat Market (Vleeshal), 1603: The fine Flemish Renaissance building nearest the cathedral is the old meat hall. It was built by the rich butchers' and leatherworkers' guilds. The meat market was on the ground floor, the leather was upstairs, and the cellar was filled with ice to keep the meat preserved. It's decorated with carved bits of early advertising—sheep and cows for sale. Today, rather than meat, the hall shows off temporary art exhibits (€5, Tue–Sat, 11:00–17:00, closed Mon, tel. 023/511-5775, www.dehallen.com).

SIGHTS

▲**Church (Grote Kerk)**—This 15th-century Gothic church (now Protestant) is worth a look, if only for its Oz-like organ (from 1738, 100 feet high). Its 5,000 pipes impressed both Handel and Mozart. Note how the organ, which fills the west end, seems to steal the show from the altar. Quirky highlights include a replica of Foucault's pendulum, the "Dog-Whipper's Chapel," and a 400-year-old cannonball.

To enter, find the small *Entrée* sign behind the church at Oude Groenmarkt 23 (€2, Mon–Sat 10:00–16:00, closed Sun to tourists, tel. 023/553-2040).

Consider attending (even part of) a **concert** to hear Holland's greatest pipe organ (regular free concerts Tue at 20:15 mid-May– mid-Oct, additional concerts Thu at 15:00 July–Aug, concerts nearly nightly at 20:15 during the organ competition in July, confirm schedule at TI or at www.bavo.nl; bring a sweater—the church isn't heated). ✪ See Grote Kerk Tour, page 193.

▲▲**Frans Hals Museum**—Haarlem is the hometown of Frans Hals, the foremost Dutch portrait painter of the 17th-century Golden Age. This refreshing museum, once an almshouse for old men back in 1610, displays many of his greatest paintings, done with his nearly Impressionistic style. You'll see group portraits and take-me-back paintings of old-time Haarlem (€7, Tue–Sat 11:00–17:00, Sun 12:00–17:00, closed Mon, Groot Heiligland 62, tel. 023/511-5775, www.franshalsmuseum.nl). Look for the 250-year-old dollhouse on display in a former chapel. ✪ See Frans Hals Museum Tour, page 202.

History Museum Haarlem—This small museum, across the street from the Frans Hals Museum, offers a glimpse of old Haarlem. Request the English version of the 10-minute video. Study the large-scale model of Haarlem in 1822 (when its fortifications were still intact), and enjoy the "time machine" computer and video display that show you various aspects of life in Haarlem at different points in history (€1, Tue–Sat 12:00–17:00, Sun 13:00–17:00, closed Mon, Groot Heiligland 47, tel. 023/542-2427). The adjacent architecture center (free) may be of interest to architects.

Corrie ten Boom House—Haarlem is home to Corrie ten Boom, popularized by *The Hiding Place,* her inspirational book and the movie that followed, about the ten Boom family's experience protecting Jews from the Nazis. Corrie ten Boom gives the other half of the Anne Frank story—the point of view of those who risked their lives to hide Dutch Jews during the Nazi occupation (1940–1945).

The clock shop was the ten Boom family business. The elderly father and his two daughters—Corrie and Betsy, both in their 50s—lived above the store and in the brick building attached in back (along Schoutensteeg alley). Corrie's bedroom was on the top floor at the back. This room was tiny to start with, but the family built a second, secret room (only about a foot deep) at the very back—"the hiding place," where they could hide six or seven Jews at a time.

Devoutly religious, the family had a long tradition of tolerance, having for generations hosted prayer meetings here in their home for both Jews and Christians.

The Gestapo, tipped off that the family was harboring Jews, burst into the ten Boom house. Finding a suspicious number of ration coupons, the Nazis arrested the family, but failed to find the six Jews in the hiding place (who later escaped). Corrie's father and sister died while in prison, but Corrie survived the Ravensbruck concentration camp to tell her story in her memoir.

The ten Boom House is open for 60-minute English tours; the tours are sometimes mixed with preaching (donation accepted, April–Oct Tue–Sat 10:00–16:00, Nov–March Tue–Sat 11:00–15:00, closed Sun–Mon, 50 yards north of Market Square at Barteljorisstraat 19; the clock-shop people get all wound up if you go inside—wait in the little side street at the door, where hourly tour times are posted; tel. 023/531-0823, www.corrietenboom.com).

▲**Teylers Museum**—Famous as the oldest museum in Holland, Teylers is a time-warp experience, filled with all sorts of fun curios for science buffs: fossils, minerals, primitive electronic gadgetry, and examples of 18th- and 19th-century technology. This place feels like a museum of a museum. They're serious about authenticity here: The presentation is perfectly preserved, right down to the original labels. Since there was no electricity in the olden days, you'll find no electric lighting...if it's dark outside, it's dark inside. The museum's benefactor, Pieter Teyler van der Hulst, was a very wealthy merchant who willed his estate, worth the equivalent of €80 million today, to a foundation whose mission was to "create and maintain a museum to stimulate art and science." (His last euro was spent in 1983, and now it's a national museum.) The museum opened in 1784, six years after Teyler's death. Add your name to the guest book that goes back literally to before Napoleon's visit here. The oval room—a temple of science and learning—is the core of the museum; the art gallery hangs paintings in the old style. While there are no English descriptions, there is an excellent audioguide (€5.50, Tue–Sat 10:00–17:00, Sun 12:00–17:00, closed Mon, Spaarne 16, tel. 023/531-9010, www.teylersmuseum.nl).

De Adriaan Windmill—Haarlem's old-time windmill, located just a 10-minute walk from the station and Teylers Museum, welcomes visitors with a short video, little museum, and fine town views (€2, Wed–Fri 13:00–16:00, Sat–Sun 10:00–16:00, closed Mon–Tue, Papentorenvest 1, tel. 023/545-0259).

Canal Cruise—Making a scenic 50-minute loop through and around Haarlem with a live guide who speaks up to four languages, these little trips by Woltheus Cruises are more relaxing

The Haarlemmermeer

The land between Haarlem and Amsterdam—where trains speed through, cattle graze, and 747s touch down—was once a lake the size of Washington, D.C.

In the 1500s, a series of high tides and storms caused the IJ River to breach its banks, flooding this sub-sea-level area and turning a bunch of shallow lakes into a single one nearly 15 feet deep, covering 70 square miles. By the 1800s, floods were licking at the borders of Haarlem and Amsterdam, and the residents needed to act. First, they dug a ring canal to channel away water (and preserve the lake's shipping business). Then, using steam engines, they pumped the lake dry, turning marshy soil into fertile ground. The Amsterdam–Haarlem train line that soon crossed the former lakebed was the country's first.

than informative (€7, May–Oct daily departures at the top of each hour from 12:00–17:00, closed Mon in May and Oct, no tours Nov–April, across canal from Teylers Museum at Spaarne 11a, tel. 023/535-7723).

Red Light District—Wander through a little Red Light District as precious as a Barbie doll—and legal since the 1980s (2 blocks northeast of Market Square, off Lange Begijnestraat, no senior or student discounts). Don't miss the mall marked by the red neon sign reading *'t Steegje* (free, on Begijnesteeg). The nearby *'t Poortje* (office park) costs €6.

Amsterdam to Haarlem Train Tour

Since you'll be commuting from Amsterdam to Haarlem, here's a tour to keep you entertained. Departing from Amsterdam, grab a seat on the right (with your back to Amsterdam, top deck if possible). Everything is on the right unless I say it's on the left.

You're riding the oldest train line in Holland. Across the harbor, behind the Amsterdam station, the tall brown skyscraper is the corporate office of **Royal Dutch Shell Oil.** The Dutch had the first multinational corporation (the United East India Company, back in the 17th century). And today, this international big-business spirit survives with huge companies such as Shell, Unilever, and Philips.

Leaving Amsterdam, you'll see the cranes and ships of its harbor—sizable, but nothing like the world's biggest in nearby Rotterdam.

On your left, a few minutes out of Amsterdam, find the old **windmill.** In front of it, the little garden plots and cottages are escapes for big-city people who probably don't even have a balcony.

Coming into the Sloterdijk Station (where trains connect for Amsterdam airport), you'll see huge office buildings, such as Dutch Telecom KPN. These grew up after the station made commuting easy.

Passing through a forest and by some houseboats, you enter a **polder**—reclaimed land. This is part of an ecologically sound farm zone, run without chemicals. Cows, pigs, and chickens run free—they're not raised in cages. The train tracks are on a dike, which provides a solid foundation not susceptible to floods. This way, the transportation system functions right through any calamity. Looking out at the distant dike, remember you're in the most densely populated country in Europe. On the horizon, sleek, modern windmills whirl.

On the right, just after the Ikea building, find a big, beige-and-white building. This is the **mint,** where currency is printed (top security, no advertising). This has long been a family business—see the name: Johan Enschede.

As the train slows down, you're passing through the Netherlands' biggest train-car maintenance facility and entering Haarlem. Look left. The domed building is a prison, built in 1901 and still in use. The windmill burned down in 1932 and was rebuilt in 2002.

When you cross the Spaarne River, you'll see the great church spire towering over Haarlem, as it has since medieval times—back when a fortified wall circled the town. Notice the white copy of the same spire capping the smaller church between the prison and the big church. This was the original sandstone steeple that stood atop the big church until structural problems forced them to move it to another church and build a new spire for the big church. Hop out into one of Holland's oldest stations. Art Nouveau decor from 1908 survives all around.

GROTE KERK TOUR

Haarlem's impressive Grote Kerk (Great Church), one of the best-known landmarks in the Netherlands, is visible from miles around, rising above the flat plain that surrounds it. From the Market Square, you see the church at a three-quarters angle, emphasizing both its length (240 feet) and its height (260 feet).

ORIENTATION

Cost: €2.

Hours: Mon–Sat 10:00–16:00, closed Sun to tourists, Sun service at 10:00 (May–Sept). There is a daily 15-minute prayer service at 12:45 and, in July–Aug, an evensong service on Sun at 19:00.

Getting There: The church is on the main square, a 10-minute walk south of the train station.

Information: Tel. 023/553-2040, www.bavo.nl.

Length of This Tour: Allow one hour.

Music: Consider attending even just part of a concert to hear Holland's greatest pipe organ. Free concerts are generally offered throughout the summer (Tue at 20:15 mid-May–mid-Oct, additional concerts Thu at 15:00 July–Aug; confirm schedule at TI or at Web site listed above). Every July, Haarlem hosts an organ festival, when Europe's top organists visit and perform throughout the month (free, concerts nearly nightly at 20:15).

Overview

After a fire destroyed the old church (1328), the Grote Kerk was built over a 150-year period (c. 1390–1540) in the late Gothic style of red and gray brick, topped with a slate-covered wood roof and a stacked tower bearing a golden crown and a rooster weathervane.

Builders raised money by cleverly hitting up both popes—back when there were two competing pontiffs, one in Avignon and one in Rome. The builders came home with two different "absolution bills," authorizing them to grant forgiveness to parishioners for donations. Apparently, Haarlem's sinners—not knowing for sure which pope was *the* pope—covered all their bases by giving twice for their forgiveness.

THE TOUR BEGINS

• *You'll enter the church from the side opposite the square. As you walk around the building, check out a few details...*

Exterior

Notice the rough buttress anchors, which were never needed. Money ran out, and the planned stone ceiling (which would have required these buttresses) was replaced by a lighter wooden one. Some windows are bricked up because the organ fills the wall.

The original stone tower crowned the church from 1522 until 1530, when they noticed that the church was sinking under its weight. It was removed and replaced by the lighter, wood-covered-with-lead version you see today. (The frugal Dutch recycled the old tower, using it to cap the Bakenesser church, a short walk away.)

Because the tower was used as a lookout by Napoleon, it was classified as part of the town's defense. As a result, the tower (but not the rest of the church) became city property, and, since Haarlem's citizens own it, they must help pay to maintain it.

The base of the church is crusted, barnacle-like, with shops—selling jewelry, souvenirs, haircuts, and artwork in the colonnaded former fish market—harkening back to medieval times, when religion and commerce were more intertwined. The little shops around the cathedral have long been church-owned and rented to bring in a little cash.

Originally Catholic, the St. Bavo Church became Protestant (Dutch Reformed) along with much of the country in the late 1500s. From then on, the anti-saint Protestants simply called it the Great Church.

If you're in Haarlem at night, you'll hear the Grote Kerk's carillon chiming a simple "de dong dong, de dong dong" ("Don't wor-ry, be hap-py") at 21:00. In days gone by, this used to warn

Grote Kerk

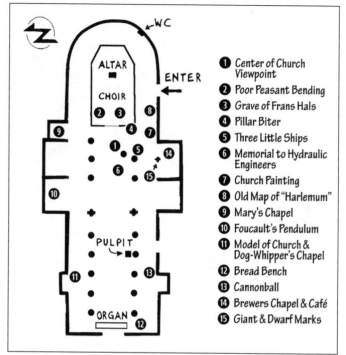

ALTAR

ENTER

CHOIR

WC

PULPIT

ORGAN

1. Center of Church Viewpoint
2. Poor Peasant Bending
3. Grave of Frans Hals
4. Pillar Biter
5. Three Little Ships
6. Memorial to Hydraulic Engineers
7. Church Painting
8. Old Map of "Harlemum"
9. Mary's Chapel
10. Foucault's Pendulum
11. Model of Church & Dog-Whipper's Chapel
12. Bread Bench
13. Cannonball
14. Brewers Chapel & Café
15. Giant & Dwarf Marks

citizens that the city gates would soon close for the night. Today, during the day, a machine and occasionally live carillonneurs play music on its bells.

• *Enter the church at Oude Groenmarkt 23 (look for the small* Entrée *sign). Stand in the center of the church and take it all in.*

Interior

Simple white walls and the black floor, brown ceiling, and mahogany-colored organ make this spacious church feel vast, light, and airy. Considering it was built during a span of 150 years, its archi-

tecture is surprisingly homogenous. Originally, much of the church was painted in bright patterns, similar to the carpet-like frescoes on some columns near the center of the church. But in 1566, Protestant extremists stripped the church of its graven images and ornate Catholic trappings, leaving it relatively stark, with minimal decoration. They whitewashed everything. The frescoes you see today were restored when the whitewash was removed in the 1980s.

Look up to see the fan-vaulted cedar ceiling from 1530. Look down to see tombstones paving the floor. And look midway up the walls to catch squatting characters. The three-story organ fills the west wall.

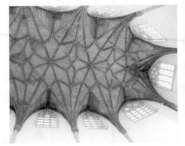

• *We'll circle the church, but first stand at the candle-lined, fence-like brass barrier and look into an enclosed area of wooden benches ("stalls") and the altar, known as the...*

Choir

After the church's foundation was laid, the choir was built first and used for worship for more than a century while the rest of the building was completed.

Today, the brass-and-wood barrier keeps tourists from entering the most sacred area, just as peasants were kept out in medieval times. While the commoners had to stand during services, local big shots got to perch their heinies on the little ledges (called misericords, carved in 1512) of the **wooden stalls** that line the choir; the eighth stall along the left-hand side shows a poor peasant bending over to bear a rich guy's bum on his back. The stalls are also decorated with the coats of arms of noble families, whose second sons traditionally became priests.

The choir's floor holds a simple slab marked with a lantern—the **Grave of Frans Hals** (Graf van Frans Hals), Haarlem's own master artist of the Golden Age. When he was a child, Hals' family moved to Haarlem, and he lived and worked here all his life, worshipping in the Grote Kerk. A friend of mayors and preachers, he chronicled middle-class citizens and tavern life, producing hundreds of masterpieces...and 10 kids. (❂ See the Frans Hals Museum Tour, page 202.)

At both ends of the brass barrier, look for the knee-level, endearing carvings of the "pillar biter." The message, aimed at those who were "more Catholic than even the Pope," was this:

Don't go overboard on devotion.

More than a thousand wealthy people are buried under the church's pavement stones. Only those with piles of money to give to the church could be buried in a way that gave them an advantage in the salvation derby. But even though the dead bodies were embalmed, they stunk. Imagine being a peasant sitting here, trying to think about God...and thinking only of the stench of well-fed bodies rotting. And the phrase "stinking rich" was born.

• *Looking down the nave (without actually walking there yet), on the left side is the...*

Pulpit

The pulpit, elaborately carved from oak in 1679, is topped with a tower-shaped roof. Brass handrails snake down the staircase, serpents fleeing the word of God. In this simply decorated Protestant church, the pulpit is perhaps the most ornate element, directing worshippers' eyes to the speaker. During the Reformation, Protestants changed the worship service. As teaching became more important than ritual, the pulpit was given a higher profile.

• *Suspended between columns, between the center of the church and the tourists' entrance, are...*

Three Little Ships

Sailing under the red-white-and-blue Dutch flag and the flag of a rearing lion, ships like these helped make Holland the world's number one sea-trading nation in the 1600s.

The biggest model ship of the three is a frigate. These fast, heavily armed, three-masted, fully rigged ships rode shotgun for merchant vessels, protecting them from pirates in their two-year journey to the Far East and back. This one has a flat-bottomed

hull, necessary to ply Amsterdam's shallow harbor. It could fire a 21-gun salute from each side. Extra cannons on the poop and forecastle made it more powerful than the average frigate. The keel has an iron saw, a Dutch military specialty for slicing through the chains that commonly blocked harbors (see the chain between two towers near the bow).

• *Three yards away, just to the right, find the...*

Memorial to Hydraulic Engineers

The marble relief shows Neptune in his water chariot. In low-lying Holland of the 1800s, when flooding could mean life or death, hydraulic engineers were heroes.

Twenty yards beyond the memorial (near where you entered, just left of the café) is a painting done when the church was commissioned. This provided a model for the architects to follow.

• *From here, circle the church counterclockwise, starting back near the tourists' entrance. On the wall near the tourists' entrance hangs an...*

Old Map of "Harlemum"

The map shows the walled city in 1688, with ramparts and a moat. Surrounding panels showcase Haarlem's 750-year history. The lower-left panel shows the 1572–1573 Siege of Haarlem (described below), as brave Haarlem women join their menfolk in battle—bombs exploding around them—to fight off invading Spanish troops.

The bottom-right panel shows knights kneeling before a king in the 12th century, while in the distance, ships sail right along the city walls. Up until the 1840s, when it was drained and reclaimed, there was a large lake (the Haarlemmermeer) standing between Haarlem and Amsterdam (see page 191). The Grote Kerk, when viewed by distant travelers, seemed to float like a stately ship on the lake, as seen in the landscape along the bottom of the map.

• *Circle around the altar to the other side of the church, to...*

Mary's Chapel (Maria Kapel)

Inside the iron cage on the back wall is an old wood-and-iron chest that served as a safe for the church's cash and precious documents—such as those papers granting the power to sell forgiveness. See the board of keys for the many doors in this huge complex. Notice also the sarcophagi. Once filled with the "stinking rich," boxes like this were buried five deep below the church floor. Such high-density burying maximized the revenue generated by selling burial spots.

Foucault's Pendulum

In the north transept, a ball on a wire hangs from the ceiling (see the brass sphere in the far right corner). When set in motion (by a church tour guide, mostly on Saturdays), it swings across a dial on the floor, recreating Foucault's pendulum experiment of 1851.

If it's swinging, stand here patiently and watch the earth rotate on its axis.

As the pendulum swings steadily back and forth, the earth rotates counterclockwise underneath it, making the pendulum appear to rotate clockwise around the dial. The earth rotates once every 24 hours, of course, but at Haarlem's latitude of 52 degrees, it makes the pendulum (appear to) sweep 360 degrees every 30 hours, 27 minutes (to knock over the bowling pin). Stand here for five minutes, and you'll see the earth move one degree.

As the world turns, find several small relief statues (in a niche on the right-hand wall) with beheaded heads and defaced faces—victims of the 1566 Iconoclast rampage, when angry Protestant extremists vandalized Dutch Catholic churches (as this once was).

Model of Church and Photo of Organist

A hundred times smaller than the church itself, this model still took a thousand work-hours to build. On the wall, some of the building materials are displayed: matchsticks, washers, screens, glue, wire, and paper clips.

Also on the wall is a photo of the organ pit, showing the organist seated at the Grote Kerk's keyboard. Three keyboards, pedals, and 65 stops (the knobs on either side of the keyboards) make the pipes sound like anything from flutes to tubas, producing an awesome majesty of sound.

Picture 10-year-old Mozart at the controls of this 5,000-pipe sound machine. In 1766, he played Haarlem at the tail end of his triumphant, three-year, whirlwind tour of Europe. He'd just returned from London, where he met J. C. Bach, the youngest son of Johann Sebastian Bach (1685–1750), the grandfather of organ music. Mozart had just written several pieces inspired by Bach, and may have tried them out here.

"Hal-le-lu-jah!" That famous four-note riff may have echoed around the church when Handel played here in 1740, the year before his famous oratorio, *Messiah*, debuted. The 20th-century organist/humanitarian Albert Schweitzer also performed here.

Pass the church's little fire pumps on wheels (from 1850). One was kept in the rafters and had access to cisterns of rainwater collected for fighting fires.

• *Ten yards farther on, the shallow niche is the...*

Dog-Whipper's Chapel

In a sculpted relief (top of column at left end of chapel, above eye level), an angry man whips an angry dog while striding over another angry dog's head. Back when churches served as rainy-day marketplaces, this man's responsibility was to keep Haarlem's dogs out of the church.

The Organ

Even silent, this organ impresses. Finished in 1738 by Amsterdam's Christian Muller, it features a mahogany-colored casing with tin pipes and gold trim, studded with statues of musicians and an eight-piece combo of angels. Lions on the top hold Haarlem's coat of arms—a sword, surrounded by stars, over a banner reading *Vicit Vim Virtus* ("Truth Overcomes Force").

There are larger pipe organs in the world, but this is one of the best.

The organist sits unseen amid the pipes, behind the section that juts out at the bottom. While the bellows generate pressurized air, the organist presses a key, which opens a valve, admitting forced air through a pipe and out its narrow opening, producing a tone. An eight-foot-long pipe plays middle C. A four-foot-long pipe plays C exactly one octave up. A 20-foot pipe rumbles the rafters. With 5,068 pipes ranging from more than 20 feet tall to just a few inches, this organ can cover eight octaves (a piano plays seven), and each key can play a variety of sounds. By pulling one of the stops (such as "flute" or "trumpet"), the organist can channel the air into certain sets of pipes tuned to play together to mimic other instruments. For maximum power, you "pull out all the stops."

Free Bread, a Cannonball in the Wall, and the Siege of Haarlem

Left of the organ, the bread bench is a rare piece of 15th-century furniture that survives here. This was where the church gave the city's poor their daily bread and lard.

Duck! On the wall (left of the chapel with the green metal gate, above eye level) sits a cannonball, placed here in 1573 to commemorate the city's finest hour—the Siege of Haarlem.

In the winter of 1572–1573, Holland was rebelling against its Spanish oppressors. Haarlem proclaimed its alliance with William of Orange (and thus, independence from Spain). In response, the angry Spanish governor—camped in Amsterdam—laid siege to Haarlem. The winter was cold, food ran low, and the city was bombarded by Spanish cannons. Inside huddled 4,000 cold, hungry Calvinists. At one point, the city's women even joined the men on the barricades, brandishing kitchen knives.

But Spain had blockaded the Haarlem Lake, and on June 12, 1573, Haarlem had to surrender. The Spanish rounded up 1,500 ringleaders and executed them to send a message to the rest of the country. Still, Haarlem's brave seven-month stand against overwhelming odds became a Dutch Alamo, inspiring their countrymen to fight on.

Following Haarlem's brave lead, other Dutch towns rebelled, including Amsterdam (see page 148). Though Holland and Spain would skirmish for another five decades, the battles soon moved southward, and Spanish troops would never again seriously penetrate the country's borders.

• *Finish in the chapel now housing the café...*

Brewers Chapel (Brouwerskapel): Giant and Dwarf Marks

The long and short of the city's 750-year history are found on the chapel's central pillar. Black lines on the column mark the height of Haarlem's shortest citizen, thigh-high (33 inches) Simon Paap, who supposedly died in a dwarf-tossing incident, and—wow!—8-foot-8-inch-tall Daniel Cajanus. Who said, "When you've seen one Gothic church, you've seen 'em all"?

FRANS HALS MUSEUM TOUR

For 200 years, Frans Hals (c. 1582–1666) was considered nothing more than just another so-so Dutch portrait painter...and many visitors to the Frans Hals Museum may agree with that lukewarm assessment.

But others may see what I did: a bold humanist who painted everyday people in their warts-and-all glory, a forerunner of Impressionist brushwork, a master of composition, and an articulate visual spokesman for his generation—the generation of the Golden Age.

Stand eye-to-eye with life-size, lifelike portraits of Haarlem's citizens—brewers, preachers, workers, bureaucrats, and housewives—and see the people who built the Golden Age, then watched it start to fade.

ORIENTATION

Cost: €7.

Hours: Tue–Sat 11:00–17:00, Sun 12:00–17:00, closed Mon.

Getting There: The museum is at Groot Heiligland 62. From the train station, walk 15 min toward the city center or take bus #4 or #73 to the Frans Hals Museum stop.

Information: While Frans Hals' masterpieces never leave Room 14, the other paintings can rotate—ask a guard if you can't locate them easily. Tel. 023/511-5775, www.franshalsmuseum.nl.

Length of This Tour: Allow one hour.

Overview

Frans Hals' paintings—located in Room 14 and other rooms nearby—are just one part of the collection. The museum fancies itself as the museum of the Golden Age, offering you the rare opportunity of enjoying 17th-century art in a 17th-century building. Well-described exhibits unfold as the rectangular museum wraps around a peaceful central courtyard. The building's layout makes sense when you realize it was built as subsidized housing for poor old men (in 1610).

Circle counterclockwise, through the art of Hals' predecessors and colleagues, to the back. The lush still lifes give a sense of how good life is and how important it is to embrace it before it all rots and falls away. Your visit begins with "Haarlem in the 17th Century," showing Dutch slice-of-life painting alongside exhibits on what concerned everyday Golden Agers: tulips, trading, linen-weaving, militias, "women power," and beer.

To see the Frans Hals paintings described in this chapter, start in Room 14, with four large Civic Guard portraits, each a masterpiece. Then see his portraits and smaller works nearby (Rooms 16–19).

THE TOUR BEGINS

• *Make your way to the large Room 14, where you're well-guarded by canvases full of companies of men in uniform. We'll start with the men in the bright red sashes.*

Banquet of the Officers of the St. George Civic Guard (1616)

In 1616, tiny Holland was the richest country on earth, and these Haarlem men are enjoying the fruits of their labor. The bright red sashes, the jaunty poses, the smiles, the rich food, the sweeping tilt of the flags...the exuberant spirit of the Golden Age. These weekend warriors have finished their ceremonial parade through town and hung their ceremonial weapons on the wall, and now they sit

down for a relaxed, after-the-show party.

The man in the middle (next to the flag-bearer, facing us) is about to carve the chicken, when the meal is interrupted. It's us, arriving late through the back door, and heads turn to greet us. Rosy-cheeked Nicolaes van der Meer (see his portrait, page 209),

Frans Hals Museum—Room 14

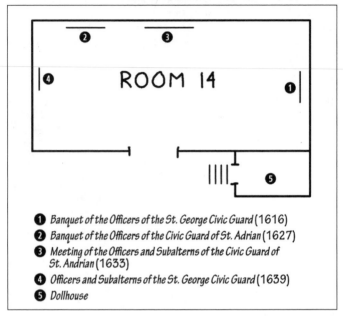

❶ *Banquet of the Officers of the St. George Civic Guard* (1616)
❷ *Banquet of the Officers of the Civic Guard of St. Adrian* (1627)
❸ *Meeting of the Officers and Subalterns of the Civic Guard of St. Andrian* (1633)
❹ *Officers and Subalterns of the St. George Civic Guard* (1639)
❺ *Dollhouse*

hand on hip, turns around with a friendly look, while the man to the right, the colonel in charge, waves us in. Frans Hals knew these men well as friends and colleagues, since he himself was a lifelong member of this Civic Guard company.

This band of brothers is united by common gestures—two men have hands on hips, three turn their palms up, two plant their hands downward, three clutch wine glasses. But mostly, they're joined by the uniform sashes. The red sashes slant both left and right, perfectly forming opposing diagonals.

With this painting, Frans Hals broke the mold of stuffy group portraits. He relegates the traditional symbolic weapons to the shelf (upper right) and breaks up the traditional chorus line of soldiers by placing the men naturally around a table. Van der Meer sticks his elbow in our faces (another Hals trademark) to define a distinct foreground, while the flag-bearer stakes out the middle ground, and a window at the back opens up to a distant, airy background.

Then Hals sets the scene in motion. A guy on the left side leans over to tell a joke to his friend. The dashing young flag-bearer in the middle turns back to listen to the bald-headed man. An ensign (standing, right side) enters and doffs his cap to Captain van der Meer. And then we barge in, interrupting the banquet, but welcomed as one of the boys.

Frans Hals
(c. 1582–1666)

At age 10, Frans Hals, the son of a weaver, moved with his family to Haarlem. He would spend the rest of his life there, rarely traveling even to nearby Amsterdam.

His early years are known to us only through his paintings of taverns and drunks, musicians and actors, done in a free and colorful style (like the Rijksmuseum's *Merry Drinker*, page 105). In 1610, he married, and joined Haarlem's St. Luke's Guild of painters. In 1612, he was admitted to the prestigious St. George Civic Guard. In 1617, Hals married again, producing (altogether) 10 children, five of whom painted.

Hals' group portrait of the St. George Civic Guard (1616) put him on the map as Haarlem's premier portrait painter. For the next five decades, he abandoned the lighthearted slice-of-life scenes of his youth and dedicated himself to chronicling Haarlem's prosperous, middle-class world of businessmen and professionals—people he knew personally, as well as professionally.

Despite his success, Hals had trouble with money. In 1654, he had to sell his belongings to pay debts, and he fought poverty the rest of his life. Commissions became scarce, as the public now preferred more elegant, flattering portraits. His final works (1650–1666) are dark and somber, with increasingly rough and simple brushwork.

In 1664, the city granted him a pension for his years of service. When he died two years later, his work quickly passed out of fashion, dismissed as mere portraits. In the 1800s, the Impressionists rediscovered him, and today he's recognized for his innovations, craftsmanship, and unique style.

Banquet of the Officers of the Civic Guard of St. Adrian (1627)

The men are bunched into two symmetrical groups, left and right, with a window in the back. The figures form a Y, with a tilted flag marking the right diagonal (echoed by several tilted ruffs), and

a slanting row of heads forming the left diagonal (echoed by several slanting sashes). The diagonals meet at the back of the table, marking the center of the composition, where the two groups of men exchange food, drink, and meaningful eye contact.

Civic Guard Portraits

The fathers of the men pictured in this room fought, suffered imprisonment, and died in the great Siege of Haarlem (1572–1573) that helped turn the tide against Spanish oppression. But their sons were bankers, merchants, traders, and sailors, boldly conquering Europe on the new frontier of capitalism. Civic Guards became less of a militia, and more a social club for upwardly mobile men. Their feasts—huge eating and drinking binges, punctuated by endless toasts, poems, skits, readings, dirty limericks, and ceremonial courses—could last days on end.

Standard Civic Guard portraits (see page 69 of Amsterdam City Walk) always showed the soldiers in the same way—two neat rows of men, with everyone looking straight out, holding medieval weapons that tell us their ranks. It took master artists like Hals and Rembrandt to turn these boring visual documents into art.

Meeting of the Officers and Subalterns of the Civic Guard of St. Adrian (1633)

Six years later, Hals painted many of these same men gathered around an outdoor table. The horizontal row of faces is punctuated by three men standing sideways, elbows out. Again, the men are united by sashes that slant in (generally) the same direction and by repeated gestures—hands on hips, hands on hearts, and so on.

Officers and Subalterns of the St. George Civic Guard (1639)

When 57-year-old Frans Hals painted this, his last Civic Guard portrait, he included himself among his St. George buddies. (Find Frans in the upper left, 2nd from left, under the number 19.)

As he got older, Hals refined and simplified his group-portrait style, using quieter colors, the classic two horizontal rows of soldiers, and the traditional symbolic weapons. You can recognize the captain (5th from the right, with white goatee, number 5) by his pike (topped with a spearhead), the lieutenants by their partisans (pikes topped with swords), and the rest by their ordinary hatchet-headed halberds.

A decade after this was painted, Holland officially ended its war with Spain (Treaty of Munster, 1648), Civic Guards lost their military purpose, businessmen preferred portraits showing themselves as elegant gentlemen rather than crusty soldiers, and the tradition of Civic Guard group portraits quickly died out.

• *Backtrack to the room just outside Room 14 to find the painting called...*

Dutch Proverbs (Vlaamsche Spreekwoorden)

This fun painting (a copy of a 17th-century work by Pieter Brueghel, the Younger) shows 72 charming Flemish scenes representing different folk sayings. Pick up the chart to identify these clever bits of everyday wisdom. True to form, this piece of Flemish art isn't preachy religious art or political propaganda; rather, it just shares the simple and decent morals of the hardworking Dutch.

• *In the next room, turn left and walk up five steps to the...*

Former Chapel

Take a look inside. You'll find a **fancy dollhouse** *(poppenhuis)*, the hobby of the lady of the house (her portrait is on the left). Handmade by finest local craftsmen, this delicately crafted dollhouse offers a glimpse of wealthy 18th-century living.

The exquisite **bed curtain,** brought back from New England, decorated the bed of a wealthy Dutch family who lived in colonial America. It's embroidered with bulb flowers known during the 17th century—and well-described in English.

• *Continue counterclockwise around the museum until you get to the hallway that is Room 17, where you're greeted by the...*

Portrait of Jacobus Zaffius (1611)

Arr-r-r-r-rh! This fierce, intense, rough-hewn man is not a pirate, but a priest, the rogue leader of an outlawed religion in Haarlem—Catholicism. In the 1600s, Haarlem was a Protestant town in the midst of a war against Catholic Spain, and Catholics were guilty by association. But Zaffius refused to be silenced. He turns to glare and snarl at the Protestant town fathers. He was so personally imposing that the city tolerated his outspokenness.

The face jumps out from a background of neutral gray-brown-black.

Frans Hals' Style

- Hals' forte is **portraits**. Of his 240 paintings, 195 are individual or group portraits, mostly of Haarlem's citizens.
- His paintings are **life-size** and **realistic**, capturing everyday people, even downright ugly people, without airbrushing out their blemishes or character flaws.
- Hals uses **rough, Impressionistic brushwork**, where a few thick, simple strokes blend at a distance to create details. He worked quickly, often making the rough sketch the final, oil version.
- His **stop-action** technique captures the sitter in midmotion. Aided by his rough brushwork, this creates a blur that suggests the person is still moving.
- Hals adds **3-D depth** to otherwise horizontal, widescreen canvases. (Men with their elbows sticking out serve to define the foreground.)
- His canvases are **unified** by people wearing matching colors, using similar poses and gestures, and gathered in symmetrical groups.
- His paintings have a **relaxed, light-hearted, even comical atmosphere**. In group portraits, the subjects interact with one another. Individual portraits meet your eyes as if meeting an old friend.
- His works show **nothing religious**—no Madonnas, Crucifixions, angels, or Bible scenes. If anything, he imbues everyday objects with heavenly beauty and grants ordinary people the status of saints.

His features are alive—head turning, mouth twisting, face wrinkling up, beard bristling. Hals captures him in action, using a slow shutter speed. The rough brushstrokes of the fur coat and beard suggest the blur of motion of this agitated individual. This is Frans Hals' first known portrait, painted when he—a late starter in the art world—was nearly 30.

• *Make a left into Room 18 to see the...*

Portraits of Nicolaes Woutersz van der Meer and his wife, Cornelia Claesdr Vooght (1631)

Hals knew Nicolaes van der Meer, a fellow Civic Guard lodge member, personally. Van der Meer was a brewer, an important post in a city where average beer consumption was six pints a day per person (man, woman, and child). He was also the mayor, so his pose is official and dignified, larger than life-size. But the face is pure Golden Age—red-cheeked and healthy, confident and intelligent, his even gaze tinged with wisdom. This mayor kept a steady

hand on the tiller of Haarlem's ship
of state.

The face is literally the focus of
this otherwise messy painting. The
ruffled collar is a tangle of simple,
figure-eight swirls of white paint;
the brocaded coat is a patchwork of
white lines; and the lace cuffs are
a few broad outlines. But out of
the rough brushwork and somber
background, van der Meer's crys-
tal-clear eyes meet ours. The finely
etched crow's feet around his eyes
suggest that Hals had seen this imposing man break into a warm
smile. Hey, I'd vote for him as my mayor.

The companion painting shows van der Meer's companion, his wife, **Cornelia.** Husband-and-wife portraits were hung

together—notice that they share the
same background, and the two figures
turn in toward each other. Still, both
people are looking out at us, not clinging to each other, suggesting a mature
partnership more than lovey-dovey newlyweds. Married couples in Golden Age
Holland divvied up the work—men ran
the business, women ran the home—and
prided themselves on their mutual independence. (Even today in progressive
Holland, fewer women join the work-
force than in many other industrial nations.) Cornelia's body is as
imposing as her husband's, with big, manly hands and a practical,
slightly suspicious look. The detail work in her ruff collar tells
us that Hals certainly could sweat the details when it suited his
purpose.

Regents of the St. Elisabeth Hospital of Haarlem (1641)

These aren't the Dutch Masters cigar boys, though it looks like
Rembrandt's famous (and later) *De Staalmeesters* (see page 111 of
the Rijksmuseum Tour). It's a board meeting, where five men in
black hats and black suits with lace collars and cuffs—the Golden
Age power suit—sit around a table in a brown room.

Pretty boring stuff, but Hals was hired to paint their portraits,
and he does his best. Behind the suits, he captures five distinct
men. The man on the far left is pondering the universe or raising
a belch. The man in the middle (facing us) looks like the classic
Golden Age poster boy, with moustache, goatee, ruddy cheeks, and

long hair. Another is clean-shaven, while the guy on the far right adds a fashion twist with moustache wax. Hals links these five unique faces with one of his trademark techniques—similar poses and gestures. The burping man and the goateed man are a mirror image of the same pose—leaning on the table, hand on chest. Several have cupped hands, several have hands laid flat, or on their chests, or on the table. And the one guy keeps working on that burp.

• *Continue to Room 19. On the wall straight ahead are the...*

Regents of the Old Men's Almshouse (1664)

These men look tired. So was Holland. So was Hals. At 82, Hals, despite years of success, was poor and dependent on the charity of the city, which granted him a small pension.

He was hired to paint the board of directors of the Old Men's Almshouse, located here in the building that now houses the Frans Hals Museum. Though Hals himself never lived in the almshouse, he fully understood what it was to be penniless and have to rely on money doled out by men like these.

The portrait is unflattering, drained of color. Somber men dressed in black peer out of a shadowy room. These men were trying to administer a dwindling budget to house and feed an aging population. Holland's Golden Age was losing its luster.

The style is nearly Impressionistic—collars, cuffs, and gloves rendered with a few messy brushstrokes of paint. Hands and faces are a patchwork of light and dark splotches. Despite the sketchiness, each face captures the man's essence.

Historians speculate that this unflattering portrait was Hals' revenge on tightwad benefactors, but the fact is that the regents were satisfied with their portrait. By the way, the man just to the right of center isn't drunk, but suffering from facial paralysis. To the end, Hals respected unvarnished reality.

• *Directly behind you, find the...*

Regentesses of the Old Men's Almshouse (1664)

These women ran the women's wing of the almshouse, located across the street. Except for a little rouge on the women's pale-as-death faces, this canvas is almost a study in gray and black, as

Hals pared his palette down to the bare essentials. The faces are subtle variations on old age. Only the woman on the right resolutely returns our gaze.

The man who painted this was old, poor, out of fashion, in failing health, perhaps bitter, and dying. In contrast with the lively group scenes of Hals' youth, these individuals stand forever isolated. They don't look at each other, each lost in their own thoughts, perhaps contemplating their own mortality (or stifling belches). Their only link to one another is the tenuous, slanting line formed by their hands, leading to the servant who enters the room with a mysterious message.

Could that message be...death? Or just that this tour is over?

The helpful Haarlem TI, just outside the train station, can nearly always find you a €25 bed in a private home (for a €6-per-person fee, plus a cut of your host's money, 2-night minimum). Avoid this if you can; it's cheaper to reserve by calling direct. Nearly every Dutch person you'll encounter speaks English.

Haarlem is most crowded in April and May (in 2006, particularly Easter weekend—April 14–16, the flower parade on April 22, and Queen's Day, celebrated this year on April 29) and in July and August.

The listed prices include breakfast (unless otherwise noted) and usually include the €1.80-per-person-per-day tourist tax. To avoid this town's louder-than-normal street noises, forgo views for a room in the back. Hotels and the TI have a useful parking brochure.

SLEEPING

In the Center

Hotels and B&Bs

$$$ Hotel Lion D'Or is a classy, 34-room business hotel with all the professional comforts and a handy location. Expect a proficient welcome (Db-€135, Fri–Sat Db-€95, extra bed-€20, air-con, some non-smoking rooms, elevator, across the street from train station at Kruisweg 34, tel. 023/532-1750, fax 023/532-9543, www.goldentulip.com, reservations@hotelliondor.nl).

$$ Hotel Amadeus, on Market Square, has 15 small, bright, and basic rooms. Some have views of the square. This characteristic hotel, ideally located above an early 20th-century dinner café, is relatively quiet, especially if you take a room in the back. Its lush old lounge/breakfast room on the second floor overlooks the square, and Mike and Inez take good care of their guests (Sb-€60,

---

Sleep Code

(€1 = about $1.20, country code: 31, area code: 023)
S = Single, **D** = Double/Twin, **T** = Triple, **Q** = Quad, **b** = bathroom, **s** = shower only. Credit cards are accepted unless otherwise noted.

To help you easily sort through these listings, I've divided the rooms into three categories, based on the price for a standard double room with bath:

$$$ **Higher Priced**—Most rooms €100 or more.
  $$ **Moderately Priced**—Most rooms between €65–100.
   $ **Lower Priced**—Most rooms €65 or less.

Db-€80–85, Tb-€105, includes tax, 2-night stay and cash get you a 5 percent discount, 10-min walk from train station, steep climb to lounge, then an elevator, Grote Markt 10, tel. 023/532-4530, fax 023/532-2328, www.amadeus-hotel.com, info@amadeus-hotel .com). The hotel also runs a six-terminal Internet café (€1.20/15 min, 25 percent discount with this book).

$$ Joops Hotel, with 30 comfortable rooms, is located just behind the Grote Kerk church (Db-€85, Fri–Sat Db-€95, 10 percent discount with this book in 2006, breakfast buffet-€9.50, Internet access in lobby, Oude Groenmarkt 20, tel. 023/532-2008, fax 023/532-9549, www.joopshotel.com, Joops@easynet.nl). Joops also rents studios with kitchenettes for two to four people in nearby Hotel Arendshoek (Db-€75, Qb-€120, elevator, contact Joops Hotel).

$ Bed-and-Breakfast House de Kiefte is your get-into-a-local-home budget option. Marjet (mar-yet) and Hans, a frank, interesting Dutch couple who speak English well, rent four bright, cheery, non-smoking rooms (rates include breakfast and travel advice) in their quiet 1892 home (Ds-€55, T-€76, Qs-€98, Quint/ b-€115, cash only, 2-night minimum, very steep stairs, family loft sleeps up to 5, kids older than 4 welcome, Coornhertstraat 3, tel. 023/532-2980, mobile 06-5474-5272, housedekiefte@gmx.net). It's a 15-minute walk or €7 taxi ride from the train station and a five-minute walk from the center. From Market Square, walk to the right of the town hall, straight out Zijlstraat, over the bridge, and take a left on the fourth street. See the photo of Marjet and Hans (doing a wheelie) on page 212.

Rooms in Restaurants

These places are all run as sidelines by restaurants, and you'll know it by the style of service and rooms. Lobbies are in the restaurant

Haarlem Hotels and Restaurants

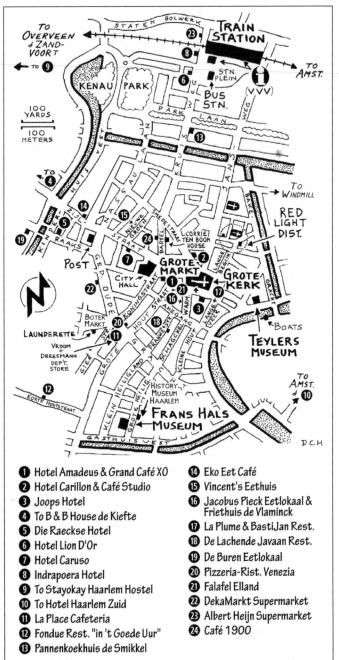

1. Hotel Amadeus & Grand Café XO
2. Hotel Carillon & Café Studio
3. Joops Hotel
4. To B & B House de Kiefte
5. Die Raeckse Hotel
6. Hotel Lion D'Or
7. Hotel Caruso
8. Indrapoera Hotel
9. To Stayokay Haarlem Hostel
10. To Hotel Haarlem Zuid
11. La Place Cafeteria
12. Fondue Rest. "in 't Goede Uur"
13. Pannenkoekhuis de Smikkel
14. Eko Eet Café
15. Vincent's Eethuis
16. Jacobus Pieck Eetlokaal & Friethuis de Vlaminck
17. La Plume & BastiJan Rest.
18. De Lachende Javaan Rest.
19. De Buren Eetlokaal
20. Pizzeria-Rist. Venezia
21. Falafel Elland
22. DekaMarkt Supermarket
23. Albert Heijn Supermarket
24. Café 1900

and there are no public spaces. Still, they are handy and—for Haarlem—inexpensive.

$$ Hotel Carillon overlooks the town square and comes with a little traffic and bell-tower chimes. Many of the 20 well-worn rooms are small, and the stairs are st-e-e-e-p. The front rooms come with more street noise and great town-square views (tiny loft S-€33, Db-€76, Tb-€92.50, Qb-€100, no elevator, 10-min walk from train station, Grote Markt 27, tel. 023/531-0591, fax 023/531-4909, www.hotelcarillon.com, info@hotelcarillon.com). A much-needed renovation is planned in 2006.

$$ Hotel Caruso rents 15 huge, plain, bright, mod rooms—which may suffer from a little commotion from revelers below—above its Italian restaurant (Db-€85, Tb-€105, Qb-€120, Reino and Nino promise a 10 percent discount with this book in 2006, Zijlstraat 56, tel. 023/542-1420).

$$ Indrapoera Hotel, a humid little place with too much carpeting, has eight cheap, handy rooms across the street from the train station (Db-€70, trains stop by midnight, Kruisweg 18, tel. 023/532-0393, yeh@yeh.speedxs.nl, Yeh family).

$$ Die Raeckse Hotel, family-run and friendly, is not as central as the others and has less character and more traffic noise—but its 21 rooms are decent and comfortable. Ask for a quiet room (Sb-€55, Db-€70–80 depending on size, Tb-€98, Qb-€115, 10 percent discount for 2-night stay except in Aug, Raaks Straat 1, tel. 023/532-6629, fax 023/531-7937, www.die-raeckse.nl, dieraeckse@zonnet.nl). A big, cheap parking garage is across the street.

Near Haarlem

$$ Hotel Haarlem Zuid, with 300 rooms and very American, is sterile, but a good value for drivers. It sits in an industrial zone a 20-minute walk from the center, on the road to the airport (Db-€80, breakfast-€12, elevator, free parking, laundry service, fitness center-€5, inexpensive hotel restaurant, Toekanweg 2, tel. 023/536-7500, fax 023/536-7980, www.hotelhaarlemzuid.nl, info@hotelhaarlemzuid.valk.nl). Bus #300 (6/hr) connects the hotel conveniently with the train station, Market Square, and the airport.

$ Stayokay Haarlem, completely renovated and with all the youth-hostel comforts, charges €19–25 for beds in four-, six-, and eight-bed dorms. They also rent simple €60 doubles (€2.50 less for members, includes sheets and breakfast, daily 7:30–24:00, Jan Gijzenpad 3, 2 miles from Haarlem station—take bus #2 from station, or a 10-min walk from Santpoort Zuid train station, tel. 023/537-3793, fax 023/537-1176, www.stayokay.com/haarlem, haarlem@stayokay.com).

Marijuana in Haarlem

Haarlem is a laid-back place for observing the Dutch approach to recreational marijuana. The town is dotted with 16 coffeeshops, where pot is casually sold and smoked by relaxed, non-criminal types. These easygoing coffeeshops are more welcoming than they may feel—bartenders are happy to answer questions from curious Yankee travelers.

If you don't like the smell of pot, avoid places sporting wildly painted walls, plants in the windows, or Rastafarian yellow, red, and green colors.

Willie Wortel Sativa Coffeeshop is one of the best established of the town's coffeeshops (daily 9:00–24:00, in front of train station at Kruisweg 46). The display case–type
menu explains what's on sale (€2.50–3.60 joints, €5 baggies, space cakes, no alcohol, only soft drinks and mellow music).

The tiny **'t Theehuis**, which feels like a hippie teahouse, was Haarlem's first coffeeshop (c. 1984). Along with a global selection of pot, it has 50 different varieties of tea on the menu, and a friendly staff (daily 13:00–22:00,

a block off Market Square at Smedestraat 25).

High Times offers smokers 12 varieties of joints in racks behind the bar (neatly prepacked in trademarked "Joint Packs," €2.50–5, daily 11:00–23:00, Internet access, Lange Veerstraat 47). They make a tobacco-free joint especially for Americans (€4.50).

EATING

In or near the Train Station

Pancakes for lunch or dinner? **Pannenkoekhuis de Smikkel** serves a selection of more than 50 pancakes for a meal (meat, cheese, etc.) and dessert. The €8 pancakes can fill two (daily 12:00–21:00, Sun from 16:00, 2 blocks in front of station, Kruisweg 57, tel. 023/532-0631).

Enjoy a sandwich or coffee surrounded by trains and 1908 architecture in the **Stations Café** (daily 6:30–20:00, between tracks #3 and #6 at the station).

On or near Zijlstraat

Eko Eet Café is great for a cheery, tasty vegetarian meal (€10–15 *menu*s, daily 11:30–21:30, Zijlstraat 39, tel. 023/532-6568).

Vincent's Eethuis, the cheapest restaurant in town, offers basic Dutch food and a friendly staff. This former St. Vincent's soup kitchen now feeds more gainfully employed locals than the poor (daily plate-€5.50, specials-€8, Mon–Fri 16:30–19:30, closed Sat–Sun, Nieuwe Groenmarkt 22).

Between the Market Square and Frans Hals Museum

Jacobus Pieck Eetlokaal is popular with locals for its fine-value "global cuisine" and peaceful garden courtyard (plate of the day-€9.50, great €5 sandwiches at lunch, cash only, good salads, Mon 10:00–17:00, Tue–Sat 10:00–22:00, closed Sun, Warmoesstraat 18, behind church, tel. 023/532-6144).

Friethuis de Vlaminck is your best bet for a cone of old-fashioned fresh "Flemish fries" (€2, Tue–Sat until 18:30, closed Sun–Mon, Warmoesstraat 3, behind church). Be creative with their dazzling array of sauces.

Pizzeria–Ristorante Venezia, run for 10 years by the same Italian family from Bari, is the place to go for pizza or pasta (€8–17 meals, pizza from €7.50, daily 13:00–23:00, facing Vroom & Dreesmann department store at Verwulft 7, 023/531-7753).

La Plume steakhouse is noisy, with a happy, local, and carnivorous crowd (€12–18 meals, daily from 17:30, Lange Veerstraat 1, tel. 023/531-3202). The relaxing outdoor seating faces the church and a lively pedestrian mall.

BastiJan serves good Mediterranean cuisine in an atmosphere of youthful elegance (€20 meals, 4-course dinner for €25, Tue–Sun from 18:00, closed Mon, Lange Veerstraat 8, tel. 023/532-6006).

De Lachende Javaan (literally "The Laughing Javanese") serves the best Indonesian food in town, in a spacious, classy, and woody dining area (I'd avoid their upstairs seating). Their €18–22 *rijsttafels* are excellent (Tue–Sun from 17:00, closed Mon, Frankestraat 27, tel. 023/532-8792).

De Buren Eetlokaal, fun and traditional, offers an old-time ambience and good Franco-Dutch food to an enthusiastic local crowd. It's just outside the center near several recommended accommodations (€10–14 meals, Thu–Mon 16:00–22:00, closed Tue–Wed, Brouwersvaart 146, tel. 023/532-7078).

Fondue Restaurant "in 't Goede Uur" (literally "in the Good Hour") is a romantic, 12-table place with classical music on the most charming street in Haarlem. Reservations are required (€17 cheese fondue, Tue–Sun 17:00–24:00, closed Mon, cash only, Korte Houtstraat 1, tel. 023/531-1174).

La Place dishes up fresh, healthy, budget food with Haarlem's best view. Sit on the top floor or roof garden of the Vroom & Dreesmann department store (Mon 11:00–18:00, Tue–Sat

9:30–18:00, Thu until 21:00, closed Sun except for 1st Sun of month 12:00–17:00, large non-smoking section, Grote Houtstraat 70, on corner of Gedempte Oude Gracht, 023/515-8700).

Falafel Elland serves the best falafel in Haarlem (€4–9 dishes—same price whether you stay or take away, daily until 22:00, Grote Houtstraat 5a).

Picnics: Shoppers have two good choices—the **DekaMarkt supermarket** near Market Square (Mon 11:00–20:00, Tue–Sat 8:30–20:00, Thu until 21:00, closed Sun, Gedempte Oude Gracht 54, between Vroom & Dreesmann department store and post office) or the **Albert Heijn supermarket** near the train station (Mon–Sat 8:00–20:00, closed Sun, Kruisweg 10).

NIGHTLIFE

Haarlem's evening scene is great. The bars around the Grote Kerk and Lange Veerstraat are colorful and lively. You'll find plenty of music. The best show in town: the café scene on Market Square. In good weather, café tables tumble happily out of the bars.

For trendy local crowds, sip a drink at **Café Studio** on Market Square (daily 12:00–4:00, next to Hotel Carillon, tel. 023/531-0033). **Grand Café XO** is another hip nightspot on the square (daily 10:00–24:00, Grote Markt 8, 023/551-1350). Tourists gawk at the old-fashioned, belt-driven ceiling fans in **Café 1900** across from the Corrie ten Boom House (daily 9:00–00:30, live music Sun night except in July, Barteljorisstraat 10, tel. 023/531-8283).

NETHERLANDS DAY TRIPS

- *The Historic Triangle*
- *Edam*
- *Arnhem*
- *Delft*
- *The Hague*

Any Netherlands native will tell you: to really experience everyday Dutch life, take a day trip out of Amsterdam. In a country as tiny as Holland, it's easy to do. Within a half hour of leaving Central Station, you can be deep in the Dutch countryside—lush, green, and filled with tulips and black-and-white cows. It's a refreshing break from urban Amsterdam. Match your interest with the village's specialty: flower auctions, wooden-shoe folk museums, fresh cheese, Delft porcelain, or modern art.

Take some time to learn a few basic Dutch phrases for the sake of politeness (see page 388), but don't obsess—just about everyone speaks English. Before you board at Central Station, check the yellow train-schedule boards or ask at the information counter to confirm the details of your trip (such as times, necessary transfers, delays, and the station you'll be using—for example, to get to Zaanse Schans, you'll get off at the Koog-Zaandijk station). For bigger cities, such as The Hague, make sure your train is heading to the main station (usually called "Centraal"), instead of a smaller satellite station. You'll find train information online at www.ns.nl.

Choosing a Day Trip

If you only have a day or two to venture outside of Amsterdam or Haarlem, this list can help you decide where to go.

Keukenhof is a don't-miss garden show, but it blooms only two months a year—March 23–May 19 in 2006 (see page 235).

The Historic Triangle is a fun trip that connects two towns and a fine open-air folk museum by steam train and boat. Allow a full day. It's a good choice for families, particularly with younger kids (see page 221).

In quiet **Edam,** you can mellow out like a hunk of aging cheese. The town has no significant sights, but its tiny main square

Netherlands Day Trips

and peaceful canals can win you over (see page 223).

The town of **Arnhem** has two major sights a fair distance apart: an open-air folk museum (Holland's original and best) and the Kröller-Müller Museum (van Gogh paintings), located in a gigantic national park (with hundreds of free bikes to get around). Seeing both sights makes for a long but satisfying day (page 226).

The **Aalsmeer Flower Auction,** close to the airport, shows you the business side of the Netherlands' beautiful flower scene (see page 235). Unlike Keukenhof's garden show, Aalsmeer is open year-round.

Delft is the lovely hometown of the painter Vermeer and the Delftware factory (page 230). You can combine a trip here with a quick visit to the neighboring city of **The Hague** (page 234).

Zaanse Schans Open-Air Museum has only one advantage over the Netherlands' other folk museums: it's a quick 15-minute trip from central Amsterdam (see page 236). But while it's convenient, it's tackier than the alternatives. With more time, I prefer the more authentic Arnhem or Enkhuizen folk museums (both described below).

The town of **Alkmaar** is fun to visit during its weekly cheese market (Friday mornings April–Aug; see page 236).

The Historic Triangle

From Amsterdam, you can take a fun all-day excursion into the "Historic Triangle." You'll start in the small town of Hoorn, catch a toot-toot steam train to the town of Medemblik, then sail on a 1920s-era boat to Enkhuizen, home of an excellent open-air folk museum (see route on map on previous page). Particularly good for families and trainspotters, the Historic Triangle trip is a ▲▲ experience and a relaxing way to pass a day. Dutch grandmothers feed snacks to towheaded toddlers, gusts of steam billow gracefully behind the engine, and cows nod sleepily in the fields.

Schedule: The Historic Triangle trip is offered from April through December (no trains Jan–March). Steam trains leave Hoorn as frequently as twice a day in July and August (daily at 11:00 and 14:20). From April through June and in September, the train runs once daily except Monday (Tue–Sun at 11:00). From October through December, the service is offered on weekends only (Sat–Sun at 11:00). Confirm train departure times (reservation tel. 0229/214-862, www.museumstoomtram .nl, info@museumstoomtram.nl). Make reservations during the summer months, particularly for weekends. Otherwise, you can normally just buy tickets as you go.

To make the 11:00 train in Hoorn, plan to leave Amsterdam's Central Station by 9:30 (train from Amsterdam to Hoorn: €7, 2/hr, 45–60 min, may require change at Amsterdam Sloterdijk station). If you start from Hoorn at 11:00 and visit the open-air museum in the afternoon, you'll likely get back to Amsterdam about 18:30 (because the museum closes at 17:00).

Cost: Allow about €43 per adult for the entire trip, including the museum and train transportation from Amsterdam to Hoorn and from Enkhuizen back to Amsterdam.

Start at Hoorn: You'll arrive in Hoorn's modern train station. There's little to see in the town of Hoorn itself; it's basically a transit point. Exit the train and find the pedestrian overpass (following *stoomtram* signs) that runs up and over the tracks, leading to the small, old-timey train station. (Both old and new trains share the same train tracks, but on opposite sides.) When you buy your tickets, they'll offer one-way seats just for the train itself. If you want to do the whole Historic Triangle trip, ask for the full-day train/ boat combo-ticket that ends at the Enkhuizen Zuiderzee Museum (€25.65 combo-ticket includes museum and saves you half a euro,

€16.15 for transport-only combo-ticket, discounts for kids; ticket does not include train ride from Zuiderzee back to Amsterdam). Hoorn's **TI** is located downtown, a two-minute walk from the station (Mon 13:00–17:00, Tue–Sun 9:30–17:00, tel. 072/511-4284, www.vvvhoorn.nl).

From Hoorn to Medemblik by Steam Train: From Hoorn, it's a 65-minute steam-train ride to Medemblik. After you choose a wooden-bench seat inside the train, you can get up and walk around—even to stand and look over small train balconies, like a whistle-stop presidential candidate. The trains are the kind that ran through Holland from 1879 through 1966; the one you'll be on dates from the 1920s. The costumed conductor walks through, giving instructions in Dutch (mostly to tell you about the train's single 5-minute stop in Twisk; if you're curious, ask him to repeat what he said in English when he passes). Keep an eye out for modern white windmills in the distance. If you see little Dutch kids waving to the train from their backyards, wave back.

Medemblik: You'll have about 50 minutes in this one-street town, which has little to offer beyond a few postcard stands; head soon to the boat dock (see below).

If you want to skip the open-air museum at Enkhuizen, and instead go directly back to Hoorn, you can catch the bus back (bus #44 or faster #39, 2/hr, 7 *strippenkaart* strips back to Hoorn).

From Medemblik to Enkhuizen by Boat: To get to the boat from the Medemblik train station, walk down the main street (Nieuwstraat) without dawdling too much; it takes 20 minutes by foot to reach the boat (departures at 13:00 and 16:30 July–Aug). Make a left before the bridge (look for *Boot veerdienst M'blik–Enkhuizen* sign) and head towards the orange building on the left side of the large canal. The historic boat will be waiting, hidden behind a building at the far end. It's a 90-minute trip to Enkhuizen. Since you won't have enough time in Medemblik to eat a meal, do as the Dutch do and eat in the boat's surprisingly comfortable dining room (€2 sandwiches, €5 hamburgers). If you've brought a picnic, grab a wicker chair and enjoy the peaceful, windswept deck. Kids can safely run around on the open spaces of the top deck, or play wooden board games in the lounge.

Enkhuizen: The boat drops you right at the entrance of the wonderful **Enkhuizen Zuiderzee Museum**, an open-air folk museum that's a ▲▲ sight. It's a low-key village patterned after a salty old Dutch fishing town, populated by people who do a

convincing job of role-playing no-nonsense 1905 villagers. You're welcome to take their picture, but they won't smile. No one said "Have a nice day" back then. You can see barrels and rope made, and eat herring hot out of the old smoker. Children enjoy playing at the dress-up chest, trying out old-time games, and making sailing ships out of old wooden shoes (€10; July–Aug daily 10:00–17:00; April–June and Sept–Oct Tue–Sun 10:00–17:00, closed Mon; Nov–March Tue–Sun 11:00–17:00, closed Mon; July–Aug free English tours at 14:00, private guide for €45, tel. 0228/351-111, www.zuiderzeemuseum.nl).

Trains make the one-hour trip between Amsterdam (or Haarlem) and Enkhuizen every half hour. To get between the museum and Enkhuizen train station, catch a shuttle boat (free with museum ticket, 4/hr, same schedule as museum) or take a pleasant 15-minute walk. Note that you don't have to do the Historic Triangle tango to visit the museum; you can take the train straight from Amsterdam, but you'd miss the steam train and boat.

Edam

For the ultimate in cuteness and peace, make your home in tiny Edam, a ▲▲ sight. It's sweet but palatable and just 30 minutes by bus from Amsterdam (2/hr).

While Edam is known today for cheese, it was once an industrious shipyard and port. But having a canal to the sea caused such severe flooding in town—cracking walls and spilling into homes—that one frustrated resident even built a floating cellar (now in Edams Museum, below). To stop the flooding, the harbor was closed off with locked gates (you'll see the gates in Dam Square next to TI). The harbor silted up, forcing the decline of the shipbuilding trade.

Edam's Wednesday market is held year-round, but it's best in July and early August, when the focus is on cheese. You, along with piles of other tourists, can meet the cheese traders and local farmers.

Tourist Information

The TI, often staffed by volunteers, is in City Hall on Dam Square. Pick up the €0.50 *Edam Holland* brochure and consider the €2.50 *A Stroll Through Edam* brochure outlining a self-guided walking tour (April–Oct Mon–Sat 10:00–17:00, Sun 12:00–16:30; Nov–March Mon–Sat 10:00–15:00, closed Sun; WC and ATM just outside, tel. 0299/315-125, www.vvv-edam.nl, info@vvv-edam.nl).

Internet Access: Edam has a two-computer Internet café close to Dam Square, called **Cor Graphics** (Mon–Sat 9:00–17:30, Sun 12:00–16:00, Voorhaven 141, tel. 0299/315-587, www.cor-graphics.com).

Arrival in Edam

To get from the bus "station" to Dam Square and the TI, head toward the gray-and-gold bell tower just east of the main square. It's a five-minute walk: With the buses behind you, go right. When you reach a tree-lined avenue (Zuidervesting), turn left. Cross two pedestrian bridges (first one is black, next is white). Turn left on Hoogstraat, cross a small drawbridge, and within 50 yards, you'll be at Dam Square.

SIGHTS

Introductory Walk—Start in Dam Square and walk over the bridge to the Edams Museum (see below). After visiting the museum, turn right down Spui (canal on your left) and walk for one block. Take a right down Prinsenstraat onto Matthijs Tinxgracht and follow this street through the cheese-market square. Peek into the old "cheese weigh house," and continue down the street to see the Church of Saint Nicholas.

Edams Museum/Historical Collection—This small, quirky museum—and a nearby 400-year-old historical home with a floating cellar (covered by the same ticket)—offer a fun peek into Edam's past. At the museum, learn about Edam's trade history upstairs, and about Fris Pottery on the top floor (€3, April–Oct Tue–Sat 10:00–16:30, Sun 13:00–16:30, closed Mon and Nov–March, historical house at Dam Square 8, museum in city hall with TI, tel. 0299/372-644, www.edamsmuseum.nl).

SLEEPING AND EATING

The TI has a list of inexpensive rooms in private homes.

$$ Hotel de Fortuna is an eccentric, canalside place with flowers and duck and bird noises. It offers steep stairs and 23 low-ceilinged rooms in several ancient buildings in the old center of Edam. It's been run by the Dekker family for more than 30 years

Sleep Code

(€1 = about $1.20, country code: 31, area code: 0299)
S = Single, **D** = Double/Twin, **T** = Triple, **Q** = Quad, **b** = bathroom,
s = shower only. Unless otherwise noted, credit cards are
accepted, breakfast is included, and hoteliers speak English.

To help you easily sort through these listings, I've divided
the rooms into three categories, based on the price for a standard double room with bath:

$$$ **Higher Priced**—Most rooms €120 or more.
$$ **Moderately Priced**—Most rooms between €80–120.
$ **Lower Priced**—Most rooms €80 or less.

(Db-€90–100, Spuistraat 3, tel. 0299/371-671, fax 0299/371-469,
www.fortuna-edam.nl, fortuna@fortuna-edam.nl). Try lunch on
their garden patio or dinner in their romantic restaurant (3-course
meal-€32.50, restaurant open Mon–Fri 12:00–15:00 & 18:00–
21:30, Sat–Sun 17:30–21:30).

$$ Damhotel, centrally located on a canal across the street
from the TI, has attractive, comfortable rooms with a plush feel (Sb-
€55, Db-€90, Tb-€125, Qb-€170, Keizersgracht 1, tel. 0299/371-
766, fax 0299/374-031, www.damhotel.nl, info@damhotel.nl).
There's a fancy restaurant/outdoor café on the ground floor.

De Prinsen Bar and Eetcafé is a good bet for a light lunch
or a midday snack. Of their two Dutch cheese samplers, the bet-

ter one is *Portie gemengde Hollandse
Kaas* (€5.50), offering a nice combo
of bread, olives, and regional cheeses.
It's a good nibbler plate for two, and
goes well with a little Belgian *beerje*
(€3.25 soups, €3.50 salads, daily
June–Aug 12:00–24:00, Sept–May
16:00–24:00, Prinsenstraat 8, tel.
0299/372-911).

Picnickers can stock up at the
Topper Supermarket/Delicatessen (Mon–Fri 9:00–18:00, Sat
9:00–17:00, Sun 9:30–17:00, located next door to cheese chop just
off Dam Square, tel. 0299/373-069).

TRANSPORTATION CONNECTIONS

Edam and **Amsterdam** are connected by direct bus #114 (2/hr, 30
min), or the slower bus #110 (every 45 min, scenic route through
the town of Volendam, 45 min).

Arnhem

Arnhem, 75 minutes southeast of Amsterdam by train, is the least user-friendly of all the Dutch day trips I recommend, mainly because its two main sights aren't close together or well connected by public transportation. But the sights are superb and worth the effort. Of all the Netherlands' folk museums, Arnhem's Open-Air Folk Museum feels the most authentic (people might speak to you first in Dutch, assuming you're a local). The Kröller-Müller Museum, in the northeast corner of the Netherlands' huge Hoge Veluwe National Park, displays a wonderful collection of modern art. The park itself boasts pristine bike paths and free white bikes for everyone—an endearing remnant of Holland's hippie past.

The open-air museum is within Arnhem's city limits, but the Kröller-Müller Museum is technically a town away.

Getting There and Around

By **car**, you can easily hit the open-air museum and Kröller-Müller Museum within a day (for directions, see "Getting There," page 227).

By **public transportation**, it's possible to get to Arnhem's two main sights in one very long but fulfilling day of sightseeing. First you'll take the train to Arnhem (2/hr from Amsterdam, 75 min, likely transfer). Once there, you'll use buses to reach the open-air museum and the Kröller-Müller Museum (specific instructions are given in listings, below). Because buses don't connect these two sights directly, you'll have to come back to Arnhem's bus station between visits, limiting the amount of time you'll have at either sight. If you like to linger, stay overnight (try the Boutique Hotel Sterrenberg, described on page 230).

Bike enthusiasts may want to rent some wheels once in Arnhem to get to the open-air museum; it's a strenuous 30-minute uphill ride to the museum, then a breezy, easy 15-minute glide back into town (ask for directions at bike shop, listed under "Arrival in Arnhem," below). Only consider biking to the park and the Kröller-Müller Museum (2 hrs each way) if your name rhymes with "Mance Larmstrong."

Tourist Information

Arnhem's inconvenient TI (a private company, not an official VVV) is a 15-minute walk from the train station. Personally, I'd skip it. It's at the downtown performance hall, the Musis Sacrum (July–Aug Tue–Fri 9:30–17:30, Sat 9:30–17:00, Sun 11:00–16:00, closed Mon; Sept–June shorter hours and closed Sun, Velperbuitensingel 25, tel. 026/442-6767, vvv.arnhem.web.nl). The TI has a free city map, and sells a detailed €4.95 regional map that includes the national park/Kröller-Müller Museum (called *Midden en Zuid Veluwe*).

Arrival in Arnhem

Arnhem's **train station** is surrounded by a sea of construction and urban blight. The station has WCs (€0.30) and lockers (€4.60/24 hrs). There's a Rijwiel **bike-rental shop** directly to the left of the train station as you exit (€7.50/day for 3-speed bike—you'll need all speeds—plus €50 refundable deposit, daily 7:00–24:00).

To orient yourself, stand with the train station behind you. The **Connex** office, which has bus information, is about 50 yards to your left (Mon–Fri 7:00–19:00, Sat 9:00–12:30 & 13:00–17:00, Sun 10:00–12:30 & 13:00–17:00, you can buy a *strippenkaart* here). The **bus station** (with docks marked by letters) is in the tunnel about 15 yards to your right. The buses to the open-air museum leave from dock Q, while buses to the national park/Kröller-Müller Museum depart from dock S (always confirm bus routes, correct platforms, and departure times at the Connex office).

SIGHTS

Arnhem Open-Air Folk Museum (Openluchtmuseum)

Arnhem has the Netherlands' first, biggest, and best folk museum, worth ▲▲. You'll enjoy a huge park of windmills, old farmhouses

(gathered from throughout the Netherlands and reassembled here), traditional crafts in action, and a pleasant education-by-immersion in Dutch culture. It's great for families.

Cost and Hours: €11.50, Easter–Oct daily 10:00–17:00, open for winter festival Nov–mid-Jan daily 11:00–16:30, closed mid-Jan–Easter, tel. 026/357-6111, www.openluchtmuseum .nl. A little tram takes travelers around the park (€1 per trip, buy at ticket office, not from driver).

Getting There: To reach the open-air museum from the Arnhem train station, take bus #3 (direction: Alteveer) or the faster #13 (4/hr, 15 min, runs July–Aug only, €1). Catch either bus at platform Q (but confirm at Connex bus information office—see "Arrival in Arnhem," above). By car from Amsterdam, take A-2 south to Utrecht, then A-12 east to Arnhem. Just before Arnhem, take the Arnhem Nord exit Openluchtmuseum (exit #26) and follow signs to the nearby museum (€3.50 parking). If driving from Haarlem, skirt Amsterdam to the south on E-9, then follow signs to Utrecht.

⊃ **Self-Guided Tour:** With limited time, just hit the highlights. First visit the entrance pavilion to get the free map or the €4 English guidebook. Ask about special events and activities, especially for kids. Consider viewing the multimedia exhibit "HollandRama" (1/hr). The café in the entrance pavilion is inexpensive, but has limited choices (€3.50 sandwiches)—eat inside the park instead (restaurants recommended below).

Start your walk by heading straight down the entrance path on the left. Walk to the one-story **farmhouse** (4.1 on map, labeled as "cheese-covered" farmhouse); step inside and enjoy the hospitality of 1745. In the "cow house," see the patterns the farmwife would make with fresh sand and seashells each summer to show off family status.

Then cross the drawbridge (4.2), dating from 1358. Stop here to look out over the pond toward the sawmill. You might see children playing with a small, rope-pulled ferryboat.

Continue across the drawbridge into the little **village,** stopping on the way at the bakery and grocery on your right (4.8). Continue to the main square, where you can play with toys from the 1800s. See if you can make the "flying Dutchman" fly, or try to ride an original "high-wheeled velocipede" without falling off. Sample a *poffertje* (mini-pancake) from the little stall in the main square. Leave the square and head toward the cottage (4.11).

Behind and to the left of the *poffertje* shop, the fisherman's cottage—with a bright and colorful interior behind a black-tarred exterior—has a rope-controlled smoke hatch, rather than a chimney. Wooden cottages like these were nicknamed "smokehouses." Leaving the cottage, walk back through the square to visit the laundry (5.1), and imagine washing your clothes here.

Hike up to the 17th-century **paper mill** (5.4), where you might see a demonstration of linen rags being turned into pulp, and then into paper. Peek upstairs at the finished paper hanging to dry. Leave the mill and turn left; walk two minutes toward the dairy factory (7.1), noticing the beautiful herb garden to your right.

The **Freia Steam-Dairy Factory** (named after Freia, the Norse goddess of agriculture) was the Netherlands' first privately owned cheese and butter factory. Sample free cheese, and try to follow the huge belt of the steam engine as it whirls through the factory. From Freia, head toward the village school (8.2). Finally, cut across the main field and climb the platform mill (15.6) for a great view. You can walk back, or if your feet deserve a break today, hop on the tram for a one-way ride back to the entrance pavilion (€1).

Eating: The park has several good budget restaurants and covered picnic areas. Its rustic Pancake House serves hearty and sweet (splittable) Dutch flapjacks. The De Kasteelboerderij Café-Restaurant at the Oud-Beijerland Manor (traditional €8 *dagmenu*, or plate of the day) is a friendly place that can feed 300 visitors at once.

Kröller-Müller Museum and Nationaal Park de Hoge Veluwe

Located near Arnhem, Nationaal Park de Hoge Veluwe is the Netherlands' largest national park (13,000 acres) and is famous for its modern-art museum, set deep in the forest.

The memorable **Kröller-Müller Museum**, a ▲▲ sight, features 55 paintings by Vincent van Gogh. The museum has been undergoing a renovation, but is set to re-open completely mid-2006; until then, you'll see a few "greatest hits" galleries, including about 30 van Goghs.

The **national park** has 1,500 white bikes that you're free to use to make your explorations more fun. At the Visitors Center (Bezoekerscentrum), you'll find nature exhibitions, maps, WCs, the self-service restaurant Monsieur Jacques, and a playground for children. While riding through the vast, green woods, make a point of getting off your bike to climb an inland sand dune.

Cost, Hours, Information: It's €6 to enter the park, €6 more for museum, and €6 for its easy parking. The museum is open Tue–Sun 10:00–17:00, closed Mon (museum tel. 031/859-1241, www.kmm.nl). The national park is open daily June–Aug 8:00–21:00, April–May and Sept 8:00–20:00, and Oct–March 9:00–18:00 (park tel. 055/378-8100, www.hogeveluwe.nl).

The village of **Otterlo** is located just outside the Hoge Veluwe national park entrance that's closest to the Kröller-Müller Museum. Otterlo is a tiny town with tandem-bike tourists zipping through on their way to the park. The town also has cafés and a meager TI (100 yards south of the town center, July–Sept Mon–Fri 9:30–16:30, Sat 10:00–15:00, closed Sun and off-season, ATM in lobby, Arnhemseweg 14, tel. 0318/591-254).

Getting There: If you want to go directly from Amsterdam to the Kröller-Müller Museum, take the train to Ede-Wageningen (2/hr, 1 hr), where bus #110 run to Otterlo *centrum*. From Otterlo, it's a 20-minute walk to the park gates (less than a mile), where you can buy your ticket and hop on a free white bike to ride to the art museum or the Visitors Center. You can also wait in

Otterlo (usually about a 30-min wait) to catch bus #106, which goes directly into the park and stops at both the Kröller-Müller Museum and the Visitors Center (last bus back to Otterlo leaves at 17:55 from Visitors Center).

From the **Arnhem central station**, the Kröller-Müller Museum is 12 miles away. There's no direct bus to the museum, so you'll go via the town of Otterlo. Take bus #107 from Arnhem two stops to Otterlo *centrum* (2/hr, 30 min, 6 *strippenkaart* strips each way, tell driver you want to get off at stop closest to Kröller-Müller Museum; make a note of return times before you head into the park). When you get off the bus in Otterlo, you can take bus #106 or walk to the park (both options described above). You can hire a taxi from Arnhem, but it's expensive (you'll have to pay the car-entrance fee to the park, plus the fare—about €40).

Sleeping near the Park: $$ Boutique Hotel Sterrenberg, located just 300 yards from the park entrance, is a Dutch designer's take on a traditional hunting lodge. With woodsy touches and modern flair, it's beautiful. Consider spending the night here if you'd like to have a relaxing time at the museum, the park, and nearby Arnhem (Sb-€53–70, Db-€115, non-smoking, elevator, restaurant with outdoor seating, swimming pool, sauna, 7 rentable bikes for guests or use white bikes within nearby park gates, 2 miles to Kröller-Müller Museum, Houtkampweg 1, tel. 0318/591-228, fax 0138/591-693, www.sterrenberg.nl).

TRANSPORTATION CONNECTIONS

From Arnhem by Train to: Amsterdam (2/hr, 75 min, likely transfer).

Delft

Peaceful as a Vermeer painting (he was born here) and lovely as its porcelain, Delft, worth ▲▲, has a special soul. Enjoy this typically Dutch town best by simply wandering around, watching people, munching local syrup waffles, or daydreaming from the canal bridges.

Multiple all-day markets are held on Thursdays (general on Market Square, flower market on Hippolytusbuurt Square) and on Saturdays (general on Brabantse Turfmarkt and Burgwal, flea market at Hippolytusbuurt Square, and sometimes an art market at Heilige Geestkerkhof).

Johannes Vermeer
(1632–1675)

The great Golden Age painter Johannes Vermeer was born in Delft, grew up near Market Square, and set a number of his paintings here. His father, an art dealer, gave Johannes a passion for painting. Late in the artist's career, with Holland fighting draining wars against England, the demand for art and luxuries went sour in the Netherlands, forcing Vermeer to downsize—he sold his big home, packed up his wife and 14 children, and moved in with his mother-in-law. He died two years later.

After centuries of relative obscurity, Vermeer and his 20-some paintings are now much appreciated. None of his paintings are in Delft, but you'll find four of his masterpieces in Amsterdam's Rijksmuseum (see page 112) and others in The Hague's Mauritshuis museum.

Planning Your Time

Consider a day of contrasts, visiting both the citified Eurocrat center of The Hague and sleepy Delft; the two are so close, they almost touch, and they're linked by a simple tram ride (see The Hague's "Transportation Connections," below). I recommend starting the day in The Hague (busy and urban, described on page 234), and mellowing out in the afternoon by Delft's canals.

Tourist Information

This TI is a tourist's dream, offering a good brochure on Delft (which includes an excellent map). They sell four different brochures for €2.20 apiece, describing self-guided walking tours (April–Sept Sun–Mon 10:00–16:00, Tue–Fri 9:00–18:00, Sat 10:00–17:00; Oct–March Mon 11:00–16:00, Tue–Sat 10:00–16:00, Sun 11:00–17:00; free Internet access, 2-minute walk north of Markt to Hyppolytusbuurt 4, tel. 015/215-4051, www.delft.nl, info@tipdelft.nl).

Arrival in Delft

From the train station (€0.50 WCs, ATM on left as you leave), walk across the canal and follow blue-and-white signs to the town center (5 min). Drivers take the Delft exit 9 off the A-13 expressway.

SIGHTS

Royal Dutch Delftware Manufactory—The blue earthenware made at Delft's Koninklijke Porceleyne Fles is famous worldwide, and the biggest tourist attraction in town. The Dutch East India Company, headquartered here, had imported many exotic goods, including Chinese porcelain. The Chinese designs became trendy and were copied by many of the local potters. Three centuries later, their descendants are still going strong, and you can see them at work in this factory. Take a self-guided tour at any time: Watch the short video, follow the small tile arrows, and feel free to stop and chat with any of the artisans (€4 entry; April–Oct daily 9:00–17:00; Nov–March Mon–Sat 9:00–17:00, closed Sun). You can also catch an English-language tour (€4 plus €4 entry fee, April–Oct daily at 10:30, 11:30, 12:45, 14:00, 15:15, and 16:00; Rotterdamsweg 196; from train station, catch bus #63, #121, or #129 and get off at TU Aula/Jaffalaan bus stop—5-min walk from factory; €3 bike-taxi ride—flag one in Dam Square; tel. 015/251-2030, www.royaldelft.com).

New Church (Nieuwe Kerk)—Delft's big Gothic church, located prominently on the Market Square, is more interesting from the outside than inside. But if you want to work off your *pannenkoeken*, you can climb the tower steps to one of its three levels (€2 to climb tower, 3 levels and 350 steps; 30-min climb to top; €2.50 church entry—not worth it, Mon–Sat 9:00–18:00, Sun 10:00–17:00, tel. 015/212-3025).

SLEEPING

(€1 = about $1.20, country code: 31, area code: 015)

$$ Herberg de Emauspoort, picture-perfect and family-run, is relaxed, friendly, and wrapped around the family's 82-year-old bakery. It's ideally located one block from Market Square. The 23 rooms, named for sea heroes and Delft artists (most you've never heard of), overlook the canal or peek into the courtyard. Romantics can stay in one of their two "Gypsy caravans" ("Pipo de Clown" or "Mammaloe"). Borrow bikes for free (Sb-€82.50, Db-€87.50, Tb-€115, Qb-€140, taxes extra, non-smoking rooms, behind church/Market Square at Vrouwenregt 9–11, tel. 015/219-0219, fax 015/214-8251, www.emauspoort.nl, emauspoort@emauspoort.nl, Johan will explain who your room was named for).

$$ Hotel Bridges House, with 10 rooms around the corner from Market Square, is wood-beamed elegant and was once the home of painter Jan Steen. It's a canalside splurge (Sb-€88–125,

Delft Manufacturing Process

Delft earthenware is made from a soupy mix of clay and water. To make plates, the glop is rotated on a spinning disk until it looks like a traditional Dutch pancake. This "pancake" is then placed in a plate mold, where a design is pressed into it.

To make vases, pitchers, cups, and figurines, the liquid clay is poured into hollow plaster molds. These porous molds work like a sponge, sucking the water out of the clay to leave a layer of dry clay along the mold walls. Once the interior walls have reached the correct thickness, all excess clay within is poured off and recycled.

After the clay object is removed from the mold, it's fired in the kiln for 24 hours. The pottery removed from the kiln is called "biscuit." Next, painters trace traditional decorations with sable-hair pencils onto the biscuit pottery; these are then painted with a black paint containing cobalt oxide. When the pottery is fired, a chemical reaction changes the black paint into the famous Delft Blue. Before the second firing, the objects are dipped into an opaque white glaze, which melts into a translucent, glasslike layer.

Db-€108–155, prices vary with the season, extra bed-€20, Oude Delft 74, tel. 015/212-4036, fax 015/213-3600, www.bridges-house .com, info@bridges-house.com, energetic owner Jan-Willem).

$$ Hotel Leeuwenbrug, a former warehouse and now a business-class hotel, has 36 clean rooms, an Old World atmosphere, and a helpful staff (Sb-€55–101, Db-€85–117, prices lower in summer—when businessmen aren't in town, ask for off-season pricing, check for deals online, strictly non-smoking, free Internet access and Wi-Fi in lobby, Koornmarkt 16, tel. 015/214-7741, fax 015/215-9759, www .leeuwenbrug.nl, sales@leeuwenbrug.nl, helpful manager Wubben).

$ 't Raedthuys, a hotel/restaurant with six tired, basic rooms, is located right on Market Square (S-€38, Ss-€42, D-€45, Ds-€54, Qb-€88, no breakfast, €5–8 lunches in a great setting, Markt 38–40, tel. 015/212-5115, fax 015/213-6069, www.raadhuisdelft.nl).

TRANSPORTATION CONNECTIONS

From Delft to: Amsterdam (trains every 10 min, 40 min), **The Hague** (trains every 10 min, 15 min, but tram is more fun: catch tram #1—marked *Scheveningen*—to The Hague's city center; purchase tickets at TI or use 5 *strippenkaart* strips for the journey).

The Hague
(Den Haag)

Locals say the money is made in Rotterdam, divided in The Hague, and spent in Amsterdam. The Hague—the Netherlands' capital, and the home of several engaging museums—is worth ▲▲. For

a day of contrasts, spend the morning in the bustle of The Hague and the afternoon in nearby idyllic Delft (see page 230).

Tourist Information: The TI is opposite the Parliament building on Hofweg 1, just north of where Spui street becomes Hofweg (Mon–Fri 10:00–18:00, Sat 10:00–17:00, Sun 12:00–17:00, toll tel. 0900-340-3505 costs €0.45/min).

SIGHTS

▲Mauritshuis—The delightful, easy-to-tour art collection stars Vermeer and Rembrandt (€7.50, Tue–Sat 10:00–17:00, Sun 11:00–17:00, closed Mon in winter, Korte Vijverberg 8, tel. 070/302-3456).

Torture Museum (Gevangenpoort)—This house of horrors shows the medieval mind at its worst (€5, Tue–Fri 11:00–17:00, Sat–Sun 12:00–17:00, closed Mon, required tours on the hour, last one at 16:00, ask ticket-taker if film and talk will be in English before you commit, tel. 070/346-0861, www.gevangenpoort.nl).

Panorama Mesdag—For a look at the 19th century's attempt at virtual reality, stand in the center of this 360-degree painting of nearby Scheveningen in the 1880s, with a 3-D, sandy-beach foreground (€4, Mon–Sat 10:00–17:00, Sun 12:00–17:00, Zeestraat 65, tel. 070/310-6665).

Peace Palace—The palace, a gift from Andrew Carnegie, houses the International Court of Justice (€5; Mon–Fri: required guided tours at 10:00, 11:00, 14:00, or 15:00; closes Sat–Sun and without warning—call ahead or check at TI and make reservation, bring ID—required to enter, tram #1 or #10 from station, tel. 070/302-4137).

Scheveningen—The Dutch Coney Island has a newly renovated pier and is liveliest on sunny summer afternoons (from the street in front of the TI, take tram #1 heading north to the end of the line; from Central Station, take tram #9).

Madurodam—The mini-Holland amusement park, with miniature city buildings that make you feel like Godzilla, is fun for kids (adults-€12, kids 4–11-€9, daily Sept–mid-March 9:00–18:00, mid-March–June until 20:00, July–Aug until 22:00, George Maduroplein 1, tram #9 from The Hague's central train station, tel. 070/416-2400, www.madurodam.nl).

TRANSPORTATION CONNECTIONS

Trains connect The Hague and **Amsterdam** every 10 minutes (45-min trip, may require transfer in Leiden to reach The Hague's main station). Trains also go to **Delft** (4/hr, 15 min), but the 15-minute tram ride is more scenic (costs 5 *strippenkaart* strips, pick up tram in front of the TI). At The Hague's TI, buy the bus and tram map (€0.50) to follow along as you go. Tram #1—marked *Delft Tanthof*—runs south to Delft every five minutes. (If you take tram #1 to the north—marked *Scheveningen Nooderstrand*—you'll reach the family-fun pier described above.)

More Day Trips

▲▲▲**Keukenhof**—This is the greatest bulb-flower garden on earth. Each spring, seven million flowers, enjoying the sandy soil of the Dutch dunes and *polderland,* conspire to make even a total garden-hater enjoy them. This 80-acre park is packed with tour groups daily; for the least crowds and the best light, go late in the day (€12.50, open March 23–May 19 in 2006, daily 8:00–19:30, last tickets sold at 18:00, tel. 0252/465-555, www.keukenhof.com).

Getting There: Take the train to Leiden, then catch bus #54 (Keukenhof Express) to the garden (allow 75 min total from Amsterdam, 45 min total from Haarlem).

▲▲**Aalsmeer Flower Auction**—Get a bird's-eye view of the huge Dutch flower industry. Wander on elevated walkways (through what's claimed to be the biggest commercial building on earth) over literally trainloads of freshly cut flowers. About half of all

the flowers exported from Holland are auctioned off here in four huge auditoriums. Stop at one of the "listening posts" for on-the-spot information (€4.50, April–Sept Mon–Fri 7:00–11:00, Oct–March Mon–Fri 7:30–11:00, closed Sat–Sun year-round, the auction wilts after 9:30 and on Thu, gift shop, cafeteria, tel. 0297/392-185, www.aalsmeer.com).

Getting There: You can reach the flower auction from Amsterdam (bus #172 from train station, 4/hr, 60 min) or from Haarlem (take bus #198 or #140 and transfer to bus #172 in Aalsmeer, 2/hr, 60 min). Aalsmeer, which is close to the airport, makes a handy last fling before catching a late-morning weekday flight out (direct bus #198 to Schiphol Airport).

▲**Alkmaar**—Holland's cheese capital is especially fun (and touristy) during its weekly cheese market (Fri April–Aug 10:00–12:30, closed winter; **TI** open April–Aug Mon–Wed 10:00–17:30, Thu–Fri 9:00–17:30, Sat 9:30–17:00, closed Sun; Sept–March Mon–Fri 10:00–17:30, Sat 9:30–17:00, closed Sun; tel. 072/511-4284, www.vvvalkmaar.nl, info@vvvalkmaar.nl).

Sleeping in Alkmaar: $ Te Laat rents two tastefully decorated rooms above a café (enter hotel through café), a two-minute walk from the cheese market (1 standard Db-€80, suite-€125, breakfast-€6.50, Laat 117, tel. 072/512-5506, fax 072/511-6081, www.telaat.com, info@telaat.com). **$ B&B Van der Klei** rents two bright rooms in a canalside house; ask for the room in the front (D-€60, breakfast in kitchen or on terrace, Luttik Oudorp 87–89, tel. 072/515-6141, wilkleij@planet.nl).

▲**Zaanse Schans Open-Air Museum**—This re-created 17th-century town puts Dutch culture—from cheesemaking to wooden-shoe carving—on a lazy Susan. Located in the town of Zaandijk, it's the easiest one-stop look at the Netherlands' traditional culture. Zaanse Schans is also a big-bus tour experience, meant to squeeze every dollar it can out of its visitors. To avoid the hordes, come early or late.

Cost, Hours, Information: Entry is free, but it costs a euro or two to visit each historical presentation—and these costs can quickly add up (listed below). Open daily 8:30–17:30, until 17:00 in winter.

The Visitors Center, located in the Zaanse Museum building, has a good, free brochure/map; ask there about the day's scheduled events (daily Feb–Oct 9:00–17:00, Nov–Jan 10:00–17:00, bike rentals, lockers, free WCs in museum, otherwise €0.50 in park, tel. 075/616-8218, www.zaanseschans.nl).

A boat tour (Rederij de Schans Rondvaart) floats visitors through the park and adjacent town (€5, departs near Mustardmill, Tue–Sun 11:00–16:00, closed Mon, 45 min, tel. 075/614-6762).

Sights: The **Zaanse Museum,** which houses the Visitors Center, has a fresh, modern multimedia presentation that explains Holland's industrial past and present, with the help of a fine included audioguide (€4.50, daily Feb–Oct 9:00–17:00, Nov–Jan 10:00–17:00, tel. 075/616-2862).

The fragrant **Bakery Museum** (Bakkerijmuseum) sells what it bakes (€1 to enter museum, €2 for treats). The **Shoemaker** (Klompenmakerij) is a major stop in the park, with a three-minute video and a fascinating live demonstration that sends wood chips flying as a machine carves a shoe (free entry). At the **Cheese Shop** (Kaasmakerij), a local farmer is evangelical about Dutch cheeses, telling you how they're made and filling you with tasty samples (free entry).

Eating: Pannenkoeken Restaurant de Kraai offers delicious traditional sweet and savory pancakes that come with all the fillings you might select for an omelet—cheese, ham, mushrooms, and so on (€5–8 dishes, daily until 18:00, closed Jan).

Getting There: It's a couldn't-be-easier 15-minute train ride from Amsterdam (4/hr, take the Alkmaar-bound train to Koog-Zaandijk). From the Koog-Zaandijk station, walk 15 minutes (following teal signs) through a commercial gauntlet of flea-market tables, candles, lace, cheese, and toys. Along the way, you'll also pass a huge, fragrant, corporate chocolate factory. If driving from Amsterdam, take A-8 (direction: Zaanstad/Purmerend), turn off at Purmerend A-7, then follow signs to Zaanse Schans (parking costs €3.50 for the first hour, €7 maximum).

▲**Rotterdam**—This city, the world's largest port, bounced back after being bombed flat in World War II. See its towering Euromast, take a harbor tour, and stroll its great pedestrian zone (**TI** tel. 0900-403-4065, toll call costs €0.35/min, www.vvv .rotterdam.nl).

Utrecht—The Nationaal Museum van Speelklok tot Pierement, which offers free and mandatory guided 55-minute tours on the hour, demonstrates musical clocks, calliopes, and street organs (€7, Tue–Sat 10:00–17:00, Sun 12:00–17:00, closed Mon, last tour at 16:00, 10-min walk from station, located on busy shopping street in city center at Steenweg 6, tel. 030/231-2789, www .museumspeelklok.nl).

Zandvoort—For a quick and easy look at the windy coastline in a shell-lover's Shangri-la, visit the beach resort of Zandvoort, a breezy 45-minute bike ride or an eight-minute car or train ride west of Haarlem (from Haarlem, follow road signs to Bloemendaal). South of the main beach, sunbathers work on all-over tans.

De Rijp—This sleepy town is worth visiting if you're driving north of Amsterdam.

Volendam, Marken, and Monnikendam—These famous towns are quaint as can be, but very touristy.

TRANSPORTATION CONNECTIONS

The Netherlands

The Netherlands is so small, level, and well-covered by trains and buses that transportation is a snap. Major cities are connected by speedy trains that come and go every 10 or 15 minutes. Buses take you where trains don't, and bicycles take you where buses don't. Bus stations and bike-rental shops cluster around train stations.

Amsterdam

Buses

The national bus system, both within and between cities, runs on a uniform system of strip tickets *(strippenkaart)*; each time you board, you (or the driver) stamp your *strippenkaart*, deducting the fare of a ride. Single-ride tickets are also available. Buy *strippenkaart* at tobacco shops, bookstores, and machines at train stations, or on the bus but you'll pay extra. For details, see page 32). If you're caught riding without a strip ticket, you have to take off your clothes.

Trains

Intercity (IC) trains are fastest, connecting big cities; *sneltreins* connect smaller towns; and *stoptreins* are pokey, milk-run trains that stop at every station. Train connections are excellent, and you'll rarely wait more than a few minutes. Round-trip tickets are discounted.

You have two options for buying train tickets in the Netherlands: at a ticket window (costs €0.50 extra), or at an automated machine (no extra charge). Some machines have instructions only in Dutch, and you can pay in euros (no credit cards). Frustratingly, the newer machines—which have instructions

Netherlands Train Lines

in English—accept only Dutch debit cards (no cash, Visa, or MasterCard). If you're having trouble, visit the yellow information booth, or enlist the help of any official-looking employees (most wear portable computers with timetables) to help you with train departure times, or to navigate your way through the older, Dutch-only machine menus. If lines are short and frustration levels high, pay the extra €0.50 to buy your ticket at the window.

The easiest way to get train schedules is online. The German Rail site has comprehensive schedules for virtually anywhere in Europe (http://bahn.hafas.de/bin/query.exe/en). Or try the Dutch Rail site (www.ns.nl). For phone information, dial 0900-9292 for local trains or 0900-9296 for international trains (€0.50/min, daily 7:00–24:00, wait through recording and hold...hold...hold...). The numbers listed in this chapter are frustrating phone trees in Dutch and—if you wait—maybe in English.

You'll find storage lockers at the north end of Amsterdam's Central Station—but during busy summer weekends, they can fill up fast, causing a line to form (€5.70/24 hours, daily 7:00–23:00, ID required).

Since 2004, smoking has been prohibited in trains and train stations.

From Amsterdam

Amsterdam's train-information center can require a long wait. Save lots of time by getting train tickets and information in a small-town station (such as Haarlem), at the airport upon arrival, or from a travel agency. Remember, you can use *strippenkaart* on any train that travels within the Netherlands.

By Train to: Schiphol Airport (6/hr, 20 min, €3.40, have coins handy to buy from a machine to avoid lines, train usually departs from track 13a), **Haarlem** (6/hr, 15 min, €3.40 one-way, €6 same-day round-trip), **The Hague/Den Haag** (6/hr, 45 min, may require switch in Leiden to get to main station), **Delft** (every 10 min, 50 min), **Arnhem** (2/hr, 75 min, transfer likely), **Rotterdam** (4/hr, 1 hr), **Bruges** (hrly, 3.5 hrs, transfer in Brussels or Antwerp's central station; transfer can be timed closely—be alert and check with conductor), **Brussels** (hrly, 3 hrs, €30–42.50), **Ostende** (hrly, 4 hrs, change in Antwerp), **London** (6–7/day, 6 hrs, with transfer to Eurostar Chunnel train in Brussels, Eurostar discounted with railpass, www.eurostar.com), **Copenhagen** (hrly, 15 hrs, requires multiple transfers), **Frankfurt** (hrly, 4–5 hrs, some are direct, others involve transfer in Köln or Duisburg), **Munich** (7/day, 7–8 hrs, transfer in Frankfurt or Düsseldorf), **Bonn** (10/day, 3 hrs, some direct but most transfer in Köln), **Bern** (5/day, 9 hrs, 1 direct but most transfer in Mannheim), **Paris** (5/day, 5 hrs, requires fast Thalys train from Brussels with €11 supplement, www.thalys .com).

By Bus: If you don't have a railpass, the cheapest way to get to Paris is by bus (Eurolines buses make the 8-hour trip 5 times daily, about €40–60 round-trip, compared to €100 second-class by train; check online for deals, bus station in Amsterdam at Julianaplein 5, Amstel Station, 5 stops by metro from Central Station, tel. 020/560-8788, www.eurolines.com).

Amsterdam's Schiphol Airport

Schiphol (SKIP-pol) Airport, like most of Holland, is English-speaking, user-friendly, and below sea level.

Information: Schiphol flight information (tel. 0900-7244-7465) can give you flight times and your airline's Amsterdam phone number for reconfirmation before going home (€0.45/min to climb through its phone tree—or visit www.schiphol.nl). To reach the airlines directly, call: KLM and Northwest, tel. 020/649-9123 or 020/474-7747; Martinair, tel. 020/601-1222; SAS, tel. 0900-746-63727; American Airlines, tel. 06/022-7844; British Airways, tel. 023/554-7555; and easyJet, tel. 023/568-4880.

Services: The ABN/AMRO **banks** offer fair rates (in arrivals and lounge area). The GWK **public-transit office** is located in Schiphol Plaza. Surf the **Internet** and make phone calls at the Communication Centre on the top level of lounge 2 (daily 6:00–20:00, behind customs—not available once you've left the security checkpoint). Convenient luggage **lockers** are at various points around the terminal—and a big bank of them is on the bottom floor—allowing you to leave your bag at the airport on a lengthy layover (both short-term and long-term lockers).

If you have extra time to kill at Schiphol, check out some **fine art**, actual Dutch Masters by Rembrandt, Vermeer, and others. The Rijksmuseum loans a dozen or so of its minor masterpieces from the Golden Age to the unique airport museum "Rijksmuseum Amsterdam Schiphol," a little art gallery behind the passport check at Holland Boulevard between piers E and F. Yes, this is really true (free, daily 7:00–20:00). To escape the crowds in the airport, follow signs for the *Panorama Terrace* to the third floor, where you'll find a quieter, locals-only cafeteria, a kids' play area, and a view terrace where you can watch planes come and go while you nurse a coffee.

Transportation Connections: The airport has a train station of its own. You can validate your Eurailpass and hit the rails immediately, or, to stretch your railpass, buy an inexpensive ticket into Amsterdam today and start the pass later.

From Schiphol Airport to Amsterdam: There's a direct **train** to Amsterdam's Central Station (every 10 min, 20 min, €3.40). The Connexxion **shuttle bus** takes you to your hotel neighborhood; since there are various routes, ask the attendant which works best for your hotel (2/hr, 20 min, €11 one-way, €17.50 round-trip, one route stops at Westerkerk near Anne Frank House and many recommended hotels, bus to other hotels may cost a couple euros more, departs from lane A7 in front of airport, tel. 020/653-4975, www.airporthotelshuttle.nl). Allow about €40 for a **taxi** to downtown Amsterdam.

From Schiphol Airport to Haarlem: The big red #300 **bus** is direct, stopping at Haarlem's train station and near the Market Square (4/hr, 40 min, €5.80—buy ticket from driver, or use 7 strips of a *strippenkaart*, departs from lane B2 in front of airport). The **train** is slightly cheaper and just as quick, but you'll have to transfer at the Amsterdam-Sloterdijk station (4/hr, 40 min, €4.55). Figure about €40 to Haarlem by taxi.

From Schiphol Airport by Train to: The Hague/Den Haag (2/hr, 30 min), **Delft** (4/hr, 45 min, transfer in The Hague or Leiden), **Rotterdam** (3/hr, 45 min). International trains to Belgium run every hour: **Brussels** (2.5 hrs), **Bruges** (3.25 hrs, change in Antwerp or Brussels).

Haarlem

From Haarlem by Train to: Amsterdam (6/hr, 15 min, €3.40 one-way, €6 same-day round-trip), **The Hague** (4/hr, 35 min), **Delft** (2/hr, 40 min), **Rotterdam** (2/hr, 50 min, may require change in Leiden), **Hoorn** (2/hr, 1 hr), **Alkmaar** (2/hr, 45 min), **Brussels** (hrly, 2.75 hrs, transfer in Rotterdam), **Bruges** (1–2/hr, 3.5 hrs, requires transfer).

To Schiphol Airport: Your options are the **bus** (4/hr, 40 min, €5.80, bus #300, departs from Haarlem's train station in "Zuidtangent" lane), **train** (4/hr, 40 min, transfer at Amsterdam-Sloterdijk station, €4.90), or **taxi** (about €45).

BELGIUM

Belgium falls through the cracks. It's nestled between Germany, France, and Britain, and it's famous for waffles, sprouts, endives, and a statue of a little boy peeing—no wonder many travelers don't even consider a stop here. But many who do visit remark that Belgium is one of Europe's best-kept secrets. There are tourists—but not as many as the country's charms merit.

Belgium is split between the French-speaking Walloons in the south and the Dutch-speaking Flemish people (60 percent of the population) in the north. Talk to locals to learn how deep the cultural rift is. Belgium's capital, Brussels, while mostly French-speaking, is officially bilingual. The country also has a small minority of German-speaking people. Because of Belgium's international importance as the capital of the European Union, more than 25 percent of its residents are foreigners.

It's here in Belgium that Europe comes together: where Romance languages meet Germanic languages, Catholics meet Protestants, and the Benelux union was established 40 years ago, planting the seed that today is sprouting into the unification of Europe. Belgium flies the flag of Europe more vigorously than any other place on the Continent.

Bruges and Brussels are the best two first bites of Belgium. Brussels is simply one of Europe's great cities. Bruges is a

How Big, How Many, How Much

- 12,000 square miles, a little larger than Maryland
- 10 million people (830 per square mile)
- €1 = about $1.20

Belgium

wonderfully preserved medieval gem that expertly nurtures the tourist industry, bringing the town a prosperity it hasn't enjoyed since 500 years ago, when—as one of the largest cities in the world—it helped lead northern Europe out of the Middle Ages.

Belgians brag that they eat as much as the Germans and as well as the French. They are among the world's leading beer consumers and carnivores. In Belgium, never bring chrysanthemums to a wedding—they symbolize death. And tweaking little kids on the ear is considered rude.

Ten million Belgians are packed into a country only a little bigger than Maryland. With 830 people per square mile, it's the second most densely populated country in Europe (after the Netherlands). This population concentration, coupled with a dense and well-lit rail and road system, causes Belgium to shine at night when viewed from space, a phenomenon NASA astronauts call the "Belgian Window."

BRUGES
Brugge

ORIENTATION

With Renoir canals, pointy, gilded architecture, vivid time-tunnel art, and stay-a-while cafés, Bruges is a heavyweight sightseeing destination, as well as a joy. Where else can you ride a bike along a canal, munch mussels and wash them down with the world's best beer, savor heavenly chocolate, and see Flemish Primitives and a Michelangelo, all within 300 yards of a bell tower that jingles every 15 minutes? And there's no language barrier.

The town is Brugge (BROO-ghah) in Flemish, and Bruges (broozh) in French and English. Its name comes from the Viking word for wharf. Right from the start, Bruges was a trading center. In the 11th century, the city grew wealthy on the cloth trade.

By the 14th century, Bruges' population was 35,000, as large as London's. As the middleman in sea trade between northern and southern Europe, it was one of the biggest cities in the world and an economic powerhouse. In addition, Bruges had become the most important cloth market in northern Europe.

In the 15th century, while England and France were slogging it out in the Hundred Years' War, Bruges was the favored residence of the powerful Dukes of Burgundy—and at peace. Commerce and the arts boomed. The artists Jan van Eyck and Hans Memling had studios here.

But by the 16th century, the harbor had silted up and the economy had collapsed. The Burgundian court left, Belgium became a minor Hapsburg possession, and Bruges' Golden Age abruptly ended. For generations, Bruges was known as a mysterious and dead city. In the 19th century, a new port, Zeebrugge, brought renewed vitality to the area. And in the 20th century, tourists discovered the town.

Today, Bruges prospers because of tourism: It's a uniquely well-preserved Gothic city and a handy gateway to Europe. It's no secret, but even with the crowds, it's the kind of city where you don't mind being a tourist.

Bruges' ultimate sight is the town itself, and the best way to enjoy it is to get lost on the back streets, away from the lace shops and ice-cream stands.

Planning Your Time

Bruges needs at least two nights and a full, well-organized day. Even non-shoppers enjoy browsing here, and the Belgian love of life makes a hectic itinerary seem a little senseless. With one day (other than a Monday, when all the museums are closed), the speedy visitor could do the Bruges blitz described below:

9:30	Climb the bell tower on Market Square.
10:00	Tour the sights on Burg Square.
11:00	Tour the Groeninge Museum.
12:00	Tour the Gruuthuse Museum.
13:00	Eat lunch and buy chocolates.
14:00	Take a short canal cruise.
14:30	Visit the Church of Our Lady and see Michelangelo's *Madonna and Child*.
15:00	Tour the Memling Museum.
16:00	Catch the De Halve Maan Brewery tour (note that their last tour runs at 15:00 in winter).
17:00	Calm down in the Begijnhof courtyard.
18:00	Ride a bike around the quiet back streets of town or take a horse-and-buggy tour.
20:00	Lose the tourists and find dinner.

If this schedule seems insane, skip the bell tower and the brewery—or stay another day.

OVERVIEW

The tourist's Bruges—and you'll be sharing it—is less than one square mile, contained within a canal (the former moat). Nearly everything of interest and importance is within a convenient cobbled swath between the train station and Market Square (a 15-min walk). Many of my quiet, charming recommended accommodations lie just beyond Market Square.

Tourist Information

The main tourist office, called **In&Uit** (literally, "In and Out"), is in the big, red concert hall on the square called 't Zand (daily 10:00–18:00, Thu until 20:00, 't Zand 34, tel. 050/448-686, www.brugge.be). The other TI is at the train station (generally Tue–Sat 10:00–13:00 & 14:00–17:00, closed Sun–Mon).

The TIs sell a great €1 Bruges visitors guide with a map and listings of all of the sights and services. You can also pick up a monthly English-language program called *events@brugge*. The TIs have information on train schedules and on the many tours available (see "Tours," below). Bikers will want the *5X on the Bike Around Bruges* map/guide (€1.50) that shows five routes through the countryside. Many hotels give out free maps with more detail than the map the TIs sell.

Arrival in Bruges

By Train: Coming in by train, you'll see the square bell tower that marks the main square. Upon arrival, stop by the station TI to pick up the €1 Bruges visitors guide (with map). The station lacks ATMs, but has lockers (€2–3.50, daily 6:00–24:00).

The best way to get to the town center is by **bus**. Buses #1, #3, #4, #6, #8, #11, #13, and #16 go directly to Market Square. Simply hop on, pay €1, and in four minutes, you're there. Buses #4 and #8 continue on to the northeast part of town (to the windmills and recommended accommodations on Carmersstraat). The **taxi** fare from the train station to most hotels is about €6.

It's a 20-minute **walk** from the station to the center—no fun with your luggage. If you want to walk to Market Square, cross the busy street and canal in front of the station, head up Oostmeers, and turn right on Zwidzandstraat. You can rent a **bike** at the station for the duration of your stay, but other bike rental shops are closer to the center (see "Helpful Hints," below).

By Car: Park at the train station for just €2.50 per day and take the bus into town. There are pricier underground parking garages at the square called 't Zand and around town (€10/day, all of them well-marked). Paid parking on the street in Bruges is limited to four hours. Driving in town is very complicated because of the one-way system.

Helpful Hints

Market Days: Bruges hosts markets on Wednesday morning (Market Square) and Saturday morning ('t Zand). On Saturday and Sunday, a flea market hops along Dijver in front of the Groeninge Museum.

Shopping: Shops are open from 9:00 to 18:00, and a little later on Friday. Grocery stores are usually closed on Sunday. The main shopping street, Steenstraat, stretches from Market Square to the square called 't Zand. The Hema department store is at Steenstraat 73 (Mon–Sat 9:00–18:00, closed Sun).

Money: Although there are no ATMs at the train station, there are plenty in town: at the post office (Markt 5), Fortis Bank (Simon Stevins Plein 3), Fortis Bank (Hoogstraat 23), KBC (Steenstraat 38), and Fortis Bank (Vlamingstraat 78).

Museum Tips

Admission prices are steep, but they include great audio-guides—so plan on spending some time and really getting into it. For information on all the museums, call 050/448-711 or visit www.brugge.be.

Combo-Tickets: The TIs and participating museums sell a museum combo-ticket (any 5 museums for €15, open-ended validity period). Since the Groeninge and Memling museums cost €8 each, art lovers will save money with this pass. Another combo-ticket offers three museums and a one-day bike rental for €15 (get bike from Koffieboontje, listed under "Helpful Hints"; sold at bike shop or TI, open-ended validity period). If you use one of these combo-tickets, you don't need to wait in any lines—simply walk directly to the turnstile, get your ticket punched, and go in.

Blue Monday: In Bruges, nearly all museums are open Tuesday through Sunday year-round from 9:30 to 17:00 and are closed on Monday. If you're in Bruges on a Monday, the following attractions are still open: bell-tower climb on Market Square, Church of Our Lady, Begijnhof, De Halve Maan Brewery Tour, Basilica of the Holy Blood, City Hall's Gothic Room, and chocolate shops and museum. You can also join a boat, bus, or walking tour, or rent a bike and pedal into the countryside.

Internet Access: The relaxing **Coffee Link,** with mellow music and pleasant art, is centrally located in a medieval mall across from the Church of Our Lady (€3/30 min, 16 terminals surrounded by sweet temptations, daily 10:00–18:00 in summer, Mariastraat 38, tel. 050/349-973, well-run by Staf).

Post Office: It's on Market Square near the bell tower (Mon–Fri 9:00–18:00, Sat 9:30–12:30, closed Sun, tel. 050/331-411).

Laundry: Bruges has three self-service launderettes, each a five-minute walk from the center; ask your hotel for the nearest one.

Bike Rental: Koffieboontje (literally "Coffee Bean"), just under the bell tower on Market Square, is the handiest place to rent bikes. They're extremely well organized—they swipe a credit-card imprint for a deposit, and you're on your way with a nearly new bike (€3.50/1 hr, €7/4 hrs, €10/24-hr day, special discount with this book in 2006: €7/24-hr day, free city maps and child seats, daily 9:00–22:00, Hallestraat 4, tel. 050/338-027, www.hotel-koffieboontje.be). The €15 bike-plus-any-three-museums combo-ticket works only with this outfit (and can save enough to pay for lunch).

Other rental places include the less central **De Ketting** (cheap at €5/day, Mon–Fri 9:00–19:00, Sat–Sun 9:00–14:00, Gentpoortstraat 23, tel. 050/344-196), and the **train station** (ticket window labeled *verhuring fietsen*, €9.50/day, €6.50/ half-day after 14:00, €20 deposit, daily 7:00–20:00, blue lockers here for day-trippers leaving bags).

Best Town View: The bell tower overlooking Market Square rewards those who climb it with the ultimate town view.

Getting Around Bruges

Most of the city is easily walkable, but you may want to take the bus or taxi between the train station and the city center (especially if you have heavy luggage).

By Bus: A €1 bus ticket is good for an hour; an all-day pass costs €3. Nearly all city buses go directly from the train station to Market Square and fan out from there. They then return to Market Square and back to the station. Note that buses returning to the station from the center leave from the library bus stop, a block off Market Square on nearby Kuiperstraat (every 5 min).

By Taxi: You'll find taxi stands at the station and on Market Square (to call a cab in the center, dial 050/334-444).

TOURS

Of Bruges

Bruges by Boat—The most relaxing and scenic (though not

informative) way to see this city of canals is by boat, with the captain narrating. (Always let them know you speak English to ensure you'll understand the spiel.) Several companies offer basically the same 30-minute tour (€5.70, 4/hr, daily 10:00–17:00). Two companies give a €0.90 discount with this book in 2006: Boten Stael (just over the canal from Memling Museum at Katelijnestraat 4, tel. 050/332-771) and Gruuthuse (Nieuwstraat 11, opposite the Groeninge Museum).

Bruges

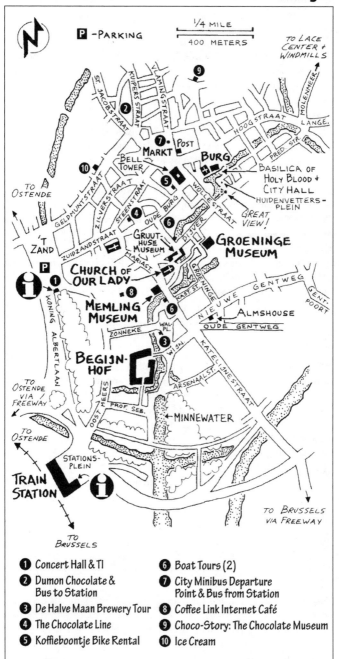

P –PARKING

¼ MILE

400 METERS

N

TO LACE
CENTER +
WINDMILLS

ST. JACOBSTRAAT

KUIPERS STRAAT

VLAMINGSTRAAT

❷ Dumon Chocolate

HOOGSTRAAT

LANGE.

MOLENMEER

❾ Choco-Story

❼ City Minibus

Post

MARKT

BELL
TOWER

BURG

BASILICA OF
HOLY BLOOD +
CITY HALL

HUIDENVETTERS-
PLEIN

❺

❿

GELDMUNTSTRAAT

SILVERSTRAAT

STEENSTRAAT

OUDE BURG

❹

WOLLESTRAAT

PI. VER

GREAT
VIEW!

TO
OSTENDE

'T
ZAND

ZUIDZANDSTRAAT

GRUUT-
HUSE
MUSEUM

GROENINGE
MUSEUM

❻

MARIAST.

GROENINGE

GENTWEG

GENT-
POORT

P

i

❶

CHURCH OF
OUR LADY

❽

MEMLING
MUSEUM

KAST ST.

NIEUWE

ALMSHOUSE

OUDE GENTWEG

KATELIJNESTRAAT

KONING ALBERTLAAN

ZONNEKE

WAL-
PL.

❻

W.SN.

❸

BEGIJN-
HOF

TO
OSTENDE
VIA
FREEWAY

OOST MEERS

PROF. SEB.

ARSENAALST.

MINNEWATER

TO
OSTENDE

STATIONS-
PLEIN

i

TRAIN
STATION

TO BRUSSELS
VIA FREEWAY

TO
BRUSSELS

❶ Concert Hall & TI

❷ Dumon Chocolate &
Bus to Station

❸ De Halve Maan Brewery Tour

❹ The Chocolate Line

❺ Koffieboontje Bike Rental

❻ Boat Tours (2)

❼ City Minibus Departure
Point & Bus from Station

❽ Coffee Link Internet Café

❾ Choco-Story: The Chocolate Museum

❿ Ice Cream

City Minibus Tour—City Tour Bruges gives a rolling overview of the town in an 18-seat, two-skylight minibus with dial-a-language headsets and video support (€11.50, 50 min). The tour leaves hourly from Market Square (10:00–20:00 in summer, until 18:00 in spring, until 17:00 in fall, less in winter, tel. 050/355-024, www.citytour.be). The narration, while clear, is slow-moving and a bit boring. But the tour is a lazy way to cruise past virtually every sight in Bruges.

Walking Tour—Local guides walk small groups through the core of town (€5, €12 for a family, 2 hrs, daily July–Aug, Sat–Sun only mid-May–June and Sept, no tours Oct–mid-May, depart from TI on 't Zand at 14:30—just drop in a few minutes early). Though earnest, the tours are heavy on history and given in two languages, so they may be less than peppy. Still, to propel you beyond the pretty gables and canal swans of Bruges, they're good medicine.

Private Guide—A private two-hour guided tour costs €45 (reserve at least 1 week in advance through TI, tel. 050/448-686). Or contact Christian and Danielle Scharle, who give two-hour walks for €50 and three-hour guided drives for €100 (Christian's mobile 0475-659-507, Danielle's mobile 0476-493-203, tmb@skynet.be).

Horse-and-Buggy Tour—The buggies around town can take you on a clip-clop tour (€30, 35 min, price is per carriage, not per person). When divided among four or five people, this can be a good value.

From Bruges

Quasimodo Countryside Tours—This company offers those with extra time two excellent, entertaining, all-day, English-only bus tours through the rarely visited Flemish countryside.

The "In Flanders Fields" tour concentrates on World War I battlefields, trenches, memorials, and poppy-splattered fields (April–Oct Tue–Sun 9:15–17:00; Nov–March Sun, Tue, and Thu only).

The other tour, "Triple Treat," focuses on Flanders' medieval past and rich culture, with tastes of chocolate, waffles, and beer (Mon, Wed, and Fri 9:15–17:00). Be ready for lots of walking.

Tours cost €50, or €40 if you're under 26 (includes a picnic lunch, 30-seat, non-smoking bus, reserve by calling tel. 050/370-470 or toll-free tel. 0800-97525, www.quasimodo.be). After making a few big-hotel pick-ups, the buses leave town at 9:15 from the Park Hotel on 't Zand.

Daytours—Tour guide Frank loves leading small groups on a fascinating "Flanders Fields Battlefield" day trip. This tour is like Quasimodo's (listed above), but more expensive. The differences: seven travelers on a minibus rather than a big busload; pick-up from any hotel or B&B (because the small bus is allowed in the town center); an included restaurant lunch rather than a picnic; and a little more serious lecturing and a stricter focus on World War I. For instance, you actually visit the In Flanders Fields Museum in Ieper (Ypres in French). Tours cost €59 (€5 discount when booked direct using this book in 2006, Wed–Sun 9:00–17:00, no tours Mon–Tue, call 050/346-060 or toll-free 0800-99133 to reserve).

Bruges by Bike—QuasiMundo Biketours Brugge leads daily bike tours around the city (departs at 10:00, 5 miles, 2.5 hrs). Their other tour, "Border by Bike," goes through the nearby countryside to Damme (departs at 13:00, 15 miles, 4 hrs). Either tour costs €20, or €17 with this book in 2006 (tel. 050/330-775, www.quasimundo .com). Both tours include bike rental, a light raincoat (if necessary), water, and a drink in a local café. Meet on Burg Square. If you already have a bike, you're welcome to join either tour for €14. For a do-it-yourself bike tour, see page 260.

Bus and Boat Tour—The Sightseeing Line offers a bus trip to Damme and a boat ride back (€16.50, April–Sept daily at 14:00, 2 hrs, leaves from the post office at Market Square, tel. 050/355-024).

SIGHTS

These sights are listed in walking order from Market Square to Burg Square to the cluster of museums around the Church of our Lady to the Begijnhof (10-min walk from beginning to end, without stops). ✪ For a self-guided walk and more information on each sight, see the Bruges City Walk, page 262.

▲**Market Square (Markt)**—Ringed by a bank, the post office, lots of restaurant terraces, great old gabled buildings, and the iconic bell tower, this is the modern heart of the city (most city buses run from near here to the train station—library bus stop, a block down Kuiperstraat). Under the bell tower are two great Belgian french-fry stands, a quadrilingual Braille description of the old town, and a metal model of the tower. In Bruges' heyday as a trading center, a canal came right up to this square.

Geldmuntstraat, just off the square, is a delightful street with many fun and practical shops and eateries.

▲▲**Bell Tower (Belfort)**—Most of this bell tower has presided over Market Square since 1300, serenading passersby with carillon music. The octagonal lantern was added in 1486, making it 290 feet high—that's 366 steps. The view is worth the climb and the €5 (daily 9:30–17:00, last entry 45 min before closing, €0.30 WC in courtyard).

▲▲**Burg Square**—This opulent square is Bruges' civic center, historically the birthplace of Bruges and the site of the ninth-century castle of the first Count of Flanders. Today, it's the scene of outdoor concerts and surrounded by six centuries of architecture.

▲**Basilica of the Holy Blood**—Originally the Chapel of Saint Basil, this church is famous for its relic of the blood of Christ, which, according to tradition, was brought to Bruges in 1150 after the Second Crusade. The lower chapel is dark and solid—a fine example of Romanesque style. The upper chapel (separate entrance, climb the stairs) is decorated Gothic. An interesting treasury museum is next to the upper chapel (treasury entry–€1.50; April–Sept Thu–Tue 9:30–11:45 & 14:00–17:45, Wed 9:30–11:45 only; Oct–March Thu–Tue 10:00–11:45 & 14:00–15:45, Wed 10:00–11:45 only; Burg Square, tel. 050/336-792, www.holyblood.org).

▲**City Hall**—This complex houses several interesting sights. Your €2.50 ticket includes an audioguide; access to a room full of old town maps and paintings; the grand, beautifully restored **Gothic Room** from 1400, starring a painted and carved wooden ceiling adorned with hanging arches (daily 9:30–17:00, Burg 12); and the less impressive **Renaissance Hall** (Brugse Vrije), basically just one ornate room with a Renaissance chimney (Tue–Sun 9:30–12:30 & 13:30–16:30, closed Mon, separate entrance—in corner of square at Burg 11a).

▲▲▲**Groeninge Museum**—This museum houses a world-class collection of mostly Flemish art, from Memling to Magritte. While there's plenty of worthwhile modern art, the highlights are the vivid and pristine Flemish Primitives. ("Primitive" here means before the Renaissance.) Flemish art is shaped by its love of detail, its merchant patrons' egos, and the power of the Church. Lose yourself in the halls of Groeninge: Gaze across 15th-century canals, into the eyes of reassuring Marys, and through town squares littered with leotards, lace, and lopped-off heads (€8, includes audioguide, Tue–Sun 9:30–17:00, closed Mon, Dijver 12, tel. 050/448-751). ○ See Groeninge Museum Tour, page 278.

▲**Gruuthuse Museum**—Once a wealthy brewer's home, this 15th-century mansion is a sprawling smattering of everything from medieval bedpans to a guillotine (€6, includes audioguide and entry to apse in Church of Our Lady, Tue–Sun 9:30–17:00, closed Mon, Dijver 17).

▲▲**Church of Our Lady**—The church stands as a memorial to the power and wealth of Bruges in its heyday. A delicate *Madonna and Child* by Michelangelo is near the apse (to the right if you're facing the altar). It's said to be the only Michelangelo statue to leave Italy in his lifetime (thanks to the wealth generated by Bruges' cloth trade). If you like tombs and church art, pay to wander through the apse (Michelangelo viewing is free, art-filled apse–€2.50, covered by €6 Gruuthuse admission, Mon–Fri 9:30–16:50, Sat 9:30–15:50, Sun 13:30–16:50 only, Mariastraat).

▲▲**Memling Museum/St. John's Hospital (Sint Janshospitaal)**—The former monastery/hospital complex has two entrances—one is to a welcoming visitors center (free), the other to the Memling Museum. The Memling Museum, in the monastery's former church, was once a medieval hospital and now contains six much-loved paintings by the greatest of the Flemish Primitives, Hans Memling. His *Mystical Wedding of St. Catherine* triptych is a

Bruges at a Glance

▲▲▲**Groeninge Museum** Top-notch collection of mainly Flemish art. **Hours:** Tue–Sun 9:30–17:00, closed Mon.

▲▲**Bell Tower** Overlooking Market Square, with 366 steps to a worthwhile view and a carillon close-up. **Hours:** Daily 9:30–17:00.

▲▲**Burg Square** Historic square with sights and impressive architecture. **Hours:** Always open.

▲▲**Memling Museum/St. John's Hospital** Art by the greatest of the Flemish Primitives. **Hours:** Tue–Sun 9:30–17:00, closed Mon.

▲▲**Church of Our Lady** Tombs and church art, including Michelangelo's *Madonna and Child*. **Hours:** Mon–Fri 9:30–16:50, Sat 9:30–15:50, Sun 13:30–16:50 only.

▲▲**Begijnhof** Benedictine nuns' peaceful courtyard and Beguine's House museum. **Hours:** Courtyard always open, museum open daily 10:00–12:00 & 13:45–17:00, shorter hours off-season.

▲▲**De Halve Maan Brewery Tour** Fun and handy tour includes beer. **Hours:** Daily on the hour 11:00–16:00, Oct–March at 11:00 and 15:00 only.

▲▲**Biking** Explore the countryside and pedal to nearby Damme.

highlight, as is the miniature gilded oak shrine to St. Ursula (€8, includes fine audioguide, Tue–Sun 9:30–17:00, closed Mon, across the street from the Church of Our Lady, Mariastraat 38). ✪ See Memling Museum Tour, page 287.

▲▲**Begijnhof**—Inhabited by Benedictine nuns, the Begijnhof courtyard (free and always open) almost makes you want to don a habit and fold your hands as you walk under its wispy trees and whisper past its frugal little homes. For a good slice of Begijnhof life, walk through the simple museum, the Beguine's House (€2, daily 10:00–12:00 & 13:45–17:00, shorter hours off-season, English explanations, Beguine's House is left of entry gate).

Minnewater—Just south of the Begijnhof is Minnewater, an idyllic world of flower boxes, canals, and swans.

Almshouses—Walking from the Begijnhof back to the town center, you might detour along Nieuwe Gentweg to visit one of about 20 almshouses in the city. At #8, go through the door marked

Hours: Koffieboontje bike-rental shop open daily 9:00–22:00 (see page 249).

▲**Market Square** Main square that is the modern heart of the city, with carillon bell tower (described above). **Hours:** Always open.

▲**Basilica of the Holy Blood** Romanesque and Gothic church housing a relic of the blood of Christ. **Hours:** April–Sept Thu–Tue 9:30–11:45 & 14:00–17:45, Wed 9:30–11:45 only; Oct–March Thu–Tue 10:00–11:45 & 14:00–15:45, Wed 10:00–11:45 only.

▲**City Hall** Beautifully restored Gothic Room from 1400, plus a Renaissance Hall. **Hours:** Gothic Room—daily 9:30–17:00; Renaissance Hall—Tue–Sun 9:30–12:30 & 13:30–16:30, closed Mon.

▲**Gruuthuse Museum** 15th-century mansion displaying an eclectic collection that includes furniture, tapestries, and lots more. **Hours:** Tue–Sun 9:30–17:00, closed Mon.

▲**Chocolate** Sample Bruges' specialty: Try Dumon, The Chocolate Line, Sweertvaegher, and on and on. **Hours:** Shops generally open 10:00–18:00.

Choco-Story: The Chocolate Museum Learn the whole delicious story of Belgium's favorite treat. **Hours:** Daily 10:00–17:00.

Godshuis de Meulenaere 1613 into the peaceful courtyard (free). This was a medieval form of housing for the poor. The rich would pay for someone's tiny room here in return for lots of prayers.

The small **Diamond Museum** at the start of Nieuwe Gent-weg is a little more interesting than reading an encyclopedia (€6, daily 10:30–17:30, Katelijnestraat 43, tel. 050/342-056, www .diamondhouse.net).

Bruges Experiences: Beer, Chocolate, Lace, and Biking

▲▲**De Halve Maan Brewery Tour**—Belgians are Europe's beer connoisseurs. This fun, handy tour is a great way to pay your respects. "The Brugse Zot" is the only beer actually brewed in Bruges, and the happy gang at this working family brewery gives entertaining and informative 45-minute, three-language tours (often by friendly Inge, €4.50 tour includes a beer, lots of very steep steps, great rooftop panorama, daily on the hour 11:00–16:00, Oct–March at 11:00 and 15:00 only, 1 block past church and canal, take a right down skinny Stoofstraat to #26 on Walplein, tel. 050/332-697, www.halvemaan.be).

During your tour, you'll learn that "the components of the beer are vitally necessary and contribute to a well-balanced life pattern. Nerves, muscles, visual sentience, and a healthy skin are stimulated by these in a positive manner. For longevity and life-long equilibrium, drink Brugse Zot in moderation!"

Their bistro, where you'll be given your included beer, serves quick, hearty lunch plates. You can eat indoors with the smell of hops, or outdoors with the smell of hops. This is a great place to wait for your tour or to linger afterward. For more on beer, see page 301.

▲**Chocolate Shops**—Bruggians are connoisseurs of fine chocolate. You'll be tempted by chocolate-filled display windows all over town. While Godiva is the best big-factory/high-price/high-quality brand, there are plenty of smaller, family-run places in Bruges that offer exquisite handmade chocolates. Each of the following chocolatiers is proud of its creative varieties. They are all generous with samples and welcome you to pick any five or six chocolates to assemble a 100-gram assortment.

Dumon: Perhaps Bruges' smoothest and creamiest chocolates are at Dumon (€1.75/100 grams). Madame Dumon and her children (Stefaan and Christophe) make their top-notch chocolate daily and sell it fresh just off Market Square (Thu–Tue 10:00–18:00, closed Wed, old chocolate molds on display in basement, Eiermarkt 6, tel. 050/346-282). Their *ganache,* a dark, creamy combo, wows chocoholics. The Dumons don't provide English labels because they believe it's best to describe their chocolates in person—and they do it with an evangelical fervor.

The Chocolate Line: Locals and tourists alike flock to The Chocolate Line (€3.40/100 grams) to taste the *gastronomique* varieties concocted by Dominique Person—the mad scientist of chocolate. His unique creations include Havana cigar (marinated in rum, cognac, and Cuban tobacco leaves—so therefore technically illegal in the U.S.), lemon grass, lavender, ginger (shaped like a Buddha), saffron curry, spicy chili, and a Moroccan mint that will take you to Marrakech. My fave: the sheets of chocolate with crunchy roasted cocoa beans. In 2006, Dominique envisions a Pop Rocks/cola chocolate. The kitchen—busy whipping up 80 varieties—is on display in the back. Enjoy the window display, renewed monthly (daily 9:30–18:00, between Church of Our Lady and Market Square at Simon Stevinplein 19, tel. 050/341-090).

Sweertvaegher: This small shop, near Burg Square, features high-quality chocolate (€2.65/100 grams) that's darker rather than sweeter, made with fresh ingredients and no preservatives (Tue–Sat 9:30–18:00, closed Sun–Mon, Philipstockstraat 29, tel. 050/338-367).

Choco-Story: The Chocolate Museum—This museum, rated ▲ for chocoholics, explains why, in the ancient Mexican world of the Mayas and the Aztecs, chocolate was considered the drink of the gods, and cocoa beans were used as a means of payment. With lots of actual arti-facts well-described in English, the museum fills you in on the production of truffles, chocolates, hollow figures, and bars of chocolate. Then you'll view a delicious little video (8 min long, repeating continuously, alternating Flemish, French, and then English; peek into the theater to check the schedule. If you have time before the next English showing, visit the exhibits in the top room). Your finale is in the "demonstration room," where—after a 10-minute cooking lesson—you get a taste (€6, daily 10:00–17:00, where Wijnzakstraat meets Sint Jansstraat at Sint Jansplein, 3-min walk from Market Square, tel. 050/612-237, www.choco-story.be). Notice how choco-laty the fine building looks from across the street.

Windmills and Lace by the Moat—A 15-minute walk from the center to the northeast end of town brings you to four windmills strung along a pleasant grassy setting on the "big moat" canal. If biking, don't miss the idyllic park along the canal.

Windmill: The St. Janshuismolen windmill is open to visitors (€2, May–Sept daily 9:30–12:30 & 13:30–17:00, closed Oct–April, at the end of Carmersstraat, between Kruispoort and Dampoort, on Bruges side of the moat).

Lace: To actually see lace being made, drop by the nearby **Lace Center** (Kant Centrum), where ladies toss bobbins madly while their eyes go bad (€2.50 includes afternoon demo and small lace museum, as well as adjacent Jeruzalem Church, Mon–Fri 10:00–12:00 & 14:00–18:00, Sat until 17:00, closed Sun, Peperstraat 3, tel. 050/330-072). The **Folklore Museum,** in the same neighborhood, is cute but forgettable (€3, Tue–Sun 9:30–17:00, closed Mon, Balstraat 43, tel. 050/448-764-044). To find either place, ask for the Jeruzalem Church (mentioned below, under "Damme Bike Ride").

A lace shop with a good reputation is **'t Apostelientje** (Mon–Fri 9:30–18:00, Sat 9:30–17:00, Sun 10:00–13:00, near Lace Center, Balstraat 11, tel. 050/337-860).

▲▲**Biking**—The Flemish word for bike is *fiets* (pronounced "feets"). While Bruges' sights are close enough for easy walking, the town is a treat for bikers. And a bike quickly gets you into dreamy back lanes without a hint of tourism. Take a peaceful evening ride through the town's nooks and crannies and around the outer canal. Consider keeping a bike for the duration of your stay. It's the way the locals get around in Bruges.

Rental shops have maps and ideas (see "Bike Rental" on page 249 for more info). The TI sells a handy *5X on the Bike Around Bruges* map/guide (€1.50) describing five different bike routes (10–18 miles) through the idyllic countryside nearby. The best trip is 30 minutes along the canal out to Damme and back (described below). The Belgium/Netherlands border is a 40-minute pedal beyond Damme.

Damme Bike Ride: For the best short bike trip out of Bruges, rent a bike and pedal four miles to the nearby town of Damme. You'll enjoy a whiff of the countryside, passing windmills and a historic church, and riding along a canal to this interesting city. Allow about two hours for the leisurely round-trip bike ride and a short stop in Damme. You can also take a bus/boat tour or a bike tour (see page 252 for both), or pedal to Damme and come back (with your bike) by boat.

From **Market or Burg Square,** head east to the weird, medieval, almost creepy **Jeruzalem Church,** built by Crusaders who'd seen the Church of the Holy Sepulchre in Jerusalem. (A button to the left of the entrance lights the church.) The **Lace Center** is next door (described above).

Continue east to the ring canal, with several **windmills** (one is open for touring, described above). Go north along the canal and exit at Damport, heading northeast on Damsevaart Zuid, which borders a canal.

From Damport, you pedal along a canal directly to Damme. There's no chance to cross the canal until you reach the town. I'd ride down on the busy right-hand side and return on the more peaceful and farm-filled left side. About halfway to Damme (on the right side) is a roadhouse inn.

Shortly before reaching town, pull over at the Uilenspiegel parking lot for a great **view of Damme,** with its houses and square church tower rising up from the fields. You can approach the city by taking the Vonderweg dirt path from the parking lot.

Damme is a tiny version of Bruges, with a smaller-but-similar City Hall, St. John's Hospital, and Our Lady Church. Grab a coffee at the café next to City Hall.

Our Lady of Damme has two statues of the Virgin Mary. To the right of the altar is a 1630 wooden statue. Mary, tall and stately, with her curly hair spilling loose, welcomes you—her eyes twinkle and crinkle as she spots you and breaks into a smile. To the right (Mary's left), watch out for the well-dressed, white-gloved Church Police (Kerk Politie). And over your left shoulder, look up at the statues in the upper nave to see Belgium's oldest wooden statue, St. Andrew, with his X-shaped cross.

Mary's rival is the statue to the left of the altar, Our Lady of the Fishermen (c. 1650, in a glass case). Remember, Damme was once a port as well. The canal you rode on once led past Bruges and out to the North Sea.

Outside, near the (climbable) church tower, is a four-faced modern sculpture by local artist Delporte. Like his work? You'll find more at his gallery, just down the road (on the west edge of town).

Cross the canal at a bridge in Damme, and return along the scenic north bank.

Near Bruges

In Flanders Fields Museum—This World War I museum, about 40 miles southwest of Bruges, provides a moving look at the battles fought near Ieper (Ypres in French). Use interactive computer displays to trace the wartime lives of individual soldiers and citizens. Powerful videos and ear-shattering audio complete the story (€7.50; April–Sept daily 10:00–18:00; Oct–March Tue–Sun 10:00–17:00, closed Mon; last entry 1 hour before closing, Grote Markt 34, Ieper, tel. 057/239-220, www.inflandersfields.be). From Bruges, catch a train to Ieper via Kortrijk (2 hrs), or take a tour (see "Tours," page 252). Drivers, take E-403 to Kortrijk, then A-19 to Ieper, following signs to Bellewaerde.

BRUGES CITY WALK

This walk, which takes you from Market Square to the Burg to the cluster of museums around the Church of Our Lady (the Groeninge, Gruuthuse, and Memling), shows you the best of Bruges in a day.

ORIENTATION

Bell Tower (Belfort): €5, daily 9:30–17:00, last entry 45 min before closing, on Market Square.

Basilica of the Holy Blood: Treasury entry-€1.50; April–Sept Thu–Tue 9:30–11:45 & 14:00–17:45, Wed 9:30–11:45 only; Oct–March Thu–Tue 10:00–11:45 & 14:00–15:45, Wed 10:00–11:45 only; Burg Square, tel. 050/336-792, www.holyblood.org.

City Hall's Gothic Room: €2.50, includes audioguide and entry to Renaissance Hall, daily 9:30–17:00, Burg 12.

Renaissance Hall (Brugse Vrije): €2.50, includes audioguide and admission to City Hall's Gothic Room, Tue–Sun 9:30–12:30 & 13:30–16:30, closed Mon, entrance in corner of square at Burg 11a.

Groeninge Museum: €8, includes audioguide, Tue–Sun 9:30–17:00, closed Mon, Dijver 12, tel. 050/448-751.

Gruuthuse Museum: €6, includes apse of Church of Our Lady, Tue–Sun 9:30–17:00, closed Mon, Dijver 17.

Church of Our Lady: Free Michelangelo, €2.50 for art-filled apse, covered by €6 Gruuthuse admission, Mon–Fri 9:30–16:50, Sat 9:30–15:50, Sun 13:30–16:50 only, Mariastraat.

Memling Museum: €8, includes fine audioguide, Tue–Sun 9:30–17:00, closed Mon, Mariastraat 38.

De Halve Maan Brewery Tour: €4.50 tour includes a beer, daily on the hour 11:00–16:00, 11:00 and 15:00 are your best times to avoid groups, Oct–March at 11:00 and 15:00 only, 1 block past church and canal, take a right down narrow Stoofstraat to #26 on Walplein, tel. 050/332-697, www.halvemaan.be.

Begijnhof: Courtyard free and always open; Beguine's House costs €2, open daily 10:00–12:00 & 13:45–17:00, shorter hours off-season.

THE WALK BEGINS

Market Square (Markt)

Ringed by a bank, the post office, lots of restaurant terraces, great old gabled buildings, and the bell tower, this is the modern heart of the city. And, in Bruges' heyday as a trading city, this was also the center. The "typical" old buildings here were rebuilt in

the 19th century in an exaggerated neo-Gothic style (Bruges is often called "more Gothic than Gothic"). This pre–Martin Luther style was a political statement for this Catholic town.

Formerly, a canal came right up to this square. Imagine boats moored where the post office stands today. In the 1300s, farmers shipped their cotton, wool, flax, and hemp to the port at Bruges. Before loading it onto outgoing boats, the industrious locals would spin, weave, and dye it into a finished product.

By 1400, the economy was shifting away from textiles and toward more refined goods, such as high-fashion items, tapestry, chairs, jewelry, and paper—a new invention (replacing parchment) that was made in Flanders with cotton that was shredded, soaked, and pressed.

The square is adorned with **flags,** including the red-white-and-blue lion flag of Bruges, the black-yellow-and-red flag of Belgium, and the blue-with-circle-of-yellow-stars flag of the European Union.

The **statue** depicts two friends, Jan Breidel and Pieter de Coninc, clutching sword and shield and looking toward France during their 1302 people's uprising against the French king. The rebels identified potential French spies by demanding they repeat two words—*schild en vriend* (shield and friend)—that only Flemish locals (or foreigners with phlegm) could pronounce. They won Flanders its freedom. Cleverly using hooks to pull knights from their horses, they scored the medieval world's first victory of foot

Bruges City Walk

1 Market Square
2 Bell Tower
3 Burg Square
4 Basilica of the Holy Blood
5 City Hall
6 Renaissance Hall
7 Crowne Plaza Hotel
8 Blinde Ezelstraat
9 Fish Market
10 Huidevettersplein
11 Postcard Canal View
12 Groeninge Museum
13 Gruuthuse Museum
14 Church of Our Lady
15 Memling Museum
16 De Halve Maan Brewery
17 Begijnhof
18 Minnewater

soldiers over horsed knights, and of common people over nobility. The French knights, thinking that fighting these Flemish peasants would be a cakewalk, had worn their dress uniforms. The peasants had a field day afterward scavenging all the golden spurs from the fallen soldiers after the Battle of the Golden Spurs (1302).

Geldmuntstraat, a block west of the square, has fun shops and eateries. Steenstraat is the main shopping street and is packed with people. Want a coffee? Stop by the Café-Brasserie Craenenburg on Market Square. Originally the house where Maximilian of Austria was imprisoned in 1488, it's been a café since 1905 (daily 8:00–23:00, Markt 16).

Bell Tower (Belfort)

Most of this bell tower has stood over Market Square since 1300. The octagonal lantern was added in 1486, making it 290 feet

high. The tower combines medieval crenellations, pointed Gothic arches, round Roman arches, flamboyant spires, and even a few small flying buttresses (two-thirds of the way up).

Try some french fries from either stand at the bottom of the tower. Look for the small metal model of the tower and the Braille description of the old town. Enter the courtyard. At the base of the bell tower, find the posted schedule of free carillon concerts (with photos of carillonneur at keyboard; normally Mon, Wed, and Sat at 21:00, sit on benches in courtyard—a great experience). There's also a WC in the courtyard.

Climb the tower (€5, 366 steps). Just before you reach the top, peek into the carillon room. The 47 bells can be played mechani-

cally with the giant barrel and movable tabs (as they are on each quarter hour), or with a manual keyboard (as they are during concerts). The carillonneur uses his fists and feet, rather than fingers. Be there on the quarter hour, when things ring. It's *bellissimo* at the top of the hour.

Atop the tower, survey the town. On the horizon, you can see the towns along the North Sea coast.

• *Leaving the bell tower, turn right (east) onto pedestrian-only Breidelstraat. Thread yourself through the lace and waffles to Burg Square.*

Burg Square

This opulent square is Bruges' historical birthplace, political center, and religious heart. Today it's the scene of outdoor concerts and local festivals.

Pan the square to see six centuries of architecture. Starting with the view of the bell tower above the rooftops, sweep counterclockwise 360 degrees. You'll go from Romanesque (the interior of the fancy, gray-brick **Basilica of the Holy Blood** in the corner), to the pointed Gothic arches and prickly steeples of the white sandstone **City Hall,** to the well-proportioned Renaissance windows of the **Old Recorder's House** (next door, under the gilded statues), to the elaborate 17th-century Baroque of the **Provost's House** (past the park behind you). The **park** at the back of the square is the site of a cathedral that was demolished during the French Revolutionary period. Today, the foundation is open to the public in the **Crowne Plaza Hotel** basement (described below).

• *Complete your spin and walk to the small, fancy, gray-and-gold building in the corner of the Burg Square.*

Basilica of the Holy Blood

The gleaming gold knights and ladies on the church's gray facade remind us that the double-decker church was built (c. 1150) by a brave Crusader to house the drops of Christ's blood he brought back from Jerusalem.

Lower Chapel: Enter the lower chapel through the door labeled *Basiliek*. Inside, the stark and dim decor reeks of the medieval piety that drove crusading Christian Europeans to persecute

Muslims. With heavy columns and round arches, the style is pure Romanesque. The annex along the right aisle displays somber statues of Christ being tortured and entombed, plus a 12th-century relief panel over a doorway showing St. Basil (a 4th-century scholarly monk) being baptized by a double-jointed priest, and a

The Legend of the Holy Blood

Several drops of Christ's blood, washed from his lifeless body by Joseph of Arimathea, were preserved in a crystal phial in Jerusalem. In 1150, the patriarch of Jerusalem gave the blood to a Flemish soldier, Derrick of Alsace, as thanks for rescuing his city from the Muslims during the Second Crusade. Derrick (also called Dedric or Thierry) returned home and donated it to the city. The old, dried blood suddenly turned to liquid, a miracle repeated every Friday for the next two centuries, and verified by thousands of pilgrims from around Europe who flocked here to adore it. The blood dried up for good in 1325.

Every year on Ascension Day (May 25 in 2006), Bruges' bankers, housewives, and waffle vendors put on old-time costumes for the parading of the phial through the city. Crusader knights re-enact the bringing of the relic, Joseph of Arimathea washes Christ's body, and ladies in medieval costume with hair tied up in horn-like hairnets come out to wave flags, while many Bruges citizens just take the day off.

man-size Dove of the Holy Spirit.

• *Go back outside and up the staircase to reach the...*

Upper Chapel: After being gutted by Napoleon's secular-humanist crusaders in 1797, the upper chapel's original Romanesque decor was redone in a neo-Gothic style. The nave is colorful, with a curved wooden ceiling, painted walls, and stained-glass windows of the dukes who ruled Flanders, along with their duchesses.

The painting at the main altar tells how the Holy Blood got here. Derrick of Alsace, having helped defend Jerusalem *(Hierosolyma)* and Bethlehem *(Bethlema)* from Muslim incursions in the Second Crusade, kneels (left) before the grateful Christian patriarch of Jerusalem, who rewards him with the relic. Derrick returns home (right) and kneels before Bruges' bishop to give him the phial of blood.

The relic itself—some red stuff preserved inside a clear, six-inch tube of rock crystal—is kept in the adjoining room (through the 3 arches). It's in the tall, silver tabernacle on the altar. (Each Friday—and increasingly on other days, too—the tabernacle's doors will be open, so you can actually see the phial of blood.) On holy days, the relic is shifted across the room, and displayed on the throne under the canopy.

The Treasury (next to Upper Chapel): For €1.50, you can see the impressive gold-and-silver, gem-studded, hexagonal reli-

quary (c. 1600, left wall) that the phial of blood is paraded around in on feast days. The phial is placed in the "casket" at the bottom of the four-foot-tall structure. On the wall, flanking the shrine, are paintings of kneeling residents who, for centuries, have tended the shrine and organized the pageantry as part of the 31-member Brotherhood of the Holy Blood. Elsewhere in the room are the Brothers' ceremonial necklaces, clothes, chalices, and so on.

In the display case by the entrance, find the lead box that protected the phial of blood from Protestant extremists (1578) and French Revolutionaries (1797) bent on destroying what, to them, was a glaring symbol of Catholic mumbo-jumbo. The broken rock-crystal tube with gold caps on either end is a replica of the phial, giving an idea of what the actual relic looks like. Opposite the reliquary are the original cartoons (from 1541) that provided the designs for the basilica's stained glass.

City Hall (Stadhuis)

Built in about 1400, when Bruges was a thriving bastion of capitalism with a population of 35,000, this building served as a model

for town halls elsewhere, including Brussels. The white sandstone facade is studded with statues of knights, nobles, and saints with prickly Gothic steeples over their heads. A colorful double band of cities' coats of arms includes those of Bruges (Brugghe) and Dunkirk (Dunquerke). Back then, Bruges' jurisdiction included many towns in present-day France. The building is still the City Hall,

and it's not unusual to see couples arriving here to get married.

Entrance Hall: The ground-level lobby (free, closed Mon) leads to a picture gallery with scenes from Belgium's history, from the Spanish king to the arrival of Napoleon, shown meeting the mayor here at the City Hall in 1803. You can pay €2.50 to climb the stairs for a look at the...

Gothic Room: Some of modern democracy's roots lie in this ornate room, where, for centuries, the city council met to discuss the town's affairs (€2.50 entry includes audioguide and Renaissance Hall). In 1464, one of Europe's first parliaments, the Estates General of the Low Countries, convened here. The fireplace at the far end bears a proclamation from 1305, which says, "All the artisans, laborers... and citizens of Bruges are free—all of them" (provided they pay their taxes).

The elaborately carved and painted wooden ceiling (a reconstruction from 1800) features Gothic-style tracery in gold, red, and black. Five dangling arches ("pendentives") hang down the center, now adorned with modern floodlights. Notice the New Testament themes carved into the circular medallions that decorate the points where the arches meet.

The **wall murals** are late-19th-century Romantic paintings depicting episodes in the city's history. Start with the biggest painting along the left wall, and work clockwise, following the numbers found on the walls:

1. Hip, hip, hooray! Everyone cheers, flags wave, trumpets blare, and dogs bark, as Bruges' knights, dressed in gold with black Flemish lions, return triumphant after driving out French oppressors and winning Flanders' independence. The Battle of the Golden Spurs (1302) is remembered every July 11.

2. Bruges' high-water mark came perhaps at this elaborate ceremony, when Philip the Good of Burgundy (seated, in black) assembled his court here in Bruges and solemnly founded the knightly Order of the Golden Fleece (1429).

3. The Crusader knight, Derrick of Alsace, returns from the Holy Land and kneels at the entrance of St. Basil's Chapel to present the relic of Christ's Holy Blood (c. 1150).

4. A nun carries a basket of bread in this scene from St. John's Hospital.

5. A town leader stands at the podium and hands a sealed document to a German businessman, renewing the Hanseatic League's business license. Membership in this club of trading cities was a key to Bruges' prosperity.

6. As peasants cheer, a messenger of the local duke proclaims the town's right to self-government (1190).

7. The mayor visits a Bruges painting studio to shake the hand of Jan van Eyck, the great Flemish Primitive painter (1433). Jan's wife, Margareta, is there, too. In the 1400s, Bruges rivaled Florence and Venice as Europe's cultural capital. See the town in the distance, out van Eyck's window.

8. Skip it.

9. City fathers grab a ceremonial trowel from a pillow to lay the fancy cornerstone of the City Hall (1376). Bruges' familiar towers stand in the background.

10. Skip it.

11. It's a typical market day at the Halls (the courtyard behind the bell tower). Arabs mingle with Germans in fur-lined coats and beards in a market where they sell everything from armor to lemons.

12. A bishop blesses a new canal (1404) as ships sail right by the city. This was Bruges in its heyday, before the silting of the harbor. At the far right, the two bearded men with moustaches are the brothers who painted these murals.

In the adjoining room, old paintings and maps show how little the city has changed through the centuries. Map #8 (on the right wall) shows in exquisite detail the city as it looked in 1562. (The map is oriented with south on top.) Find the bell tower, the Church of Our Lady, and Burg Square, which back then was bounded on the north by a cathedral. Notice the canal (on the west) leading from the North Sea right to Market Square. A moat circled the 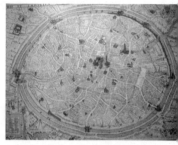 city with its gates, unfinished wall, and 28 windmills (4 of which survive today). The mills pumped water to the town's fountains, made paper, ground grain, and functioned as the motor of the Middle Ages. Most locals own a copy of this map that shows how their neighborhood looked 400 years ago.

• *Back on the square, leaving the City Hall, turn right and go to the corner.*

Renaissance Hall (Brugse Vrije)

This elaborately decorated room has a grand Renaissance chimney carved from oak by Bruges' Renaissance man, Lancelot Blondeel, in 1531. If you're into heraldry, the symbolism makes this room  worth a five-minute stop. If you're not, you'll wonder where the rest of the museum is.

The centerpiece of the incredible carving is the Holy Roman Emperor Charles V. The hometown duke, on the far left, is related to Charles V. By making the connection to the Holy Roman Emperor clear, this carved family tree of Bruges' nobility helped substantiate their power. Notice the closely guarded family jewels. And check out the expressive little cherubs.

Crowne Plaza Hotel

One of the city's newest buildings (1992) sits atop the ruins of the town's oldest structures. In about A.D. 900, when Viking ships regularly docked here to rape and pillage, Baldwin Iron Arm built a fort *(castrum)* to protect his Flemish people. In 950, the fort was converted into St. Donatian's Church, which became one of the city's largest.

Ask politely at the hotel's reception desk to see the archaeological site—ruins of the fort and the church—in the basement. If there's no conference, they'll let you walk down the stairs and have a peek.

In the basement of the modern hotel are conference rooms lined with old stone walls and display cases of objects found in the ruins of earlier structures. On the immediate left hangs a document announcing the *Vente de Materiaux* (sale of material). When Napoleon destroyed the church in the early 1800s, its bricks were auctioned off. A local builder bought them at auction, and now the pieces of the old cathedral are embedded in other buildings throughout Bruges.

See oak pilings once driven into this former peat bog to support the fort and shore up its moat. Paintings show the immensity of the church that replaced it. The curved stone walls you walk among are from the foundations of the ambulatory around the church altar.

Excavators found a town water hole—a bonanza for archaeologists—turning up the refuse of a thousand years of habitation: pottery, animal skulls, rosary beads, dice, coins, keys, thimbles, pipes, spoons, and Delftware.

Don't miss the 14th-century painted sarcophagi—painted quickly for burial, with the crucifixion on the west ends and the Virgin and Child on the east.

• *Back on Burg Square, walk south under the Goldfinger family down the alleyway called...*

Blinde Ezelstraat

Midway down on the left side (knee level), see an original iron hinge from the city's south gate, back when the city was ringed by a moat and closed up at 22:00. On the right wall at eye level, a black patch shows just how grimy the city had become before a 1960s cleaning. Despite the cleaning and a few fanciful reconstructions, the city looks today much as it did in centuries past.

The name "Blinde Ezelstraat" means "Blind Donkey Street." In medieval times, the donkeys, carrying fish from the North Sea on their backs, were stopped here so that their owners could put blinders on them. Otherwise, the donkeys wouldn't cross the water between the old city and the fish market.

• *Cross the bridge over what was the 13th-century city moat. On your left are the arcades of the...*

Fish Market (Vismarkt)

The North Sea is just 12 miles away, and the fresh catch is sold here (Tue–Sat 6:00–13:00). Once a thriving market, today it's mostly souvenirs...and the big catch is the tourists.

• *Take an immediate right (west), entering a courtyard called...*

Huidevettersplein

This tiny, picturesque, restaurant-filled square was originally the headquarters of the town's skinners and tanners. On the facade of the Hotel Duc de Bourgogne, six old relief panels show scenes from the leather tanners—once a leading Bruges industry. First, they tan the hides in a bath of acid; then, with tongs, they pull it out to dry; then they beat it to make it soft; and finally, they scrape and clean it to make it ready for sale.

• *Continue a few steps to Rozenhoedkaai street, where you can look back to your right and get a great...*

Postcard Canal View

The bell tower reflected in a quiet canal lined with old houses—the essence of Bruges. Seeing buildings rising straight from the water

makes you understand why this was the Venice of the North. Can you see the bell tower's tilt? It leans about four feet. The tilt has been carefully monitored since 1740, but no change has been detected.

Looking left (west) down the Dijver canal (past a flea market on weekends) looms the huge spire of the Church of Our Lady, the tallest brick spire in the Low Countries. Between you and the church is the Europa College (a postgraduate institution for training future "Eurocrats" about the laws, economics, and politics of the European Union) and two fine museums.

Groeninge Museum

This sumptuous collection of paintings takes you from 1400 to 1945. The highlights are its Flemish Primitives, with all their glorious detail. ✪ See Groeninge Museum Tour, page 278.

Gruuthuse Museum

This 15th-century mansion of a wealthy Bruges merchant displays period furniture, tapestries, coins, and musical instruments. Nowhere in the city do you get such an intimate look at the materialistic revolution of Bruges' glory days.

With the help of the excellent and included audioguide, browse through rooms of secular objects that are both functional and beautiful. Here are some highlights:

On the left, in the first room (or **Great Hall**), the big fireplace, oak table, and tapestries attest to the wealth of Louis Gruuthuse, who got rich providing a special herb used to spice up beer.

Tapestries like the ones you see here were a famous Flemish export product, made in local factories out of raw wool imported from England and silk from the Orient (via Italy). Both beautiful and useful (as insulation), they adorned many homes and palaces throughout Europe.

These **four tapestries** (of 9 originals) tell a worldly story of youthful lust that upsets our stereotypes about supposed medieval piousness. The first tapestry, the *Soup-Eating Lady* (on the left), shows a shepherd girl with a bowl of soup in her lap. The horny shepherd lad cuts a slice of bread (foreplay in medieval symbolism) and saucily asks (read the archaic French cartoon bubbles) if he can "dip into the goodies in her lap," if you catch my drift. On the right, a woman brazenly strips off her socks to dangle her feet in water, while another woman lifts her dress to pee.

The next tapestry (as you're moving clockwise), called *The Dance*, shows couples freely dancing together under the apple tree of temptation. *The Wedding Parade* (opposite wall) shows where all this wantonness leads—marriage. Music plays, the table is set, and the meat's on the BBQ as the bride and groom enter... reluctantly. The bride smiles, but she's closely escorted by two men, while the scared groom (center) gulps nervously.

From here, the next stop is *Old Age* (smaller tapestry), and the aged shepherd is tangled in a wolf trap. "Alas," reads the French caption, "he was once so lively, but marriage caught him, and now he's trapped in its net."

In Room 2, see the **Bust of Charles V** (on top of an oak chest) and ponder the series of marriages that made Charles (1500–1558), the grandson of a Flemish girl, the powerful ruler of most of Europe, including Bruges. Mary of Burgundy (and Flanders) married powerful Maximilian I of Austria. Their son Philip married Juana, the daughter of Ferdinand and Isabel of Spain, and when little Charles was born to them, he inherited all his grandparents' lands, and more. Charles' son, Philip II (see his bust opposite), a devout Catholic, brought persecution and war to the Protestant Low Countries.

• *Facing Philip, climb the stairs on the left to the third floor, pass through Room 10, and cross the open mezzanine. In the far left corner of Room 16, find a chapel.*

The Gruuthuse mansion abuts the Church of Our Lady and has a convenient little **chapel** with a window overlooking the interior of the huge church. In their private box seats above the choir, the family could attend services without leaving home. From the balcony, you can look down on two reclining gold statues in the church, marking the tombs of Charles the Bold and his daughter, Mary of Burgundy (the grandmother of powerful Charles V).

The last room (ground floor, directly below) deals with old-time justice. In 1796, the enlightened city of Bruges chose the new-fangled **guillotine** as its humane form of execution. This 346-pound model was tested on sheep before being bloodied twice by executions on the Market Square. Also see the branding irons, a small workbench for slicing off evil-doers' members, and posts used to chain up criminals for public humiliation.

Leaving the museum, contemplate the mountain of bricks that towers 400 feet above, as it has for 600 years. You're heading for that church.

• *Take the interesting back way to the church. At the Arentshuis Museum entrance, duck under the arch at #16 and into a quiet courtyard. Veer right and cross a tiny 19th-century bridge.*

From the bridge, look up at the corner of the Gruuthuse mansion, where there's a teeny-tiny window, a toll-keeper's lookout. The bridge gives you a close-up look at Our Lady's big buttresses and round apse. The church entrance is around the front.

Church of Our Lady

This church stands as a memorial to the power and wealth of Bruges in its heyday.

A delicate **Madonna and Child by Michelangelo** (1504) is near the apse (to the right as you enter), somewhat overwhelmed by the ornate Baroque niche it sits in. It's said to be the only Michelangelo statue to leave Italy in his lifetime, bought in Tuscany by a wealthy Bruges businessman, who's buried beneath it.

As Michelangelo chipped away at the masterpiece of his youth, *David*, he took breaks by carving this (1504). Mary, slightly smaller than life-size, sits, while young Jesus stands in front of her. Their expressions are mirror images—serene, but a bit melancholy, with downcast eyes, as though pondering the young child's dangerous future. Though they're lost in thought, their hands instinctively link, tenderly. The white Carrara marble is highly polished, something Michelangelo only did when he was certain he'd gotten it right.

If you like tombs and church art, pay €2.50 to wander through the apse (also covered by €6 Gruuthuse admission). The highlight is the reclining statues marking the tombs of the last local rulers of Bruges, Mary of Burgundy, and her father, Charles the Bold. The dog and lion at their feet are symbols of fidelity and courage.

In 1482, when 25-year-old Mary of Burgundy tumbled from a horse and died, she left behind a toddler son and a husband who was heir to the Holy Roman Empire. Beside her lies her father, Charles the Bold, who also died prematurely, in war. Their twin deaths meant Bruges belonged to Austria, and would soon be swallowed up by the empire and ruled from afar by Hapsburgs—who didn't understand or care about its problems. Trade routes shifted, and goods soon flowed through Antwerp, then Amsterdam, as Bruges' North Sea port silted up. After these developments, Bruges began four centuries of economic decline. The city was eventually moth-balled, and later discovered by modern-day tourists to be remarkably well-pickled—which explains its modern-day affluence.

The balcony to the left of the main altar is part of the Gruuthuse mansion next door, providing the noble family with prime seats for Mass.

Excavations in 1979 turned up fascinating grave paintings on the tombs below and near the altar. Dating from the 13th century, these show Mary represented as Queen of Heaven (on a throne, carrying a crown and scepter) and Mother of God (with the baby Jesus on her lap). Since Mary is in charge of advocating with Jesus for your salvation, she's a good person to have painted on the wall of your tomb. Tombs also show lots of angels—generally patron saints of the dead person—swinging thuribles (incense burners).

• Just across Mariastraat from the church entrance is the entry to the St. John's Hospital's Visitors Center (with good Internet café and a €0.30 public WC). The entrance to the Memling Museum, which fills that hospital's church, is 20 yards south on Mariastraat.

Memling Museum

This medieval hospital contains some much-loved paintings by the greatest of the Flemish Primitives, Hans Memling. His *Mystical Wedding of St. Catherine* triptych deserves a close look. Catherine and her "mystical groom," the baby Jesus, are flanked by a headless John the Baptist and a pensive John the Evangelist. The chairs are there so you can study it. If you know the Book of Revelation, you'll understand St. John's wild and intricate vision. The St. Ursula Shrine, an ornate little mini-church in the same room, is filled with impressive detail. ✪ See Memling Museum Tour, page 287.

• Continue south about 150 yards on Mariastraat. Turn right on Walstraat, which leads into the pleasant square called Walplein, where you'll find the...

De Halve Maan Brewery Tour

If you like beer, take a tour here (Walplein 26). See page 257.

• From here, the lacy cuteness of Bruges crescendos as you approach the Begijnhof.

Begijnhof

Begijnhofs (pronounced gutturally: buh-HHHINE-hof) were built to house women of the lay order, called Beguines, who spent their lives in piety and service without having to take the same vows a nun would. For military and other reasons, there were more women than men in the medieval Low Countries. The order of Beguines offered women (often single or widowed) a dignified place to live and work. When  the order died out, many Begijnhofs were taken over by towns for subsidized housing. Today, single religious women live in the small homes. Benedictine nuns live in a building nearby. Tour the simple museum to get a sense of Beguine life.

In the church, the rope that dangles from the ceiling is yanked by a nun at about 17:15 to announce a sung vespers service.

• Exiting opposite the way you entered, you'll hook left and see a lake.

Minnewater

Just south of the Begijnhof is Minnewater (literally, "Water of Love"), a peaceful, lake-filled park with canals and swans. This was once far from quaint—a busy harbor where small boats shuttled cargo from the big, ocean-going ships into town. From this point, the cargo was transferred again to flat-bottomed boats that went through the town's canals to their respective warehouses and Market Square.

When locals see these swans, they remember the 15th-century mayor—famous for his long neck—who collaborated with the Austrians. The townsfolk beheaded him as a traitor. The Austrians warned them that similarly long-necked swans would inhabit the place to forever remind them of this murder. And they do.

• *You're a five-minute walk from the train station, where you can catch a bus to Market Square, or a 15-minute walk from Market Square—take your pick.*

GROENINGE MUSEUM TOUR

In the 1400s, Bruges was northern Europe's richest, most cosmopolitan, and most cultured city. New ideas, fads, and painting techniques were imported and exported with each shipload. Beautiful paintings were soon an affordable luxury, like fancy clothes or furniture. Internationally known artists set up studios in Bruges, producing portraits and altarpieces for wealthy merchants from all over Europe.

The Groeninge Museum, understandably, has one of the world's best collections of the art produced in the city and surrounding area. This early Flemish art is less appreciated and understood today than the Italian Renaissance art produced a century later. But by selecting eleven masterpieces, we'll get an introduction to this subtle, technically advanced, and beautiful style. Hey, if you can master the museum's name (HHHROON-ih-guh), you can certainly handle the art.

ORIENTATION

Cost: €8, includes audioguide.
Hours: Tue–Sun 9:30–17:00, closed Mon.
Getting There: The museum is at Dijver 12, near the Gruuthuse Museum and Church of Our Lady.
Information: Tel. 050/448-751.
Length of this Tour: Allow one hour.

Overview
The included audioguide allows you to wander as you like. Use this chapter as background to the huge collection's highlights, then browse, punching in the numbers of the paintings you'd like to learn more about.

THE TOUR BEGINS

• *In Room 1, look for...*

Attributed to Hieronymus Bosch (c. 1450–1516)— *Last Judgment* (late 15th century)

It's the end of the world, and Christ descends in a bubble to pass judgment on puny humans. Little
naked people dance and cavort in
a theme park of medieval symbolism, desperately trying to squeeze
in their last bit of fun. Meanwhile,
some wicked souls are being
punished, victims either of their
own stupidity or of genetically
engineered demons. The good get
sent to the left panel to frolic in
the innocence of Paradise, while
the rest are damned to hell (right

panel) to be tortured under a burning sky. Bosch paints the scenes
with a high horizon line, making it seem that the chaos extends
forever.

The bizarre work of Bosch (who, by the way, was not from
Bruges) is open to many interpretations, but some see it as a warning for the turbulent times. It was the dawn of a new age. Secular
ideas and materialism were encroaching, and the pious and serene
medieval world was shattering into chaos.

Gerard David (c. 1455–1523)—*Judgment of Cambyses* (1498)

That's gotta hurt.

A man is stretched across a table and skinned alive in a very
businesslike manner. The crowd hardly notices, and a dog just

scratches himself. According to legend,
the man was a judge arrested for corruption (left panel) and flayed (right
panel), then his skin was draped (right
panel background) over the new judge's
throne.

Gerard David, Memling's successor
as the city's leading artist, painted this
for the City Hall. City councilors could
ponder what might happen to them if
they abused their office.

By David's time, Bruges was in serious decline, with a failing
economy and struggles against the powerful Austrian Hapsburg
family. The Primitive style was also fading. Italian art was popular,

Flemish Primitives

Despite the "Primitive" label, the Low Countries of the 1400s (along with Venice and Florence) produced the most refined art in Europe. Here are some common features of Flemish Primitive art:

- **Primitive 3-D perspective:** Expect unnaturally cramped-looking rooms, oddly slanted tables, and flat, cardboard-cutout people with stiff posture. Yes, these works are more primitive (hence the label) than those with the later Italian Renaissance perspective.
- **Realism:** Everyday bankers and clothmakers in their Sunday best are painted with clinical, warts-and-all precision. Even saints and heavenly visions are brought down to earth.
- **Details:** Like meticulous Bruges craftsmen, painters used fine-point brushes to capture almost microscopic details—flower petals, wrinkled foreheads, intricately patterned clothes, the sparkle in a ruby. The closer you get to a painting, the better it looks.
- **Oil painted on wood:** They were the pioneers of new-fangled oil-based paint (while Italy still used egg-yolk tempera), working on wood before canvas became popular.
- **Portraits and altarpieces:** Wealthy merchants and clergymen paid to have themselves painted either alone or mingling with saints.
- **Symbolism:** In earlier times, everyone understood that a dog symbolized fidelity, a lily meant chastity, and a rose was love.
- **Materialism:** Rich Flanders celebrated the beauty of luxury goods—the latest Italian dresses, jewels, carpets, oak tables—and the ordinary beauty that radiates from flesh-and-blood people.

so David tries to spice up his retro-Primitive work with pseudo-Renaissance knickknacks—*putti* (baby angels, over the judgment throne), Roman-style medallions, and garlands. But he couldn't quite master the Italian specialty of 3-D perspective. We view the flayed man at an angle from slightly above, but the table he lies on is shown more from the side.

• *Head to Room 2 for...*

Jan van Eyck (c. 1390–1441)—
Virgin and Child with Canon Joris van der Paele (1436)
Jan van Eyck was the world's first and greatest oil painter, and this is his masterpiece—three debatable but defensible assertions.

Mary, in a magnificent red gown, sits playing with her little baby, Jesus. Jesus glances up as St. George, the dragon-slaying knight, enters the room, tips his cap, and says, "I'd like to introduce my namesake, George (Joris)." Mary glances down at the kneeling Joris, a church official dressed in white. Joris takes off his glasses and looks up from his prayer book to see a bishop in blue,  St. Donatian, patron of the church he hopes to be buried in.

Canon Joris, who hired van Eyck, is not a pretty sight. He's old and wrinkled, with a double chin, weird earlobes, and bloodshot eyes. But the portrait isn't unflattering, it just shows unvarnished reality with crystal clarity.

Van Eyck brings Mary and the saints down from heaven and into a typical (rich) Bruges home. He strips off their haloes, banishes all angels, and pulls the plug on heavenly radiance. If this is a religious painting, then where's God?

He's in the details. From the bishop's damask robe and Mary's wispy hair to the folds in Jesus' baby fat and the oriental carpet to "Adonai" (Lord) written on St. George's breastplate, the painting is as complex and beautiful as God's creation. The color scheme— red Mary, white canon, and blue-and-gold saints—are Bruges' city colors, from its coat of arms.

Mary, crowned with a jeweled "halo" and surrounded by beautiful things, makes an appearance in 1400s Bruges, where she can be adored in all her human beauty by Canon Joris...and by us, reflected in the mirror-like shield on St. George's back.

Jan van Eyck—*Portrait of Margareta van Eyck* (1439)

At 35, shortly after moving to Bruges, Jan van Eyck married 20-
 year-old Margareta. They had two kids, and after Jan died, Margareta took charge of his studio of assistants and kept it running until her death. This portrait (age 33), when paired with a matching self-portrait of Jan, was one of Europe's first husband-and-wife companion sets.

She sits half-turned, looking out of the frame. (Jan might have seen this "where-have-you-been?" expression in the window late one night.) She's dressed in a red, fur-lined coat, and we catch a glimpse of her wedding ring. Her hair is invisible—very fashionable at the time—pulled back tightly, bunched into horn-like hairnets, and draped with a headdress. Stray hairs along the perimeter were plucked to achieve the high forehead look.

This simple portrait is revolutionary—one of history's first individual portraits that wasn't of a saint, king, duke, or pope, or part of a religious work. It signals the advent of humanism, celebrating the glory of ordinary people. Van Eyck proudly signed the work on the original frame, with his motto saying he painted it "*als ik kan*" *(ALC IXH KAN)*..."as good as I can."

Rogier van der Weyden (c. 1399–1464)— St. Luke Drawing the Virgin's Portrait (c. 1435)

Rogier van der Weyden, the other giant among the Flemish Primitives, adds the human touch to van Eyck's rather detached precision.

As Mary prepares to nurse, baby Jesus can't contain his glee, wiggling his fingers and toes, anticipating lunch. Mary, dressed in everyday clothes, can't hide her love as she tilts her head down with a proud smile. Meanwhile, St. Luke (the patron saint of painters, who was said to have experienced this vision) looks on intently with a sketch pad in his hand, trying to catch the scene. These small gestures, movements, and facial expressions add an element of human emotion that later artists would amplify.

The painting is neatly divided by a spacious view out the window, showing a river stretching off to a spacious horizon. Van der Weyden experimented with 3-D effects like this, though ultimately it's just window-dressing.

Rogier van der Weyden—Duke Philip the Good (c. 1450)

Tall, lean, and elegant, this charismatic Duke transformed Bruges from a commercial powerhouse to a cultural one. In 1425, Philip moved his court to Bruges, making it the de facto capital of a Burgundian empire stretching from Amsterdam to Switzerland.

Philip wears a big hat to hide his hair, a fashion trend he himself set. He's also wearing the gold-chain necklace of the Order of the Golden Fleece, a distinguished knightly honor he gave himself. He inaugurated the Golden Fleece in a lavish ceremony at the Bruges City Hall, complete with parades, jousting, and festive pies that contained live people hiding inside to surprise his guests.

As a lover of painting, hunting, fine clothes, and many mistresses, Philip was a role model for Italian princes, such as Lorenzo the Magnificent—the *uomo universale,* or Renaissance Man.

Oil Paint

Take vegetable oil pressed from linseeds (flax), blend in dry powdered pigments, whip to a paste the consistency of room-temperature butter, then brush onto a panel of whitewashed oak—you're painting in oils. First popularized in the early 1400s, oil eventually overshadowed egg-yolk-based tempera. Though tempera was great for making fine lines shaded with simple blocks of color, oil could blend colors together seamlessly.

Watch a master create a single dog's hair: He paints a dark stroke of brown, then lets it dry. Then comes a second layer painted over it, of translucent orange. The brown shows through, blending with the orange to match the color of a collie. Finally, he applies a third, transparent layer (a "glaze"), giving the collie her healthy sheen.

Many great artists were not necessarily great painters (e.g., Michelangelo). Van Eyck, Rembrandt, Hals, Velázquez, and Rubens were master painters, meticulously building objects with successive layers of paint...but they're not everyone's favorite artists.

Hugo van der Goes (c. 1430–c. 1482)—
Death of the Virgin (c. 1470)

The long death watch is over—their beloved Mary has passed on, and the disciples are bleary-eyed and dazed with grief, as though hit with a spiritual two-by-four. Each etched face is a study in sadness, as they all have their own way of coping—lighting a candle, fidgeting, praying, or just staring off into space. Blues and reds dominate, and there's little eye-catching ornamentation, which lets the lined faces and expressive hand gestures do the talking.

Hugo van der Goes painted this, his last major work, the same year he attempted suicide. Hugo had built a successful career in Ghent, then abruptly dropped out to join a monastery. His paintings became increasingly emotionally charged, and his personality more troubled.

Above the bed floats a heavenly vision, as Jesus and the angels prepare to receive Mary's soul. Their smooth skin and serene expressions contrast with the gritty, wrinkled death pallor on earth. Caught up in their own grief, the disciples can't see the silver lining.

Jan Provoost (c. 1465–1529)—*Death and the Miser*

A Bruges businessman in his office strikes a deal with Death. The grinning skeleton lays coins on the table, and in return, the man—

looking unhealthy and with fear in his eyes—reaches across the divide in the panels to give Death a promissory note, then marks the transaction in his ledger book. He's trading away a few years of his life for a little more money. The worried man on the right (the artist's self-portrait) says, "Don't do it."

Jan Provoost (also known as Provost) worked for businessmen like this. He knew their offices, full of moneybags, paperwork, and books. Bruges' materialistic capitalism was at odds with Christian poverty, and society was divided over whether to praise or condemn it. Ironically, this painting's flip side is a religious work bought and paid for by...rich merchants.

Petrus Christus (c. 1420–c. 1475)— *Annunciation and Nativity* (1452)

Italian art was soon all the rage. Ships from Genoa and Venice would unload Renaissance paintings, wowing the Northerners with their window-on-the-world, 3-D realism. Petrus Christus,

one of Jan van Eyck's students, studied the Italian style and set out to conquer space.

The focus of his *Annunciation* panel is not the winged angel announcing Jesus' coming birth, and not the swooning, astonished Mary—it's the empty space between them. Your eye focuses back across the floor tiles and through the open doorway to gabled houses on a quiet canal in the far distance.

No Joke

An enthusiastic American teenager approaches the ticket seller at the Groeninge Museum:
"This is the Torture Museum, right?!"
"No," the ticket man replies, "it's art."
"Oh..." mumbles the kid, "art...."
And he walks away, not realizing that, for him, the Groeninge Museum would be torture.

In the *Nativity* panel, the three angels hovering overhead really should be bigger, and the porch over the group looks a little rickety. Compared to the work of Florence's Renaissance painters, this is quite...primitive.

• *Fast-forward a few centuries, past paintings by no-name artists from Bruges' years of decline, to a couple of Belgium's 20th-century masters in Room 9...*

Paul Delvaux (1897–1994)— *Serenity* (1970)

Perhaps there's some vague connection between van Eyck's medieval symbols and the Surrealist images of Paul Delvaux. Regardless, Delvaux gained fame for his nudes sleepwalking through moonlit, video-game landscapes.

René Magritte (1898–1967)—*The Assault* (c. 1932)

Magritte had his own private reserve of symbolic images. The

cloudy sky, female torso, windows, and horsebell (the ball with the slit) appear in other works as well. They're arranged here side by side as if they should mean something, but they—as well as the title— only serve to short-circuit your thoughts when you try to make sense of them. Magritte paints real objects with photographic clarity, then jumbles them together in new and provocative ways.

Scenes of Bruges

Remember that Jan van Eyck, Petrus Christus, Hans Memling, Gerard David, Jan Provoost, and possibly Rogier van der Weyden (for a few years) all lived and worked in Bruges.

In addition, many other artists included scenes of the picturesque city in their art, proving that the city looks today much as it did way back when. Enjoy the many painted scenes of old Bruges as a slice-of-life peek into the city and its people back in its glory days.

MEMLING
MUSEUM
TOUR

Located in the former hospital wards and church of St. John's
Hospital (Sint Janshospitaal), the Memling Museum displays sur-
gical instruments, documents, and visual aids, offering a glimpse
into medieval medicine as you work your way to the museum's
climax: several of Hans Memling's glowing masterpieces.

ORIENTATION

Cost: €8, includes fine audioguide.
Hours: Tue–Sun 9:30–17:00, closed Mon.
Getting There: The museum is at Mariastraat 38, across the street
    from the Church of Our Lady.
Length of this Tour: Allow one hour.

Overview

Hans Memling's art was the culmination of Bruges' Flemish
Primitive style. His serene, soft-focus, motionless scenes capture
a medieval piety that was quickly fading. The popular style made
Memling (c. 1430–1494) one of Bruges' wealthiest citizens, and
his work was gobbled up by visiting Italian merchants, who took it
home with them, cross-pollinating European art.

    The displays are all on one floor of the former church, with
the Memlings in a chapel at the far end.

THE TOUR BEGINS

The Church as a Hospital

Some 500 years ago, the nave of this former church was lined
with beds filled with the sick and dying. Nuns served as nurses.
At the far end was the high altar, which once displayed Memling's

Some Memling Trademarks

- Serene symmetry, with little motion or emotion
- Serious faces that are realistic but timeless, with blemishes airbrushed out
- Eye-catching details like precious carpets, mirrors, and brocaded clothes
- Glowing colors, even lighting, no shadows
- Cityscape backgrounds

St. John Altarpiece (which we'll see). Bed-ridden patients could gaze on this peaceful, colorful vision and gain a moment's comfort from their agonies.

As the museum displays make clear, medicine of the day was

well-intentioned, but very crude. In many ways, this was less a hospital than a hospice, helping the down-and-out make the transition from this world to the next. Religious art (displayed further along in the museum) was therapeutic, addressing the patients' mental and spiritual health. The numerous Crucifixions reminded

the sufferers that Christ could feel their pain, having lived it himself.

• *Continue on the ground floor through the displays of religious art—past paintings that make you thankful for modern medicine—to the final two rooms, displaying Memling's paintings. A large triptych (3-paneled altarpiece) dominates the room.*

St. John Altarpiece
(a.k.a. *The Mystical Marriage of St. Catherine*, 1474)

Sick and dying patients lay in their beds in the hospital and looked at this colorful, three-part work, which sat atop the hospital/church's high altar. The piece was dedicated to the hospital's patron

saints, John the Baptist and John the Evangelist (see the inscription along the bottom frame), but Memling broadened the focus to take in a vision of heaven and the end of the world.

Central Panel: Mary, with baby Jesus on her lap,

sits in a canopied chair, crowned by hovering blue angels. It's an imaginary gathering of conversing saints *(sacra conversazione)*, though nobody in this meditative group is saying a word or even exchanging meaningful eye contact.

Mary is flanked by the two Johns—John the Baptist to the

left, and John the Evangelist (in red) to the right. Everyone else sits symmetrically around Mary. An organist angel to the left is matched by a book-holding acolyte to the right. St. Catherine (left, in white, red, and gold) balances St. Barbara, in green, who's absorbed in her book. Behind them, classical columns are also perfectly balanced left and right.

At the center of it all, Jesus tips the balance by leaning over to place a ring on Catherine's finger, sealing the "mystical marriage" between them.

St. Catherine of Alexandria, born rich, smart, and pagan to Roman parents, joined the outlawed Christian faith. She spoke out against pagan Rome, attracting the attention of the emperor, Maxentius, who sent 50 philosophers to talk some sense into her—but she countered every argument, even converting the emperor's own wife. Maxentius killed his wife, then asked Catherine to marry him. She refused, determined to remain true to the man she'd already "married" in a mystical vision—Christ.

Frustrated, Maxentius ordered Catherine to be stretched across a large, spiked wheel (the rather quaint-looking object at her feet), but the wheel flew apart, sparing her and killing many of her torturers. So they just cut her head off, which is why she has a sword, along with her "catherine wheel."

Looking through the columns, we see scenes of Bruges. Just to the right of the chair's canopy, the wooden contraption is a crane, used to hoist barrels from barges on Kraanplein.

Left Panel—The Beheading of John the Baptist: Even this gruesome scene, with blood still spurting from John's severed neck, becomes serene under Memling's gentle brush. Everyone is solemn, graceful, and emotionless—including both halves of the decapitated John. Memling depicts Salomé (in green) receiving the head on her silver platter with a humble servant's downcast eyes, as if accepting her role in God's wonderful, if sometimes painful, plan.

In the background left, we can look into Herod's palace, where he sits at a banquet table with his wife while Salomé dances modestly in front of him. Herod's lust is only hinted at with the naked statues—a man between two women—that adorn the palace exterior.

Right Panel—John the Evangelist's Vision of the Apocalypse: John sits on a high, rocky bluff on the island of Patmos and sees the end of the world as we know it...and he feels fine.

Overhead in a rainbow bubble, God appears on his throne, resting his hand on a sealed book. A lamb steps up to open the seals, unleashing the awful events at the end of time. Standing at the bottom of the rainbow, an angel in green gestures to John and says, "Write this down." John starts to dip his quill into the inkwell (his other hand holds the quill-sharpener), but he pauses, absolutely transfixed, experiencing the Apocalypse now.

He sees wars, fires, and plagues on the horizon, the Virgin in the sky rebuking a red dragon, and many other wonders. Fervent fundamentalists should bring their Bibles along, because there are many specific references brought to life in a literal way.

In the center ride the dreaded Four Horsemen, wreaking havoc on the cosmos (galloping over either islands or clouds). Horseman #4 is a skeleton, followed by a human-eating monster head. Helpless mortals on the right seek shelter in the rocks, but find none.

Memling has been criticized for building a career by copying the formulas of his predecessors, but this panel is a complete original. Its theme had never been so fully expressed, and the bright, contrasting colors and vivid imagery are almost modern. In the *St. John Altarpiece,* Memling shows us the full range of his palette, from medieval grace to Renaissance symmetry, from the real to the surreal.

• *In a glass case, find the...*

St. Ursula Shrine (c. 1489)

On October 21, 1489, the mortal remains of St. Ursula were brought here to the church and placed in this gilded oak shrine, built specially for the occasion and decorated with paintings by Memling. Ursula, yet another Christian martyred by the ancient Romans, became a sensation in the Middle Ages when builders in Germany's Köln (Cologne) unearthed a huge pile of bones believed to belong to her and her 11,000 slaughtered cohorts.

The shrine, carved of wood and covered with gold, looks like a miniature Gothic Church (similar to the hospital church). Memling was asked to fill in the "church's" stained-glass windows with six arch-shaped paintings telling Ursula's well-known legend.

• *Circle counterclockwise from the room entrance to get the story...*

1. Ursula—in white and blue—arrives by boat at the city of Köln and enters through the city gate. She's on a pilgrimage to Rome, accompanied by 11,000 (female) virgins. That night (look in the 2 windows of the house in the background, right), an angel appears and tells her this trip will mean her death, but she is undaunted.

2. Continuing up the Rhine, they arrive in Basel. (Memling knew the Rhine, having grown up near it.) Memling condenses the 11,000 virgins to a more manageable 11, making each one pure enough for a thousand. From Basel, they set out on foot (in the background, right) over the snowy Alps.

3. They arrive in Rome—formally portrayed by a round Renaissance tower decorated with *putti* (little angels)—where Ursula falls to her knees before the Pope at the church steps. Kneeling behind Ursula is her fiancé, Etherus, the pagan prince of England. She has agreed to marry him only if he becomes a Christian and refrains from the marriage bed long enough for her to make this three-year pilgrimage as a virgin (making, I guess, number 11,001). Inside the church on the right side, he is baptized a Christian.

4. They head back home. Here, they're leaving Basel, boarding ships to go north on the Rhine. The pope was so inspired by these virgins that he joined them. These "crowd" scenes are hardly realistic—more like a collage of individual poses and faces. And Memling tells the story with extremely minimal acting. Perhaps his inspiration was the pomp and ceremony of Bruges parades, introduced by the Burgundian dukes. He would have seen *tableaux vivants,* where Brugeois would pose in costume like human statues to enact an event from the Bible or from city history. (American "living Christmas crèches" carry on this dying art form.)

5. Back in Köln, a surprise awaits them—the city has been taken over by vicious Huns. They grab Etherus and stab him. He dies in Ursula's arms.

6. The Hun king (in red with turban and beard) woos Ursula, placing his hand over his heart, but she says, "No way." So a Hun

soldier draws his arrow and prepares to shoot her dead. Even here, at the climax of the story, there are no histrionics. Even the dog just sits down, crosses his paws, and watches. The whole shrine cycle is as posed, motionless, and colorful as the *tableaux vivants* that may have inaugurated the shrine here in this church in 1489.

In the background behind Ursula, a Bruges couple looks on sympathetically. This may be Memling himself (in red coat with fur lining) and his wife, Anna, who bore him three children. Behind them, Memling renders an accurate city skyline of Köln, including a side view of the Köln Cathedral (missing its still-unfinished tall spires).

• *In the small adjoining room, find several more Memlings.*

Portrait of a Young Woman (1480)

Memling's bread-and-butter was portraits done for families of wealthy merchants (especially visiting Italians and Portuguese). This portrait takes us right back to that time.

The young woman looks out the frame as if she were looking out a window. Her hands rest on the "sill," with the fingertips sticking over. The frame is original, but the banner and van Eyck–like lettering are not.

Her clothes look somewhat simple, but were high-class in their day. A dark damask dress is brightened by a red sash and a detachable white collar. She's pulled her hair into a tight bun at the back, pinned there with a fez-like cap and draped with a transparent veil. She's shaved her hairline and plucked her brows to get that clean, high-forehead look. Her ensemble is animated by a well-placed necklace of small stones.

Memling accentuates her fashionably pale complexion and gives her a pensive, sober expression, portraying her like a medieval saint. Still, she keeps her personality, with distinct features like the broad nose, neck tendons, and realistic hands. She peers out from her subtly painted veil, which sweeps down over the side of her face. What's she thinking?

Diptych of Martin van Nieuwenhove (1489)

Three-dimensional effects—borrowed from the Italian Renaissance style—enliven this traditional two-panel altarpiece. Both Mary-

and-Child and the 23-year-old Martin, though in different panels, inhabit the same room.

Stand right in front of Mary, facing her directly. If you line up the paintings' horizons (seen in the distance, out the room's windows), you'll see that both panels depict the same room—a room with two windows at the back and two along the right wall.

Want proof? In the convex mirror on the back wall (just to the left of Mary), the scene is reflected back at us, showing Mary and Martin from behind, silhouetted in the two "windows" of the picture frames. Apparently, Mary makes house calls, appearing right in the living room of the young donor Martin, the wealthy, unique-looking heir to his father's business.

SLEEPING

Bruges is a great place to sleep, with Gothic spires out your window, no traffic noise, and the cheerily out-of-tune carillon heralding each new day at 8:00 sharp. (Thankfully, the bell tower is silent from 22:00 to 8:00.)

Most Bruges accommodations are located between the train station and the old center, with the most distant (and best) being a few blocks to the north and east of Market Square.

B&Bs offer the best value (listed after "Hotels," below). All are on quiet streets and (with a few exceptions) keep the same prices throughout the year.

Bruges is most crowded Friday and Saturday evenings Easter through October, with July and August weekends being worst. Many hotels charge a bit more on Friday and Saturday, and won't let you stay just one night if it's a Saturday.

Hotels

$$$ Hotel Heritage offers 24 rooms, with chandeliers that seem hung especially for you, in a solid and completely modernized old building. Tastefully decorated and offering all the amenities, it's one of those places that does everything just right yet still feels warm and inviting (Db-€176, superior Db-€220, deluxe Db-€266, singles take a double for nearly the same cost, suites available, skipping their fine breakfast saves €15 per person, non-smoking, air-con, elevator, free Internet access in lobby, sauna, tanning bed, fitness room, bike rental for €6.50/half-day, Niklaas Desparsstraat 11, a block north of Market Square, tel. 050/444-444, fax 050/444-440, www.hotel-heritage.com, info@hotel-heritage.com, run by cheery and hardworking Johan and Isabelle).

$$$ Hotel Egmond is a creaky mansion quietly located in the middle of the idyllic Minnewater. Its eight 18th-century rooms are

Sleep Code

(€1 = about $1.20, country code: 32)
S = Single, **D** = Double/Twin, **T** = Triple, **Q** = Quad, **b** = bathroom,
s = shower only. Everyone speaks English. Unless otherwise
noted, credit cards are accepted and breakfast is included.

To help you easily sort through these listings, I've divided
the rooms into three categories, based on the price for a standard double room with bath:

$$$ **Higher Priced**—Most rooms €120 or more.
$$ **Moderately Priced**—Most rooms between €75–120.
$ **Lower Priced**—Most rooms €75 or less.

plain, with small modern baths shoehorned in, and the guests-only
garden is just waiting for a tea party. This hotel is ideal for romantics
who want a countryside setting and the convenience of being just a
five-minute walk from town (Sb-€92, small twin Db-€112, larger
Db-€120–130, Tb-€150, cash only, Minnewater 15, tel. 050/341-
445, fax 050/342-940, www.egmond.be, info@egmond.be).

$$$ **Crowne Plaza Hotel Brugge** is the most modern,
comfortable, and central hotel option. With 96 air-conditioned
rooms, it's just like a fancy American hotel (Db-€254–276, prices
drop as low as €200 on weekdays and off-season, breakfast-€21,
elevator, pool, Burg 10, tel. 050/446-844, fax 050/446-868, www
.crowneplaza.com).

$$ **Hotel Adornes** is small and classy—a great value. This
17th-century canalside house has 20 rooms with full modern bath-
rooms, free parking (reserve in advance), free loaner bikes, and
a cellar lounge with games and videos (Db-€90–120 depending
on size, singles take a double for nearly the same cost, Tb-€135,
Qb-€145, elevator, near Carmersstraat at St. Annarei 26, tel.
050/341-336, fax 050/342-085, www.adornes.be, info@adornes.be,
Nathalie runs the family business). For canal views and open-beam
ambience at no additional cost, request room #15, #16, or #17.

$$ **Hotel Patritius,** family-run and centrally located, is a
grand, circa-1830, neoclassical mansion with 16 stately rooms, a
plush lounge and chandeliered breakfast room, and a courtyard
garden. This is the best value in its price range (Db-€80–105
depending on size, Tb-€140, about €10 more Fri–Sat, non-smok-
ing, free parking, Riddersstraat 11, tel. 050/338-454, fax 050/339-
634, www.hotelpatritius.be, info@hotelpatritius.be, Garrett and
Elvi Spaey).

$$ **Hotel Botaniek,** quietly located a block from Astrid Park,
rents nine rooms (Db-€89 weekday special for Rick Steves' readers,

Bruges Hotels

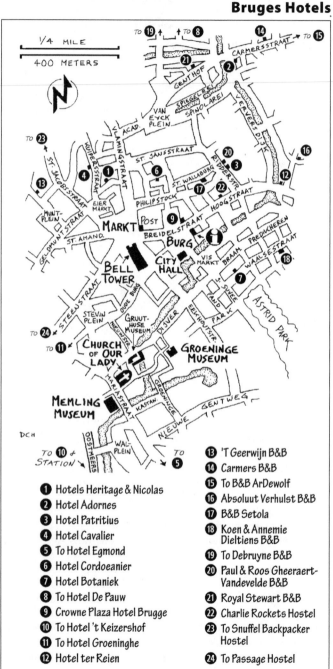

1 Hotels Heritage & Nicolas
2 Hotel Adornes
3 Hotel Patritius
4 Hotel Cavalier
5 To Hotel Egmond
6 Hotel Cordoeanier
7 Hotel Botaniek
8 To Hotel De Pauw
9 Crowne Plaza Hotel Brugge
10 To Hotel 't Keizershof
11 To Hotel Groeninghe
12 Hotel ter Reien
13 'T Geerwijn B&B
14 Carmers B&B
15 To B&B ArDewolf
16 Absoluut Verhulst B&B
17 B&B Setola
18 Koen & Annemie Dieltiens B&B
19 To Debruyne B&B
20 Paul & Roos Gheeraert-Vandevelde B&B
21 Royal Stewart B&B
22 Charlie Rockets Hostel
23 To Snuffel Backpacker Hostel
24 To Passage Hostel

€95 on weekends; Tb-€106, Qb-€115, less for longer and off-season stays, free museum discount card, elevator, Waalsestraat 23, tel. 050/341-424, fax 050/345-939, www.botaniek.be, info@botaniek .be).

$$ Hotel Groeninghe has eight charming, Old World rooms in a good location close to 't Zand. It's run by friendly Laurence (Sb-€70, Db-€85, Tb-€110, no elevator, Korte Vulderstraat 29, tel. 050/343-255, fax 050/340-769, www.hotelgroeninghe.be, hotelgroeninghe@pandora.be)

$$ Hotel ter Reien is big and basic, with 26 rooms overlooking a canal in the center (Db-€80, €5 extra for canal view, Langestraat 1, tel. 050/349-100, www.hotelterreien.be, info@hotelterreien.be).

$ Hotel Cordoeanier, a family-run hotel, rents 22 bright, simple, modern rooms on a quiet street two blocks off Market Square. It's the best cheap hotel in town (Sb-€59, Db-€65, Tb-€75, Qb-€88, Quint/b-€101, €5 extra on Fri–Sat, Cordoeanierstraat 16–18, tel. 050/339-051, fax 050/346-111, www.cordoeanier.be, info@cordoeanier.be, Kris, Veerle, Guy, and family). Their "holiday house" across the street sleeps up to 10 for €250 a night (includes a kitchen; cheaper for longer stays).

$ Hotel Cavalier, with more stairs than character, rents eight decent rooms and serves a hearty buffet breakfast in a once-royal setting (Sb-€52, Db-€64, Tb-€78, Qb-€85, 2 lofty "backpackers' doubles" on 4th floor-€42 or €47, Kuipersstraat 25, tel. 050/330-207, fax 050/347-199, www.hotelcavalier.be, run by friendly Viviane de Clerck).

$ Hotel de Pauw is tall, skinny, and family-run, with straight-forward rooms, on a quiet street across from a church (Sb-€60, Db-€65–68, renovated Db-€75, free and easy street parking or pay garage, Sint Gilliskerkhof 8, tel. 050/337-118, fax 050/345-140, www.hoteldepauw.be, info@hoteldepauw.be, Philippe and Hilde).

$ Hotel Nicolas feels like an old-time boarding house that missed Bruges' affluence bandwagon. Its 14 big, plain rooms are a good value, and the location is ideal—on a quiet street a block off Market Square (Sb-€49, Db-€58, Tb-€70, Niklaas Desparsstraat 9, tel. 050/335-502, hotel.nicolas@telenet.be).

Near the Train Station: **$ Hotel 't Keizershof** is a dollhouse of a hotel that lives by its motto, "Spend a night...not a fortune." It's simple and tidy, with seven small, cheery, old-time rooms split between two floors, with a shower and toilet on each (S-€25, D-€40, T-€62, Q-€72, cash only, free and easy parking, laun-dry service-€7.50, Oostmeers 126, a block in front of station, tel. 050/338-728, www.hotelkeizershof.be, hotel.keizershof@belgacom .net, Stefaan and Hilde).

Bed-and-Breakfasts

These B&Bs, run by people who enjoy their work, offer a better value than hotels. Most families rent out their entire top floor—generally three rooms and a small sitting area. And most are mod and stylish, in medieval shells. Each is central, with lots of stairs and €60 doubles you'd pay €100 for in a hotel. Most places charge extra for one-night stays. Parking is generally easy on the street (pay 9:00–19:00, free overnight).

$ Absoluut Verhulst is a great, modern-feeling B&B in a 400-year-old house, run by friendly Frieda and Benno (Sb-€50, Db-€75, huge and lofty suite-€95 for 2, €115 for 3, and €140 for 4, 1-night stays pay €10 more, cash only, 5-min walk east of Market Square at Verbrand Nieuwland 1, tel. & fax 050/334-515, www.b-bverhulst.com, b-b.verhulst@pandora.be).

$ B&B Setola, run by Lut and Bruno Setola, offers three modern rooms and a spacious breakfast/living room in their house (Sb-€55, Db-€60, Tb-€80, 1-night stays pay €10 more, family deals, cash only, non-smoking, 6-min walk from Market Square, Sint Walburgastraat 12, tel. 050/334-977, fax 050/332-551, www.bedandbreakfast-bruges.com, setola@bedandbreakfast-bruges.com).

$ Koen and Annemie Dieltiens are a friendly couple who enjoy getting to know their guests while sharing a wealth of information on Bruges. You'll eat a hearty breakfast around a big table in their comfortable house (Sb-€55, Db-€60, Tb-€80, 1-night stays pay €10 more, cash only, non-smoking, Waalse Straat 40, 3 blocks southeast of Burg Square, tel. 050/334-294, fax 050/335-230, www.bedandbreakfastbruges.be, dieltiens@bedandbreakfastbruges.be).

$ Debruyne B&B, run by Marie-Rose and her architect husband, Ronny, offers artsy, original decor (check out the elephant-size white doors—Ronny's design) and genuine warmth. If Gothic is getting old, this is refreshingly modern (Sb-€55, Db-€60, Tb-€80, 1-night stays pay €10 more, cash only, non-smoking, free Internet access in lobby, 7-min walk north of Market Square, 2 blocks from the little church at Lange Raamstraat 18, tel. 050/347-606, fax 050/340-285, www.bedandbreakfastbruges.com, marie.debruyne@advalvas.be).

$ Paul and Roos Gheeraert-Vandevelde live in a neoclassical mansion and rent huge, bright, comfy rooms (Sb-€55, Db-€60, Tb-€80, cash only, strictly non-smoking, fridges in rooms, Riddersstraat 9, 4-min walk east of Market Square, tel. 050/335-627, fax 050/345-201, www.bb-bruges.be, bb-bruges@skynet.be).

$ 't Geerwijn B&B, run by Chris Deloof, offers homey rooms in the old center. Check out the fun, lofty A-frame room upstairs (Ds/Db-€60, Tb-€75, pleasant breakfast room and a royal lounge, cash only, non-smoking, Geerwijnstraat 14, tel. 050/340-544, fax

050/343-721, www.geerwijn.be, chris.deloof@scarlet.be).

$ Carmers B&B, owned by the Van Nevel family, rents three attractive rooms with built-in beds on the top floor of a 16th-century house (D-€50–53, Db-€60, 1-night stays pay €10 more, third person-€17, cash only, non-smoking, 10-min walk from Market Square, or bus #4 or #14 from train station or Market Square to Carmersbridge, Carmersstraat 13, tel. 050/346-860, fax 050/347-616, www.brugesbb.com, robert.vannevel@advalvas.be). Affable Robert, who works at the Memling Museum, enthusiastically shares the culture and history of Bruges with his guests.

$ B&B ArDewolf is a family-friendly place with a boarding-house feel, run by Nicole and Arnold. It's in a stately, quiet neighborhood at the far edge of the old town, near the windmills and moat (S-€35, D-€40, T-€60, Q-€70, Quint/b-€80, cash only, Oostproosse 9, tel. 050/338-366, www.ardewolf.be, info@ardewolf.be). This is good for drivers, but a long walk from the center. From the train station, take bus #4 to Sasplein. Walk to the path behind the first windmill and turn left on Oostproosse.

$ Royal Stewart B&B, run by Scottish Maggie and her husband, Gilbert, has three thoughtfully decorated rooms in a quiet, almost cloistered 17th-century house that was inhabited by nuns until 1953 (S-€45, D/Db-€57, Tb-€80, cash only, non-smoking, pleasant breakfast rooms, Genthof 25–27, 5-min walk from Market Square, tel. & fax 050/337-918, www.royalstewart.be, r.stewart@pandora.be).

Hostels

Bruges has several good hostels offering beds for around €10–12 in two- to eight-bed rooms. Breakfast is about €3 extra. The American-style **Charlie Rockets** hostel and bar is the liveliest and most central. The ground floor feels like a 19th-century sports bar, with a foosball-and-movie-posters party ambience. Upstairs is an industrial-strength pile of hostel dorms (75 beds, €16 per bed with sheets, 4–6 beds per room, D-€42, cash only, lockers, Hoogstraat 19, tel. 050/330-660, fax 050/343-630, www.charlierockets.com). Other small, loose, and central places are **Snuffel Backpacker Hostel** (€13–17, Ezelstraat 47, tel. 050/333-133, www.snuffel.be) and the funky **Passage** (€12, 4–7 beds per room, D-€45, Db-€60, Dweerstraat 26, tel. 050/340-232, www.passagebruges.com).

EATING

Belgium is where France meets the North, and you'll find a good mix of both Flemish and French influences in Bruges and Brussels.

Belgian Specialties

These are popular throughout Belgium.

Moules: Mussels are served everywhere, either cooked plain *(nature)*, with white wine *(vin blanc)*, with shallots or onions *(marinière)*, or in a tomato sauce *(provençale)*. You get a big-enough-for-two bucket and a pile of fries. Go local by using one empty shell to tweeze out the rest of the *moules*. When the mollusks are in season, from about mid-July through April, you'll get the big Dutch mussels. Locals take a break in May and June, when only the puny Danish kind is available.

Frites: Belgian fries *(Vlaamse frites,* or Flemish fries) taste so good because they're deep-fried twice—once to cook, and once to brown. The natives eat them with mayonnaise, not ketchup.

Flemish Specialties

These specialties are traditional to Bruges, but available in Brussels.

Carbonnade: Rich beef stew flavored with onions and beer.

Chou rouge à la flamande: Red cabbage with onions and prunes.

Flamiche: Cheese pie with onions.

Flemish asparagus: White asparagus (fresh in springtime) in cream sauce.

Lapin à la flamande: Marinated rabbit braised in onions and prunes.

Soupe à la bière: Beer soup.

Stoemp: Mashed potatoes and vegetables.

Waterzooi: Creamy meat stew (chicken, eel, or fish).
...à la flamande: Anything cooked in the local Flemish style.

Brussels Specialties

These specialties are "native" to Brussels (which tends toward French cuisine), but you'll find them in Bruges, too.

Anguilles au vert: Eel in green herb sauce.

Caricoles: Sea snails. Very local, seasonal, and hard to find, these are usually sold hot by street vendors.

Cheeses: Remoudou and Djotte de Nivelles are made locally.

Choux de Bruxelles: Brussels sprouts (in cream sauce).

Crevettes: Shrimp, often served as croquettes (minced and stuffed in breaded, deep-fried rolls).

Croque monsieur: Grilled ham-and-cheese sandwich.

Endive: Typical Belgian vegetable (also called *chicoree* or *chicon*) served as a side dish.

Filet américain: Beware—for some reason, steak tartare (raw) is called "American."

Tartine de fromage blanc: Open-face cream-cheese sandwich, often enjoyed with a cherry Kriek beer.

...à la brabançonne: Anything cooked in the local Brabant (Brussels) style, such as *faisant* (pheasant) *à la brabançonne.*

Desserts and Snacks

Gaufres: Waffles, sold hot in small shops.

Dame blanche: Hot-fudge sundae.

Spekuloos: Spicy gingerbread biscuits served with coffee.

Pralines: Filled Belgian chocolates.

Pistolets: Round croissants.

Cramique: Currant roll.

Craquelin: Currant roll with sugar sprinkles.

Belgian Beers

Belgium has about 120 different varieties of beer and 580 different brands, more than any other country...and the locals take their beers as seriously as the French regard their wines. Even small café menus include six to eight varieties. Connoisseurs and novices alike can be confused by the many choices, and casual drinkers probably won't like every kind offered, since some varieties don't even taste like beer. Belgian beer is generally yeastier and higher in alcohol than beers in other countries.

In Belgium, certain beers are paired with certain dishes. To bring out their flavor, different beers are served at cold, cool, or room temperature, and each has its own distinctive glass. Whether wide-mouthed, tall, and fluted, with or without a stem, the glass is meant to highlight the beer's qualities. One of my favorite Belgian beer experiences is drinking a Kwak beer in its traditional tall glass. The glass, which widens at the base, stands in a wooden holder, and you pick the whole apparatus up—frame and glass—and drink. As you near the end, the beer in the wide bottom comes out at you quickly, with a "Kwak! Kwak! Kwak!"

To get a draft beer in Bruges, where Flemish is the dominant language, ask for *een pintje* (a pint, pronounced ayn pinch-ya), and in Brussels, where French prevails, request *une bière* (oon bee-yair). Cheers is *proost* or *gezondheid* in Flemish, and *santé* (sahn-tay) in French. The colorful cardboard coasters make nice, free souvenirs.

Here's a breakdown of types of beer, with some common brand names you'll find either on tap or in bottles. (Some beers require a second fermentation in the bottle, so they're only available in bottles.) This list is just a start, and you'll find many beers that don't fall into these neat categories. For encyclopedic information on Belgian beers, visit www.belgianstyle.com or www.beerhunter.com.

Ales (Blonde/Red/Amber/Brown): Ales are easily recognized by their color. Try a blonde or golden ale (Leffe Blonde, Duvel, Kwak), a rare and bitter sour red (Rodenbach), an amber (Palm, De Koninck), or a brown (Leffe Bruin).

Lagers: These are the light, sparkling, Budweiser-type beers. Popular brands include Jupiler, Stella Artois, and Maes.

Lambics: Perhaps the most unusual and least beer-like, *lambics* are stored for years in wooden casks, fermenting from wild yeasts that occur naturally in the air. Tasting more like a dry and bitter cider or champagne, pure *lambic* is often blended with fruits or herbs to improve the taste. Homebrewed *lambics*—such as *gueuze*, *faro*, *lambic doux*, and *lambic blanche*—are on tap in old cafés. Only *gueuze*, a blend of aged and young ale, is sold commercially in bottles. Some brand names include Cantillon, Lindemans, and Mort-Subite (literally, "Sudden Death").

Fruit *lambics* include those made with cherries *(kriek)*, raspberries *(frambozen)*, peaches *(peche)*, or black currants *(casis)*. The result for each is a tart beer, similar to a dry pink champagne. People who don't usually enjoy beer tend to like these fruit-flavored varieties.

White *(Witte):* Based on wheat instead of hops, these milky-yellow summertime beers are often served with a lemon slice. White beer, similar to a Hefeweizen in the United States, is often flavored with spices such as orange peel or coriander. Hoegaarden or Dentergems are names to look for.

Trappist Beers: For centuries, between their vespers and matins, Trappist monks have been brewing heavily fermented, malty beers. Three typical Trappist beers (from the Westmalle monastery) are *Trippel*, with a blonde color, served cold with a frothy head; *Dubbel*, which is dark, sweet, and served cool; and *Single*, made especially by the monks for the monks, and considered a fair trade for a life of celibacy. Other Trappist monasteries include Rochefort, Chimay, Westvleteren, and Orval.

Strong Beers: The potent brands include Duvel (meaning "devil," because of its high octane, camouflaged by a pale color), Verboten Vrucht (literally, "Forbidden Fruit," with Adam and Eve on the label), and the not-for-the-fainthearted brands of Judas, Satan, and Lucifer. Gouden Carolus is considered the strongest beer in Belgium, and Delerium Tremens speaks for itself.

Restaurants in Bruges

Bruges' specialties include mussels cooked a variety of ways (one order can feed two), fish dishes, grilled meats, and french fries. Don't eat before 19:30 unless you like eating alone. Tax and service are always included in your bill. You can't get free tap water; Belgian restaurateurs are emphatic about that. While tap water comes with a smile in Holland, France, and Germany, it's not the case in Belgium, where you'll either pay for water, enjoy the beer, or go thirsty.

You'll find plenty of affordable, touristy restaurants on floodlit squares and along dreamy canals. Bruges feeds 3.5 million tourists a year, and most are seduced by a high-profile location. These can be fine experiences for the magical setting and views, but the quality of food and service is low. I wouldn't blame you for eating at one of these places, but I won't recommend any. I prefer the candle-cool bistros that flicker on back streets. Here are my favorites:

Rock Fort is a chic, eight-table spot with a modern, fresh coziness and a high-powered respect for good food. Two young chefs, Peter Laloo and Hermes Vanliefde, give their French cuisine a creative and gourmet twist. Reservations are required for dinner but not lunch. This place is a winner (€11 Mon–Fri lunch special with coffee, beautifully presented €15–20 dinner plates, open Mon–Fri 12:00–14:30 & 18:30–23:00, closed Sat–Sun, great pastas and salads, Langestraat 15, tel. 050/334-113). They also run the Barsalon restaurant next door.

Barsalon Tapas Bar, more than a tapas bar, is the brain-child of Peter Laloo from Rock Fort (listed above), allowing him to spread his creative cooking energy. This long, skinny slice of L.A. thrives late into the evening with Bruges' beautiful people. Choose between the long bar, comfy stools, and bigger tables in back. Come early for fewer crowds. The playful menu comes with €6 "tapas" dishes taking you from Spain to Japan (3 fill 2 hungry travelers) and more elaborate €14 plates—and don't overlook their daily "suggestions" board with some special wines by the glass and a "teaser" sampler plate of desserts. Barsalon shares the same kitchen, hours, and dressy local clientele as the adjacent Rock Fort.

Bruges Restaurants

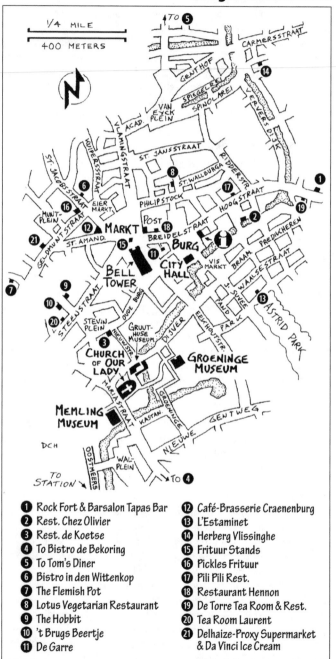

1. Rock Fort & Barsalon Tapas Bar
2. Rest. Chez Olivier
3. Rest. de Koetse
4. To Bistro de Bekoring
5. To Tom's Diner
6. Bistro in den Wittenkop
7. The Flemish Pot
8. Lotus Vegetarian Restaurant
9. The Hobbit
10. 't Brugs Beertje
11. De Garre
12. Café-Brasserie Craenenburg
13. L'Estaminet
14. Herberg Vlissinghe
15. Frituur Stands
16. Pickles Frituur
17. Pili Pili Rest.
18. Restaurant Hennon
19. De Torre Tea Room & Rest.
20. Tea Room Laurent
21. Delhaize-Proxy Supermarket & Da Vinci Ice Cream

Restaurant Chez Olivier, with 10 classy, white-tableclothed tables, is considered the best fancy French cuisine splurge in town. While delicate Anne serves, her French husband, Olivier, is busy cooking up whatever he found freshest that day. While you can order à la carte, it's wise to go with the recommended daily *menu* (€34 for 3-course lunch, €45 for 3-course dinner, €55 for 4-course dinner, wine adds €15–20, Mon–Wed and Fri–Sat 12:00–13:30 & 19:00–21:30, closed Sun and Thu, reserve for dinner, Meestraat 9, tel. 050/333-659).

De Torre, a tea room and restaurant, has a fresh interior and a scenic, shady, canalside terrace. I'd eat here only to be along a canal (€10 3-course lunch, €22–35 dinner *menu*s, Thu–Mon 10:00–22:00, closed Tue–Wed, Langestraat 8, tel. 050/342-946).

Pili Pili is a mod and inviting pasta place, where Reinout and Tom prepare and serve 10 different pastas and great salads at very reasonable prices. The place is clean, low-key, and brimming with quality (€9 lunch plate with wine, €12.50 pasta and wine dinner, Thu–Tue 12:00–14:30 & 18:00–22:30, closed Sun afternoon and Wed, Hoogstraat 17, tel. 050/491-149).

Restaurant de Koetse is a good bet for central, affordable, quality, local-style food. The feeling is traditional, yet fun and kid-friendly. The cuisine is Belgian and French, with a stress on grilled meat, seafood, and mussels (€27 3-course meals, €20 plates include vegetables and a salad, Fri–Wed 12:00–15:00 & 18:00–22:00, closed Thu, non-smoking section, Oude Burg 31, tel. 050/337-680).

Bistro de Bekoring, cute, candlelit, and Gothic, fills two almshouses with people thankful for good food. Rotund and friendly Chef Roland and his wife, Gerda, love to tempt people—as the name of their bistro implies. They serve traditional Flemish food (especially eel and beer-soaked stew) from a small menu to people who like holding hands as they dine (€12 weekday lunch, €32 dinners, Wed–Sat from 12:00 and from 18:30, closed Sun–Tue, out past the Begijnhof at Arsenaalstraat 53, tel. 050/344-157).

Bistro in den Wittenkop, very Flemish, is a cluttered, laid-back, old-time place specializing in the local favorites. While Lieve cooks, his wife Daniel serves in a cool-and-jazzy, candlelit Flemish ambience (€16–20 main courses, Tue–Sat 12:00–14:00 & 18:00–21:30, closed Sun–Mon, terrace in back, Sint Jakobsstraat 14, tel. 050/332-059).

The Flemish Pot (a.k.a. The Little Pancake House) is a hard-working eatery serving up traditional peasant-style Flemish meals. They crank out pancake meals (savory and sweet) and homemade *wafels* for lunch. Then, at 18:00, enthusiastic chefs Mario and Rik stow their waffle irons and pull out a traditional menu of vintage Flemish plates (€25 dinner *menu*, Fri–Wed 12:00–22:00, closed

Thu, family friendly, just off Geldmuntstraat at Helmstraat 3, tel. 050/340-086).

Lotus Vegetarian Restaurant serves serious lunch plates (€9 *plat du jour* offered daily), salads, and homemade chocolate cake in a smoke-free, bustling, and upscale setting without a trace of tie-dye (Mon–Sat 11:45–14:00, closed Sun, just off north of Burg at Wapenmakersstraat 5, tel. 050/331-078).

The Hobbit, featuring an entertaining menu, is always busy with happy eaters. For a swinging deal, try the all-you-can-eat spareribs with salad for €13. It's nothing fancy, just good, basic food in a fun, traditional grill house (daily 18:00–24:00, family-friendly, Kemelstraat 8–10, tel. 050/335-520).

Tom's Diner, a "bistro eetcafé," glows with a love of food in a quiet, cobbled residential area a 10-minute walk from the center. Young chef Tom gives traditional dishes a delightful modern twist, and your meal comes gorgeously presented in a "high food" style. The "diner" comes with Creedence Clearwater Revival soft rock, rusty 1960s kitsch knickknacks under 16th-century beams, and friendly and helpful service (hearty yet delicate €15 plates, Thu–Mon 18:00–24:00, closed Tue–Wed, reserve on weekends, north of Market Square near Sint-Gilliskerk at West-Gistelhof 23, tel. 050/333-382).

Market Square Restaurants: Most tourists seem to be eating on the Market Square with the bell tower high overhead and horse carriages clip-clopping by. The square is ringed by tourist traps with aggressive waiters expert at getting you to consume more than you realized. Still, if you order smartly, you can have a memorable meal or drink here on one of the finest squares in Europe at a reasonable price. Consider **Café-Brasserie Craenenburg**, with a straightforward menu, where you can get a pasta and beer for €10 or €12 and spend all the time you want ogling the magic of Bruges (daily 8:00–23:00, Markt 16, tel. 050/333-402).

Bars Offering Light Meals, Beer, and Ambience

Stop into one of the city's atmospheric bars for a light meal or a drink with great Bruges ambience. For information on beer, see page 301.

The 't Brugs Beertje is the place for a huge selection of Belgian beers. While any pub or restaurant carries the basic beers, you'll find a selection of more than 300 types, including brews to suit any season here. They serve only two light meals: pâté or a traditional cheese plate (5 cheeses, bread, and salad for €9; Thu–Tue 16:00–24:00, closed Wed, Kemelstraat 5, tel. 050/339-616, run by fun-loving manager Daisy).

De Garre is another good place to gain an appreciation of the Belgian beer culture. Rather than a noisy pub scene, it has a dressy, sit-down-and-focus-on-your-friend-and-the-fine-beer vibe (great selection, daily 12:00–24:00, off Breidelstraat between Burg and Markt, on tiny Garre alley, tel. 050/341-029). Don't come here expecting to eat anything more than grilled cheese sandwiches... this is for beer and camaraderie.

L'Estaminet is a youthful, brown-café-feeling, jazz-filled eatery. Almost intimidating in its lack of tourists, it's popular with local students who come for the Tolkien-chic ambience and hearty €7 spaghetti and good salads. It has more beer than wine, a super characteristic interior, and a relaxed patio facing the peaceful Astrid Park under an all-weather canopy (Tue–Sun 11:30–24:00, closed Mon, Park 5, tel. 050/330-916).

Herberg Vlissinghe is the oldest pub in town (1515), where Bruno keeps things simple and laid-back, serving just hot snacks (lasagna and grilled cheese sandwiches), but great beer in the best old-time tavern atmosphere in town. This must have been the Dutch Masters' rec room. The garden outside comes with a boules court—free for guests to watch or play (Wed–Sun open from 11:00 on, closed Mon–Tue, Blekersstraat 2, tel. 050/343-737).

Fries, Fast Food, and Picnics

Local french fries *(frites)* are a treat. Proud and traditional *frituurs* serve tubs of fries and various local-style shish kebabs. Belgians dip their *frites* in mayonnaise, but ketchup is there for the Yankees (along with spicier sauces). For a quick, cheap, and scenic meal, hit a *frituur* and sit on the steps or benches overlooking Market Square (convenience benches are about 50 yards past the post office).

Market Square Frituur: Twin take-away french fries carts are on the Market Square at the base of the bell tower (daily 10:00–24:00).

Pickles Frituur, a block off Market Square, is handy for sit-down fries. Its forte is greasy, fast, deep-fried Flemish corn dogs. The "menu 2" comes with three traditional gut bombs: shrimp, chicken, and "spicy gypsie" (daily 11:30–24:00, at the corner of Geldmuntstraat and Sint Jakobstraat, tel. 050/337-957).

Delhaize-Proxy Supermarket is ideal for picnics (push-button produce pricer lets you buy as little as one mushroom, Mon–Sat 9:00–19:00, closed Sun, 3 blocks off the Market Square on Geldmuntstraat). For midnight munchies, you'll find Indian-run corner grocery stores.

Belgian Waffles and Ice Cream

While Americans think of "Belgian" waffles for breakfast, the Belgians (who don't eat waffles or pancakes for breakfast) think of *wafels* as Liège-style (dense, sweet, eaten plain, and heated up) and Brussels-style (lighter, often with powdered sugar or whipped

cream and strawberry, served in teahouses only in the afternoons from 14:00–18:00). You'll see waffles sold at restaurants and take-away stands.

For good Liège-style *wafels* (€2), stop by **Restaurant Hennon**—their waffles and other dishes are made with fresh ingredients (€2.50–6 plates, Tue–Sun 9:00–18:30, closed Mon, between Market Square and Burg at Breidelstraat 16). You can also try **Tea Room Laurent** for waffles and pancakes (€4–8 plates, Steenstraat 79) and the **Flemish Pot** (listed above).

Da Vinci Ice Cream, the local favorite for good homemade ice cream, has creative flavors and a great, fun ambience. As you approach, you'll see a line of happy lickers. Before ordering, ask to sample the Ferrero Rocher (chocolate, nuts, and crunchy cookie) and Bacio Bianco—rice with white chocolate (daily 10:00–24:00, Geldmuntstraat 34, run by Sylvia from Austria).

Nightlife

Herberg Vlissinghe, listed above for light meals, is a great place to just nurse a beer.

Charlie Rockets is an American-style bar—lively and central—with foosball games, darts, and five pool tables in the inviting back room. It also runs a youth hostel upstairs and therefore is filled with a young, international crowd (a block off Market Square at Hoogstraat 19). Nearby is **De Versteende Nacht Jazzcafe,** another youthful, more local hangout devoted to music and drinking (Langestraat 11).

Night-time Bike Ride: Great as these pubs are, my favorite way to spend a late summer twilight evening in Bruges is on a rental bike, savoring the cobbled wonders of its back streets, far from the touristic commotion.

Evening Carillon Concerts: The tiny courtyard behind the bell tower has a few benches where people can enjoy the free carillon concerts (generally Mon, Wed, and Sat at 21:00 in the summer, schedule posted on the wall).

BRUSSELS

ORIENTATION

Six hundred years ago, Brussels was just a nice place to stop and buy a waffle on the way to Bruges. With no strategic importance, it was allowed to grow as a free trading town. Today, it's a city of 1.25 million, the capital of Belgium, the headquarters of NATO, and the center of the European Union.

The Bruxelloise are cultured and genteel—even a bit snobby. As the unofficial capital of Europe, the city is multicultural, hosting politicians and businessmen from around the globe and featuring a world of ethnic restaurants.

Brussels enjoyed a Golden Age of peace and prosperity (1400–1550) while England and France were duking it out in the Hundred Years' War. It was then that many of the fine structures that distinguish the city today were built. In the 1800s, Brussels had another growth spurt, fueled by industrialization, exploited wealth from the Belgian Congo, and the exhilaration of the country's recent independence (1830).

Brussels speaks French. Bone up on *bonjour* and *s'il vous plaît*. Though the city (and country) is officially bilingual and filled with foreign visitors, 80 percent of the locals speak French first and English second. Language aside, the whole feel of the town is urban French, not rural Flemish.

Because Brussels sits smack-dab between Belgium's two linguistic groups (60 percent of Belgians speak Flemish, 40 percent speak French), most of Brussels' street signs and maps are in both languages. In this chapter, French names are generally used.

Tourists zipping between Amsterdam and Paris by train usually miss Brussels, but its rich, chocolaty mix of food and culture pleasantly surprises those who stop.

Brussels Overview

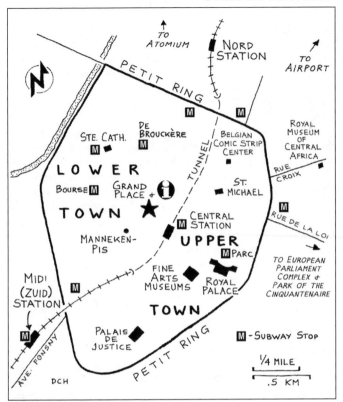

Planning Your Time

Brussels is low on great sights and high on ambience. On a quick trip, a day and a night are enough for a good first taste. It could even be done as a day trip by train from Bruges (2/hr, 1 hr) or a stopover on the Amsterdam–Paris or Amsterdam–Bruges ride (hourly trains); for specifics, see the sidebar. The main reason to stop—the Grand Place—takes only a few minutes to see. With very limited time, skip the indoor sights and enjoy a coffee or a beer on the square.

Art lovers and novices alike can spend a couple of enjoyable hours at the Royal Museums of Fine Arts of Belgium (twin museums—ancient and modern—covered by the same ticket), and even the tone-deaf can appreciate the Musical Instruments Museum. To see the impressive auto and military museums (side by side), plan on a three-hour excursion from the town center.

OVERVIEW

(area code: 02)

Central Brussels is surrounded by a ring of roads (which replaced the old city wall) called the Pentagon. (Romantics think it looks more like a heart.) All hotels and nearly all the sights I mention are within this circle. The epicenter holds the main square (the Grand Place), the TI, and Central Station (all within 3 blocks of each other).

What isn't so apparent from maps is that Brussels is a city divided by altitude. A ridgeline that runs north–south splits the town into the Upper Town (east half, elevation 200 feet) and Lower Town (west, at sea level), with the Central Station in between. The Upper Town, traditionally the home of nobility and the rich, has big marble palaces, broad boulevards, and the major museums. The Lower Town, with the Grand Place (Grote Markt in Flemish), narrow streets, old buildings, modern shops, colorful eateries, and the famous peeing-boy statue, has more character.

Outside the Pentagon-shaped center, sprawling suburbs and vast green zones contain some tourist attractions, including the European Parliament and the Park of the Cinquantenaire, along with Autoworld and the Royal Museum of the Army and Military History.

Tourist Information

Although the TI at Rue du Marché-aux-Herbes 63 is for all of Belgium, it does Brussels fine (July–Aug daily 9:00–19:00; Sept–June Mon–Fri 9:00–18:00, Sat–Sun 9:00–13:00 & 14:00–18:00; Jan–March closed Sun afternoon; downhill 3 blocks from Central Station, tel. 02/504-0390, www.belgium-tourism.be; 2 fun Europe stores are across the street). A Brussels-only TI is in the Town Hall on the Grand Place (summer daily 9:00–18:00; winter Mon–Sat 9:00–18:00, Sun 9:00–14:00; closed Sun Jan–Easter; tel. 02/513-8940, www.brusselsdiscovery.com).

The TIs have countless fliers. Day-trippers should pick up a city map and a public transit map. The €3 *Brussels Guide & Map* booklet is worthwhile if you want a series of neighborhood walks (the Grand Place, plus 3 others farther afield), a map of greater Brussels, and a more complete explanation of the city's many museums. For current listings of concerts and other entertainment options, pick up *The Bulletin* magazine, which has the monthly "What's On" inside. The **Brussels Card**, which provides unlimited public transportation and free entrance to most museums, is worthwhile if you plan to sightsee like mad for three days (€30/3 days).

Remember that the TI at Rue du Marché-aux-Herbes 63

Brussels in Three Hours

Brussels makes a great stopover between trains. First check your bag at the Central Station and confirm your departure time and station (factoring in any necessary transit time to a different departure station) before heading into town.

Here are some suggestions on how to spend a short visit.

1. Plant yourself at a café on the Grand Place and watch the parade of tourists from around the world, while you enjoy a meal of Belgian clichés: mussels, *frites* with mayonnaise, a waffle *(gaufre)*, chocolates, and a Belgian beer. Or...

2. Take my Grand Place Walk (see page 327), then have your meal. Or...

3. Tour the Royal Museums of Fine Arts and/or the Musical Instruments Museum in the Upper Town. Or...

4. Combine elements of all of the above—quickly—by doing the "Brussels Blitz." Ready, set, go: Head directly for the Grand Place and take my Grand Place Walk (described on page 327). To streamline, skip the *Manneken-Pis* until later, and end the walk at the Bourse, where you'll catch bus #95 or #96 to Place Royale. Enjoy a handful of masterpieces at the Royal Museums of Fine Arts, then do the Upper Town Walk (page 338), which ends back at the *Manneken-Pis* and the Grand Place. Buy a box of chocolates and a bottle of Belgian beer, and pop the top as your train pulls out of the station. Ahhh!

covers all of Belgium. If your next destination is Bruges, get your Bruges information here.

Arrival in Brussels

By Train: Brussels can't decide which of its three stations (Central, Nord, and Midi) is the main one. Most international trains use the Nord and Midi Stations. The Eurostar leaves from the Midi Station (also called Zuid, or South), getting you to London in less than three hours. The area around the Midi Station is a rough-and-tumble immigrant neighborhood (marked by its towering Ferris wheel); the area around the Nord Station is a seedy red light district. The Central Station, nearest to the sights and my recommended hotels, has handy services: a small grocery store, fast food, waiting rooms, and luggage storage (near track 1, €3.20/bag). Normally, only Belgian and Amsterdam trains stop at Central. Don't assume your train stops at more than one station; ask your conductor.

If you arrive at Nord or Midi, take a connecting train to the Central Station. Trains zip under the city, connecting all three stations every two minutes or so. It's an easy three-minute chore to

French Phrases

Though many people in Brussels speak English, it's helpful to know some French phrases. (When using the phonetics, try to nasalize the "n" sound.)

Good day.	*Bonjour.*	bohn-zhoor
Mrs.	*Madame*	mah-dahm
Mr.	*Monsieur*	muhs-yur
Please?	*S'il vous plaît?*	see voo play
Thank you.	*Merci.*	mehr-see
You're welcome.	*De rien.*	duh ree-ahn
Excuse me.	*Pardon.*	par-dohn
Yes. / No.	*Oui. / Non.*	wee / nohn
Okay.	*D'accord.*	dah-kor
Cheers!	*Santé!*	sahn-tay
Goodbye.	*Au revoir.*	oh vwahr
women / men	*dames / hommes*	dahm / ohm
one / two / three	*un / deux / trois*	uhn / duh / twah
Do you speak English?	*Parlez-vous anglais?*	par-lay voo ahn-glay

connect from Nord or Midi to Central. The €1.40 ticket between the stations is covered by any train ticket into or out of Brussels (or use your railpass). Scan the departures board for trains leaving in the next few minutes and note which ones stop at Central. As you wait on the platform for your train, watch the track notice board that tells which train is approaching. They zip in and out constantly. Anxious travelers, who think their train has arrived early, often board the wrong train on the right track.

To get to the Grand Place from Central Station, exit the station from the top floor (to the left of the ticket windows), and you'll see Le Meridien Hôtel across the street. Pass through the arch of Le Meridien Hôtel, turn right, and walk downhill one block to a small square with a fountain. For the Grand Place, turn left at the far end of the square and walk a half-block on Rue de la Colline. Or, to head directly to the all-Belgium TI, exit the small square at the far end and continue straight for one block to Rue du Marché-aux-Herbes 63. Note that the hop-on, hop-off bus companies depart from just in front of the Central Station (you'll meet ticket hustlers as you leave). You could hop on one of these buses upon arrival to orient yourself from the top deck (see "Tours," below).

By Plane: See the Transportation Connections chapter, page 365.

Helpful Hints

Theft Alert: While I euphemistically describe Brussels as "earthy," it's also undeniably seedier than many European cities. Expect more grime on buildings, street people, and Gypsy ladies cradling their babies with a fake arm (while her hidden real arm rifles your pockets). Muggings do occur. Some locals warn that it's not safe to be out late, especially after the Métro shuts down at midnight; troublemakers prey on people who missed that last ride. As in any other big city, use common sense and consider taking a taxi back to your hotel at night.

Sightseeing Schedules: Brussels' most important museums are closed on Monday. But, of course, the city's single best sight—the Grand Place—is always open. You can also enjoy a bus tour any day of the week. Most important, this is a city to browse and wander.

Laundry: There's a launderette at Rue du Midi 65 (daily 7:00–21:00).

Department Store: Hema is at Nieuwstraat 13 (Mon–Sat 9:30–18:30, closed Sun).

Travel Agency and Discount Flights: The Connections Agency has a line on the cheapest transportation connections—plane and train—which they book for a €10 fee (Mon–Fri 9:30–18:30, Sat 10:00–17:00, closed Sun, free coffee and WC, Rue du Midi 19, tel. 02/550-0130, www.connections.be).

Getting Around Brussels

Most of central Brussels' sights are walkable. But public transport is handy for connecting the train stations, climbing to the Upper Town (bus #95 or #96 from the Bourse), or visiting sights outside of the central core. To reach these outlying sights, such as the European Parliament, take the Métro or jump on a hop-on, hop-off tour bus from Central Station (described under "Tours," below; check tour bus route map to make sure it covers the sights you want to see). On summer weekends, a charming old-time trolley goes out to the Royal Museum of Central Africa (see page 325).

By Métro, Bus, Tram, and Train: A single €1.50 ticket is good for one hour on all public transportation—Métro, buses, trams, and even trains shuttling between Brussels' three train stations (notice the time when you first stamp it, stamp it again if you transfer lines, buy single tickets on bus or at Métro stations). Deals are available at the TI at Rue de Marché-aux-Herbes 63 and at Métro stations: an all-day pass for €4 (cheaper than 3 single tickets; on Sat–Sun and holidays, this pass covers 2 people); a pack of five single tickets for €6.50 (saving you €0.20 per ticket); or a 10-ride card for €10. The free *Métro Tram Bus Plan* is excellent; pick it up at either TI or any Métro station. Transit info: tel. 02/515-2000.

Near the Grand Place are two transportation hubs: Central Station and the Bourse. Those staying in hotels northwest of the Grand Place have good access to the Métro system at the De Brouckère and Ste. Catherine stops.

By Taxi: Cabbies charge a €2.50 drop fee, and then €1.20 per additional kilometer. After 22:00, you'll be hit with a €2 surcharge. You'll pay about €10 to ride from the center to the European Parliament. Convenient taxi stands are at the Bourse (near Grand Place) and at Place du Grand Sablon (in the Upper Town). To call a cab, try Taxi Bleu (tel. 02/268-0000).

TOURS

Hop-on, Hop-off Bus Tours—Two different companies offer nearly identical city tours. The 90-minute loop and recorded narration give you a once-over-lightly of the city from the top deck (open on sunny days) of a double-decker bus. While you can hop on and off for 24 hours with one ticket, schedules are sparse (about 2 per hour, times listed on each flier; both companies run roughly Sun–Thu 10:00–16:00, Fri–Sat 10:00–17:00). Except for the trip out to the European Parliament and Cinquantenaire Park (military and auto museums), I'd just stay on to enjoy the views and the minimal commentary. The fiercely competitive companies often both have hustlers at the Central Station trying to get you on board (offering "student" discounts to customers of all ages). The handiest starting points are the Central Station and the Bourse. The companies are **City Tours** (€16, tel. 02/513-7744, www.brussels-city-tours.com) and **Golden Tours** (€15, mobile 0486-053-981, www.goldentours.be).

Bus Tours—City Tours also offers a typical three-hour, guided (in up to 5 languages) bus tour, providing an easy way to get the grand perspective on Brussels. You start with a walk around the Grand Place, then jump on a tour bus (€25.50, April–Oct daily at 10:00, 11:00, and 14:00; Nov–March daily at 10:00 and 14:00; depart from their office a block off Grand Place at Rue de la Colline 8; you can buy tickets there, at TI, or in your hotel; tel. 02/513-7744, www.brussels-city-tours.com). You'll get off the bus at a lace workshop (shopping stop) and at the Atomium (picture stop).

Private Guide—Claude Janssens is good (€92/half-day, €173/day, mobile 0485-025-423, claude.janssens@pandora.be).

SIGHTS

On and near Grand Place

Brussels' Grand Place area sights, listed briefly below, are described in more detail in the ○ Grand Place Walk on page 327.

▲▲▲**Grand Place**—Brussels' main square, aptly called Grand Place (grahn plahs, "Grote Markt" in Flemish), is the heart of the old town and Brussels' greatest sight. Any time of day, it's worth swinging by to see what's going on. Concerts, flower markets, sound-and-light shows, endless people-watching—it entertains (as do the streets around it).

The museums on the square are well-advertised, but dull. The **Town Hall** (Hôtel de Ville), with the tallest spire, is the square's centerpiece, but the interior is no big deal to see (€3, visits only by 30-min English tour; Mon–Sat at 15:15, Sun at 12:15, no Sun tour Oct–March). Opposite the City Museum is the **Brewery Museum,** with one room of old brewing paraphernalia and one room of new, plus a beer video in English. It's pretty lame...but a good excuse for a beer (€4 includes an unnamed local beer, daily 10:00–17:00, sometimes open later July–Sept, Grand Place 10). The **Museum of Cocoa and Chocolate,** to the right of Town Hall, is a delightful concept. But at €5 for a meager set of displays, a second-rate video, a look at a "chocolate master" at work, and a choco-sample, it's overpriced for most (Tue–Sun 10:00–16:30, last entry 16:00, closed Mon, Rue de la Tête d'Or 9).

▲**Chocolate Shops on Grand Place**—For many, the best thing about Grand Place is the chocolate sold at the four venerable chocolate shops: Godiva, Neuhaus, Galler, and Leonidas (shops generally open daily 9:00–22:00). Each has inviting displays and sells mixes of 100 grams (your choice of 6–8 pieces) or individual pieces for about €1. It takes a lot of sampling to judge. See the "choco-crawl" described in the Grand Place Walk (page 327).

Brussels

IIII – STAIRS

Ⓜ – SUBWAY STOP

Ⓑ – TOUR BUS DEPARTURE POINTS (2)

••• – 5 MIN. WALK – CENTRAL
STATION TO GRAND PLACE

200 YARDS

200 METERS

Grand Place

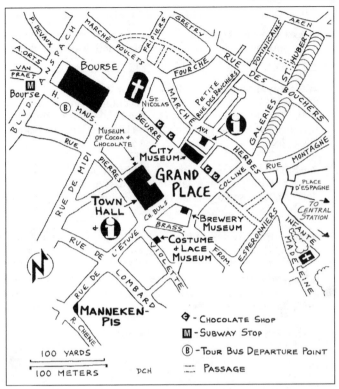

City Museum (Musée de la Ville de Bruxelles)—This museum, opposite the Town Hall, is in a neo-Gothic building (1875) called the Maison du Roi, or King's House (in which no king ever lived). The top floor displays a chronological history of the city and an enjoyable room full of costumes the *Manneken-Pis* statue (see below) has dampened. The middle floor features maps and models of 13th- and 17th-century Brussels. The bottom floor has some tapestries and paintings (€3, Tue–Sun 10:00–17:00, closed Mon, Grand Place, tel. 02/279-4350). With the new BELvue Museum covering Belgian history so well (see page 322), this is hardly worth a visit.

Manneken-Pis—Brussels is a great city, but its mascot (apparently symbolizing the city's irreverence and love of the good life) is a statue of a little boy urinating. Read up on his story at any postcard stand. It's three short blocks off Grand Place, but, for exact directions, take my Grand Place Walk (page 327) or just ask a local, *"Où est le Manneken-Pis?"* The little squirt may be wearing some clever outfit, as costumes are sent to Brussels from around the world.

Brussels at a Glance

▲▲▲**Grand Place** Main square and spirited heart of the old town, surrounded by mediocre museums and delectable chocolate shops. **Hours:** Always open.

▲▲▲**Royal Museums of Fine Arts of Belgium** Twin museums displaying ancient art (14th–18th centuries) and modern art (19th–20th centuries). **Hours:** Tue–Sun 10:00–17:00, closed Mon, half the rooms close for lunch 12:00–13:00, the other half closes 13:00–14:00.

▲▲**BELvue Museum** Interesting Belgian history museum with a focus on the popular royal family. **Hours:** April–Sept Tue–Sun 10:00–18:00, closed Mon; Oct–March Tue–Sun 10:00–17:00, closed Mon.

▲**Chocolate on Grand Place** Choco-crawl through Godiva, Neuhaus, Galler, and Leonidas. **Hours:** Generally daily 9:00–22:00.

▲**Musical Instruments Museum** More than 1,500 instruments, complete with audio. **Hours:** Tue–Fri 9:30–17:00, Sat–Sun 10:00–17:00, closed Mon.

▲**St. Michael's Cathedral** White-stone Gothic church where Belgian royals are married and buried. **Hours:** Daily 8:00–18:00.

Cases full of these are on display in the City Museum (described above).

Costume and Lace Museum—This is worthwhile only to those who have devoted their lives to the making of lace (€3, Mon–Tue and Thu–Fri 10:00–12:30 & 13:30–17:00, Sat–Sun 14:00–17:00, closed Wed, Rue Violette 12, a block off Grand Place, tel. 02/213-4450).

Upper Town

Brussels' grandiose Upper Town, with its huge palace, is described in the ✪ Upper Town Walk on page 338. Along that walk, you'll pass the following sights.

▲▲▲**Royal Museums of Fine Arts of Belgium (Musées Royaux des Beaux-Arts de Belgique)**—These are two separate museums, connected by a tunnel and covered by the same €5 ticket (enter either through the main foyer). The Museum of Ancient Art—featuring Flemish and Belgian art of the 14th–18th centuries—is packed with a dazzling collection of masterpieces by van der Weyden, Brueghel, Bosch, and Rubens. The Museum of Modern Art gives an easy-to-enjoy walk through the art of the 19th and 20th centuries, from

▲**Belgian Comic Strip Center** Hometown heroes the Smurfs, Tintin, and Lucky Luke, plus many more. **Hours:** Tue–Sun 10:00–18:00, closed Mon.

▲**European Parliament** Soaring home of Europe's governing body. **Hours:** Tours Mon–Thu at 10:00 and 15:00, Fri at 10:00 only.

▲**Park of the Cinquantenaire** Belgium's sprawling tribute to independence, near the European Parliament. **Hours:** Always open.

▲**Autoworld** Hundreds of historic vehicles, including Mr. Benz's 1886 motorized tricycle. **Hours:** Daily April–Sept 10:00–18:00, Oct–March 10:00–17:00.

▲**Royal Army and Military History Museum** Vast collection of weaponry and uniforms. **Hours:** Tue–Sun 9:00–12:00 & 13:00–16:45, closed Mon.

▲**Royal Museum of Central Africa** Excellent but far-flung exhibit about the former "Belgian Congo," featuring ethnology, artifacts, and wildlife. **Hours:** Tue–Fri 10:00–17:00, Sat–Sun 10:00–18:00, closed Mon.

neoclassical to Surrealism. Highlights here include works by Seurat, Gauguin, David, and Magritte. The Patio, between the two museums, features tapestries from the 1500s (Tue–Sun 10:00–17:00, closed Mon, half the rooms close for lunch 12:00–13:00, the other half close 13:00–14:00, last entry 16:30, free first Wed of the month after 13:00, audioguide-€2.50, tour booklet-€2.50, decent cafeteria with salad bar, Rue de la Régence 3, tel. 02/508-3211, www.fine-arts-museum.be). ✪ See Royal Museums of Fine Arts of Belgium Tour, page 347.

▲**Musical Instruments Museum (Musée des Instruments de Musique)**—One of Europe's best musical museums is housed in one of Brussels' most impressive Art Nouveau buildings, the newly renovated Old English department store. Inside, you'll be given a pair of headphones and set free to wander several levels: folk instruments

from around the world on the ground floor, a history of Western musical instruments on the first, and an entire floor devoted to strings and pianos on the second. It has more than 1,500 instruments—from Egyptian harps to medieval lutes to groundbreaking harpsichords to the Brussels-built saxophone. As you approach an instrument, you hear it playing on your headphones (which actually work...most of the time). The museum is skimpy on English information—except for a €16 visitors guide—but the music you'll hear is an international language (€5, Tue–Fri 9:30–17:00, Sat–Sun 10:00–17:00, closed Mon, last entry 30 min before closing, Rue Montagne de la Cour 2, just downhill and toward Grand Place from the Royal Museums of Fine Arts, tel. 02/545-0130, www.mim.fgov.be). The sixth floor has a restaurant, a terrace, and a great view of Brussels (€8–14 lunches, same hours as museum, pick up free access pass at museum entrance).

▲▲BELvue Museum—This brilliant museum, filling two floors of the king's former guest house, offers far and away the best look in town at Belgian history. The exhibit, with lots of real historical artifacts, illustrates the short sweep of this nation's story, from its 1830 inception to today: kings, Congo, Art Nouveau, wars, and an intimate chance to get to know the generally much-loved royal family with intimate family photos. To make the most of your visit, read the extensive flier translating all of the descriptions (€3, €5 combo-ticket includes Coudenberg Palace; April–Sept Tue–Sun 10:00–18:00, closed Mon; Oct–March Tue–Sun 10:00–17:00, closed Mon; to the right of the palace at place des Palais 7, tel. 02/545-0800, www.musbellevue.be).

Coudenberg Palace—The BELvue Museum stands atop the barren archeological remains of a 12th-century Brussels palace. While well-lit and well-described, the ruins still aren't much to see. The best thing is the orientation video you see before descending (€4, €5 combo-ticket includes BELvue Museum, same hours as BELvue).

North of Central Station

▲**St. Michael's Cathedral**—St. Michael's Cathedral has been the center of Belgium's religious life for nearly 1,000 years. Belgium is Catholic. While the Netherlands went in a Protestant direction in the 1500s, Belgium remains 80 percent Catholic (although only about 20 percent go to Mass). One of Europe's classic Gothic churches, built between roughly 1200 and 1500, Brussels' cathedral is made from white stone and topped by twin towers (open daily 8:00–18:00).

The church is where royal weddings and funerals take place. Photographs (to the right of the entrance) show the funeral of the popular King Baudouin, who died in 1993. He was succeeded by his younger brother, Albert II (whose face is on Belgium's euro coins). Albert will be succeeded by his son, Prince Philippe. Formerly, the ruler was always a man. But in 1992, the constitution was changed, making it clear that the oldest child—boy or girl—would take the throne. In 1999, Prince Philippe and his bride, Mathilde—after a civil ceremony at the Town Hall—paraded up here for a two-hour Catholic ceremony with all the trimmings. They had a baby girl in 2001, and she is in line to become Belgium's Queen Elisabeth.

Before leaving, enjoy the great view from the outside porch of the Town Hall spire with its gold statue of St. Michael.

▲**Belgian Comic Strip Center (Centre Belge de la Bande Dessinée)**—Belgium has produced some of the world's most popular comic characters, including the Smurfs, Tintin, and Lucky Luke. You'll find these, and many less famous Belgian comics, at the Comic Strip Center.

Just pop into the lobby to see the museum's groundbreaking Art Nouveau building (a former department store designed in 1903 by Belgian architect Victor Horta), browse through comics in the bookshop, and snap a photo with a three-foot-tall Smurf... and that's enough for many people. Kids especially might find the museum, like, totally boring. But those who appreciate art in general will enjoy this sometimes humorous, sometimes probing, often beautiful medium. The displays are in French and Flemish, but they loan out a helpful, if hard-to-follow, English guidebook.

You'll see how comics are made, watch early animated films (such as *Gertie the Dinosaur,* c. 1909), and see a sprawling exhibit on Tintin (the intrepid boy reporter with the button eyes and wavy shock of hair, launched in 1929 by Hergé and much loved by older Europeans). The top floor is dedicated to "serious" comics, where more adult themes and high-quality drawing aspire to turn kid's stuff into that "Ninth Art." These works can be grimly realistic, openly erotic or graphic, or darker in tone, featuring flawed antiheroes (€6.50, Tue–Sun 10:00–18:00, closed Mon, Rue des Sables 20, tel. 02/219-1980).

Away from the Center

▲**European Parliament**—Europe's governing body now welcomes visitors. This towering complex of glass skyscrapers is a cacophony of black-suited politicians speaking 20 different Euro-languages. It's exciting just to be here—a mouse in the corner of a place that

charts the future of Europe "with
respect for all political thinking...
consolidating democracy in the
spirit of peace and solidarity."
The 732 parliament members,
representing 25 countries, shape
Europe with a €100 billion budget
(from import duties, sales tax, and
a cut of each member country's
GDP).

The only way in is to take the 30-minute **tour** (free, Mon–Thu
at 10:00 and 15:00, Fri only at 10:00; before making the trip, confirm the tour time by calling 02/284-3457). From the Bourse in
downtown Brussels, catch bus #95 or #96 to Place du Luxembourg
(this square has lots of restaurants, good for a €10 lunch). To get
from Place du Luxembourg to Infopoint, where the tours start, go
behind the old train station and cross the temporary footbridge
through the construction site. Infopoint will be on your left. Go
down the steps by Infopoint and find the visitors entrance, across
the street on the right-hand side.

At the appointed time, enter the main hall through the double
doors and meet your escort, who equips you with an audioguide and
takes you to a balcony overlooking the huge "hemi-cycle" where
the members of the European Parliament sit. Here you'll listen to a
political-science lesson about the all-Europe system of governance.
You'll learn how early visionary utopians (like Churchill, who in
1946 called for a "United States of Europe" to avoid future wars)
led the way as Europe gradually evolved into the European Union
(1992).

▲**Park of the Cinquantenaire (Parc du Cinquantenaire)**—The
19th-century Belgian king Leopold wanted Brussels to rival Paris.
In 1880, he celebrated the 50th anniversary *(cinquantenaire)* of
Belgian independence by building a huge monumental arch flanked
by massive exhibition halls, which today house Autoworld and the
military museum (see listings below). The Métro stop nearest the
museums is the Merode stop (300 yards behind the statue crown-
ing the big arch).

▲**Autoworld**—Starting with Mr. Benz's motorized tricycle
of 1886, you'll stroll through a giant hall filled with 400 historic cars. It's well-described in English (€6, daily April–Sept
10:00–18:00, Oct–March 10:00–17:00, in Palais Mondial, Parc
du Cinquantenaire 11, Métro: Merode, tel. 02/736-4165, www
.autoworld.be).

▲**Royal Army and Military History Museum (Musée Royal de
l'Armée et d'Histoire Militaire)**—Wander through an enormous
collection of 19th-century weaponry and uniforms, and a giant

hall dedicated to warplanes of the 20th century. There's a good display about the Belgian struggle for independence in the early 1800s. Don't miss the primitive tanks from World War I—able to break through the stalemated "Western Front," but so clumsy that they couldn't do anything once in enemy territory. This place is filled with real, tangible history...but precious little English. Use the map to get the most out of your visit (free, Tue–Sun 9:00–12:00 & 13:00–16:45, closed Mon, Parc du Cinquantenaire 3, tel. 02/737-7811, www.klm-mra.be). While most of the museum closes at lunch, the huge airplane hall stays open.

Royal Belgian Institute of Natural Sciences (Institut Royal des Sciences Naturelles de Belgique)—Dinosaur enthusiasts come to this museum for the world's largest collection of iguanodon skeletons (€4, Tue–Fri 9:30–16:45, Sat–Sun 10:00–18:00, closed Mon, last entry 30 min before closing, Rue Vautier 29, bus #34 from the Bourse, tel. 02/627-4238, www.naturalsciences.be).

Antoine Wiertz Museum—Next to the Royal Belgian Institute of Natural Sciences (described above) is a collection of works by Antoine Wiertz. This 19th-century Romantic artist painted some of the world's largest canvases, with themes ranging from biblical to political (free, Tue–Sun 10:00–12:00 & 13:00–17:00, closed Mon and every other weekend, Rue Vautier 62, bus #34 from the Bourse, tel. 02/648-1718).

▲Royal Museum of Central Africa (Musée Royal de l'Afrique Centrale)—Remember the Belgian Congo? Just east of the city center, this fine museum covers the Congo and much more of Africa, including ethnography, sculptures, jewelry, colonial history, flora, and fauna. You'll learn about both the history of Belgian adventure in the Congo (when it was the king's private plantation) and the region's natural wonders. Unfortunately, there's barely a word of English (€4, Tue–Fri 10:00–17:00, Sat–Sun 10:00–18:00, closed Mon, Leuvensesteenweg 13, tel. 02/769-5211, www.africamuseum .be). The museum, housed in an immense palace, is surrounded by a vast and well-kept park. A trip out here puts you in a lush, wooded oasis a world away from the big, noisy city. To get here, take Métro #1B to Montgomery (direction: Stockel) and then catch tram #44 to its final stop, Tervuren. From there, walk 200 yards through the park to the palace. If visiting on a summer weekend, ask at either TI in Brussels about the vintage trolley that offers an idyllic connection from the city center.

Atomium—This giant, silvery molecule—with escalators connecting the various "atoms," and a view from the top sphere—was the cheesy symbol of the 1958 Universal Exhibition (€9, daily 10:00–18:00, on outskirts of town, Métro: Heysel and walk 5 min, tel. 02/475-4775, www.atomium.be).

Mini-Europe—This kid-pleasing sight, sharing a park with the Atomium, has 1:25-scale models of 350 famous European landmarks, such as Big Ben, the Eiffel Tower, and Venice. The new "Spirit of Europe" section is an interactive educational exhibit about the European Union (€11.80, Easter–Dec daily 9:30–18:00, July–Aug until 20:00, closed Jan–Easter, Métro: Heysel and walk 5 min, tel. 02/474-1313, www.minieurope.com).

GRAND PLACE WALK

This walk takes in Brussels' delightful old center. After exploring the Grand Place itself, we'll loop a couple blocks north, see the Bourse, and then end south of the Grand Place at the *Manneken-Pis*.

ORIENTATION

Length of This Walk: Allow two hours.

Brewery Museum: €4, daily 10:00–17:00, sometimes open later July–Sept, Grand Place 10.

City Museum: €3, Tue–Sun 10:00–17:00, closed Mon, Grand Place, tel. 02/279-4350.

Chocolate Shops: Generally open daily 9:00–22:00, along the north side of the Grand Place.

Church of St. Nicolas: Rue de Tabora 6, tel. 02/734-9027.

THE WALK BEGINS

The Grand Place

This colorful cobblestone square is the heart—historically and geographically—of heart-shaped Brussels. As the town's market square for a thousand years, this was where farmers and merchants sold their wares in open-air stalls, enticing travelers from the main east–west highway across Belgium, which ran a block north of the square. Today, shops and cafés sell chocolates, *gaufres* (waffles), beer, mussels, fries, lace, and flowers.

Brussels was born about a thousand years ago around a long-gone castle put up by Germans to fight off the French (long before either of those countries actually existed). The villagers supplied the needs of the soldiers. The city grew up on the banks of the Senne (not Seine) River, which today is completely bricked over.

Grand Place Walk

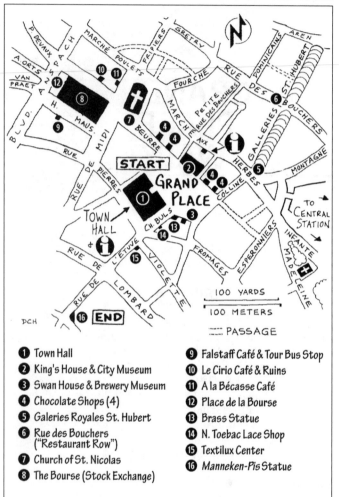

❶ Town Hall
❷ King's House & City Museum
❸ Swan House & Brewery Museum
❹ Chocolate Shops (4)
❺ Galeries Royales St. Hubert
❻ Rue des Bouchers ("Restaurant Row")
❼ Church of St. Nicolas
❽ The Bourse (Stock Exchange)
❾ Falstaff Café & Tour Bus Stop
❿ Le Cirio Café & Ruins
⓫ A la Bécasse Café
⓬ Place de la Bourse
⓭ Brass Statue
⓮ N. Toebac Lace Shop
⓯ Textilux Center
⓰ Manneken-Pis Statue

The river crossed the main road from Köln to Bruges.

Pan the square to get oriented. The **Town Hall** (Hôtel de Ville) dominates the square with its 300-foot-tall tower topped by a golden statue of St. Michael slaying a devil. This was where the city council met to rule this free trading town. Brussels proudly maintained its self-governing independence while dukes, kings, and clergymen ruled much of Europe. These days, the

The Grand Place: Center of Brussels

Face the Town Hall, with your back to the King's House. You're facing roughly southwest. The TI is one block behind you, and "restaurant row" is another block beyond that. To your right a block away, catch a glimpse of the Bourse building (with buses, taxis, cafés). The Upper Town is to your left, rising up the hill beyond the Central Station. Over your left shoulder a few blocks away is St. Michael's Cathedral. And most important? The *Manneken-Pis* is three blocks ahead, down the street that runs along the left side of the Town Hall.

Town Hall hosts weddings—Crown Prince Philippe got married here in 1999. (The Belgian government demands that all marriages first be performed in simple civil ceremonies.)

Opposite the Town Hall is the impressive, gray **King's House** (Maison du Roi), used by the Hapsburg kings not as a house, but as an administrative center. Rebuilt in the 1890s, the stately, Baroque-style building turns to prickly neo-Gothic at the top. Inside is the mildly interesting City Museum (described below).

The fancy smaller buildings giving the square its uniquely grand medieval character are former **guild halls** (now mostly shops and restaurants), their impressive gabled roofs topped with statues. Once the home offices for the town's different professions (bakers, brewers, tanners, and *Manneken-Pis*-corkscrew-makers), they all date from shortly after 1695—the year French king  Louis XIV's troops surrounded the city, sighted their cannons on the Town Hall spire, and managed to level everything around it (4,000 wooden buildings)—except the spire itself. As a matter of pride, these Brussels businessmen rebuilt their offices better than ever—all within seven years. They're in stone, taller, and with ornamented gables and classical statues.

The **Swan House** (#9, just to the left of the Town Hall) once housed a bar where Karl Marx and Frederick Engels met in February 1848 to write their *Communist Manifesto*. Later that year, when the treatise sparked socialist revolution around Europe, Brussels exiled them. Today, the proletarian bar is one of the city's most expensive restaurants. Next door (#10) was and still is the brewers' guild, now housing the **Brewery Museum** (see page 317).

The **statues** on the rooftops each come with their own uninteresting legend, but the Bruxelloise have earthier explanations: "What's that smell?" say the statues on the roof of the Swan House, "Someone farted." "Yeah," says the golden man riding a horse atop the Brewery Museum next door, "it was that guy over there," and he points north across the square to another statue. "It wasn't me," says that statue, "it was him—way over there." Follow his gaze to the southwest corner of the square, where a statue of St. Nicholas...hangs his head in shame.

• *In the King's House (across from the Town Hall) is the only museum of any importance on the square...*

City Museum

The museum's top floor has a roomful of goofy costumes the *Manneken* statue has pissed through, the middle floor features maps and models of old Brussels, and the bottom floor has a few old paintings and tapestries. Most visitors aim straight for the *Manneken-Pis* outfits.

But be sure to find the model of the city in the 13th century, on the second floor. (To follow the directions in this description, uphill is east.) The largest structure is St. Michael's Cathedral (northeast). The Upper Town hasn't a hint of its monumental future. The

Grand Place's embryonic beginning is roughly in the center of town, amid a cluster of houses.

The city was a port town—see the crane unloading barges—since it was at this point that the shallow Senne became navigable. Grain from the area was processed in the watermills, then shipped downstream to the North Sea.

By the 1200s, Brussels—though tiny by today's standards—was an important commercial center, and St. Michael's was the region's religious hub. Still, most of the area inside the

2.5-mile-long city wall was farmland, dotted with a few churches, towers, markets, and convents (such as the Carmelite convent hugging the south wall).

The model in the far end of the room shows the city a couple centuries later—much bigger, but still within its same wall.

Taste Treats on the Grand Place

Cafés: Mussels in Brussels, Belgian fries, yeasty local beers, waffles...if all you do is plop down at a café on the square, try some of these specialties, and watch the world go by—hey, that's a great afternoon in Brussels.

The outdoor cafés are casual and come with fair prices (a good Belgian beer costs €3.50—with no cover or service charge). Have a seat, and a waiter will serve you. The half dozen or so cafés are all roughly equal in price and quality for simple drinks and foods—check the posted menus.

Choco-Crawl: The best chocolate shops all lie along the north (uphill) side of the square, starting with Godiva at the high end (that is, higher in both altitude and price). The cost goes down slightly as you descend to the other shops. Each shop has a mouth-watering display case of 20 or so chocolates and sells mixes of 100 grams—your choice of 6–8 pieces—for about €4, or individual pieces for about

€1. Pralines are filled chocolates—uniquely Belgian (and totally different from the French praline). The shops are generally open daily from 9:00 to 22:00.

Godiva, with the top reputation internationally, is synonymous with fine Belgian chocolate. Now owned by an American, Godiva still has its management and the original factory (built in 1926) in Belgium. This store, at Grand Place 22, was Godiva's first

(est. 1937). The almond and honey goes way beyond almond roca.

Neuhaus, a few doors down at #27, has been encouraging local chocoholics since 1857. Look through the glass floor at the old-time choco-kitchen in the basement, and check out the historic photos on the walls. The enticing varieties are described in English, and Neuhaus publishes a fine little pamphlet (free, on the counter) explaining the products. The "caprice" (toffee with vanilla crème) tastes like Easter. Neuhaus claims to be the inventor of the filled chocolate.

History of Chocolate

In 1519, Montezuma served Cortés a cup of hot cocoa (*xocoatl*) made from cocoa beans, which were native to the New World. It ignited a food fad in Europe. By 1700, elegant "chocolate houses" in Europe's capitals served hot chocolate (with milk and sugar added) to wealthy aristocrats. By the 1850s, the process of making chocolate candies for eating was developed, and Brussels, with a long tradition of quality handmade luxuries, was at the forefront.

Cocoa beans are husked, fermented, and roasted, then ground into chocolate paste. (Chocolate straight from the bean is very bitter.) The vegetable fat is pressed out to make cocoa butter. Cocoa butter and chocolate paste are mixed together and sweetened with sugar to make chocolates. In 1876, a Swiss man named Henry Nestlé added concentrated milk, creating milk chocolate—a lighter, sweeter variation, with less pure chocolate.

Galler, just off the square at Rue au Beurre 44, is more homey and less famous because it doesn't export. Still family-run (and the royal favorite), it proudly serves less sugary chocolate—dark. The new top-end choice, 85 percent pure chocolate, is called simply "Black 85"—and worth a sample if you like chocolate without the sweetness. Galler's products are well-described in English.

At **Leonidas,** a half-block off the square at Rue au Beurre 34, most locals sacrifice 10 percent in quality to double their take by getting their fix here (machine-made, only €1.60/100 grams). White chocolate is the specialty.

• *Exit the Grand Place next to Godiva (from the northeast, or uphill, corner of the square) and go north one block on Rue de la Colline to Rue du Marché-aux-Herbes, which was once the main east–west highway through Belgium. Looking to the right, notice that it's all uphill from here, past the Gothic church to the Upper Town, another four blocks (and 200-foot elevation gain) beyond. Straight ahead, you enter the arcaded shopping mall called...*

Galeries Royales St. Hubert

Europe's oldest still-operating shopping mall was built in 1847 and served as the glass-covered model for others. It celebrated the town's new modern attitude (having recently gained its independence from the Netherlands). Built at the start of a century of expansion and industrialization, the mall demonstrated efficient modern living, with elegant apartments upstairs above fine shops, theaters, and cafés.

Looking down the arcade, you'll notice that it bends halfway down, designed to lure shoppers further. Its iron-and-glass look is still popular today, but the decorative columns, cameos, and pastel colors evoke a more elegant time. It's neo-Renaissance, like a pastel Florentine palace.

There's no Gap (yet), no Foot Locker, no Karmelkorn. Instead, you'll find hat, cane, and, umbrella stores that sell...hats, canes, and umbrellas—that's it, all made on the premises. At **Philippe**, have shoes made especially for the curves of your feet by a family that's done it for generations. Since 1857, **Neuhaus** has sold chocolates from here at its flagship store, where many locals buy their pralines. Across from Neuhaus, the **Taverne du Passage** restaurant serves the same local specialties that singer Jacques Brel used to come here for: *croquettes de crevettes* (shrimp croquettes), *tête de veau* (calf's head), *anguilles au vert* (eels with herb sauce), and *fondue au fromage* (cheese fondue; €10–20 meals, daily 12:00–24:00, closed Wed–Thu June–July).

• *Midway down the mall, where the two sections bend, turn left and exit the mall onto...*

Rue des Bouchers

Yikes! During meal times, this street is absolutely crawling with visitors browsing through wall-to-wall, midlevel-quality restaurants. Brussels is known worldwide for its food, serving all kinds of cuisine, but specializing in seafood (particularly mussels and shrimp). You'll have plenty to choose from along this table-clogged "restaurant row." To get an idea of prices, compare their posted *menus*—the fixed-price, several-course meal offered by most restaurants.

Many diners here are day-trippers. Colin from London, Marie from Paris, Martje from Holland, and Dietrich from Bonn could easily all "do lunch" together in Brussels—just three hours away.

The first intersection, with Petite Rue des Bouchers, is the heart of the restaurant quarter (and home to the recommended Chez Leon—see page 359), which sprawls for several blocks around. The street names tell what sorts of shops used to stand here—butchers *(bouchers)*, herbs, chickens, and cheese.

• *At this intersection, turn right onto Petite Rue des Bouchers and walk straight back to the Grand Place. At the Grand Place, turn right (west) on Rue du Beurre. Comparison-shop a little more at the Galler and Leonidas chocolate stores and pass by the "Is it raining?" fountain. A block along, at the intersection with Rue du Midi, is the...*

Church of St. Nicolas

Since the 12th century, there's been a church here. Inside, see rough stones in some of the arches from the early church. Outside, notice the barnacle-like shops, such as De Witte Jewelers, built right into the church. The church was rebuilt 300 years ago with money provided by the town's jewelers. As thanks, they were given these shops with apartments upstairs. Close to God, this was prime real estate. And jewelers are still here.

• *Just west of the church, the big neoclassical building you run into is the back entrance of...*

The Bourse (Stock Exchange) and Art Nouveau Cafés

The stock exchange was built in the 1870s in a neo-everything style.

Several **historic cafés** huddle around the Bourse. To the right are the recommended woody, atmospheric Le Cirio and A la Bécasse cafés (see page 363). To the left is the Falstaff Café. Some Brussels cafés, like the Falstaff, are still decorated in the early-20th-century style called Art Nouveau. Ironwork columns twist and bend like flower stems, and lots of Tiffany-style stained glass and mirrors make them light and spacious. Slender, elegant, willowy Gibson Girls decorate the wallpaper, while waiters in bowties glide by.

The **ruins** under glass on the right side of the Bourse are from a 13th-century convent.

• *Circle around to the front of the Bourse, crossed by busy Boulevard Anspach. Note that the street in front of the Falstaff Café is a convenient place to catch a hop-on, hop-off bus tour (see page 316).*

Place de la Bourse and Boulevard Anspach

Brussels is the political nerve center of Europe (only Washington, D.C., has more lobbyists), and there are several hundred demonstrations a year. When the local team wins a soccer match or some political group wants to make a statement, this is where people flock to wave flags and honk horns.

It's also where the old town meets the new. To the right along Boulevard Anspach are two shopping malls and several first-run movie theaters. Rue Neuve, which parallels Anspach, is a pedestrian-only shopping street.

Boulevard Anspach covers the still-flowing Senne River (which was open until 1850). Remember that Brussels was once a port, with North Sea boats coming as far as this point to unload their goods. But with frequent cholera epidemics killing thousands of its citizens, the city decided to cover up its stinky river.

• *For efficient sightseeing, consider catching a bus (#95 or #96) from along the side of the Bourse to the Place Royale, where you can follow my*

Lace

In the 1500s, rich men and women decided that lace collars, sleeves, headdresses, and veils were fashionable. For the next 200 years, the fashion raged (peaking in about 1700). It all had to be made by hand, and many women earned extra income from the demand. The French Revolution of 1789 suddenly made lace for men undemocratic and unmanly. Then, in about 1800, machines replaced human hands and, except for ornamental pieces, the fashion died out.

These days, handmade lace is usually also homemade—not produced in factories, but at home by dedicated, sharp-eyed hobbyists who love their work. Unlike knitting, it requires total concentration as they follow intricate patterns. Women create their own patterns or trace tried-and-true designs. A piece of lace takes days, not hours, to make—which is why a handmade tablecloth can easily sell for €250.

There are two basic lace-making techniques: bobbin lace (which originated in Bruges) and needle lace. To make bobbin lace, women juggle many different strands tied to bobbins, "weaving" a design by overlapping the threads. Because of the difficulties, the resulting pattern is usually rather rough and simple compared with other techniques.

Needle lace is more like sewing—stitching pre-made bits onto a pattern. For example, the "Renaissance" design is made by sewing a pre-made ribbon onto a pattern in a fancy design. This would then be attached as a fringe to a piece of linen—to make a fancy tablecloth, for instance.

In the "Princess" design, pre-made pieces are stitched onto a cotton net, making anything from a small doily to a full wedding veil.

"Rose point"—no longer practiced—used authentic bits of handmade antique lace as an ornament in a frame or filling a pendant. Antique pieces can be very expensive.

Upper Town Walk (see page 338), also ending at the Manneken-Pis. *But if you'd rather stay in the Lower Town, return to the Grand Place.*

From the Grand Place to the *Manneken-Pis*

• *Leave the square kitty-corner, heading south down the street running along the left side of the Town Hall, Rue Charles Buls (which soon changes its name to Stoofstraat). Just five yards off the square, under the arch, is a well-polished, well-loved brass statue.*

You'll see tourists and locals rubbing a **brass statue** of a reclining man. This was Mayor Evrard 't Serclaes, who in 1356 bravely refused to surrender the keys of the city to invaders, and so was tortured and killed. Touch him, and his misfortune becomes your good luck. Judging by the reverence with which locals go through this ritual, there must be something to it.

The **N. Toebac Lace Shop** is a welcoming place with fine lace, a knowledgable staff, and an interesting three-minute video. Brussels is perhaps the best-known city for traditional lacemaking, and this shop still sells handmade pieces in the old style: lace clothing, doilies, tablecloths, and ornamental pieces (daily 9:30–19:30, Rue Charles Buls 10). The shop gives travelers with this book a 15 percent discount in 2006. If you buy more than €125, you get a further 18 percent tax rebate. For more on lace, the Costume and Lace Museum is a block away and just around the corner (see page 320).

A block farther down the street, step into **Textilux Center** (Rue Lombard 41) for a good look at Belgian tapestries—both traditional wall-hangings and modern goods, such as tapestry purses and luggage in traditional designs.

• *Follow the crowds, noticing the excitement build, as in another block you reach the...*

Manneken-Pis

Even with low expectations, this bronze statue is smaller than you'd think—the little squirt's under two feet tall, practically the size of a newborn. Still, the little peeing boy is an appropriately low-key symbol for the earthy Bruxelloise. The statue was made in 1619 to provide drinking water for the neighborhood. Sometimes, *Manneken-Pis* is dressed in one of the 700 different costumes that

Tapestries

In 1500, tapestry workshops in Brussels were famous, cranking out high-quality tapestries for the walls of Europe's palaces. They were functional (as insulation and propaganda for a church, king, or nobleman) and beautiful—an intricate design formed by colored thread. Even great painters (such as Rubens and Raphael) designed tapestries, which rivaled Renaissance canvases.

First, they stretched neutral-colored threads (made from imported English wool) vertically over a loom. A tapestry design is made with the horizontal weave, from colored threads that interlace the vertical so they (mostly) cover it. Tapestry-making is much more difficult than basic weaving because each horizontal thread is only as long as the detail it's meant to create, so a single horizontal row can be made up of many individual pieces of thread. The weavers follow a pattern designed by an artist, called a "cartoon."

Flanders and Paris (the Gobelins workshop) were the two centers of tapestry-making until the art died out, along with Europe's noble class.

visiting VIPs have brought for him (including an Elvis Pissley outfit).

There are several different legends about *Manneken*—take your pick. He was a naughty boy who peed inside a witch's house, so she froze him. A rich man lost his son and declared, "Find my son, and we'll make a statue of him doing what he did when found." Or—the locals' favorite version—the little tyke loved his beer, which came in handy when a fire threatened the wooden city: He bravely put it out. Want the truth? The city commissioned it to show the joie de vivre of living in Brussels—where

happy people eat, drink...and drink...and then pee.

The scene is made interesting by the crowds that gather. Hang out for a while and watch the commotion this little guy makes as tour groups come and go. When I was there, a Russian man marveled at the statue, shook his head, and said, "He never stop!"

UPPER TOWN WALK

The Upper Town has always had a more aristocratic feel than the medieval, commercial streets of the Lower Town. With broad boulevards, big marble buildings, palaces, museums, and so many things called "royal," it also seems much newer and a bit more sterile. But in fact, the Upper Town has a history that stretches back to Brussels' beginnings.

Use this 10-stop walk to get acquainted with a less touristed part of town, sample some world-class museums, see the palace, explore art galleries, and stand on a viewpoint to get the lay of the land.

The tour starts half a block from the one essential art sight in town, the Royal Museums of Fine Arts of Belgium, which include the ancient- and modern-art museums. Consider a visit while you're here (some rooms close during lunch, closed Mon, see tour on page 347). The Musical Instruments Museum is also in the neighborhood (also closed Mon, see page 321).

ORIENTATION

Length of This Walk: Allow 90 minutes.

Getting There: The walk begins at Place Royale in the Upper Town. There are several ways to get there:

    1. From the Grand Place, it's a 15-minute uphill walk (follow your map).

    2. From the Bourse, in front of the Falstaff Café, buses #95 and #96 leave every few minutes for Place Royale (bus signs call it "Royale"; buy ticket from driver, validate it in machine).

    3. Catch a taxi (figure on €5 from the Bourse).

4. Hop off here during a hop-on, hop-off bus tour (see page 316).

Route Overview: From Place Royale, walk south along the ridge, popping into a stained-glass-filled Gothic church, and on to the best view of the city from the towering Palace of Justice. Then backtrack a bit and descend through the well-worn tapestries of the Sablon Quarter's antiques, art, and cafés, and on to the foot of the hill at the *Manneken-Pis.*

Cuisine Art: For lunch, try the restaurant on the top floor of the Musical Instruments Museum (open to the public, with a great view) or the two recommended eateries near Place du Grand Sablon (see page 345).

THE WALK BEGINS

❶ Place Royale

At the crest of the hill sits Place Royale, enclosed by white, neo-classical buildings forming a mirror image around a cobblestone square, with a big, green statue of a horseman in the center.

The statue—a Belgium-born Crusader, Godfrey de Bouillon (who led the First Crusade in 1096)—rides forward carrying a flag, gazing down on the Town Hall spire. If Godfrey turned and looked left down Rue de la Régence, he'd see the domed Palace of Justice at the end of the boulevard. Over his right shoulder, just outside the square, is the Royal Palace, the king's residence.

In the 1800s, as Belgium exerted itself to industrialize and modernize, this area was rebuilt as a sign that Brussels had arrived as a world capital. Broad vistas down wide boulevards ending in gleaming white, Greek-columned monuments—the look was all the rage, seen at Versailles, London, Washington, D.C....and here.

The cupola of the Church of St. Jacques sur Coudenberg—the central portion of the square's ring of buildings—makes the church look more like a bank building. But St. Jacques goes back much further than this building (from 1787). It originated in the 13th century near a 12th-century castle. Nobles chose to build their mansions in the neighborhood, and later, so did the king.

The Musical Instruments Museum (see page 321) is 30 yards downhill from the square, housed in an early-20th-century, iron-and-glass former department store. Its Art Nouveau facade was a deliberate attempt to get beyond the retro-looking Greek columns

Upper Town Walk

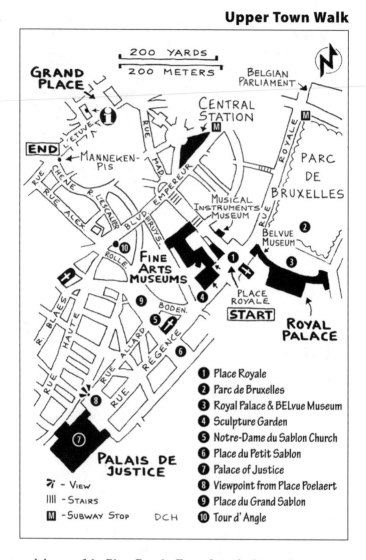

❶ Place Royale
❷ Parc de Bruxelles
❸ Royal Palace & BELvue Museum
❹ Sculpture Garden
❺ Notre-Dame du Sablon Church
❻ Place du Petit Sablon
❼ Palace of Justice
❽ Viewpoint from Place Poelaert
❾ Place du Grand Sablon
❿ Tour d'Angle

↗ – View
|||| – Stairs
Ⓜ – Subway Stop   DCH

and domes of the Place Royale. Even if you don't visit the museum, you can ride the elevator up to the museum café for a superb Lower Town view.

• *Brussels' world-class Royal Museums of Fine Arts of Belgium are 30 yards south of Place Royale on Rue de la Régence. But before heading south, exit Place Royale on the north side (to Godfrey's right), which opens up to a large, tree-lined park.*

❷ Parc de Bruxelles

Copying Versailles, the Hapsburg empress Maria Theresa of
Austria (Marie-Antoinette's
mom) had this symmetrical park
laid out in 1776, when she ruled
(but never visited) the city. This
is just one of many large parks in
a city that expanded with an eye
to city planning.

At the far (north) end of the
park (no need to actually walk
there) is the Parliament building.
Which parliament? The city hosts several—the EU Parliament,
the Belgian Parliament, and several local, city-council-type parliaments. This is the Belgian Parliament, often seen on nightly news-
casts as a backdrop for the country's politicians.

In 1830, Belgian patriots rose up and converged on the park,
where they attacked the troops of the Dutch king. This was the
first blow in a short, almost bloodless revolution that drove out
the foreign-born king and gave the Belgians independence...and a
different foreign-born king.

• *The long building facing the park is the...*

❸ Royal Palace (Palais Royale)

After Belgium struck out twice trying to convince someone to
be their new king, Leopold I (r. 1831–1865), a nobleman from
Germany, agreed. Leopold was a steadying influence as the country modernized. His son rebuilt this palace—near the site of earlier
palaces, dating back to the 10th century—by linking together a
row of townhouse mansions with a unifying facade (around 1870).

Leopold's great-great-great-grandnephew, King Albert II,
today uses the palace as an office. (His head is on Belgium's euro
coins.) Albert and his wife, Queen

Paola, live in a palace north of
here (near the Atomium) and on
the French Riviera. If the Belgian
flag (black-yellow-red) is flying
from the palace, the king is somewhere in Belgium.

Albert II (born 1932) is a
figurehead king, as in so many
European democracies, but he
serves an important function as a common bond between bicker-
ing Flemish and Walloons. His son, Prince Philippe, is slated to
succeed him, though Philippe—awkward and stand-offish—is not
as popular as his wife, Mathilde, a Belgian native. Their little girl,

Elisabeth, born in 2001, will become the first Belgian queen.

The bulk of the palace is off-limits to tourists (except in Aug), but you can see an impressive exhibit on Belgian history and the royal family in the adjacent BELvue Museum (see page 322).

• *Return to Place Royale, then continue south along Rue de la Régence, noticing the entrance to the Royal Museums of Fine Arts of Belgium (see tour on page 347). Just past the museums, on the right, you'll see a...*

❹ Sculpture Garden (Jardin de Sculpture)

This pleasant public garden—starring a statue by Rodin's contemporary, Aristide Maillol—looks like a great way to descend into the Sablon Quarter, but the gates at the bottom are often locked.

• *A hundred yards farther along, you reach the top of the Sablon neighborhood, dominated by the...*

❺ Notre-Dame du Sablon Church

The round, rose, stained-glass windows in the clerestory of this 14th-century Flamboyant Gothic church are nice by day, but the real thrill is at night, when the church is lit from inside. It glows like a lantern, enjoyed by locals at the cafés in the surrounding square.

Step inside. The glorious apse behind the altar—bathed in stained-glass light—is what Gothic is all about. Next to the altar, see a small wooden **statue of Mary** dressed in white with a lace veil. This is a copy, made after iconoclastic Protestant vandals destroyed the

original. The original statue was thought to have had miraculous powers, saving the town from plagues. In 1348, when the statue was in Antwerp, it spoke to a godly woman named Beatrix, prompting her to board a boat (see the small **wooden boat,** high above the entry door) and steal the statue away from Antwerp. When they tried to stop her, the Mary statue froze the Antwerp citizens in their tracks.

Beatrix and the statue arrived here, the Bruxelloise welcomed her with a joyous parade, and this large church was erected in her honor. Every summer, in Brussels' famous Ommegang, locals in tights and flamboyant costumes recreate the joyous arrival. With colorful banners and large puppets, they carry Mary from here through the city streets to the climax on the Grand Place.

• *On the other side of Rue de la Régence from the church is a leafy, fenced-off garden called the...*

❻ Place du Petit Sablon

This is a pleasant refuge from the busy street, part of why this neighborhood is considered so livable. The 48 small statues atop the wrought-iron fence represent the guilds—weavers, brewers, and butchers—of medieval Brussels. Inside the garden, 10 large statues represent hometown thinkers of the 16th century—a time of great intellectual accomplishments in

Brussels. Gerardus Mercator (1512–1594), the Belgian mapmaker who devised a way to show the spherical Earth on a flat surface, holds a globe.

• *We'll visit the Sablon neighborhood below the church later, but before losing elevation, let's continue along Rue de la Régence, passing the Music Academy and Brussels' main synagogue (its sidewalk fortified with concrete posts to keep car bombs at a distance), before reaching the long-scaffolded...*

❼ Palace of Justice (Palais de Justice)

This domed mountain of marble sits on the edge of the Upper Town ridge, dominating the Brussels skyline. Built in wedding-cake layers of Greek columns, it's topped with a dome taller than St. Peter's in Rome, rising up 340 feet. Covering more than six

acres, it's the size of a baseball stadium. Everyone seems to pooh-pooh this over-the-top monument, but I find it jaw-dropping.

The palace was built in the time of King Leopold II (son of Leo I, r. 1865–1909), and epitomizes the brassy, look-at-me grandeur of his reign. Leopold became obscenely wealthy by turning Africa's Congo region—80 times the size of Belgium—into his personal colony.

Whip-wielding Belgian masters forced African slaves to tend lucrative rubber plantations, exploiting the new craze for bicycle tires. Leopold spent much of this wealth expanding and beautifying the city of Brussels.

Leo's architect, Joseph Poelaert (1817–1879), wrestled with the mathematics of the building's construction for 20 years before it finally drove him mad. He ended up in an insane asylum, leaving the project to be completed by others in 1883. The dome, often covered with maintenance scaffolding, is somewhat shaky.

The building serves as a Hall of Justice, where major court cases are tried. If you pop into the lobby, you may see lawyers in black robes buzzing about.

• *One of the best views of Brussels is immediately to the right of the Palace of Justice.*

❽ Viewpoint from Place Poelaert

You're standing 200 feet above the former Senne River Valley. Gazing west over the Lower Town, pan the valley from right (north) to left:

Near you is the stubby **clock tower** of the Minimen Church (which hosts lunchtime concerts in the summer). To the left of that, in the distance, past a tall square skyscraper, comes the lacy white Town Hall **spire** (marking the Grand Place).

In the far distance, six miles away, you can see one of the city's landmarks, the **Atomium**. (No doubt, someone atop it is looking back at you.) The Atomium's nine steel balls form the shape of an iron molecule the size of the Palace of Justice behind you. Built for a 1958 World's Fair, it's now a middle-aged symbol of the dawn of the Atomic Era.

Next (closer to you) comes the **black-steepled roof** of the Notre-Dame de la Chapelle church, the city's oldest (from 1134, with a spire that starts Gothic and ends Baroque). On the distant horizon, see **five boxy skyscrapers**, part of the residential sprawl of this city of 1.2 million, which now covers 62 square miles. The **green dome** belongs to the Basilica of Koekelberg (fourth biggest in the world). And finally  (panning quickly to the left), you see a **black glass skyscraper** marking the Midi (or South) train station.

At your feet lies the **Marolles neighborhood**. Once a funky, poor place where locals developed their own quirky dialog, it remains somewhat seedy—and famous for its sprawling flea market (daily 7:00–13:00, best on weekends). Two of the streets just below you—Rue Haute and Rue Blaes—are lined with secondhand shops. An **elevator** connects Place Poelaert with the Marolles neighborhood (free, daily 6:00–23:00). People who brake for garage sales may want to cut out of this walk early and head to the Marolles from here.

Gazing off into the distance to the far left (south), you can't quite see the suburb of **Waterloo**, 10 miles away. But try to imagine it, because it was there that history turned. On the morning of June 18, 1815, Napoleon waited two hours for the ground to dry before sending his troops into battle. That delay may have cost him the battle. His 72,000 soldiers could have defeated Wellington's 68,000. But the two-hour delay was just enough time for Wellington's reinforcements to arrive—45,000 Prussian troops. Napoleon had to surrender, his rule of Europe ended, and Belgium was placed under a Dutch king—until the Belgians won their independence in the 1830 revolution.

Behind you, in Place Poelaert, are two memorials to the two World Wars, both of which passed through Belgium with deadly force.

• *Backtrack east, descending to Place du Grand Sablon by walking down Rue Ernest Allard.*

❾ Place du Grand Sablon

The Sablon neighborhood features cafés and restaurants, antiques stores, and art galleries. Every weekend, there's an antiques market

on the square. On warm summer evenings, the square sparks magic, as sophisticated locals sip apéritifs at the café tables, admiring the glowing stained glass of the church.

Chocolatier Wittamer (on the far side of the square, at #6) often has elaborate window displays.

Le Pain Quotidien serves healthy lunches, fresh-baked goods, and coffee in an unstuffy atmosphere (11 Rue des Sablons 11, on near side of square, close to church; see page 363). The café at the base of the sloping square (the *Café Leffe* sign) offers cheap, no-nonsense meals any time of day. For a classy lunch, try **L'Estrille du Vieux Bruxelles**, a block downhill from Place du Grand Sablon (Rue de Rollebeek 7, see page 363).

• *Sloping Place du Grand Sablon funnels downhill into the pedestrian-only street called Rue de Rollebeek, which leads past fun shops and the recommended L'Estrille restaurant to the busy Boulevard de l'Empereur. To the right on the boulevard, just past the bowling alley, is the...*

❿ Tour d'Angle

This "Corner Tower" is a rare surviving section of Brussels' 13th-century city wall. The plan of the old town (on a plaque on the ruin) shows how this was one of seven gates along the 2.5-mile-long wall that enclosed Brussels, one of Europe's great cities.

• *Continue downhill several blocks. When you hit level ground, turn right on Rue L'Etuve, which leads directly back to the Grand Place. A block along, you'll run into our old friend* Manneken-Pis, *eternally relieving himself (if you're urine-ing to learn more about this leaky little tyke, see page 336).*

ROYAL MUSEUMS OF FINE ARTS OF BELGIUM TOUR

(Musées Royaux des Beaux-Arts de Belgique)

Two large buildings, each housing an art museum (ancient and modern), contain a vast collection covering the entire history of Western painting. The collection, while enjoyable, can be overwhelming. So, here's a "Top 10" list highlighting the museum's strength: Flemish and Belgian artists.

ORIENTATION

Cost: €5, same ticket covers both museums, free first Wed of the month after 13:00.

Hours: Tue–Sun 10:00–17:00, closed Mon, half the rooms close for lunch 12:00–13:00, the other half close 13:00–14:00, last entry at 16:30.

Getting There: The museums are at Rue de la Régence 3 in the Upper Town, just a five-minute walk uphill from Central Station (or take bus #27, #38, #60, #71, #95, or #96). You'll also encounter the museums if you take my Upper Town Walk on page 338.

Information: Consider the excellent €2.50 audioguide or the €2.50 tour booklet *(Twenty Masterpieces of the Art of Painting: A Brief Guided Tour)*. You can also choose among four self-guided tours, each marked with a different color: blue for the 15th and 16th centuries, brown for the 17th and 18th, yellow for the 19th, and green for the 20th. Tel. 02/508-3211, www.fine-arts-museum.be.

Length of This Tour: Allow one hour.

Cuisine Art: The Greshem, a restaurant and tea room, is nearby at Place Royale (daily 11:00–18:00).

Overview

Though there are technically two museums—Ancient Art (pre-1800) and Modern Art (post-1800)—they're connected and covered by the same ticket. Recent renovations have allowed the museum to display more of its collection of 17th-century Flemish and Dutch art, as well as open a new area called the Patio (located between the 2 museums)

to show off its 16th-century Flemish tapestries. But be warned that in 2006, the impressive main hall will be under renovation as they restore it to its original grand gallery function.

The museum sprawls over several wings and a dozen floors, and to see it all is a logistical nightmare. But armed with the museum's free map (supplemented with the audioguide), you'll breeze through the maze with these 10 stops as guideposts.

THE TOUR BEGINS

• *Start with the Flemish masters, one floor up in the Ancient Art Museum, and follow the blue tour signs. In Room 11, you'll find...*

ANCIENT ART

Rogier van der Weyden (c. 1399–1464)—*Portrait of Anthony of Burgundy (Portrait d' Antoine de Bourgogne)*

Anthony was known in his day as the Great Bastard, the bravest and most distinguished of the many bastards fathered by prolific

Duke Philip the Good (a Renaissance prince whose sense of style impressed Florence's young Lorenzo the Magnificent, patron of the arts).

Anthony, a member of the Archers Guild, fingers the arrow like a bow-string. From his gold necklace dangles a Golden Fleece, one of Europe's more prestigious knightly honors. Wearing a black cloak, a bowl-cut hairdo, and a dark-red cap, with his pale face and hand emerging from a dark background, the man who'd been called a bastard all his life gazes to the distance, his clear, sad eyes lit with a speckle of white paint.

Van der Weyden, Brussels' official portrait painter, faithfully rendered life-size, lifelike portraits of wealthy traders, bankers, and craftsmen. Here he captures the wrinkles in Anthony's neck, and the faint shadow his chin casts on his Adam's apple. Van der Weyden had also painted Philip the Good, and young Anthony's long, elegant face and full lips are a mirror image—pretty convincing DNA evidence in a paternity suit.

Capitalist Flanders in the 1400s was one of the richest, most cultured, and progressive areas in Europe, rivaling Florence and Venice.

• *In Room 14, find...*

Hans Memling (c. 1430–1494)—*Martyrdom of St. Sebastian (Volets d'un Triptyque)*

Serene Sebastian is filled with arrows by a serene firing squad in a serene landscape. Sebastian, a Roman captain who'd converted to Christianity, was ordered to be shot to death. (He miraculously survived, so they clubbed him to death.)

Ready, freeze! Like a *tableaux vivant* (popular with Philip the Good's crowd), the well-dressed archers and saint freeze this moment in the martyrdom so the crowd can applaud the colorful costumes and painted cityscape backdrop.

Hans Memling, along with his former employer, Rogier van der Weyden, are called Flemish Primitives. Why "Primitive"? For the lack of 3-D realism so admired in Italy at the time. Sebastian's arm is tied to a branch that's not arching overhead, as it should be, but instead is behind him. An archer aims slightly behind, not at, Sebastian. The other archer strings his bow in a stilted pose. But Memling is clearly a master of detail, and the faces, beautiful textiles, and hazy landscape combine to create a meditative mood appropriate to the church altar in Bruges where this was once placed.

• *In Room 31, look for...*

Pieter Brueghel I, the Elder (c. 1527–1569)— *The Census at Bethlehem*

Perched at treetop level, you have a bird's-eye view over a snow-covered village near Brussels. The canals are frozen over, but life goes on, with everyone doing something. Kids throw snowballs and sled across the ice. A crowd gathers at the inn (lower left), where a woman holds a pan to catch blood while a man slaughters a pig. Most everyone has his or her back to us or head covered, so the figures speak through poses and motions.

Into the scene rides a woman on a donkey led by a man—it's Mary and husband Joseph hoping to find a room at the inn (or at least a manger), because Mary's going into labor.

The year is 1566—the same year that Protestant extremists throughout the Low Countries vandalized Catholic churches, tearing down "idolatrous" statues and paintings of the Virgin Mary. Brueghel (more discreetly) brings Mary down to earth from her Triumphant Coronation in heaven, and places Jesus' birth in the humble here and now. The busy villagers put their heads down and work, oblivious to the future Mother of God and the wonder about to take place.

Brueghel the Elder was famous for his landscapes filled with crowds of peasants in motion. His religious paintings place the miraculous in everyday settings.

In this room, you'll see Brueghel's works, as well as those of his less famous sons. Pieter Brueghel II, the younger Pieter, copied dad's style (and even some paintings, like the *Census at Bethlehem*). Another son, Jan, was known as the "Velvet Brueghel" for his glossy still lifes of flower arrangements.

• *Leave the blue tour and walk into the adjacent rooms to follow the brown tour signs. You'll find lots of Rubens in Rooms 52 and 53.*

Peter Paul Rubens (1577–1640)—*The Ascent to Calvary (La Montée au Calvaire)*

Life-size figures scale this 18-foot-tall canvas on the way to Christ's Crucifixion. The scene ripples with motion, from the windblown clothes to steroid-enhanced muscles to billowing flags and a troubled sky. Christ stumbles, and might get trampled by the surging crowd. Veronica kneels to gently wipe his bloody head.

This 200-square-foot canvas was manufactured by Rubens at his studio in Antwerp. Hiring top-notch assistants, Rubens could crank out large altarpieces for the area's Catholic churches. First, Rubens himself did a small-scale sketch in oil (like many such studies in Room 52). He would then make other sketches, highlighting individual details. His assistants would reproduce it on the large canvas, and Rubens would then add in the final touches.

This work is from late in Rubens' long and very successful

career. He got a second wind in his 50s, when he married 16-year-old Hélène Fourment. She was the model in this painting for Veronica, who consoles the faltering Christ.

• *To get to the Modern Art wing, return to the ground floor and the large main entrance hall of the Ancient Museum. From there, a passage-way leads to Modern Art. Once in the Modern Art wing (entering on Level -2), take the elevator to the top floor (Level +3) and work your way down the museum's eight floors. Follow the yellow tour signs.*

MODERN ART

Panorama

At the very top of Level +3 is a great view westward over Brussels' Lower Town. See the Town Hall spire and, two miles away, the twin green domes of the gigantic basilica built by Leopold II. Looking as far right (north) as you can, you can make out the Atomium on the horizon.

• *Watch Impressionism turn to Post-Impressionism in this wing, which features both. Paul Gauguin and Georges Seurat emerged from Paris' Impressionist community to forge their own styles. Here on Level +3, visit with...*

Georges Seurat (1859–1891)— *The Seine at Grand-Jatte* (*La Seine à la Grande-Jatte,* 1888)

Seurat paints a Sunday-in-the-park view from his favorite island in the Seine. Taking Impressionism to its extreme, he builds the scene out of small points of primary colors that blend at a distance to form objects. The bright colors capture the dazzling, sunlit atmosphere of this hazy day.

Paul Gauguin (1848–1903)—*Breton Calvary* (*Calvaire Breton,* 1889; a.k.a *The Green Christ/Le Christ Vert*)

Paul Gauguin returned to the bold, black, coloring-book outlines of more "primitive" (pre-3-D) art. The Christian statue and countryside look less like Brittany and more like primitive Tahiti, where Gauguin would soon settle.

• *Descend one floor to Level +2.*

James Ensor (1860–1949)—*Shocked Masks* (1883)

At 22, James Ensor, an acclaimed child prodigy, proudly presented his lively Impressionist-style works to the Brussels Salon for exhi-

bition. They were flatly rejected.

The artist withdrew from public view and, in seclusion, painted *Shocked Masks*, a dark and murky scene set in a small room of an ordinary couple wearing grotesque masks. Once again, everyone disliked this disturbing canvas and heaped more criticism on him. For the next six decades, Ensor painted the world as he saw it—full of bizarre, carnival-masked, stupid-looking crowds of cruel strangers who mock the viewer.

• *Down one more floor (Level +1), you'll find...*

Jacques-Louis David (1748–1825)—*The Death of Marat* (1793)

In a scene ripped from the day's headlines, Marat—a well-known crusading French journalist—has been stabbed to death in his

bathtub by Charlotte Corday, a conservative fanatic. Marat's life drains out of him, turning the bathwater red. With his last strength, he pens a final, patriotic, "*Vive la Révolution*" message to his fellow patriots. Corday, a young noblewoman angered by Marat's campaign to behead the French king, was arrested and guillotined three days later.

Jacques-Louis David, one of Marat's fellow Revolutionaries, set to work painting a tribute to his fallen comrade. (He signed the painting: "*À Marat*"—"To Marat.")

David makes it a secular *pietà*, with the brave writer as a martyred Christ in a classic dangling-arm pose. Still, the deathly pallor and harsh lighting pull no punches for in-your-face realism.

David, the official art director of the French Revolution, supervised propaganda and the costumes worn for patriotic parades. A year later (1794), his extreme brand of Revolution (which included guillotining thousands of supposed enemies) was squelched by moderates, and David was jailed. He emerged again as Napoleon's court painter. When Napoleon was exiled in 1815, so was David, spending his last years in Brussels.

• *Leave the yellow tour route, proceed to Level -5, and follow the green tour to see...*

Paul Delvaux (1897–1994)

Delvaux, who studied, worked, and taught in Brussels, gained fame for his Surrealistic nudes sleepwalking through moonlit, video-game landscapes. They cast long shadows, wandering bare-breasted among classical ruins. Some women grow roots.

• *Proceed to Level -6 to see art by the Surrealists Joan Miró, Salvador Dalí, Max Ernst, Yves Tanguy, and Roberto Matta, as well as works by...*

René Magritte (1898–1967)

Magritte paints real objects with photographic clarity, then jumbles them together in new and provocative ways.

Magritte had his own private reserve of symbolic images. You'll see clouds, blue sky, windows, the female torso, men in bowler hats, rocks, and castles arranged side by side as if they should mean something. People morph into animals or inanimate objects. The juxtaposition only short-circuits your brain when you try to make sense of it.

Magritte also trained and worked in Brussels. Though he's world-famous now, it took decades before his peculiar brand of Surrealism caught on.

SLEEPING

Normal hotel prices are high in central Brussels. But if you arrive in July, August, or on a Friday or Saturday night any other time, the city's fancy business-class hotels rent rooms for half price, making them your best budget bet. Otherwise, you do have budget options. The modern hostels are especially good and rent double rooms. And I've found a few fine little family-run hotels that offer good prices throughout the year. April, May, September, and October are very crowded, and finding a room without a reservation can be impossible.

Business Hotels with Summer Rates

The fancy hotels of Brussels (Db-€150–200) survive because of the business and diplomatic trade. But they're desperately empty in July and August (sometimes June, too) and on weekends (most Fri, Sat, and—to a lesser extent—Sun nights). If you ask for a summer/weekend rate, you'll save about a third. If you go through the TI, you'll save up to two-thirds. Three-star hotels in the center abound with amazing summer rates—you can rent a double room with enough comforts to keep a diplomat happy, including a fancy breakfast, for about €60.

The TI assured me that every day in July and August, there are tons of business-class hotel rooms on the push list. You'll get a big discount by just showing up at either TI (for same-day booking only). In July and August and on any Friday or Saturday—trust me—your best value is to arrive without a reservation, walk from the Central Station down to either TI, and let them book you a room within a few blocks. You cannot book these deals in advance. They are only for the bold who show up without a reservation. The later you arrive, the lower the prices drop.

Sleep Code

(€1 = about $1.20, country code: 32)
S = Single, **D** = Double/Twin, **T** = Triple, **Q** = Quad, **b** = bathroom,
s = shower only. Everyone speaks English and accepts credit
cards. Unless otherwise noted, breakfast is included.

To help you easily sort through these listings, I've divided
the rooms into three categories, based on the price for a standard double room with bath:

$$$ Higher Priced—Most rooms €100 or more.
  $$ Moderately Priced—Most rooms between €80–100.
    $ Lower Priced—Most rooms €80 or less.

These seasonal rates apply only to business-class hotels. Because
of this, budget accommodations, which charge the same throughout the year, go from being a good value one day (say, a Thursday in
summer) to a bad value the next (a Friday in summer).

Hotels near the Grand Place

$$$ Hotel Ibis has six locations in or near Brussels; the best is
well-situated halfway between the Central Station and the Grand
Place. It's a sprawling, modern place offering 184 quiet, simple,
industrial-strength-yet-comfy rooms (Sb/Db-€129 Mon–Thu,
€109 Fri–Sun, rooms €20 more in Sept, €20 less Jan–Feb and
July–Aug, extra bed-€16, breakfast-€10, non-smoking rooms, air-
con, elevator, Grasmarkt 100, tel. 02/514-4040, fax 02/514-5067,
www.ibishotel.com, h1046@accor.com).

$$$ Hotel le Dixseptième, a four-star luxury hotel ideally
located a block below Central Station, is an expensive oasis in the
heart of town. Prim, proper, and peaceful, with chandeliers and
squeaky hardwood floors, it comes with all the comforts in its 24
rooms, each decorated with a different theme (only 4 standard Db-
€180, the rest are Db suites-€260–340, extra bed-€30, see Web site
for discounts, non-smoking rooms, air-con, elevator, free Internet
in lobby, Rue de la Madeleine 25, tel. 02/517-1717, fax 02/502-6424,
www.ledixseptieme.be, info@ledixseptieme.be).

$$$ Hotel la Madeleine, on the small square between Central
Station and the Grand Place, rents 52 plain, overpriced rooms.
While not terribly clean, it has a great location and a friendly staff
(S-€52, no shower at all for this room; Ss-€75, Sb-€99, Db-€110;
"executive" rooms: Sb-€120, Db-€125, Tb-€135; see Web site for
deals, request a quieter back room when you reserve, elevator, Rue
de la Montagne 22, tel. 02/513-2973, fax 02/502-1350, www.hotel
-la-madeleine.be, info@hotel-la-madeleine.be).

Brussels Hotels

IIII - Stairs
Ⓜ - Subway Stop
Ⓑ - Tour Bus Departure Points (2)
••• - 5 Min. Walk - Central
        Station to Grand Place

200 YARDS
200 METERS

DCH

❶ Hotel la Madeleine
❷ Hotel the Moon
❸ Hotel Ibis
❹ Hotel Opéra
❺ Hotel le Dixseptième
❻ Hotel la Légende
❼ Hotel Welcome
❽ Hotel Noga
❾ Citadines Sainte-
    Catherine Apart'hotel
❿ Bruegel Hostel
⓫ To Sleepwell Hostel
⓬ To Jacques Brel Hostel

$$$ **Hotel la Légende** rents 26 rooms with a dormitory ambience a block from the *Manneken-Pis* statue. Although it's on a busy road, it has a pleasant courtyard. The furnishings are basic, but the location and price are right, and the rooms are comfortable enough (Db-€89, or €76 in July–Aug, Tb-€129, Qb-€139, weekends are cheaper, elevator, Rue du Lombard 35, tel. 02/512-8290, fax 02/512-3493, www.hotellalegende.com, info@hotellalegende .com).

$$ **Hotel the Moon** is concrete and efficient, with 17 fresh if industrial-strength rooms and almost no public spaces. Although it has absolutely no character, you'll sleep fine and it's super-convenient, right in the old center (Sb-€65, Db-€80, Tb-€100, €5 less on weekends, €15 less in July–Aug, Rue de la Montagne 4, tel. 02/508-1580, fax 02/508-1585, hotelthemoon@hotmail.com).

$$ **Hotel Opéra,** on a great, people-filled street near the Grand Place, is professional, dark, and standardized, with street noise and 49 boxy rooms (Sb-€68, Db-€85, or €65 in July–Aug, Tb-€93, Qb-€107, 10 percent less than top rates with this book in 2006, courtyard rooms are quieter, elevator, Internet in lobby, Rue Gretry 53, tel. 02/219-4343, fax 02/219-1720, www.hotel-opera.be, reception@hotel-opera.be).

Hotels Around the Fish Market

The next four listings are a 10-minute walk from the intensity of the old center, near the Ste. Catherine Métro stop. This charming neighborhood, called "the village in Brussels," faces the canalside fish market and has many of the town's best restaurants.

$$$ **Citadines Sainte-Catherine Apart'hotel,** part of a Europe-wide chain, is a huge "apart-hotel" with modern, ship-shape rooms. Choose from efficiency studios with fold-out double beds or two-room apartments with a bedroom and a fold-out couch in the living room. All 163 units come with a kitchen, stocked cupboards, a stereo, and everything you need to settle right in (1- or 2-person studio-€120, or €60 in slow times, apartment for up to 4 people-€150, 10 percent cheaper by the week, 50 percent cheaper by the month, breakfast-€13, parking-€10, 51 Quai au Bois à Brûler, tel. 02/221-1411, fax 02/221-1599, www.citadines.com, stecatherine@citadines.com).

$$$ **Hotel Noga** feels extremely homey, with 19 rooms, a welcoming game room, and old photos of Belgian royalty lining the hallways. It's carefully run by Frederich Faucher and his son, Mourad (Sb-€80–85, Db-€100, Tb-€130, Qb-€155, all rooms about 20 percent less Fri–Sat and every day in Aug, 5 percent discount if you pay in cash, very quiet, Internet access in lobby, Rue du Beguinage 38, tel. 02/218-6763, fax 02/218-1603, www.nogahotel .com, info@nogahotel.com).

$$ Hotel Welcome, owned by an energetic bundle of hospitality named Meester Smeesters, offers outrageously creative rooms tastefully decorated with artifacts he's picked up in his world travels. Each of the 16 fun-loving rooms has a different geographic theme—from India to Japan to Bali (Sb-€85, standard Db-€95, deluxe Db-€120, Db "Egypt" junior suite-€130, huge Db "Silk Road" suite-€180, Tb-€145, Qb-€160, much lower rates in Aug, elevator, parking-€10, airport shuttle available, 23 Quai au Bois à Brûler, tel. 02/219-9546, fax 02/217-1887, www.hotelwelcome.com, info@hotelwelcome.com, run by Sophie and Michel Smeesters, plus Vanessa). Take a tour of Michel's rooms on the Web.

Hostels

Three classy and modern hostels—in buildings that could double as small, state-of-the-art, minimum-security prisons—are within a 10-minute walk of the Central Station. Each accepts people of all ages, serves cheap and hot meals, takes credit cards, and charges about the same price. All rates include breakfast and showers down the hall.

$ Bruegel Hostel, a fortress of cleanliness, is handiest and most comfortable. Of its many rooms, 22 are bunk-bed doubles (S-€26, D-€41, beds in quads or dorms-€17.30, nonmembers pay €3 extra per night, reception open 7:00–10:00 & 14:00–24:00, Rue de St. Esprit 2, midway between Midi and Central stations, behind Chapelle church, tel. 02/511-0436, fax 02/512-0711, www.vjh.be, brussel@vjh.be).

$ Sleepwell, surrounded by high-rise parking lots, is also comfortable (S-€26.50, D-€40, T-€53, dorm beds-€12–15.50, nonsmoking, Internet in lobby, walking tours-€2.50/person, Rue de Damier 23, tel. 02/218-5050, fax 02/218-1313, www.sleepwell.be, info@sleepwell.be).

$ Jacques Brel is a little farther out, but it's still a reasonable walk from everything (180 beds, S-€26, D-€41, T-€52, Q-€70, dorm bed-€15.30, includes breakfast and sheets, no curfew, nonsmoking rooms, laundry, Rue de la Sablonnière 30, tel. 02/218-0187, fax 02/217-2005, www.laj.be, brussels.brel@laj.be).

EATING

For many, the obvious eating tip in Brussels is simply to enjoy the Grand Place. My vote for northern Europe's grandest medieval square is lined with hardworking eateries that serve the predictable dishes to tourist crowds. Of course, you won't get the best quality or prices—but, after all, it's the Grand Place. Locals advise eating well elsewhere and enjoying a Grand Place perch for dessert or a drink.

Brussels is known for both its high-quality, French-style cuisine and for multicultural variety. Seafood—fish, eel, shrimp, and oyster—is especially well-prepared here. For more on Belgian cuisine, see page 300.

Mussels in Brussels

Mussels are available all over town. For an atmospheric cellar or a table right on the Grand Place, eat at **'t Kelderke**. Its one steamy vault under the square is always packed with both natives and tourists—a real Brussels fixture. It serves local specialties, including mussels (a splittable kilo bucket—just more than 2 pounds—for €17.50–20.50; daily 12:00–24:00, no reservations, Grand Place 15, tel. 02/513-7344). Also see Restaurant Chez Leon, below.

Rue des Bouchers ("Restaurant Row")

Brussels' restaurant streets, two blocks north of the Grand Place, are touristy and notorious for aggressively sucking you in and ripping you off. But the area is an exhilarating spectacle and fun for at least a walk. Order carefully, understand the prices thoroughly, and watch your wallet.

The touristy **Restaurant Chez Leon** is a mussels factory, slamming out piles of good, cheap buckets since 1893. It's big and welcoming, with busy green-aproned waiters offering a "Formula

Brussels Restaurants

① 't Kelderke
② Aux Armes de Bruxelles
③ Restaurant Chez Leon
④ Rest. Vincent & de l'Ogenblik
⑤ Bij den Boer & Rest. Jacques
⑥ La Marie Joseph
⑦ Restaurant le Loup-Galant
⑧ La Pain Quotidien Bakery
⑨ L'Estrille du Vieux Bruxelles
⑩ La Maison des Crêpes
⑪ Belga Queen Brasserie

⑫ Osteria a l'Ombra
⑬ Le Cirio Café
⑭ A la Bécasse Café
⑮ A la Mort Subite Bar
⑯ Panos Sandwiches
⑰ Au Suisse Deli
⑱ Restaurant le Pre Sale
⑲ La Villette Restaurant
⑳ AD Delhaize Grocery
㉑ Super GB Grocery

Leon" for €12.85—a light meal consisting of a small bucket of mussels, fries, and a beer. They also offer a €22.95 *menu* that comes with a starter, a large bucket of mussels, fries, and beer (daily 12:00–23:00, non-smoking section, kids eat free, Rue des Bouchers 18, tel. 02/511-1415). In the family portrait of Leon's brother Honoré (hanging in the corner), the wife actually looks like a mussel.

Aux Armes de Bruxelles is a venerable restaurant that has been serving reliably good food to the Bruxelloise in a dressy setting for generations. This is another food factory with white-suited waiters serving an older clientele impressed by the restaurant's reputation (€29.50–45 *menu*s, €23 lunch *menu*, Tue–Sun 12:00–23:00, closed Mon, indoor seating only, Rue des Bouchers 13, tel. 02/511-5550).

At **Restaurant Vincent**, you enter through the kitchen—say hello to owners Michel and Jacques—and end up in their 1905-era establishment. Enjoy a €27.50 *menu* and Old World ambience with the natives (daily 12:00–14:30 & 18:30–23:00, Rue des Dominicains 8–10, tel. 02/511-2607).

Restaurant de l'Ogenblik, a remarkably peaceful eddy just off the raging restaurant row, fills an early-20th-century space in the corner of an arcade. The dressy waiters serve well-presented, near-gourmet French and international cuisine (€25 plates, closed Sun, Galerie des Princes 1, tel. 02/511-6151).

Belga Queen Brasserie bills itself as a "wonderfood palace." A huge, trendy brasserie filling a palatial former bank building, it's *the* place for Brussels' beautiful people. While quite expensive, the food is excellent, service is sharp, and the experience memorable—from the french fries served in silver cones to the double-decker platters of iced shellfish to the transparent toilets stalls (which become opaque only after you nervously lock the door). The high-powered trendiness can make you feel a little gawky, but if you've got the money, this is a great splurge (€20–30 entrées, €30–50 *menu*s, daily 12:00–14:00 & 19:00–24:00, call to reserve, 2 seatings: about 19:30 and 21:30, Rue Fosse-aux-Loups 32, tel. 02/217-2187). The vault downstairs is a plush cigar and cocktail lounge. For a quick bite or slurp here, grab a stool at the white-marble oyster bar.

More Eateries near the Grand Place

La Maison des Crêpes, a little eatery, looks underwhelming but serves delicious €8 crêpes (savory and sweet) and salads half a block south of the Bourse. It has a brown café ambience, and even though it's just a few steps away from the tourist bustle, it feels laid-back and local (good beers, sidewalk seating, daily 11:30–23:00, Rue du Midi 13).

Osteria a l'Ombra, a true Italian joint across the lane from the TI a block off the Grand Place, is perfect for anyone needing a quality bowl of pasta with a fine glass of Italian wine, served by ponytailed Italian stallions. It's pricey, but the woody bistro ambience and tasty food make it a good value. If you choose an entrée (about €15), you get your choice of pasta or salad included in the price. While the ground-floor seating is fine, also consider sitting upstairs (Mon–Fri 12:00–14:30 & 18:30–23:30, Sat 18:30–23:30, closed Sun, Rue des Harengs 2, tel. 02/511-6710).

Sandwiches: You'll find sandwich shops throughout Brussels. **Panos** is a good sandwich chain (Mon–Fri 7:30–19:00, Sat–Sun 9:00–19:00; on Grasmarkt, across from entrance of Galeries Royales St. Hubert). The 129-year-old **Au Suisse** deli is a traditional spot for a drink and a sandwich (closed Sun, across from the Bourse at Boulevard Anspach 73).

Groceries: Two supermarkets are about a block from the Bourse and a few blocks from the Grand Place. **AD Delhaize** is at the intersection of Anspach and Marché-aux-Poulets (Mon–Sat 9:00–20:00, Fri until 21:00, Sun 9:00–18:00), and **Super GB** is half a block away at Halles and Marché-aux-Poulets (Mon–Sat 9:00–20:00, Fri until 21:00, closed Sun).

Around the Sainte Catherine Fish Market

A 10-minute walk from the old center puts you in "the village within the city" area of Sainte Catherine (Métro: Ste. Catherine). The historic fish market here has spawned a tradition of fine restaurants specializing mostly in seafood. The old fish canal survives, and if you walk around it, you'll see plenty of enticing restaurants. Make the circuit, considering these very good yet very different eating options.

Bij den Boer, a fun, noisy eatery popular with locals and tourists, feels like a traditional and very successful brasserie. The specialty: fish (€25 4-course *menu*, Mon–Sat 12:00–14:30 & 18:00–22:30, closed Sun, Quai aux Briques 60, tel. 02/512-6122). Its neighbor, **Restaurant Jacques** (at #44), also has a good reputation.

La Marie Joseph, stylish and modern, serves fancy fish and fries. They earn raves from the natives (€20–25 plates, non-smoking area, Tue–Sun 12:00–15:00 & 18:30–23:00, closed Mon, no reservations, Quai au Bois à Brûler 47, tel. 02/218-0596).

Restaurant le Loup-Galant, a block beyond the fish market, is wonderfully Bruxelloise, with a rustic-yet-dressy charm. They serve fine contemporary Belgian cuisine from a menu that changes monthly depending on what's in season (€25 3-course *menu* of the week, €10.50 *plat du jour,* Tue–Sat 12:00–14:00 & 19:00–22:00, closed Sun–Mon, air-con, few tourists, reservations wise, Quai aux Barques 4, tel. 02/219-9998).

Restaurant le Pre Sale is noisy, high-energy, and family-friendly. A Brussels fixture for its traditional local cuisine, it fills a former butcher shop with happy eaters and a busy open kitchen (big shareable €20 pots of mussels come with a salad, €15 meals, closed Mon–Tue, a block off the fish market at Rue de Flandre 20, tel. 02/513-6545).

La Villette Restaurant is a more romantic, low-energy eatery serving Belgian cuisine. It has a charming red-and-white-tablecloth interior and good outdoor seating facing a small square (€15 meals, closed Sun, Rue du Vieux Marché-aux-Grains 3, tel. 02/512-7550).

Near Place du Grand Sablon

La Pain Quotidien (literally, "The Daily Bread") is a mod, rustic, woody bakery that extends out back into a tented terrace. You'll find classy open-face sandwiches (*tartines*, about €8), soups, and salads (about €12)—expensive, but fresh and tasty (daily 8:00–18:00, Rue des Sablons 11, tel. 02/513-5154).

L'Estrille du Vieux Bruxelles is a dressy, half-timbered restaurant just downhill from Place du Grand Sablon, serving a fine lunch special (€12) and two tasting *menus* (€23 and €33). Each tasting *menu* comes with six classic French dishes in one delicious course—so a couple ordering both *menus* can experience a dozen different taste treats (kids' menu, Mon–Sat 12:00–14:00 & 19:00–22:00, closed Sun, Rue de Rollebeek 7, tel. 02/512-5857).

Sampling Belgian Beer with Food and Ambience

Looking for a good spot to enjoy that famous Belgian beer? Brussels is full of atmospheric cafés to savor. The eateries lining the Grand Place are touristy, but the setting—plush old medieval guild halls fronting all that cobbled wonder—is hard to beat. I've listed three places a few minutes' walk off the square, with magical, old-time feel. For a few euros, you can generally get a cold-meat plate, an open-face sandwich, or a salad.

All varieties of Belgian beer are available, but Brussels' most unusual beers are *lambic*-based. Look for *lambic doux, lambic blanche, gueuze* (pronounced "kurrs"), and *faro*, as well as fruit-flavored *lambic*s, such as *Kriek* and *Framboise*. These beers look and taste more like a dry, somewhat bitter cider. The brewer doesn't add yeast—the beer ferments naturally from yeast found floating only in the marshy air around Brussels. For more on Belgian beer, see page 301.

At **Le Cirio,** across from the Bourse, the dark wooden tables boast the skid marks of over a century's worth of beer steins (nightly 22:00–1:00 in the morning, Rue de la Bourse 18–20, tel. 02/512-1395).

A la Bécasse is lower profile than Le Cirio, with a simple wood-panel and wood-table decor that appeals to both poor students and lunching businessmen. The home-brewed *lambic doux* is served in a clay jar. It's just around the corner from Le Cirio, towards the Grand Place, hidden away at the end of a courtyard (daily from 10:00, Rue de Tabora 11, tel. 02/511-0006).

A la Mort Subite, north of the restaurant streets, is a classic old bar that has retained its 1928 decor... and many of its 1928 customers (Rue Montagne-aux-Herbes Potagères 7, tel. 02/513-1318).

 Named after the "sudden death" playoff that workingmen used to end their lunchtime dice games, it still has an unpretentious, working-class feel. The decor is simple, with wood tables, grimy yellow wallpaper, and some-other-era garland trim. Tiny metal plates on the walls mark spots where gas-powered flames once flickered—used by patrons to light their cigars. A typical lunch or snack here is a *tartine* (open-face sandwich, €4) spread with *fromage blanc* (cream cheese) or pressed meat. Eat it with one of the home-brewed, *lambic*-based beers. This is a good place to try the Kriek (cherry-flavored) beer. The Bruxellois claim it goes well with sandwiches.

TRANSPORTATION CONNECTIONS

Belgium

Belgium's train system is slick, efficient, and non-smoking. Consider these rail deals for traveling within the country (www.b-rail.be):

- **Youths** under age 26 can get a Go Pass: €43 for 10 rides anywhere in Belgium.
- **Seniors** (age 65-plus) can get a same-day round-trip ticket to anywhere in Belgium for €3.50 (valid daily, weekdays after 9:00).
- Those traveling on the **weekend** should request the weekend discount for round-trips (50 percent off, valid Fri after 19:00).

Note that if you have a bike, you'll pay extra to bring it on the train (€4.20 one-way, €7.20 round-trip).

Bruges

Trains
From Bruges by Train to: Brussels (2/hr, usually at :31 and :57, 1 hr, €10), **Ghent** (2/hr, 40 min), **Ostende** (3/hr, 15 min), **Köln** (6/day, 3.5 hrs), **Paris** (hrly via Brussels, 2.5 hrs, must pay supplement of €11 2nd class, €20 1st class—even with a railpass), **Amsterdam** (hrly, 3.5 hrs, transfer in Antwerp or Brussels), **Amsterdam's Schiphol Airport** (hrly, 3.5 hrs, transfer in Antwerp or Brussels, €35). Train info: tel. 050/302-424.

Trains from London: Bruges is an ideal "Welcome to Europe" stop after London. Take the Eurostar train from London to Brussels (9/day, 2.75 hrs), then transfer, backtracking to Bruges (2/hr, 1 hr, entire trip is covered by same Eurostar ticket; see Eurostar details below).

Belgian Train Lines

Brussels

Trains

Brussels has three train stations: Central, Midi, and Nord (described on page 313). Be sure you're clear on which station or stations your train uses.

From Brussels by Train to: Bruges (2/hr, 1 hr; from any of Brussels' train stations, catch IC train—direction: Ostende or Knokke-Blankenberge), **Amsterdam** (stopping at Amsterdam's Schiphol Airport on the way, hrly, 3 hrs, from Central, Midi, or Nord—sometimes from just 1 station, but sometimes all 3), **Berlin** (7/day, 7.5–8 hrs, from Central or Midi, transfer in Köln; or 12-hr night train from Midi), **Frankfurt** (9/day, 5.5 hrs, from Midi; or transfer in Köln from Central, Midi, and Nord), **Munich** (9/day, 8.5–9.5 hrs; from Central, Midi, and Nord, most transfer in Köln and sometimes also Mannheim), **Rome** (3/day, 17 hrs; from Nord, transfer in Milan, Zürich, or Paris), **Paris** (fast Thalys trains zip to

Eurostar Routes

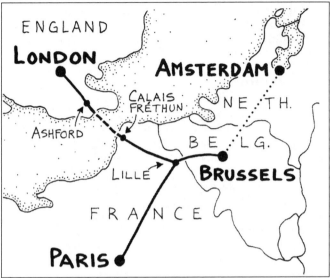

Paris hrly, 1.5 hrs, from Midi—it's best to book by 20:00 the day before, or risk limited availability on same day). When booking Thalys (and similar express) trains to or from Paris, Amsterdam, and Köln, even railpass-holders need to pay the supplement of €11 for second class or €20 for first class. The first-class supplement generally gets you a meal on board. Train info: tel. 02/528-2828 (long wait), www.thalys.com.

By Eurostar to/from London: Brussels and London are three hours apart by Eurostar train (9/day). In 2005, full-fare one-way tickets cost $255 for second class and $375 for first class (full-fare tickets are exchangeable and fully refundable, even after your departure date). The cheaper second-class "Leisure" rates start at $90 one-way for midday, midweek travel (no refund or exchange). Railpass-holders get discounts ($75 one-way for 2nd class, $135 one-way for 1st class).

You can check and book fares by phone or online in the U.S. (order online at www.ricksteves.com/rail/eurostar.htm, prices listed in dollars; or order by phone at U.S. tel. 800-EUROSTAR) or in Belgium (www.eurostar.com, prices listed in euros; Belgian tel. 0900-10177—this expensive toll line costs €0.50/min from pay phone and €1.50/min from hotel). While tickets are usually cheaper if purchased in the U.S., fares offered in Europe follow different discount rules—so it can be worth it to check www.eurostar .com before purchasing. If you buy from a U.S. company, you'll pay for ticket delivery in the U.S. In Europe, you can buy your

Eurostar ticket at any major train station in any country or at any travel agency that handles train tickets (expect a booking fee).

By Bus to: London (cost can vary, but generally €50 one-way, €75 round-trip, about 9 hrs, Eurolines tel. 02/203-0707 in Brussels, www.eurolines.com).

Brussels Airport

The clear winner for getting to and from the airport (9 miles from downtown Brussels) is the Airport Express shuttle train that runs from Brussels Midi and Central stations (€2.60, 4/hr, 25 min, daily 6:00–23:00). If you're connecting the airport with Bruges, take this shuttle train and transfer in Brussels. Figure on spending €35 for a taxi between downtown Brussels and the airport. Airport info: tel. 0900-70000, www.brusselsairport.be.

Virgin Express flies cheaply between Brussels and London (hrly, starting at €50), plus Milan, Rome, Geneva, Nice, Lisbon, Barcelona, Madrid, Athens, and more (Belgian tel. 02/752-0505, www.virgin-express.com). Bmi british midland has inexpensive flights from Brussels to the British Isles (www.flybmi.com). Non-discount airlines, such as Brussels Airlines (www.flysn.com), Lufthansa (www.lufthansa.com), Finnair (www.finnair.com), and Alitalia (www.alitalia.com), offer daily flights from Brussels Airport.

HISTORY

TWENTY CENTURIES IN FOUR PAGES

A.D. 1–1300—Romans and Invasions

When Rome falls (c. 400), the Low Countries shatter into a patchwork of local dukedoms, ravaged by Viking raids. Out of this poor, agricultural, and feudal landscape emerge three self-governing urban centers—Amsterdam, Bruges, and Brussels—each in a prime location for trade. Amsterdam and Bruges sit where rivers flow into the North Sea, while Brussels hugs a main trading highway.

Sights

- Amsterdam's Dam Square
- Exhibits in Amsterdam History Museum
- Haarlem's Market Square
- Bruges' original fort and church ruins
- Bruges' Basilica of the Holy Blood (1150)
- Brussels' St. Michael's Cathedral, model in the City Museum, and Tour d'Angle (tower) from city wall

1300–1500—Booming Trade Towns

Bruges, the midway port between North Sea and Mediterranean trade, becomes one of Europe's busiest and richest cities. Amsterdam augments its beer and herring trade with budding capitalism: banking, loans, and speculation in stock and futures.

Brussels sells waffles and beer to passing travelers. Politically, the Low Countries are united by marriage with the cultured empire of the Dukes of Burgundy.

Sights

- Churches: Amsterdam's Old Church (Oude Kerk) and New Church (Nieuwe Kerk), and Haarlem's Grote Kerk
- Amsterdam's Waag (in Red Light District), the Mint Tower from original city wall, and the wooden house at Begijnhof 34
- Bruges' bell tower, the Gothic Room in the City Hall, and the Church of Our Lady
- Flemish "Primitive" art (van Eyck, Memling, van der Weyden) in Bruges' Groeninge and Memling museums, and in Brussels' Royal Museums of Fine Arts of Belgium
- Brussels' Grand Place, medieval street Rue des Bouchers (Restaurant Row), and Notre-Dame du Sablon Church

1500s—Protestants vs. Catholics, Freedom-Fighters vs. Spanish Rulers

Protestantism spreads through the Low Countries, particularly

in Holland (while Belgium remains more Catholic). Thanks to other royal marriages, the Low Countries are ruled from afar by the very Catholic Hapsburg family in Spain. In 1566, angry Protestants rise up against Spain and Catholicism, vandalizing Catholic churches and deposing Spanish governors. King Philip II of Spain sends troops to restore order and brutally punish the rebel-heretics, beginning the Eighty Years' War, also known as the Dutch War of Independence (1568–1648).

Sights

- Amsterdam's whitewashed, simply decorated, post-Iconoclasm churches
- Civic Guard portraits in Amsterdam History Museum
- Mementos of the Siege of Haarlem in Haarlem's Grote Kerk
- Brussels' tapestry designs

1600s—Holland's Golden Age

Holland gains its independence from the Hapsburgs (officially in

1648), while Belgium languishes under Spanish rule. Amsterdam invents the global economy, as its hardy sailors ply the open seas, trading in Indonesian spices and South American sugar. Establishing colonies all over the world, they also conceive the African slave trade. Their combined nautical and capitalist skills make Amsterdam the world's wealthiest city.

Sights

- Amsterdam's Rijksmuseum and Haarlem's Frans Hals Museum—paintings by Rembrandt, Hals, Vermeer, and Steen
- Old townhouses and gables in Amsterdam's Jordaan neighborhood and Red Light District
- Amsterdam's Begijnhof, Royal Palace, Westerkerk, and Rembrandt's house
- Brussels' *Manneken-Pis*
- Lace (popularity peaks c. 1700)

1700s—Elegant Decline

Holland and Belgium are both surpassed by the rise of superpowers France and England. Wars with those powers drain their economies and scuttle Holland's fleet. Still, they survive as bankers, small manufacturers, and craftsmen in luxury goods—but on a small scale fitting their geographical size. They hit rock-bottom in 1795, when French troops occupy the Low Countries (1795–1815), and Europe's powers subsequently saddle them with a monarchy.

Sights

- Amsterdam's Amstelkring Museum (hidden church), Willet-Holthuysen Museum (Herengracht Canal Mansion), and Jewish Historical Museum synagogues
- Brussels' Grand Place guildhalls

1800s—Revival

Though slow to join the Industrial Revolution, Holland picks up speed by century's end. A canal to the North Sea rejuvenates Amsterdam's port, railroads lace cities together, and Amsterdam hosts a World Exhibition. Belgium—having been placed under a Dutch king—revolts, gains its independence (1830), and picks its own king, a German this time. Wealth from its colony in Africa's Congo region helps rebuild Brussels in grand style.

Sights

- Amsterdam's Central Station, Rijksmuseum, and Magna Plaza
- Van Gogh paintings at the Van Gogh Museum
- Indonesian foods from the colonial era
- Brussels' Upper Town buildings and boulevards
- Brussels' Galeries Royales St. Hubert
- Chocolate

1900s—Invasions by Germans, Hippies, and Immigrants

Belgium is a major battleground in both World Wars. Holland,

neutral in World War I, suffers brutal occupation under the Nazis in World War II. After the war, Brussels becomes the center of the budding movement toward European economic unity. In Amsterdam, postwar prosperity and a tolerant atmosphere in the 1960s and 1970s make it a global magnet for hippies, freaks, and your co-authors. In the 1970s and 1980s, Amsterdam and Brussels are flooded with immigrants from former colonies, causing friction, but diversifying the population.

Sights

- Amsterdam's Beurs, Tuschinski Theater, and National Monument on Dam Square
- Amsterdam's Anne Frank House and Dutch Resistance Museum
- Amsterdam's Heineken Brewery, rock-and-roll clubs Paradiso and Melkweg, and the new "Stopera" opera house

- Haarlem's Corrie ten Boom House
- Paintings by René Magritte in Bruges' Groeninge Museum and Brussels' Royal Museums of Fine Arts of Belgium
- Brussels' Atomium and European Parliament quarter

THE NETHERLANDS AND BELGIUM— A TIMELINE

57 B.C.   Julius Caesar invades the Low Countries, conquering local Batavian, Frisian, and Belgae tribes, beginning four centuries of Roman rule.

A.D. 406   Frankish tribes from Germany drive out the last Roman legions as Rome's Europe-wide empire collapses. Christian missionaries work to prevent the area from reverting to paganism.

c. 800   Charlemagne, born in Belgium, rules the Low Countries as part of a large North European empire. After his death, his grandsons divide the kingdom and bicker among themselves.

c. 880–1000   Vikings rape and pillage the Low Countries during two centuries of raids.

c. 900   The Low Countries are a patchwork of small dukedoms ruled by bishops and local counts (of Holland, Flanders, Brabant, and so on), who owe allegiance to greater kings in France, Germany, and England.

c. 1250   In Amsterdam, fishermen build a dike (dam) where the Amstel River flows into the North Sea, creating a prime trading port. Soon the town gains independence and trading privileges from the local count and bishop. Meanwhile, Bruges becomes a major weaver of textiles, and Brussels becomes a minor trading town along the Germany–Bruges highway.

c. 1300   Italian and Portuguese sailors forge a coast-hugging trade route from the Mediterranean to the North Sea, with Bruges as the final stop.

1302   In Bruges, Flemish rebels drive out French rulers at the Battle of the Golden Spurs.

1345   Amsterdam experiences the Miracle of the Host, when a flame-resistant communion wafer causes miracles and attracts pilgrims.

1384   The discovery of a process to cure herring with salt makes Amsterdam a major fish exporter (to augment its thriving beer trade).

1384	Mary of Flanders marries Duke Philip the Bold of Burgundy, turning Holland and Belgium into part of a Burgundian empire that eventually stretches from Amsterdam to Switzerland.
c. 1400	Bruges is Europe's greatest trade city, the middleman between North and South.
1433	Burgundy's empire peaks when Duke Philip the Good takes over the titles of the local counts. His cultured court makes the Low Countries a center of art, literature, ideas, and pageantry.
1482	Mary of Burgundy, the last heir to the Burgundian throne, falls from a horse and dies. Her possessions (including Holland and Belgium) pass to her Austrian husband, Maximilian, and get swallowed up in his family's large Holy Roman Empire, ruled from Austria and later Spain.
1492	Columbus' voyage demonstrates the potential wealth of New World trade.
1517	The German Martin Luther's 95 theses inspire Protestantism, which becomes popular in the Low Countries (especially Holland). Later, refugees of religious persecution, including Calvinists and Anabaptists (such as the Amish and Mennonites), find a home in tolerant Amsterdam.
1519	King Charles V (1500–1558), the grandson of Mary of Burgundy and Maximilian, inherits all of his family's combined possessions. Charles rules Holland and Belgium, as well as Austria, Spain, Germany, Spain's New World colonies, and much more. A staunch Catholic, Charles battles rebellious Protestant princes.
1535	On Amsterdam's Dam Square, Anabaptist rebels are hanged, drawn, and quartered.
1540	Emperor Charles' son, Philip of Spain, invites the Inquisition to Spain.
1556	Philip II, based in Spain, succeeds his father as ruler of the Netherlands and intensifies the wars on Protestants (especially Calvinists).
1566	In a wave of anti-Catholic and anti-Spanish fury, extreme Protestants storm Catholic churches, vandalizing religious objects and converting the churches to Protestant (the Iconoclasm). Philip II sends soldiers to the Low Countries to establish order and punish rebels and heretics.
1568	Holland's Protestant counts rally around William "The Silent" of Orange, demanding freedom from

Spanish Hapsburg rule (the Beggars' Revolt). This begins 80 years of on-again-off-again war with Spain, called...the Eighty Years' War.

1572–1573 The Spanish conquer Haarlem after a long siege, but Haarlem's brave stand inspires other towns to carry on the fight.

1578 Amsterdam switches sides (the Alteration), joining the Protestant independence movement. Extreme Calvinists control the city for several decades, officially outlawing Catholic services. Within a few years, Spanish troops are driven south out of Holland, and future battles take place mostly on Belgian soil.

1580 Holland and Belgium go separate ways in the war. Holland's towns and counts form a Protestant military alliance against Catholic Spain (the United Provinces), while Belgium remains Catholic, with Brussels as the capital of Spanish Hapsburg rule.

1585 Antwerp, Northern Europe's greatest trading city (pop. 150,000), falls to Spanish troops. In the chaos, business plummets, and many Protestant merchants leave town. Industrious Amsterdam steps in to fill the vacuum of trade.

1588 Elizabeth I of England defeats the Spanish Armada (navy), breaking Spain's monopoly on overseas trade.

1602 The Dutch East India Company (V.O.C.), a government-subsidized trading company, is formed, soon followed by the West India Company (1622). Together, they make Amsterdam (pop. 100,000) the center of a global trading empire, spawning Holland's Golden Age (c. 1600–1650).

1609 Henry Hudson's *Half Moon*, sailing for the Dutch East India Company, departs Amsterdam in search of a western passage to the Orient. Instead, Hudson finds the island of Manhattan, which soon becomes New Amsterdam (New York, 1625).

1616 Frans Hals paints the *St. George Civic Guards* (Frans Hals Museum, Haarlem).

1620 Pilgrims from England stop in Holland on their way to America.

1631 Rembrandt moves to Amsterdam, a wealthy city of 120,000 people, including René Descartes (1596–1650) and Erasmus (1585–1638), plus many different religious sects and a thriving Jewish Quarter.

1637	After a decade of insanely lucrative trade in tulip bulbs ("tulip mania"), the market crashes.
1648	The Treaty of Munster (and the Treaty of Westphalia) officially ends the Eighty Years' War with Spain. The United Provinces (today's Netherlands) are now an independent nation.
1652–1654	Holland battles England over control of the seas. This is the first of three wars with England (also in 1665 and 1672) that sap Holland's wealth.
1672–1678	Louis XIV of France invades Holland and gets 15 miles from Amsterdam, but is finally stopped when the citizens open the Amstel locks and flood the city. After another draining war with France (1701–1713), England and France overtake Holland in overseas trade.
1689	Holland's William of Orange is invited by England's Parliament to replace the despot they'd deposed. He, ruling with wife Mary, becomes King William III of England.
1695	Louis XIV of France bombs and incinerates Brussels, punishing them for allying against him.
1776	The American Revolution inspires European democrats and worries nobles.
1787	Holland's budding democratic movement, the Patriots, is suppressed and exiled when Prussian troops invade Holland.
1789	French Revolution begins.
1795	France, battling Europe's monarchs to keep their Revolution alive, invades and occupies Holland (establishing the "Batavian Republic," 1795–1806) and Belgium.
1806	Napoleon Bonaparte, who turned France's Revolution into a dictatorship, proclaims his brother, Louis Napoleon, to be King of Holland (1806–1810).
1815	After Napoleon's defeat at Waterloo (near Brussels), Europe's nobles decide that the Low Countries should be a monarchy, ruled jointly by a Dutch prince, who becomes King William I. (Today's Queen Beatrix is descended from him.)
1830	Belgium rebels against the Dutch-born king, becoming an independent country under King Leopold I.
1860	The novel *Max Havelaar,* by the Dutch writer Multatuli, exposes the dark side of Holland's repressive colonial rule in Indonesia.

1876   The North Sea Canal opens after 52 years of building, revitalizing Amsterdam's port. In the next decade, the city builds the Centraal Station, Rijksmuseum, and Concertgebouw, and hosts a World Exhibition (1883) that attracts three million visitors.

1881   King Leopold II of Belgium acquires Africa's Congo region, tapping its wealth to rebuild Brussels with broad boulevards and big marble buildings (neoclassical style).

1914   In World War I, Holland remains neutral, while Belgium becomes the horrific battleground where Germany dukes it out with England and France— for example, at Ieper (Ypres in French).

1932   The Dutch Zuiderzee dike is completed, making the former arm of the North Sea into a freshwater lake (the IJsselmeer) and creating many square kilometers of reclaimed land.

1940–1945   Nazi Germany bombs Holland's Rotterdam and easily occupies the Netherlands and Belgium (1940). Belgium's king officially surrenders, while Holland's Queen Wilhelmina (1880–1962) flees to England. In Amsterdam, Anne Frank and her Jewish family go into hiding in an attempt to avoid arrest by the Nazis (1942–1944). Late in the war, Belgium is the site of Germany's last-gasp offensive, the Battle of the Bulge (1944–1945).

1945   Holland and Belgium are liberated by Allied troops.

1949   Indonesia gains its independence from Holland.

1953   Major floods in Holland kill almost 2,000 people, prompting more dams and storm barriers (the Delta Project, 1958–1997).

1957   Belgium and the Netherlands join the EEC (Common Market)—the forerunner of today's European Union—with headquarters in Brussels.

1960   The Benelux economic union between Belgium, the Netherlands, and Luxembourg—first proposed in 1944—becomes fully operational. Belgium, after years of protests, grants independence to the Belgian Congo.

1967   Amsterdam is Europe's center for hippies and the youth movement.

1975   Suriname (Dutch Guyana) gains its independence from Holland, and many emigrants flock to Holland.

1980   Queen Beatrix (b. 1938) becomes ruler of Holland.

1992   Belgium and the Netherlands sign the Treaty of Maastricht, which creates the European Union (EU).

1995   Floods in the Netherlands cause a billion dollars in damage.

2002   Anti-immigration politician Pim Fortuyn is assassinated.

2004   An Islamist radical kills Dutch filmmaker Theo van Gogh (Vincent's great-grandnephew) on an Amsterdam street because of his film *Submission*, discussing violence against women in Muslim societies.

2005   Dutch voters speak for all Europe by voting for a referendum that slows the adoption of a European Constitution.

2006   You arrive in Amsterdam, Bruges, and Brussels and make your own history.

APPENDIX

Let's Talk Telephones

Here's a primer on making phone calls. For information specific to the Netherlands and Belgium, see "Telephones" in the Introduction.

Making Calls Within a European Country: About half of all European countries use area codes (like we do in much of the U.S.); the other half use a direct-dial system without area codes.

To make calls within a country that uses a direct-dial system (Belgium, the Czech Republic, Denmark, France, Italy, Portugal, Norway, Spain, and Switzerland), you dial the same number whether you're calling across the country or across the street.

In countries that use area codes (such as the Netherlands, Austria, Britain, Finland, Germany, Ireland, and Sweden), you dial the local number when calling within a city, and you add the area code if calling long-distance within the country.

Making International Calls: You always start with the international access code (011 if you're calling from the U.S. or Canada, or 00 from Europe), then dial the country code of the country you're calling (see chart below).

What you dial next depends on the phone system of the country you're calling. If the country uses area codes, drop the initial 0 of the area code, then dial the rest of the number.

Countries that use direct-dial systems (no area codes) vary in how they're accessed internationally by phone. For instance, if you're making an international call to the Czech Republic, Denmark, Italy, Norway, Portugal, or Spain, simply dial the international access code, country code, and the local phone number. But if you're calling Belgium, France, or Switzerland, drop the initial 0 of the local phone number.

European Calling Chart

Just smile and dial, using this key:
AC = Area Code, LN = Local Number.

European Country	Calling long distance within ...	Calling from the U.S.A./ Canada to ...	Calling from a European country to ...
Austria	AC + LN	011 + 43 + AC (without the initial zero) + LN	00 + 43 + AC (without the initial zero) + LN
Belgium	LN	011 + 32 + LN (without initial zero)	00 + 32 + LN (without initial zero)
Britain	AC + LN	011 + 44 + AC (without initial zero) + LN	00 + 44 + AC (without initial zero) + LN
Croatia	AC + LN	011 + 385 + AC (without initial zero) + LN	00 + 385 + AC (without initial zero) + LN
Czech Republic	LN	011 + 420 + LN	00 + 420 + LN
Denmark	LN	011 + 45 + LN	00 + 45 + LN
Finland	AC + LN	011 + 358 + AC (without initial zero) + LN	00 + 358 + AC (without initial zero) + LN
France	LN	011 + 33 + LN (without initial zero)	00 + 33 + LN (without initial zero)
Germany	AC + LN	011 + 49 + AC (without initial zero) + LN	00 + 49 + AC (without initial zero) + LN
Greece	LN	011 + 30 + LN	00 + 30 + LN
Hungary	06 + AC + LN	011 + 36 + AC + LN	00 + 36 + AC + LN
Ireland	AC + LN	011 + 353 + AC (without initial zero) + LN	00 + 353 + AC (without initial zero) + LN
Italy	LN	011 + 39 + LN	00 + 39 + LN

European Country	Calling long distance within ...	Calling from the U.S.A./ Canada to ...	Calling from a European country to ...
Netherlands	AC + LN	011 + 31 + AC (without initial zero) + LN	00 + 31 + AC (without initial zero) + LN
Norway	LN	011 + 47 + LN	00 + 47 + LN
Poland	AC + LN	011 + 48 + AC (without initial zero) + LN	00 + 48 + AC (without initial zero) + LN
Portugal	LN	011 + 351 + LN	00 + 351 + LN
Slovakia	AC + LN	011 + 421 + AC (without initial zero) + LN	00 + 421 + AC (without initial zero) + LN
Slovenia	AC + LN	011 + 386 + AC (without initial zero) + LN	00 + 386 + AC (without initial zero) + LN
Spain	LN	011 + 34 + LN	00 + 34 + LN
Sweden	AC + LN	011 + 46 + AC (without initial zero) + LN	00 + 46 + AC (without initial zero) + LN
Switzerland	LN	011 + 41 + LN (without initial zero)	00 + 41 + LN (without initial zero)
Turkey	AC (if no initial zero is included, add one) + LN	011 + 90 + AC (without initial zero) + LN	00 + 90 + AC (without initial zero) + LN

- The instructions above apply whether you're calling a fixed phone or mobile phone.
- The international access codes (the first numbers you dial when making an international call) are 011 if you're calling from the U.S.A./Canada, or 00 if you're calling from anywhere in Europe.
- To call the U.S.A. or Canada from Europe, dial 00, then 1 (the country code for the U.S.A. and Canada), then the area code and number. In short, 00 + 1 + AC + LN = Hi, Mom!

Country Codes

After you've dialed the international access code (00 if you're calling from Europe, 011 if calling from the United States or Canada), dial the code of the country you're calling.

Austria—43	Italy—39
Belgium—32	Morocco—212
Britain—44	Netherlands—31
Canada—1	Norway—47
Croatia—385	Poland—48
Czech Rep.—420	Portugal—351
Denmark—45	Slovakia—421
Estonia—372	Slovenia—386
Finland—358	Spain—34
France—33	Sweden—46
Germany—49	Switzerland—41
Gibraltar—350	Turkey—90
Greece—30	U.S.A.—1
Ireland—353	

U.S. Embassies

The Netherlands

U.S. Embassy: Lange Voorhout 102, The Hague (Mon–Fri 8:15–17:00, closed Sat–Sun, tel. 070/310-2209, www.usemb.nl).

U.S. Consulate: Museumplein 19, Amsterdam (for passport concerns, open Mon–Fri 8:30–11:30, closed Sat–Sun, tel. 020/575-5309, http://netherlands.usembassy.gov/consular_visa.html, consularamster@state.gov).

Belgium

U.S. Embassy: Regentlaan 27 Boulevard du Régent, Brussels (Mon–Fri 9:00–18:00, closed Sat–Sun; passport services Mon–Fri 13:30–16:30, closed Sat–Sun, tel. 02/508-2111, www.usembassy.be).

Festivals and Public Holidays in 2006

Here's a partial list of festivals and public holidays in the Netherlands and Belgium. For more information on holidays, see www.holland .com, www.visitbelgium.com and www.whatsonwhen.com.

Jan 1	New Year's Day
Mid-Feb	Carnival (Mardi Gras)
April 16 and 17	Easter Sunday and Monday
April 22	Flower Parade (www.bloomencorso -bollenstreek.nl), Haarlem
April 29	Queen's Day (Koninginnedag), birthday of the late Queen Mother Juliana, party in the streets of Amsterdam (it's usually

2006

JANUARY

S	M	T	W	T	F	S
1	2	3	4	5	6	7
8	9	10	11	12	13	14
15	16	17	18	19	20	21
22	23	24	25	26	27	28
29	30	31				

FEBRUARY

S	M	T	W	T	F	S
			1	2	3	4
5	6	7	8	9	10	11
12	13	14	15	16	17	18
19	20	21	22	23	24	25
26	27	28				

MARCH

S	M	T	W	T	F	S
			1	2	3	4
5	6	7	8	9	10	11
12	13	14	15	16	17	18
19	20	21	22	23	24	25
26	27	28	29	30	31	

APRIL

S	M	T	W	T	F	S
						1
2	3	4	5	6	7	8
9	10	11	12	13	14	15
16	17	18	19	20	21	22
23/30	24	25	26	27	28	29

MAY

S	M	T	W	T	F	S
	1	2	3	4	5	6
7	8	9	10	11	12	13
14	15	16	17	18	19	20
21	22	23	24	25	26	27
28	29	30	31			

JUNE

S	M	T	W	T	F	S
				1	2	3
4	5	6	7	8	9	10
11	12	13	14	15	16	17
18	19	20	21	22	23	24
25	26	27	28	29	30	

JULY

S	M	T	W	T	F	S
						1
2	3	4	5	6	7	8
9	10	11	12	13	14	15
16	17	18	19	20	21	22
23/30	24/31	25	26	27	28	29

AUGUST

S	M	T	W	T	F	S
		1	2	3	4	5
6	7	8	9	10	11	12
13	14	15	16	17	18	19
20	21	22	23	24	25	26
27	28	29	30	31		

SEPTEMBER

S	M	T	W	T	F	S
					1	2
3	4	5	6	7	8	9
10	11	12	13	14	15	16
17	18	19	20	21	22	23
24	25	26	27	28	29	30

OCTOBER

S	M	T	W	T	F	S
1	2	3	4	5	6	7
8	9	10	11	12	13	14
15	16	17	18	19	20	21
22	23	24	25	26	27	28
29	30	31				

NOVEMBER

S	M	T	W	T	F	S
			1	2	3	4
5	6	7	8	9	10	11
12	13	14	15	16	17	18
19	20	21	22	23	24	25
26	27	28	29	30		

DECEMBER

S	M	T	W	T	F	S
					1	2
3	4	5	6	7	8	9
10	11	12	13	14	15	16
17	18	19	20	21	22	23
24/31	25	26	27	28	29	30

on April 30, but that's a Sunday in 2006, so the party will be on the 29th)

May 1   Labor Day

May 4   Remembrance of WWII Dead (Dodenherdendking), Netherlands

May 5   Liberation Day in Netherlands (Bevrijdingsdag)

May 25   Procession of the Holy Blood in Bruges; Ascension in Netherlands and Belgium

May (1st week)   Kunst RAI—contemporary-art exhibition (www.kunstrai.nl), Netherlands

May (2nd Sat)   National Windmill Day (sails whirl, many mills open to public), Netherlands

June 3–4   Pentecost weekend

June 5	Whit Monday (7 weeks after Easter)
July 14–16	North Sea Jazz Festival (www.northseajazz.nl), The Hague
June 23	Grachtenloop (run around canals, www.grachtenloop.nl), Amsterdam
Month of June	Holland Arts Festival (concerts, theater, etc., www.hollandfestival.nl); Amsterdam Roots Festival—Oosterpark (ethnic food, music, world culture; www.amsterdamroots.nl)
July 21	Independence Day, Belgium
Aug 15	Assumption Day, Procession in Bruges
Aug 15	Carpet of Flowers (celebrated even years), Brussels
Mid-Aug	Prinsengracht canal concert on barges, Amsterdam
Aug	Festival on the canals, held every five years, next in 2009 (Reiefeesten, www.reiefeest.be), Bruges
Summer 2006	Ommegang festival—pomp and pageantry (www.visitbelgium.com/mediaroom/Ommegang.htm), Brussels
Sept (1st week)	Flower parade on canals, Aalsmeer to Amsterdam
Mid-Sept	Jordaan Festival—neighborhood street party (www.jordaanfestival.nl), Amsterdam
Nov 1	All Saints' Day
Nov 11	Armistice Day
Dec 5	Sinterklaas and Zwarte Piet arrive, procession and presents, Netherlands
Dec 25	Christmas

Climate

First line, average daily low temperature; second line, average daily high; third line, days of no rain.

J	F	M	A	M	J	J	A	S	O	N	D

Amsterdam

J	F	M	A	M	J	J	A	S	O	N	D
30°	31°	35°	40°	45°	52°	55°	55°	51°	43°	37°	33°
41°	42°	49°	55°	64°	70°	72°	71°	66°	56°	48°	41°
8	9	16	14	16	16	14	12	11	11	10	9

Brussels

J	F	M	A	M	J	J	A	S	O	N	D
30°	32°	34°	40°	45°	53°	55°	55°	52°	45°	38°	32°
41°	44°	51°	58°	65°	71°	73°	72°	69°	60°	48°	42°
9	11	14	12	15	15	13	12	15	13	10	11

Numbers and Stumblers

- Europeans write a few of their numbers differently than we do. 1 = 1, 4 = 4, 7 = 7. Learn the difference or miss your train.
- In Europe, dates appear as day/month/year, so Christmas is 25/12/06.
- Commas are decimal points and decimals commas. A dollar and a half is 1,50, and there are 5.280 feet in a mile.
- When pointing, use your whole hand, palm down.
- When counting with fingers, start with your thumb. If you hold up your first finger to request one item, you'll probably get two.
- What Americans call the second floor of a building is the first floor in Europe.
- Europeans keep the left "lane" open for passing on escalators and moving sidewalks. Keep to the right.

Metric Conversion (approximate)

1 inch = 25 millimeters

1 foot = 0.3 meter

1 yard = 0.9 meter

1 mile = 1.6 kilometers

1 centimeter = 0.4 inch

1 meter = 39.4 inches

1 kilometer = .62 mile

32°F = 0°C

82°F = about 28°C

1 ounce = 28 grams

1 kilogram = 2.2 pounds

1 quart = 0.95 liter

1 square yard = 0.8 square meter

1 acre = 0.4 hectare

Temperature Conversion: Fahrenheit and Celsius

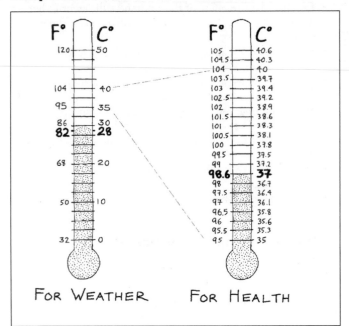

Europe takes its temperature using the Celsius scale, while we opt for Fahrenheit. For weather, remember that 28°C is 82°F—perfect. For health, 37°C is just right.

Dutch Phrases

You won't need to learn Dutch, but knowing a few phrases can help if you're traveling off the beaten path. Taking a few moments to learn the pleasantries (such as please and thank you) will improve your connections with locals even in the bigger cities.

To pronounce the difficult Dutch "g" (indicated in phonetics by hhh) make a hard, guttural, clear-your-throat sound, similar to the "ch" in the Scottish word "loch."

English	Dutch	Pronunciation
Hello.	*Hallo.*	hol-LOH
Good day.	*Dag.*	dahhh
Good morning.	*Goeiemorgen.*	hhhoy-ah MOR-hhhen
Good afternoon.	*Goeiemiddag.*	hhhoy-ah MIT-tahhh
Good evening.	*Goeieavond.*	hhhoy-ah AH-vond
Ma'am	*Mevrouw*	meh-frow
Sir	*Meneer*	men-ear
Yes	*Ja*	yah
No	*Nee*	nay
Please	*Alstublieft*	AHL-stoo-bleeft
Thank you.	*Dank u wel.*	dahnk oo vehl
Excuse me.	*Pardon.*	par-DOHN
Do you speak English?	*Spreekt u Engels?*	spraykt oo ENG-gels
Okay.	*Oké.*	"okay"
Goodbye.	*Tot ziens.*	toht zeens
one / two	*een / twee*	ayn / t'vay
three / four	*drie / vier*	dree / feer
five / six	*vijf / zes*	fife / ses
seven / eight	*zeven / acht*	say-fen / ahcht
nine / ten	*negen / tien*	nay-hhhen / teen
What does it cost?	*Wat kost?*	vaht kost
I would like...	*Ik wil graag...*	ik vil hhhrahhh
...a room.	*...een kamer.*	un kah-mer
...a ticket.	*...een kaart.*	un kart
...a bike.	*...een fiets.*	un feets
Where is...?	*Waar is...?*	vahr is
...the station	*...het station*	het sta-tsee-on
...the tourist info office	*...de VVV*	duh vay vay vay
left / right	*links / rechts*	links / rechts
open / closed	*open / gesloten*	"open" / hhhe-sloh-ten

In the Restaurant

The Dutch have an all-purpose word, alstublieft (AHL-stoo-bleeft), that means: "Please," or "Here you are," (if handing you something), or "Thanks," (if taking payment from you), or "You're welcome" (when handing you change). Here are other words that might come in handy at restaurants, particularly if you're day-tripping to small towns:

English	Dutch	Pronunciation
I would like...	*Ik wil graag...*	ik vil hhhrahhh
...a cup of coffee	*...kopje koffee.*	kop-yeh "coffee"
non-smoking	*niet-roken*	neet roh-ken
smoking	*roken*	roh-ken
with / without	*met / buiten*	met / bow-ten
and / or	*en / of*	en / of
bread	*brood*	broht
salad	*sla*	slah
cheese	*kaas*	kahs
meat	*vlees*	flays
chicken	*kip*	kip
fish	*vis*	fis
egg	*ei*	eye
fruit	*vrucht*	frucht
pastries	*gebak*	hhhe-bak
I am vegetarian.	*Ik ben vegetarish.*	ik ben vay-hhhe-tah-rish
Tasty.	*Lekker.*	lek-ker
Enjoy!	*Smakelijk!*	smak-kuh-luk
Cheers!	*Proost!*	prohst

Making Your Hotel Reservation

Most hotel managers know basic "hotel English." Faxing or e-mailing are the preferred methods for reserving a room. They're more accurate than telephoning and much faster than writing a letter. Use this handy form for your fax or find it online at www.ricksteves.com/reservation. Photocopy and fax away.

One-Page Fax

To: _____ @ _____
          hotel   *fax*

From: _____ @ _____
          name   *fax*

Today's date: _____ / _____ / _____
            day   *month*   *year*

Dear Hotel _____ ,
Please make this reservation for me:

Name: _____

Total # of people: _____ # of rooms: _____ # of nights: _____

Arriving: _____ / _____ / _____   My time of arrival (24-hr clock): _____
       day *month* *year*   (I will telephone if I will be late)

Departing: _____ / _____ / _____
       day *month* *year*

Room(s): Single _____ Double _____ Twin _____ Triple _____ Quad _____

With: Toilet _____ Shower _____ Bath _____ Sink only _____

Special needs: View ___ Quiet ___ Cheapest ___ Ground Floor ___

Please fax, mail, or e-mail confirmation of my reservation, along with the type of room reserved and the price. Please also inform me of your cancellation policy. After I hear from you, I will quickly send my credit-card information as a deposit to hold the room. Thank you.

_____
Signature

_____
Name

_____
Address

_____
City   *State*   *Zip Code*   *Country*

_____
E-mail Address

INDEX

CREDITS

Researcher
To help update this book, Rick relied on the help of…

Jennifer Hauseman
Jennifer Hauseman, an editor and researcher for Rick Steves, originally hails from the East Coast, but has since become an honorary Seattleite. While in the Low Countries, Jen enjoyed researching by bike with Rick, sampling vending-machine *stroop-wafels,* and being mistaken for a *Nederlandse* in and around Amsterdam.

Start your trip at
www.ricksteves.com

Rick Steves' website is packed with over 3,000 pages of timely travel information. It's also your gateway to getting FREE monthly travel news from Rick—and more!

Free Monthly European Travel News

Fresh articles on Europe's most interesting destinations and happenings. Rick will even send you an e-mail every month (often direct from Europe) with his latest discoveries!

Timely Travel Tips

Rick Steves' best money-and-stress-saving tips on trip planning, packing, transportation, hotels, health, safety, finances, hurdling the language barrier…and more.

Travelers' Graffiti Wall

Candid advice and opinions from thousands of travelers on everything listed above, plus whatever topics are hot at the moment (discount flights, packing tips, scams…you name it).

Rick's Annual Guide to European Railpasses

The clearest, most comprehensive guide to the confusing array of railpass options out there, and how to choo-choose the railpass that best fits your itinerary and budget. Then you can order your railpass (and get a bunch of great freebies) online from us!

Great Gear at the Rick Steves Travel Store

Enjoy bargains on Rick's guidebooks, planning maps and TV series DVDs—and on his custom-designed carry-on bags, wheeled bags, day bags and light-packing accessories.

Rick Steves Tours

Every year more than 6,000 lucky travelers explore Europe on a Rick Steves tour. Learn more about our 30 different one-to-three-week itineraries, read uncensored feedback from our tour alums, and sign up for your dream trip online!

Rick on Radio and TV

Read the scripts and run clips from public television's "Rick Steves' Europe" and public radio's "Travel with Rick Steves."

Respect for Your Privacy

Ordering online from us is secure. When you buy something from us, join a tour, or subscribe to Rick's free monthly travel news e-mails, we promise to never share your name, information, or e-mail address with anyone else. You won't be spammed!

Have fun raising your Travel I.Q. at
www.ricksteves.com

Travel smart...carry on!

The latest generation of Rick Steves' carry-on travel bags is easily the best—benefiting from two decades of on-the-road attention to what really matter maximum quality and strength; practical, flexible features; and no unnecessary frills. You won't find a better value anywhere!

Convertible, expandable, and carry-on-size:
Rick Steves' Back Door Bag $99

This is the same bag that Rick Steves lives out of for three months every summer. It's made of rugged water-resistant 1000 denier Cordura nylon, and best of all, it converts easily from a smart-looking suitcase to a handy backpack with comfortably-curved shoulder straps and a padded waistbelt.

This roomy, versatile 9" x 21" x 14" bag has a large 2600 cubic-inch main compartment, plus three outside pockets (small, medium and huge) that are perfect for often-used items. And the cinch-tight compression straps will keep your load compact and close to your back—not sagging like a sack of potatoes.

Wishing you had even more room to bring home souvenirs? Pull open the ful perimeter expando-zipper and its capacity jumps from 2600 to 3000 cubic inche When you want to use it as a suitcase or check it as luggage (required when "expanded"), the straps and belt hide away in a zippered compartment in the back.

Attention travelers under 5'4" tall: This bag also comes in an inch-shorter version, for a compact-friendlier fit between the waistbelt and shoulder straps.

Convenient, expandable, and carry-on-size:
Rick Steves' Wheeled Bag $129

At 9" x 21" x 14" our sturdy Rick Steves' Wheeled Bag is rucksack-soft in front, but the rest is lined with a hard ABS-lexan shell to give maximum protection to your belongings. We've spared no expense on moving parts, splurging on an extra-long button-release handle and big, tough inline skate wheels for easy rolling on rough surfaces.

Wishing you had even more room to bring home souvenirs? Pull open the full-perimeter expando-zipper and its capacity jumps from 2600 to 3000 cubic inches.

Rick Steves' Wheeled Bag has exactly the same three-outside-pocket configuration as our Back Door Bag, plus a handy "add-a-bag" strap and full lining.

Our Back Door Bags and Wheeled Bags come in blac navy, blue spruce, evergreen and merlot.

For great deals on a wide selection of travel goodies, begin your next trip at the Rick Steves Travel Store!

Visit the Rick Steves Travel Store at
www.ricksteves.com

Rick Steves

More *Savvy*. More *Surprising*. More Fun.

COUNTRY GUIDES 2006

England
France
Germany & Austria
Great Britain
Ireland
Italy
Portugal
Scandinavia
Spain
Switzerland

CITY GUIDES 2006

Amsterdam, Bruges & Brussels
Florence & Tuscany
London
Paris
Prague & The Czech Republic
Provence & The French Riviera
Rome
Venice

BEST OF GUIDES

Best of Eastern Europe
Best of Europe

As the #1 authority on European travel, Rick gives you inside information on what to visit, where to stay, and how to get there—economically and hassle-free.

www.ricksteves.com

PHRASE BOOKS & DICTIONARIES

French
French, Italian & German
German
Italian
Portuguese
Spanish

MORE EUROPE FROM RICK STEVES

Easy Access Europe
Europe 101
Europe Through the Back Door
Postcards from Europe

RICK STEVES' EUROPE DVDs

All 43 Shows 2000-2005
Britain
Eastern Europe
France & Benelux
Germany, The Swiss Alps & Travel Skills
Ireland
Italy
Spain & Portugal

PLANNING MAPS

Britain & Ireland
Europe
France
Germany, Austria & Switzerland
Italy
Spain & Portugal

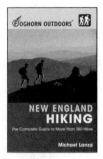
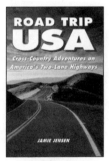

For a complete list of Rick Steves' guidebooks, see page 6.

Avalon Travel Publishing
1400 65th Street, Suite 250
Emeryville, CA 94608

AVALON
publishing group incorporated

Avalon Travel Publishing is an Imprint of Avalon Publishing Group, Inc.

Printed in the U.S.A. by Worzalla
First printing February 2006

Portions of this book were originally published in *Rick Steves' Mona Winks* © 2001, 1998, 1996, 1993, 1988 by Rick Steves and Gene Openshaw; and in *Rick Steves' France* © 2004, 2003, 2002, 2001, 2000 by Rick Steves and Steve Smith.

ISBN(10) 1-56691-719-0 • ISBN(13) 978-1-56691-719-3
ISSN 1543-012X

For the latest on Rick's lectures, books, tours, public radio show, and public television series, contact Europe Through the Back Door, Box 2009, Edmonds, WA 98020, tel. 425/771-8303, fax 425/771-0833, www.ricksteves.com, rick@ricksteves.com.

Europe Through the Back Door Managing Editor: Risa Laib
ETBD Editors: Jennifer Hauseman, Cameron Hewitt, Kevin Yip
Avalon Travel Publishing Series Manager and Editor: Patrick Collins
Avalon Travel Publishing Project Editor: Madhu Prasher
Research Assistance: Jennifer Hauseman
Copy Editor: Matthew Reed Baker
Indexer: Laura Welcome
Production & Typesetting: Patrick David Barber, Holly McGuire
Cover Design: Kari Gim, Laura Mazer
Interior Design: Jane Musser, Amber Pirker, Laura Mazer
Maps and Graphics: David C. Hoerlein, Laura VanDeventer, Lauren Mills, Mike Morgenfeld
Photography: Rick Steves, Dominic Bonuccelli, Gene Openshaw, Jennifer Hauseman
Front matter color photos: p. i, Amsterdam at Night, © Rick Steves; p. viii, Amsterdam © Rick Steves
Cover Photos: front image, Market Square, Bruges © Doug McKinlay/Lonely Planet Images; back image: Red tulip field in Lisse © Izzet Keribar/Lonely Planet Images